P9-BYA-993

WHERE DO WE GO FROM HERE?

A Guidebook for Cell Group Churches

Ralph W. Neighbour, Jr.
with **Lorna Jenkins**

WHERE DO WE GO FROM HERE?
A Guidebook for Cell Group Churches

Copyright © 1990 by Ralph W. Neighbour, Jr.

Unless stated otherwise, the Scripture quotations in this book
are from the New American Standard Bible.
Copyright © The Lockman Foundation, 1960, 1962, 1963, 1968, 1971,
1972, 1973, 1975, 1977.
Used by Permission.

Library of Congress Catalog Card Number: 90-071778
ISBN Number: 1-880828-54-5

Published by Touch Publications, Inc.
Box 19888
Houston, TX 77224
1-800-735-5865

Available in Asia from:
Touch Resource
#06-00/07-00
66/68 East Coast Road
Singapore 1542

Printed in the Republic of Singapore
by BAC Printers

A SUGGESTION FROM DR. DAVID FINNELL

Professor Of Evangelism, Columbia Biblical Seminary
& Graduate School Of Missions

This book may be the second most important book you have ever read. That doesn't mean it will be easy to read. Quite the contrary!

I'm not referring to the writing style. It's well written, often captivating. But to some, it will be difficult to read because of our excess baggage of tradition and culture.

Let me make a suggestion: before you begin this book, agree with me to do four things:

First, lay the book aside and pray the Holy Spirit will guide and instruct you according to His will. Certainly, we can all agree this is a fair and non-threatening request.

Second, deposit the baggage of your church's tradition and your cultural heritage at the end of the book. You may reclaim it when you arrive there. Some of that baggage is good, and some is excess weight that will burden your spiritual journey. Let the sole measure and authority for your evaluation of this book be according to God's word under the tutelage of the Holy Spirit.

Third, agree to read the entire book.

A majority of the readers will find sections that will take them out of their present "comfort zones." Those at either end of the theological poles may find passages that will raise questions for them. Don't stop—to understand the book, *you must finish it.*

Pastors of traditional churches may be offended at some points. If you are one of them and fail to capture the spirit of love that the author has for you—read on! Leaders of churches who are not doing any evangelism may be overwhelmed—but read on!

You don't have to agree with everything written here in order to benefit from the book. There are some points made where I am still unsure and searching. But, I challenge you: if you disagree, use *scriptural exegesis* as your basis for disagreement, rather than your tradition and heritage.

Fourth, when you reclaim your baggage at the end, don't just pick up your bags and walk on. Open your luggage and examine it. See if there are any items you may no longer need—items that will just add to your burden and make your journey more difficult. Lighten your load! Consider where you are going, and move on to the fulfillment of the task God has called you to complete.

I hope your curiosity has been aroused. I don't think you will be disappointed. *This may be the second most important book you will ever read.*

Now, put the book down for a moment and prayerfully prepare yourself to read it!

TABLE OF CONTENTS

Preface 6

PART 1: A LOOK AT THE CURRENT SITUATION 9
  1 The Journey Into New Church Life.....................................11
  2 The Roadblock: The "P.B.D." Church.................................38
  3 Poor Lost Sheep: P.B.D. Groups 59
  4 My Journey Into The Cell Church.....................................78

PART 2: THEOLOGY BREEDS METHODOLOGY 93
  5 Community: The Reason For Cells.....................................94
  6 About *Oikos*...114
  7 Putting Cells In The Kingdoms.......................................122
  8 Grace Gifts In Cell Group Life 139
  9 Gifts Belong In Cell Groups 146
  10 The Holy Spirit In The Cell Group...................................160
  11 The Listening Room 172
  12 Children In The Cells 181

PART 3: THE STRUCTURE OF A CELL GROUP CHURCH...........193
  13 Cell, Congregation, and Celebration 197
  14 More About Shepherd Groups 209
  15 The Dynamics Of Shepherd Groups.................................223
  16 Cell Evangelism Explained 239
  17 All About Share Groups 254
  18 What About Finances? 262
  19 Children's Cell Groups..267
  20 "He Set A Child In The Midst".......................................297
  21 Equipping Children's Cell Leaders 313
  22 Cell Groups For Teenagers...330
  23 Expanding Cells Into The City.......................................336
  24 Equipping *All* The Ministers.......................................358
  25 Organizing For The Harvest...378
  26 Transitioning A P.B.D. Church 404
  27 How To Plant A Cell Group Church..................................423
  28 TOUCH Tools To Use..441
Endnotes..453
Index 461

PREFACE

I am convinced that the traditional church worldwide is being slowly replaced by an act of God. Developments taking place today are as powerful as the upheaval in 1517 during the time of Martin Luther. One cannot say that Luther *caused* the first Reformation. He was only the tinder that lit the fire; the dead wood was ready to burn.

Historians have examined the forces which came into play at that moment of time. The development of the printing press, the seething impatience with the greed of Rome, the growing disillusionment about philosophical systems, the emergence of scientific methods, all made that century a time of transition. The church was reformed by the hand of God to prepare it for the new world that was about to exist.

The Catholicism of the Dark Ages was simply incompetent to cope with the new environment. The reformed church was a child of its time. It faced each new event with power from above. To be sure, it didn't come out of the old mold far enough—and the more conservative branches retained enough of the old ways to *burn at the stake* those who did go farther out.

The styles of church life so appropriate for the Reformation period are now impotent. The church is impotent. It cannot reproduce unless it first physically fathers new children. I have roamed this earth since 1974, and the impotence is everywhere.

It is time for the second Reformation. The people of earth have moved into a new era, one which never existed before in all the history of man. Change comes faster and faster, and the church becomes more and more irrelevant to cope with the changes.

I pen these words on my way back to the United States from Singapore. Just a speedboat ride away from that modern world class city is the Indonesian island of Batam. It's not large—about double the size of Singapore. I met a Muslim man there who was over one hundred years old, and who had never seen the opposite side of the jungle-covered island.

The peace and quiet of fishing villages that have existed for a century is about to disappear. The local inhabitants are being given $75 for each shack in their *kampong* and 50¢ for each coconut tree and told to move out to make way for resort hotels to be constructed. Both Singapore and Indonesia are sinking a billion dollars each into the development of Batam. All the land has been gobbled up by speculators. *By 2000 A.D., the entire island will become a teeming city!*

Cities of a million people will spring up during the next 20 years all over the earth. How can they be reached for Christ? Most certainly, *not* through planting existing church forms in them! That's why God is quietly ignoring religious power structures and those who make their living from preserving them.

I am going on 62 as I write, and I have felt for years like those old men in the Gospels who wanted to live long enough to see the Messiah with their own eyes. I have longed to see the new church in all its glory before I go to Glory. Praise God, it's here! He has launched a new form of church life called the "cell group church." At this stage, it's still pure enough to reach the exploding population of our day. This book is all about what I have seen and learned in the last 25 years concerning this new form of church.

The chapters will describe the problem with the old and will prepare the reader for the new by first discussing the theology of the cell group structure. Finally, I will tell everything I can think of which might help those who are ready to journey into the second Reformation—concepts which have been gleaned from many men and many groups in many nations.

Spare me the phone calls that begin, "Where is a cell group church in my area?" If there's one near you, you already know about it. Its detractors delight in slinging mud at it, and its members delight in harvesting the unchurched. If there's *not* one near you, take a trip. Visit one of the churches mentioned in this book, or better yet, *start one yourself!*

I had men come to see my experimental church in Houston by the droves. Most successful churches do what I did: they hold Pastors' Conferences to satisfy the curious. However, few men whom I have spent precious hours talking to or holding seminars for have ever done anything with what they learned. On the other hand, I have asked every cell group pastor I have met on my journeys, "When you started, did you make a trip to see a model of what you have here? Did you attend someone's seminar before you started?" In each and every case, the answer has been "No. I went to my knees and got marching orders from my Lord. I had no choice. He taught me as I went along."

Among the thousands of these books which will be distributed, approximately 2% of the readers will close the pages as they read and seek the face of their Lord. He will appoint them to be a part of the new, rather than a preserver of the impotent. Lay the book aside and *just do it!* Then—as you need it—read chapters that share "how to do it" things.

After you have some battle scars, take that trip! Like those veteran missionaries who return to Columbia Biblical Seminary on furloughs, you will know what you're looking for is worth the investment of time you will require. I'm thinking just now of Jim Romaine, one of my doctoral students. With 15 tough years in Turkey under his belt, he drilled and grilled me in every class. How I love him! His new insights into God's activity in forming cell group churches will guide his coming years there, and I will avidly read his newsletters.

There are other materials you will want to peruse when you finish reading this book. They are mentioned in the back pages. Get them and use them for a time as models to get started. But don't keep ordering my materials! Create your own—and as you do, you have my permission to plagiarize my writings and training materials and paste them into your own equipping manuals. All I ask is that you send me what you produce so *I* can plagiarize from *you!* The goal, my dear reader, is to harvest this generation before it goes into eternity without the Master.

Let's covenant now to pray for each other. The first birds in the air fly alone, and I can testify that it has been lonely up there. Drop a letter to the address on the copyright page, and let me know what the Lord is doing to you on the journey.

Ralph W. Neighbour, Jr.
Houston, Texas and Singapore

1

A LOOK AT

THE CURRENT

SITUATION

May they also be in us so that the world may believe that you have sent me. I have given them the glory that you gave me, that they may be one as we are one: I in them and you in me. May they be brought to complete unity to let the world know that you sent me and have loved them even as you have loved me.

• John 17:21-23

1 THE JOURNEY INTO NEW CHURCH LIFE

Before we begin our journey together, let me give you the conclusion. With great love and affection, we shall examine the lifestyle of traditional church structures we have all known since childhood, and we shall find them wanting. Or, to put it more clearly, the Holy Spirit is finding them wanting. I repeat: we make this examination with sensitivity and compassion, in the same way a doctor examines an old friend who has a terminal disease. Sadly, I weep within as did Jeremiah over his beloved Israel as I write about the traditional church. I also seek to withdraw from those who are filled with anger and criticism of it. Such negative spirits never become a part of what this book is about. Their motives are not pure enough for the Spirit of God to bless them.

We shall use *the church in the New Testament* as a yardstick to evaluate today's congregations. In so doing, we will see how far we have strayed from where we started. This study will also explain why today's "churchianity" is slowly dying from its own terminal disease, diagnosed as the deadly "Program Base Design."

Next, we are going to observe what the Holy Spirit is beginning to do in our generation to raise up the beautiful Bride of Christ in a more appropriate form—one with the ability to harvest the billions of newborns of this generation. To distinguish between the traditional church as we have known it and these new life forms, we shall call them the "Cell Group Churches."

They are growing like mushrooms in the rich soil of a dark night. A recent estimate by a Nashville church-watcher puts the number of new, innovative cell group churches in America alone in the thousands. Only a few of them existed in 1979. They are a recent activity of the Spirit. They are new wineskins, and they hold a new wine—the wine of God's activity in a world we must bring to Jesus' feet as we minister to this generation.

The Awesome Population Explosion And The Church

As this book is published, approximately four thousand days separate us from the year 2000. According to the latest United Nations projections, the world's population is currently estimated to be in excess of five billion people. It will exceed six billion at the end of this decade, increasing to eight billion and more by the year 2025. The preponderance of that growth will occur in the developing countries. The Director of the U. N. Centre for Human Settlements in Nairobi writes:

> The urban share of total world population, which was estimated at less than 30 percent in 1950, had steady growth to 36.9 percent in 1970 and 41.6 percent in 1985. Now it is projected to surpass the 50 percent mark just after the turn of the century and to approach 60 percent in the year 2025...in 1950, four out of the five largest urban agglomerations were located in the industrialized world...today, of the world's 10 largest urban agglomerations, only two—Tokyo/Yokohama and New York/ Northeastern New Jersey—are situated in a developed region...at the top of the list are...Mexico City, with 26.3 million; Sao Paolo, with 24 million; Calcutta, with 16.6; Greater Bombay, with 16; Seoul and Shanghai, with 13.5 million each; and not much further behind will be Rio de Janeiro, Delhi, Greater Buenos Aires, Cairo/Giza/ Imbaba, Jakarta, Baghdad, Teheran, Karachi, Istanbul, Dacca, Manila, Beijing, all with populations between 10 and 13 million people.[1]

The Population Reference Bureau has prepared charts of this astonishing urban growth, projecting that Africa will have five times as many cities of one million or more in the year 2000 than it had in 1950.[2] As we observe this explosion and implosion of people, it becomes quickly obvious that the world is being impacted by young people. In Asian cities like Singapore, people below 15 years of age form 23.4 per cent of the population while those above 60 comprise 8.1 percent.[3]

All this points to an important fact. The population explosion is taking place in the non-Christian world. We are not alone in seeking to reach these exploding metropolises. Other world religions are alert to the importance of these days and are hard at work making converts. Dr. Charles Deevers, missionary dentist in Abidjan, Ivory Coast, reports Muslims are greeting incoming buses and trains, snagging rural people coming to live in the city. They are offered food, shelter, and assistance in getting a job. As a result, thousands are being snatched away from the message of Christ within minutes of their arrival.[4] We have entered an era of history when evangelism must be sharpened and honed to cut into the darkness of a burgeoning non-Christian world.

Our evangelism must take new forms and shapes if it is to keep up with the need of our day! The crusades, the evangelistic preaching activities of local churches, must not slow down. But we must add another dimension if we are to keep up with the exploding population. We must plant a new type of church that can think in terms of multiplication, not addition.

NET ADDITIONS TO WORLD POPULATION
AT 25 YEAR INTERVALS, 1900-2100

Source: Population Division, United Nations

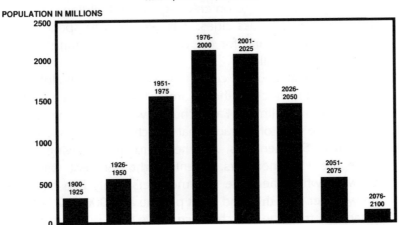

This graph shares the alarming situation. Never before in history—and never again before 2100 A.D.—will the earth's population grow so fast! The church *as we know it* is simply not capable of harvesting such an increase.

Church Structures Are Woefully Inadequate

In the light of this population explosion in the world, we must conclude that current models of church planting are inadequate. Several reasons may be given:

5%
OVER 350 MEMBERS

28%
151-350 MEMBERS

33%
UNDER 50 MEMBERS

33%
51-150 MEMBERS

1. The form of church planting we are now using in major urban centers is taken from a rural concept of church life. It is not appropriate for urban structures. The kaleidoscope of cultures which intertwine in the cities requires an urban form for church life.

2. We cannot afford to continue planting congregations in urban areas which are limited by parish boundaries or "church fields." This is a rural mind set, inappropriate for world class cities. (See graph on opposite page.)

3. We cannot afford to go on erecting church buildings in small districts of world class cities. It is senseless to spend huge amounts for land and for the construction of "starter buildings" every few miles.

4. The traditional church, consisting of a church building, a pastor, and a flock gathered from the "parish area," has specific growth limits. Each church will plateau at certain points. One third of all traditional churches in the world today plateau at 50 members. Another third quit growing when there are 150 members. Twenty-eight per cent will stop growing when there are 350 members. Only five per cent grow larger than this, and most plateau at 1,000 or 2,000.[5] It is sad, but true: the church structure we have duplicated over and over in this century is shockingly inefficient! The buildings are empty for most of the week. The members aren't equipped to minister to hurting people. Everything centers on activities within the church buildings.

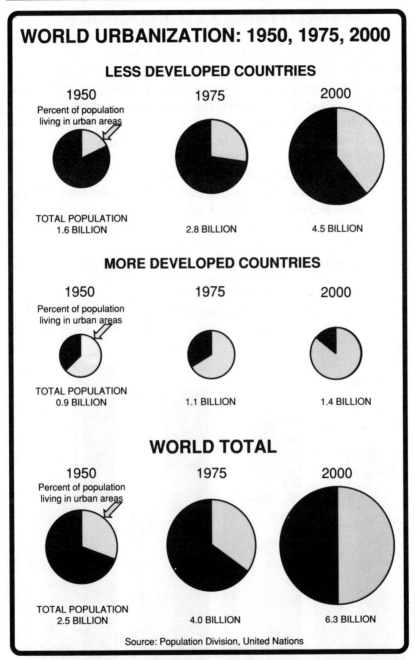

WORLD URBANIZATION: 1950, 1975, 2000

LESS DEVELOPED COUNTRIES

1950
Percent of population living in urban areas

1975

2000

TOTAL POPULATION
1.6 BILLION

2.8 BILLION

4.5 BILLION

MORE DEVELOPED COUNTRIES

1950
Percent of population living in urban areas

1975

2000

TOTAL POPULATION
0.9 BILLION

1.1 BILLION

1.4 BILLION

WORLD TOTAL

1950
Percent of population living in urban areas

1975

2000

TOTAL POPULATION
2.5 BILLION

4.0 BILLION

6.3 BILLION

Source: Population Division, United Nations

As the earth's population explodes, it also *implodes*. By the end of the century, one half of all humanity will live in urban areas. Our rural concept of church life must be abandoned.

American Churches Are In Deep Recession

According the The World Almanac and Book of Facts for 1990, four adults out of every ten Americans (40%) attended a church or synagogue in a typical week in 1987. In 1958, that figure was 49%. The average for the nation is skewed by the larger church attendance in the smaller communities. The *Houston Chronicle* has estimated that only 30% of Houstonians darken the door of a church on an average Sunday.

While two thirds of U. S. adults (65%) said they were *members* of a church or synagogue, the current percentage is the lowest ever recorded. Roman Catholics have been particularly hard hit, losing one sixth of their members in only 18 years.

U. S. POPULATION AND CHURCH MEMBERSHIP
Source: The World Almanac and Book of Facts, 1990

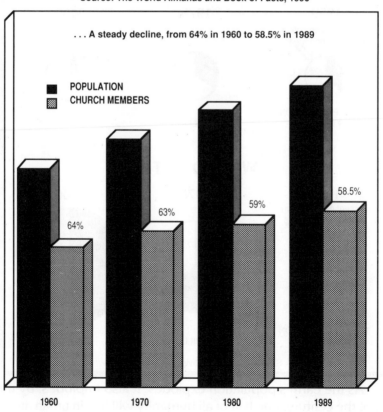

. . . A steady decline, from 64% in 1960 to 58.5% in 1989

■ POPULATION
▨ CHURCH MEMBERS

64%   63%   59%   58.5%

1960   1970   1980   1989

Sunday School, the highly touted "arm of evangelism" of the local church, is no longer impacting the society. Many churches today are registering larger attendance in their worship services than in their Sunday Schools—a clear reversal for evangelicals.

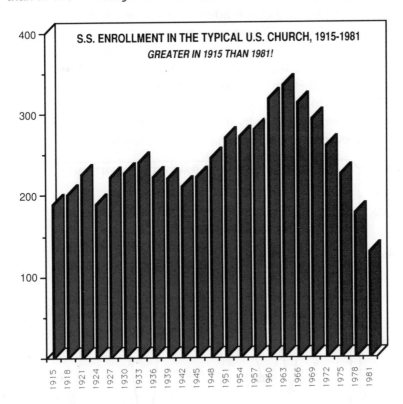

S.S. ENROLLMENT IN THE TYPICAL U.S. CHURCH, 1915-1981
GREATER IN 1915 THAN 1981!

What happened to it? In *Growth, a New Vision for the Sunday School*, the authors provide these insights:

> The focus of the Sunday School changed from those "outside" to those "inside" . . . . Leadership of the Sunday School shifted from the laity to professionals . . . . There developed a loss of community and sense of belonging . . . . The Sunday School became less and less of a priority for the church.[6]

The graph above is taken from this book, and clearly documents the failure of Sunday School to remain relevant to the changing American society at the end of the century.

Along with the decline of the backbone of the church program, the evangelistic thrust subtly changed. With little of significance to offer the unbeliever in the "here and now," the most popular programs for training Christians to evangelize clearly emphasized that the advantages of becoming a Christian come *after you die:* "If you were to die today and God were to say, 'Why should I let you into my heaven,' what would your answer be?" *Have we nothing to offer between now and then?* Unfortunately, this isn't appropriate for a generation more inter- ested in how to "live it up" than how eternity will be spent. Our loss of converts is shown by the decline in annual baptisms within the most evangelistic denomination in the nation:

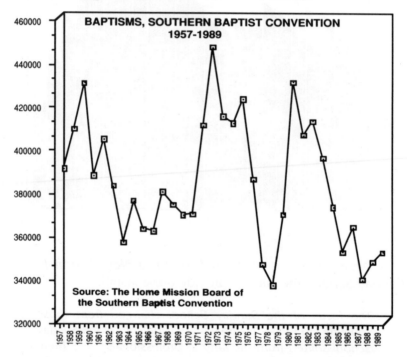

BAPTISMS, SOUTHERN BAPTIST CONVENTION 1957-1989

Source: The Home Mission Board of the Southern Baptist Convention

The church in America has spent so much time discipling itself that it has become an ignored appendage to a large portion of the nation's population. To forecast just *how* a society can look at irrelevant religion, one should examine New Zealand and Australia, where no more than 10% of the citizens attend church, or England, where hundreds of church buildings stand unused.[7]

Televangelists Disgraced, Pastors Fired

Emerging Trends indicates that public opinion of television evangelists in general is at an all-time low. 65% of viewers feel these men have "no special relationship with God," and nearly 70% feel they are "insincere." It is too soon to measure the damage these men have done to the future of organized religion in America, but it is already affirmed that contributions to many valid Christian causes have been severely damaged.[8]

Bruce Grubbs of the Southern Baptist Sunday School Board reports that over an 18-month period that ended in early 1989, more than 2,100 Southern Baptist ministers were dismissed, a 31% increase over a similar period that ended in early 1985.[9] So many clergy are being released by frustrated congregations that special non-credit schools are being set up to reequip the wounded. T. D. Hall of Fort Worth had over 80 applicants for his Emmaus Road school when it opened—mostly pastors who simply could not please their churches. Many of these fine men have returned to a new style of ministry, planting new cell group churches.

Some want to explain away these dismissals as the fault of exceptional preachers who reach church members through the media, making the local pastor's preaching and teaching look shabby in comparison. The *Emerging Trends* poll doesn't bear this out. A more realistic evaluation may simply be that the old ways of "doing church" in the 1990's neither satisfies those who are inside nor outside the structures.

Most popular of all forms of traditional church life just now are the "Megachurches." These city-wide congregations have bled the life out of neighborhood churches in the same way that grocery chains drove the "Mom and Pop" corner stores out of business 30 years ago. Plush, ornate auditoriums and subsidized ski trips for the Yuppies appeal to the social side of Americans, but do little to touch the broken lives of the unchurched. These churches attract some who desire to "get lost" in the largeness, and their Sunday Schools are filled with members who average a twice-a-month attendance. Since their activities are extremely building-centered, they choke off growth by growing large enough that they can no longer afford to add further space to their facilities. Few options remain for the American church!

God's Solution: A New Lifestyle For The Church

There is a more effective pattern in our world today than planting traditional churches. The Holy Spirit is the author of this pattern, and it has sprouted up like mushrooms all over the globe. It is called the "cell group church."

While cell group churches also develop successfully in towns and villages, they grow most rapidly when used in an urban context. Given the proper soil to take root, they are capable of exploding to astonishing sizes. The entire Christian world is aware that the Yoido Full Gospel Church in Seoul is fast reaching a membership of seven hundred thousand people. How many know, however, that the largest Presbyterian and Methodist churches in the world are *also* cell group churches located in Seoul?

Harvesting In World Class Cities

Why are cell group churches more appropriate for world class cities? Why do they grow so much faster? There are several reasons:

1. They are more **efficient** than traditional churches. In the traditional church, only ten to fifteen per cent of the membership are engaged in the tasks required to make the church function. After the teachers, administrators, musicians, etc., have been culled out of the total membership, the rest are expected to be faithful members. If an automobile engine were rated at fifteen per cent efficiency, it would never see the light of day. The contrast between this misuse of Christians and the New Testament church, where one hundred per cent were involved, is scandalous.[10]

2. They are based on the scriptural concept of **community**. The essence of community is a sense of belonging.[11] There is a powerful Christian camaraderie established when people belong to each other in a cell group. It cannot be equaled in a church which assembles people in large groups. Some have adopted the term "Basic Christian Community" to describe the cells of this new style of church. People look after one another, and they share the ministry of reaching the unconverted as a community task.

3. They focus on the importance of **prayer** for their ministries. Half nights of prayer are commonplace among cell groups. As much as one third to one half of the time spent in their gatherings is devoted to prayer. Because they expect God to answer prayer, they often experience healing of bodies and the restoration of broken lives in their gatherings.

4. They **penetrate** deeply into the structures of the city, reaching people in a more personal way than the traditional church will ever be able to do. While the traditional church compresses as much as ninety per cent of all service to the Lord into the church buildings, the statistic is exactly reversed in the cell group church. The life of the church is to be found in the home meetings, which typically move from one residence to another on a weekly basis.

5. When one reads church history, the term **"movement"** is often used. It is the only proper word to use when describing this global phenomenon. A worldwide movement has been launched by the Holy Spirit, and He is paying no attention to denominational lines. Instead, He is finding those who are not imprisoned by the past, who have a hot heart for reaching the lost, and who are ready to acknowledge every Christian is a minister! Unlike those traditions which commission missionaries to *establish* a certain type of church, cell group churches are truly *planted*. They are indigenous to their soils in a manner that has caused them to be bitterly criticized by many missionaries and pastors, who view them from without as a threat to the status quo. In reality, they are exactly that. They are not only the new wine, but the new wineskins. There are vast differences, as well as striking similarities, between the cell group churches of the earth. Their structures are truly flexible, able to adapt to their environment. Each one has had to be shaped within its special culture impacted by history, economics, and political situations. All of them in the third world are truly indigenous, unlike the more traditional churches which have always exported, intact, the Reformation churches of Europe and England, or the program-based styles developed in America. They have a vision for reaching the entire city, not just one part of it. The term "movement" is continually heard when interviewing church planters who are committed to the cell group church. There are no parish

boundaries, no delimiting "church fields." A cell group church sees the entire metropolis as an area teeming with unreached people, and they seek to insert a cell in every neighborhood within it.

6. They are not circumscribed by the size of a church building. It is obvious that most traditional churches are limited by the size of their buildings. For some, the original edifice is used for generations. For others, a spurt of growth requires a massive building fund drive and a small addition of space. The success of the church is measured by how packed the auditorium is, rather than by the number of people who are brought to personal faith. When cell group churches do construct space, it is clearly created for the purpose of *equipping*, and not for *attracting*, members.

7. Their evangelism includes the powerful witness of Christ working within His body, beyond the traditional, cognitive presentation of the plan of salvation. The "ungifted" and the "unbelievers" of I Corinthians 14:24-26 are once again, as in the early church, exposed to the amazing power of the body of Christ, where all are involved in the process of edification. *Once again, it has become commonplace for these seekers to fall on their faces and say, "Surely God is among you!"* This "new" form of evangelism is as old as the book of Acts!

The Answer To Non-Christian Cultures

It is important to recognize that the cell groups of the earth have developed most rapidly in a non-Christian context. Why has this form of church life been so powerful in such an environment?

1. Because of its ability to deeply penetrate pagan communities. Instead of one church building in an area of a city, the cell group church has scores of "points of light" within the neighborhoods. These are often viewed with curiosity by nearby dwellers. For example, when I served as a missionary in Viet Nam, we had only to begin singing in one of the member's homes to fill the room with curious neighbors. Their observation of our lifestyle was a powerful testimony, drawing them to listen as the Bible exposed them to the Light of the World.

2. Because the gospel is offered by non-professional hands, the hands of friends or neighbors, not outsiders. Suspicion of the Christian clergy is not present when people in the community are the bearers of the gospel. It is not uncommon for cells to see conversions on a weekly basis. In the case

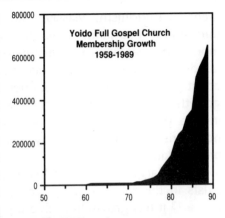

of the *Eglise Protestante Baptiste Oeuvres et Mission* in Abidjan, their rate of cell multiplication is two months and two weeks.[12]

3. Because the cell groups are battlefields where people are set free from strongholds. It is commonplace for a cell group meeting to focus on a Biblical teaching related to a life problem. Whereas the traditional church would focus on this with a sermon and an admonition, the cells call each member to be accountable. As in the days of Wesley's class meetings, it is commonplace for the cell leader to ask each person present, "What is the state of your life concerning this issue?" In the intimacy of the cell, people can wrestle with personal sin, long standing habits, and find release. Personal victory spawns deeper awarenesses of God's power and reality.

4. Because it can powerfully meet the needs of pagans. Indeed, it focuses on needs as the key method of making contacts with the unreached. One of my students from India, Dr. Samuel Raj, told me the first thing he does when he enters an unevangelized Hindu area is to seek out a family where someone is sick or demented. He teaches and prays in that home until the power of God sets the prisoner free. The impact on the neighbors causes the first cell group to develop, and the new work is on its way to being solidly established.

Examples of Cell Group Churches: Korea

The Buddhist world of Korea has a centuries-old commitment to Buddhism. Massive statues of the Buddha are found throughout the land. Tens of thousands have journeyed to mountain areas where shrines have been erected. A little over a hundred years ago, the first missionaries arrived to evangelize this country. While the land responded to the Christian message, the growth was slow. Then the cell group church movement came to invade the strongholds of paganism. The growth among the non-Christian community by cell group churches has been breathtaking!

The largest single local church in the history of Christianity exists in this land. It is the Yoido Full Gospel Church in Seoul, Korea.[13] It has grown from five people who gathered in a tent in 1958, to a congregation of over 600,000 in 1989.[14] After spurts of growth using more traditional church methodology, Dr. Cho instituted cell groups in 1964. In the first five years, without cells, the congregation grew to about 3,800 people. By September, 1980, the congregation had 141,000 members.[15] *For the past nine years the church has averaged a growth of 140 members every single day.* In a personal interview with Dr. Cho in 1984, he explained he was seeking to curb the growth of the congregation by selecting capable men from his pastoral staff and giving them 5,000 members to launch a new church. The church's Prayer Mountain now registers over two and a half million people each year.[16] The amount of time spent in prayer by this congregation exceeds any other single activity of their weekly schedule.

If this church were the *only* cell group congregation showing such growth in Seoul, it might be ignored as the fruit of a dynamic pastor's personality, but this is not the case. There are dozens of other churches who use the cell group pattern, and all are growing at an amazing rate. Today, the world's two largest Presbyterian churches, along with the largest Methodist church, are cell group congregations in Seoul. All are multiplying at a rate which far outstrips sister Korean churches who do not take advantage of a cell group structure.

Seoul's skyline after dark is filled with neon crosses, mounted on the tops of buildings where a church exists. There are literally thousands of them! A Presbyterian pastor said to me, "Most of those crosses mark small churches with fewer than fifty members. They never seem to grow beyond that figure." Those who seek to discount the amazing growth of the cell group churches in Korea must understand not *all* their churches are growing at the same rate. The difference is quite clear: *when all the believers are equipped and involved in ministry, there is a radical difference between them and traditional churches nearby in terms of growth.*

Examples of Cell Group Churches: Japan

Strongly resistant to the Christian message, the Japanese have not accepted the traditional Christian church. The teachings of Shintoism and Buddhism are well woven into the culture. The powerful control of the "web society" in this land strangles the individual Japanese who tries to break out of the life of the community, school, family, and nation. The concept of a building, a pastor, and programs conducted in the name of Jesus has been seen as "Western."

For many years, missionaries working in Japan have concluded the culture will not support large churches. As a result, some church planters do not even *expect* a church to grow larger than twenty people. As one Japanese student said to me recently, "In my country, a thirty-member congregation is considered a megachurch."

That was before the introduction of the cell group church movement! It is now evident that these older patterns have been out of tune with the Japanese situation, and the new cell group pattern fits it perfectly.

Datin Solhein has said: "...home churches, cell groups, and other patterns seemingly must be developed, for these have often been the key to the growth of new religions."[17]

An illustration of what can happen is reported by Pat Hansen, newly assigned Church Planter in Tokyo. After this American appointee finished his language study, he was seconded to a fellow OMF missionary for a three year apprenticeship. His mentor was a newly appointed Korean pastor with vast experience in developing cell group churches. Pat discovered the lifestyle of his equipper would require significant changes in his own life as a cell group church planter.

First of all, he had to adjust his prayer life. He began to share in a weekly schedule which included hours and hours of prayer, including all night sessions. Second, he observed how his Korean associate made contacts for the new cell group church. His home was filled night and day with Japanese unbelievers. He contacted them in the neighborhoods, at the shops, in nearby eating houses, and invited them to his home. (Japanese prejudice against Koreans is so strong it took weeks for this pastor to find a place to rent!) Soon, merely curious Japanese became interested seekers for Christ. Bible studies developed in the rooms of the Korean couple. As the first converts were established, the first cell group was formed. It was followed by a second, a third, a fourth, a fifth, and a sixth. In about thirty-five months, the newly planted cell group church saw over sixty conversions and is now on its way to having hundreds in the fold. Recently, this Korean pastor took Japanese pastors to Korea to see the cell group churches there.

Yonggi Cho sent a Korean woman to plant the first cell group church in Japan just a few years ago. From that humble beginning, the cells have grown and grown.[18] He is now committed to have ten million converted Japanese in cell groups by the year 2000. Peter Wagner has viewed Cho's strategy of penetration and is convinced it will succeed.[19] In any culture—*every* culture—there is both a need and a desire in the hearts of people to live in a community of love and acceptance.

The significance of the cell group as an indigenous church planting method is the use of *hoza* in the rapidly expanding Rissho Koseikai religion. Masao Takenaka, Professor of Sociology of Religion at Doshisha University writes:

> *Hoza is a kind of informal discussion and dialogue circle which takes place daily...It provides an opportunity for the believers not only to know each other but to share one another's burdens and personal problems. This indicates that in modern society where people have left the homeland of traditional religion, they need a common ground to share their own problems. It clearly indicates that such a small circle of sharing each other's problems is one of the most important functions of religion in modern society.[20]*

Thus, the potential of Christianity spreading into the Japanese culture is greatly enhanced by restructuring the life of the church to be relational, small group, and home centered. Many missionaries believe that in the decade of the 1990's, the harvest will finally begin in Japan. Sadly, Sokka Gakkai did after World War 2 what the church could have done, harvesting *millions.*

Examples of Cell Group Churches: Singapore

When I served as a missionary in Singapore in the mid-1970's, about two per cent of the citizens were related to Christian churches. The most significant harvest was taking place in small cell groups among high school students, sponsored by Youth for Christ. Nearly all of the churches looked with disdain on the ministry of this parachurch group. In reality, they were in the cell group church planting business! I worked with dozens of their small groups, meeting with them after school hours. Literally thousands of young people became "closet Christians" during this time. They feared punishment within their Buddhist homes if parents discovered they had become believers.

When they finished school and gained the independence of a young adult, they were still unattached to a church. The traditional churches, for the most part, reluctantly beckoned them to enter the front doors of their sanctuaries. There was a limited response to this cool reception. It was at this point the cell group church came to the republic.

The Assemblies of God sponsored a young man to plant a church there. He chose to use the cell group method. Soon a church numbering over five thousand existed.

The pattern was to be replicated by others. For example, a Baptist pastor, Lawrence Khong, developed a cell group church in 1986 which grew to 4,500 in about four years.[21] The Faith Community Baptist Church utilizes two floors of an office building to house its ever increasing staff of workers who guide and train the cell group workers. They are presently seeking to build an auditorium large enough to house the cell membership for their weekly "Celebrations."

One of their most powerful harvest tools is a banquet for the Buddhist parents of men and women in the cells. Held in one of the largest banquet halls in the republic, as many as 2,500 have attended the formal Chinese ten-course meal. A Christian movie star from Hong Kong was one of those who came to share in this activity. After she gave her testimony, Pastor Khong explained to the parents how they could become believers. Scores responded, and the cell groups became healing stations for the cleavage in family life caused by the children first following Christ. The Chinese speaking services of this church are growing at a rate unequaled by any of the traditional Chinese churches in the city. Their Cantonese speaking congregation, which meets separately from those who speak English, has a significant witness among those who are not bilingual.

The Church of Praise is a new congregation, pastored by a ministry team headed by Albert Kang. Their "*Oikos* Groups" are expanding weekly. "Zone Pastors," responsible for 25 cells, seek to multiply the cells about every six months.

Examples of Cell Group Churches: Thailand

Into this powerful core of Buddhism came a young professor who had been converted while studying for his Ph.D. in Economics in Melbourne. Chareonwonsak Kriengsak returned to Bangkok with a vision of reaching the entire nation for Christ through cell groups.[22] He formed a movement called the "Hope of God" and established one small cell in his own residence. Soon, the "Hope of Bangkok" church had exploded across the city. Literally hundreds were converted in a few months of time. Kriengsak eventually left his teaching post at the university to shepherd the hundreds of cells. On Sunday, hundreds of cell group leaders stand in line to turn in their reports and offerings before attending one of the multiple worship services held in a leased shopping center. The congregation has recently paid cash for a choice piece of land in Bangkok for the erection of a praise center, astonishing everyone by raising the millions required in just one short week.

Although jealous traditional pastors in the community accuse him of being a cult or growing only by robbing their memberships, his actual statistics demonstrate that over *eighty-five per cent* of his cell group members are composed of converts. His movement has now passed the five thousand mark in Bangkok, only a handful of years after it was launched.

The "Hope of God" movement has now opened new work in many other Thai cities. It openly seeks to involve existing Christians in these new works, thus drawing bitter criticism from churches in the area.

Such criticism is heard from traditional pastors in every area where a thriving cell group church exists. In Seoul, the Assemblies of God pastors severed fellowship with Cho, accusing him of doctrinal error. The same thing has happened in the Ivory Coast, in Togo, in Singapore, in Brisbane and London.

This accusation can only be understood by recognizing that churches, numbering 30 or 40 members, which have been in existence for years and which have failed to reach the lost, do not instill vision in members who truly want to serve the Lord and not just support a preacher. "Rescuing" them from stagnant situations has been understandably unpopular with traditional church workers, but it has resulted in rapidly growing cell groups who reach the lost in unprecedented numbers. This conflict is probably going to become more and more severe in the years ahead as the new structures replace the old. The cell church will always be seen as competitive, and its gains will be viewed as a loss to others. This is particularly true when a single church becomes so large that it equals the total memberships of all other churches in a city. (The fact that those other churches are *still* in existence, in spite of the growth, should make it obvious that only a few of the sheep have moved to the new pasture.)

Examples of Cell Group Churches: Mainland China

The expansion of the church under the persecution of the Communist regime in China has been through the use of cells. Recent reports indicate the movement is still expanding, still underground, still cynical of the government and unwilling to "go public." Yonggi Cho is scheduled to preach in China, the Lord willing. He told me his reports reveal there are between fifty and seventy-five million people meeting in these small groups at the present time. Mainland China is living proof of the way the church must exist under adverse circumstances. From century to century, the cell group church has preserved the Christian community from those who would oppress it. China is the contemporary illustration that it still works.

Dramatic stories have been reported by men who have the trust of these groups and move among them when visiting the mainland. One report is of a cave in the side of a mountain used for the clustering of one hundred and fifty cell group members to hear the teaching of the scriptures. One cell group community sent one of its members from a small village to a large city a hundred miles away to pick up a cache of Bibles which had been smuggled in from Hong Kong. Upon returning to the village, he was caught by the police with them in his possession. The villagers were ordered to bring their honey buckets full of human urine to a horse trough in the center of the community. The man was then immersed in the fluid until he was nearly drowned. As frantic relatives sought to revive him, the political leaders warned the unknown cell group members that if they attempted such a thing again, the person so caught would be put to death. Such persecution has only served to strengthen the commitment of precious Christians who can only meet in the secrecy of their cell group meetings.

Reports from the cell churches include stories of many miracles which are taking place, including a well documented statement about the raising of a cell group member from death while the members circled his coffin, earnestly praying for his recovery. The small village was so stunned by the miracle that nearly every person made a commitment to follow Christ.

Examples of Cell Group Churches: Macau

Pastor Lam wears two hats. He is attached to Campus Crusade for Christ, and he also pastors a cell group church of 2,000 members. This Godly man struggles in a mobile society where there is a constant turnover of those arriving from China, departing for permanent residency overseas in a year or two. His pattern is to guide the cells into a full year of evangelism, followed by a full year of equipping the converts. Before they depart, they are able to win enough new people to Christ to cause the cells to multiply. Traditional churches in Macau struggle to gather 50 to 75 members, and the turnover of pastors and missionaries using the traditional church forms is horrendous.

Examples of Cell Group Churches: Hong Kong

Within little more than a year, two separate groups have launched cell group church movements in this colony, which will return to China's control in 1997. One of those groups has a training center for those who are ready to serve the Lord full time in the cells. On the fifth floor of a tenement building, thirteen students meet with their mentors each morning. After their training, they spend the rest of the day evangelizing the Cantonese grass roots community and forming cells from converts. Their leadership includes highly trained men who are quietly forming a church for the coming political transition. This is the beginning of a movement which will be vital to the witness of our Lord in the years ahead—one which deserves your prayer support!

Examples of Cell Group Churches: Africa

The *Eglise Protestante Baptiste Œuvres et Mission* is now in its fifteenth year of life. It is headquartered in Abidjan, Ivory Coast, but has networked into every major city and dozens of villages within the nation. It was launched in 1975, but it was not until 1983 that the pastor, Dion Robert, fully developed a cell group pattern for growth. He had been struggling with how to use cells in his church from the very beginning, but only traditional church models surrounded him. When he finally developed the pattern, he grew from 638 to 23,000 in only eight years.[23]

As in all other effective cell group churches, there were several ingredients which caused this church to grow so rapidly. One ingredient was the amazing *commitment to the vision* by the pastor. Another was his determination to *make the cell groups the heart and soul of church life,* instead of a "holding tank" for people gathered by other means. A third was a theology that called for *complete surrender to the Lordship of Christ* by all who entered cell groups. Finally, a *carefully developed organizational structure* was put into place to minister to the cells. This included outreach ministries which could be performed by cell members, putting them in contact with many different groups within the community. *(A later chapter is devoted to explaining more about this structure.)*

I first visited this work in Easter of 1988 to serve as one of the preachers at the annual "Retreat" held in one of the largest stadiums in Abidjan. The total estimated audience for the five services held over three days was 80,000 people. In preparation for this evangelistic harvesting event, the cells had been divided in half to make room for the expected conversions. Ninety-nine percent of those who attended were cell group members and unbelievers they had been cultivating for weeks or months.

Thousands of conversions were recorded. The harvest was handled by the carefully trained cell group members who did all the counseling and enrolled them in the groups.

This is a totally indigenous church which has none of the flavor instilled in African churches by Western missionaries. At the same time, it is uncanny to see the way it has developed a similar lifestyle to other cell groups located on other continents half a world away. This church has now established cell church extensions in several other African nations and even works in Paris with Francophone Africans who have migrated there.

Examples of Cell Group Churches: England

ICHTHUS Fellowship in southeast London has penetrated the residents of that area, deliberately forming cells by using a "checkerboard pattern." After cells are planted on the "red" squares, they are challenged to create a cell in the "black" space between them. The growth of this movement, under the brilliant direction of the Ministry Team led by Roger Forster, has been rapid.[24] It has also been strengthened by their use of numerous church buildings, many of which have been unused for more than a generation. The wardens of these structures are glad to have someone use them in exchange for maintaining them. This ministry has grown so large it can no longer assemble all the cells in one place for a monthly "Celebration." They sponsor several Sunday evening Celebrations in different parts of the area.

Along with nearly all mature cell group movements, ICHTHUS has found it necessary to open its own internal equipping center for developing new workers. Each year it offers one month and one year apprenticeship programs. Those taking the one year training (called "Network") often live in ICHTHUS House, which provides bedrooms and training rooms for those who come from many parts of the earth to serve and be trained. These students spend several hours each morning being taught by members of the Ministry Team and the rest of the day forming new cell groups in unreached areas of the city.

Unwilling to limit its vision to London, ICHTHUS has a launching center in Cyprus for planting cells in Islamic areas. Its ministry in Turkey involves those in "Network" as a part of their course work. This vision is so ingrained in the members that I found it burning in the heart of every single member I interviewed while living among them for a week. They have a great vision and see their church as a *movement,* not just a *parish church.* In October, 1990, they had 200 cells in 32 London congregations and three congregations in the Middle East.

Examples of Cell Group Churches: Australia

Australia has imported all its religious structures from Britain or the United States (including the Mormon cult)—with one exception. The Christian Outreach Centre movement began in Brisbane. It is a cell group church movement which has now penetrated dozens of cities across the vast continent. The mother church in Brisbane is planning to construct a 40,000 seat auditorium to accommodate the Celebrations of its cells. This growth has taken place in a period of less than twenty-five years. It's built around a principle: *every Christian is a minister!*

Les Scarborough, a Baptist, has formed a cell group church in the foothills west of Sydney. The St. Marys Baptist Church has developed cells which cluster regionally into congregations. Les faithfully meets with men within the church who have been tutored by him to preach and teach. Together, they shape a common sermon to be delivered in seven different locations each Sunday. They have constructed a special type of house in one subdivision which houses a lay pastor, with a large room on one end for use as a training and worship center for cells in the neighborhood. So significant is their reputation that the government has built a two million dollar school on twenty acres of land for their use in providing Christian education to those living in the region.

Examples of Cell Group Churches: South America

In Santiago, Chile, the Pentecostal granddaddy of all cell group churches numbers over 40,000. In Brazil, at least one cell group church has erected a 25,000 seat auditorium. Cell group churches exist all over the continent, both among evangelicals and Roman Catholics, who call them *Communidades de Base.* A Baptist pastor in Cali, Columbia, calls his cells *Grupos de Amor,* reaching out to touch an area of slum dwellers along a major river in the city. When a flood wiped away the shacks in this slum, cell group members made mattresses from sheets filled with straw. They loaded them on a flatbed truck and drove down the riverside, giving them to those who had lost their shanties. They also announced they were going to form cell groups and pointed to a huge tree as the place where those who were interested could meet them on the following Friday night. They thought ten or twenty might respond: they were stunned when *over one hundred* showed up! They quickly sent an S.O.S. to the students at a nearby Baptist seminary, who provided assistance in forming groups among the poor.

Examples of Cell Group Churches: The United States

In America, Portland's New Hope Community Church has set a goal to reach 100,000 people by the year 2000 through "Tender Loving Care Groups." Pastor Dale Galloway tells of the crucial decision he made to totally scrap the traditional form of the church. He had started out to blend the cell group church with the traditional structure he had used to begin the work. Slowly, he realized he was trying to mix oil and water. He called in his staff and informed them their titles would change from "Minister of Education" and "Minister of Music" to "Zone Ministers." *He rightly realized that it is not possible to have a church built around programs and build people at the same time!*

Scores of other models from the American scene could be given in this report. Because the book dedicates itself to suggesting how cells should be formed in this culture, other examples will be mentioned from time to time in the text.

Cell group churches are springing up in all parts of the nation. They do not yet attract the attention of denominational leaders because they are in the formative stages. Well equipped men, like Dr. Lynn Reddick of Augusta, Georgia, are experimenting with ways to use cells effectively in America's culture. His vision is to spread "In Focus" churches everywhere. He already has sent church members to Alaska and Haiti to plant cell group churches. Our office in Houston receives daily calls for help and advice from pastors and church members who are with-drawing from traditional church life to form cell group churches.

Cell Group Churches And "Third Wave" Theology

The significance of cell group churches has, in the minds of many evangelicals, been downgraded because of the close alignment between cell group churches and what is popularly called the "signs and wonders" movement. This is, indeed, unfortunate. For those whose church life is formed around meeting in church buildings, there seems to be a limited vision of what is *needed* to bring the unreached to saving faith.

Many who scoff at manifestations of the power of God, manifested to set men free in our day, do not have unchurched friends. The more one leaves the insulation of the church office, the books, and the churched, the more the need for the *power* of God to do the *work* of God is recognized.

Physical, emotional, and spiritual healing is constantly experienced by those who live together in the cell group church. Building up one another through using spiritual gifts is their life-style. Without the real power of God, a ministry to the abused, the abandoned, and the possessed is a farce. Cell group churches are not to be seen as Pentecostal or charismatic, but as *biblical.*

I submit we should confess that the traditional church has little need for the power required when assaulting the gates of hell. However, when cells begin to invade Satan's territories, they discover that evil forces are real! Peter Wagner writes,

> *The most typical reaction of non-Pentecostals to spiritism has been one of polemics, and the kind of polemics which indicates that they do not take the validity of spiritism very seriously . . . . Spiritism is not simply ignorance, superstition and chicanery. A Christianity which does not recognize it as a manifestation of the powers of darkness will continue to be impotent in this particular field of evangelism.* [25]

Dr. Charles H. Kraft has written *Christianity With Power* to plead with evangelicals to rethink their cognitive views of how ministry is to be done. He explains,

. . . I am writing as an Evangelical to Evangelicals about a new understanding and experience of Christianity. I have long been part of a branch of Christianity that I feel has believed correctly and accomplished much for God in nearly all areas except that of spiritual power. So I am not about to give up the good things that have been a part of my own Evangelical Christian experience for nearly half a century. Indeed, these good things are more meaningful to me than ever before. But I have now experienced more of what Jesus expected of us than my Evangelical heritage had provided for me.[26]

Spiritual power is the birthright of believers—*all* believers, from the most mature to the most recent convert. Jesus' ministry would have been impossible without constant manifestations of power from on high. In the Great Commission, He began by saying, *"all power is given unto me,"* and ended by saying, *"I am with you always..."* Cell churches are constantly touching the evil within their world and constantly needing spiritual power.

Conclusions

1. We must recognize the activity of the Holy Spirit in the cell group movement and seek to use it for the harvest of precious souls. No other form of church life promises to harvest at the same rate the population is growing.

2. We must allow new missionaries, new pastors, and new churches to experiment with the creation of cell group churches. Many traditional denominational structures and mission boards are not open to the experimentation required to develop new concepts. Most pastors have too vested an interest in their careers, their incomes, and their reputations to participate in this new form of church life. They are to be excused with love from being participants—but respectfully asked to refrain from vilifying what the Holy Spirit is doing! They are reminded of Gamaliel's words about the young church in the book of Acts: if it's of the Lord, it can't be stopped, and if it's not, why bother to fight it?

3. We must actively abandon the hope that stagnant churches can be renewed by painful restructuring and the tacking on of cell group church principles. According to Jesus, it's not

possible to put new wine in old wineskins! The plan for the stagnant church must begin with the *wineskin,* not the new wine. A church cannot effectively mix traditional patterns of church life with cell group patterns. There must be a deliberate transition. After devoting nearly a quarter of a century to the attempt to help "renew the churches," I am a total skeptic that it can be done. The only hope for old wineskins is to pour out the wine they contain into new ones and *throw the leaky things away!*

2 THE ROADBLOCK: THE "P.B.D." CHURCH

Many of God's people are sincerely seeking for a better way to experience church life. They are recognizing they have not found it in the traditional church. We are now in a transitional period in the life of the people of God. It's the beginning of the Second Reformation, and it will go on for a long time to come.

Current Attempts At New Structures

Other more traditional church styles are being tested in this period of unrest. The "Megachurch" has become the contemporary "supermarket" for churchgoers. Other groups are seeking their destiny in the "Praise Churches," which provide overhead projectors to display the newest in worship songs. There are the "Restoration Churches," seeking to provide people with a more personal experience of the Holy Spirit's activity. Blends of the older charismatic churches continue to crop up, some almost cult-like in their control of their memberships. It's all a part of the contemporary search for spirituality among the people of God. With each new experiment, the traditional church loses ground.

In all of these attempts, a basic flaw in church life is still evident: *they're all "large group" structures.* In every case, the members still drive to the meeting place from their homes. When these churches use small groups, they use them as "holding tanks" for members. As one pastor ruefully said to me, "There are 22,000 'cruisematics' in this city, bouncing among the churches.

Each Sunday, they attend the one with the most exciting guest speaker or singer. I'm using small groups to hang on to my share of them." Such use of groups by pastors is theologically evil. Such groups develop into navel-gazing clusters of impotent Christians who "Bible study" themselves to death, ignoring the cry of unreached persons. In examining these groups, I frequently hear the comment, "We have so many needs among ourselves! There just isn't time to reach out to new people." In the background, I can hear Beelzebub snickering!

None of these models recognizes the basic flaw in a church lifestyle built upon a "Program Base Design," a term we shall refer to as "P.B.D." The term describes a structure of church life that is neither biblical nor efficient. It's used by nearly one hundred per cent of all traditional churches today, whether they are Evangelical, Liturgical, Pentecostal, or "Fullness" in their theology. It has taken a century for this virus to infect the church worldwide, and it may take another half-century before it finally succeeds in decimating the structures it infects.

"Program Base Design" churches rightly acknowledge that the foundation of their church is Jesus Christ. *What they build upon that foundation is their error,* an error which utterly annihilates what makes the church *authentic.*

To reveal the horror of P.B.D. structures, we shall first view the church in its purest form as revealed in the New Testament.

The Early Church

In the Old Testament, the Tabernacle and the Temple were both referred to as "the house of God" (cf. 1Chronicles 6:48, 25:6, Ezra 5:2, 15). In the New Testament, the concept of "house of God" radically changes. Peter sees believers as "living stones" that are being built up as a "spiritual house" (I Peter 2:5). Thus, "the house of God" is no longer seen as an edifice made by joining stones, but by *joining human lives.* Further, the builder of the house is Jesus Himself, who said in Matthew 16:18, "I will *build* my church." This construction is not to be the work of skilled specialists as was the case in the erection of the Tabernacle. The Lord Himself is to become the builder. The stones He will select for the walls are called *ecclesia,* "called out ones," also translated "church."

The Foundation Of The Church Is Christ;
The Walls Are Formed From The Living Stones

A significant word appears in Jesus' teaching. The Greek word for "build" used in Matthew 16:18 is *oikodomeo*. It is frequently used as a verb to describe the construction of an edifice (Matthew 23:29, 26:61), or, used as a noun, as the building itself (Matthew 24:1). However, it refers most often to construction using material called "living stones." In 1 Corinthians 3:9 Paul says, "...you are...God's *building*." In Acts 20:32, Paul uses the verb form to say that God is the One "who can *build* you up..." Ephesians 2:21 tells us "In him the whole *building* is joined together and rises to become a holy temple in the Lord." Hebrews 3:6 says, "But Christ is faithful as a son over God's house. And we are his *house,* if we hold on to our courage and the hope of which we boast."

As we shall see, *oikodomeo* also describes the main work of the living stones themselves: "Therefore encourage one another and *build each other up,* just as in fact you are doing" (1 Thessalonians 5:11); "From him the whole body, joined and held together by every supporting ligament, grows and *builds itself up* in love, as each part does its work" (Ephesians 4:12).

It is obvious that Jesus intended to be the builder of the church, but just as obvious that the "living stones" were to be empowered by Him to share in the building up, or edifying, of all nearby stones. Consider the lifestyle of such a church: a tight relationship exists between every "living stone" and each contiguous stone. United by the cement of love, the stones know the life of Christ flowing His grace-gifts into them, empowering them to continually build up one another.

The Church Is A Body, Christ Is The Head

Another picture of the church likens it to the human body. Christ now becomes the head, the *ecclesia* the body parts. The Holy Spirit immerses each new believer into the body, properly connected at conversion as a working, functional member. Paul explains in 1 Corinthians 12:14-19 that the unity of this body is such that one body part never says, "I have no need of you" to another member. As the hand and foot and stomach must interact, even so the members of the body of Christ must live in intimacy. The members are united into a whole. There is freedom from diversity, a oneness of mind or feeling, exactly like that of a human body. Once again, the concept of bodily parts being responsible for building up (oikodomeo) one another becomes the focus of their lifestyle (Ephesians 4:15-16).

The Greek word *katartizo* used in Mark 1:19 for mending nets is translated "equipping" in Ephesians 4:12: each body member is to participate in helping other body members be repaired for service. In Galatians 6:1, the "spiritual ones" are again described as mending other body parts that are damaged, restoring them for ministry.

In a study of the early church, one observes that this is theory which was put into practice without a great amount of instruction. Paul describes the mutual building up of believers in 1 Corinthians 14. His order is for every single Christian to use spiritual gifts for the purpose of building up the church. He scoffs at the idea of exercising gifts for personal enjoyment. The word *oikodomeo* appears six times in his teaching (verses 3, 4, 5, 12, 17, 26) as he bears down on the fact that *each one* (absolutely no exceptions!) is to participate in the ministry of building the body: "When you assemble, *each one* has a psalm, has a teaching, has a revelation, has a tongue, has an interpretation. Let all things be done for edification (building up)." The word for "each one" used here does not mean, "each one of you who desires to enter into ministry," but "every single person in the group is to be a participant in the building up." Neither physical nor spiritual youthfulness are to be reasons for exempting Christians from participating. All are to exercise spiritual gifts to edify the others.

The early church did exactly that! Recognizing there cannot be total participation by every member when the gatherings are only made up of large, impersonal groups, the people of God moved from house to house in small groups. By moving among their residences, they became intimately acquainted with each person's surroundings.

Excavations in Jerusalem reflect that only the wealthy had homes with second-floor "Upper Rooms." For the rest, residences would usually not accommodate more than ten to twelve persons. Meeting in small cells—without seasoned leaders—these groups built up one another through mutual ministries.

These house churches functioned from their inception as the nucleus of the Christian community. The Lord of the church *intended* it to be that way; if He had desired it to be otherwise, He could have shaped its lifestyle differently. There were many organizations in His culture that assembled members into halls or specially constructed auditoriums. Guilds had their own edifices. Synagogues had dotted the countryside for generations, gathering members in impersonal large groups. Pagan temples were also common. Nevertheless, Jesus shaped the church to meet in *homes*. His own disciples were gathered together with Him in a *home setting* when He served them their last supper together.

The Home Ministry Of Jesus

It's significant that in Jesus' ministry he operated out of homes, not formal buildings. He often taught his disciples in houses (Mark 2:1; 7:14-27; 9:33; 10:2-12; Matthew 13:36). We frequently see Him in the homes of others, including Peter, Matthew, a ruler, Simon the leper, Simon and Andrew, Levi, a pharisee, Jairus, Zacchaeus, and Martha. He referred to the owner of a large home in Jerusalem who would consider his upper room Jesus' "guest room" (Mark 14:14).

While "the Son of man had no place to lay His head," at the same time He taught in Mark 10:29-30 that "no one who has left home or brothers or sisters or mother or father or children or fields for me and the gospel will fail to receive a hundred times as much in this present age (homes, brothers, sisters, mothers, children and fields...)."

His itinerant servants took this literally. They lived with families in homes wherever they went. In fact, living in a home was a prime strategy for bringing people to personal faith. In Luke 10, Jesus assigned the seventy disciples to go to Perea to enter homes, offering peace to all who lived within. When they found a "man of peace" (one desiring to find peace), they remained in that home, eating and drinking whatever was set before them. In this way, a household would be converted to Christ—and another house church would be formed.

Peter's vision came at the house of Simon in Joppa. It was in the house of Mary the mother of John that Christians gathered to pray. Paul's conversion took place in the house of Judas, as

Ananias prayed with him. We see him staying in homes wherever he served, including the house of Jason—who, as host, had to pay his bail when he was jailed. He lived in the house of Lydia after her household had been converted and ate in the jailer's house after his whole family had come to believe in God. There are many more who hosted the Apostle, including Titius Justus, Crispus, Philip, Gaius, Aquila and Priscilla.

There is a very important reason for the early church to be shaped in homes. *It is in this location that values are shared.* It may be possible to transmit *information* in a neutral building, but few *values* are implanted there. Value systems are ingrained through living together in a household. Something stirs deep within when life is shared between the young and old, the strong and the weak, the wise and the foolish. In the house groups, all participated and all were impacted by the values of the others as Christ lived within them.

The Impact Of House Groups

The lifestyle of the first Christians meeting in house groups was so powerful that daily conversions took place. The total involvement of Christians in house groups overwhelmed outsiders: "But if all prophesy, and an unbeliever or an ungifted man enters, he is convicted *by all;* he is called to account *by all;* the secrets of his heart are disclosed; and so he will fall on his face and worship God, declaring that God is certainly among you" (I Corinthians 14:24-25). This may be termed "Body Life Evangelism." The simple witness of the life of Jesus, observed as it flowed in His body with power and reality, caused the most hardened skeptics to confess Him as their Lord.

In that early church, there were no specialists. Apart from the teaching of the Apostles, leadership was not emphasized to any great extent. Details were handled by those who were closest at hand as needs arose.

Our Lord knows there are two factors in spiritual growth. One is *receiving* His power; the other is becoming the *channel* of it. Maturity only occurs when both are experienced. The greatest men and women among the house churches were those who *served,* not those who *led.*

Every household had a "father," a man respected and

obeyed. At the same time, a good father would encourage the development of all within the household. He would not be a tyrant in it. Only at the end of the New Testament era do we find a house church with a petty dictator, and he is soundly rebuked by John (3 John 9-11). The domination of one person over others limits the possibility of growth. This was not permitted in the early church. It is important to realize that cults universally control their members, while the true body of Christ desires to see each member grow into wholeness of life.

The house groups were not independent from one another. They networked together from the first hour of their existence. This city-wide federation shows that the "house churches" combined to form a "local church." Paul twice refers to "the church of God which is in Corinth" (1 Corinthians 1:2 and 2 Corinthians 1:1), indicating a general relationship existed between all the believers there. Again, he speaks of the "church of the Thessalonians" (1 Thessalonians 1:1 and 2 Thessalonians 1:1). He also refers to "the *whole* church" in Romans 16:23. In 1 Corinthians 11, the city-wide gathering of the house groups for the Love Feast created a scandal of lovelessness. In Acts 20:6-12, Paul's visit to Troas occasioned a gathering of all the house groups to break bread and hear the Apostle teach them.

The Church's Servants

As the movement developed, equippers of the saints for the work of their ministry arose from within the house groups. Ephesians 4:11-12 specifically states that Christ Himself "gave some to be apostles, some to be prophets, some to be evangelists, and some to be pastors and teachers, *to prepare God's people for works of service,* so that the body of Christ may be built up . . ." Nothing is ever said about Paul or anyone else in the church appointing any of *these* men. This silence is significant. These men earned their positions by demonstrating the anointing of God on their equipping ministries.

The first task of an "equipper" is to model the lifestyle that is to be transferred to members of the body. Thus, Paul's comments about bishops/elders and deacons dealt with their *characters*, not their *duties.*

In all probability, the role of "deacon" was assigned by the home group itself to one in their midst who modelled a servant life. This man (or woman, as in the case of Phoebe in Cenchrea) has no job description in all of scripture. When one discards the clutter of ecclesiasticism developed through the centuries, the reason for the lack of a job description becomes clear. When house groups met, they shared the Love Feast. "Deacon" means literally, "one who waits on tables." Had not Jesus said, "The greatest among you is the one who serves"? Had He Himself not washed feet at the last supper? Clearly, the godly man or woman in the midst of the house group was awarded this title, and respectfully permitted to serve the Lord's Supper, perhaps the entire meal, to the rest.

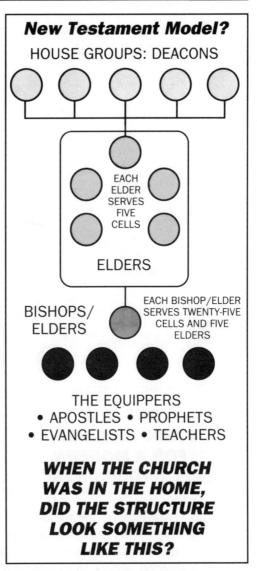

New Testament Model?

HOUSE GROUPS: DEACONS

EACH ELDER SERVES FIVE CELLS

ELDERS

BISHOPS/ ELDERS

EACH BISHOP/ELDER SERVES TWENTY-FIVE CELLS AND FIVE ELDERS

THE EQUIPPERS
• APOSTLES • PROPHETS
• EVANGELISTS • TEACHERS

WHEN THE CHURCH WAS IN THE HOME, DID THE STRUCTURE LOOK SOMETHING LIKE THIS?

As we examine the life of the current cell group church structures around the world, we can reflect some practical light on the tasks of the offices mentioned in the New Testament. These cell group churches share common church structures needed for their celebrations. Each cell has a servant-leader. For every five cells, there is a pastoral figure (often called a "Zone Servant") to counsel and guide the ministries. For every 25 cells and five Zone

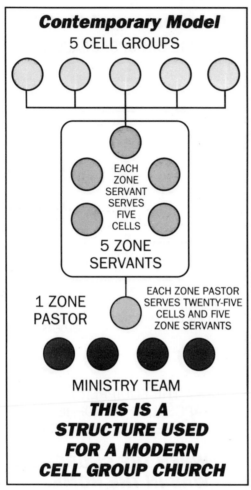

Contemporary Model

5 CELL GROUPS

EACH ZONE SERVANT SERVES FIVE CELLS

5 ZONE SERVANTS

1 ZONE PASTOR

EACH ZONE PASTOR SERVES TWENTY-FIVE CELLS AND FIVE ZONE SERVANTS

MINISTRY TEAM

THIS IS A STRUCTURE USED FOR A MODERN CELL GROUP CHURCH

Servants, there must be a person to shepherd this flock of two to three hundred (often called a "Zone Pastor"). Working with the entire city-wide local church, men who are recognized as equippers provide guidance, teaching, and equipping to all the cells, called the "Ministry Team."

While it is a matter of speculation, we may well consider the offices mentioned by Paul in the light of the universal pattern for churches in his day. In each area, the church originated when home groups clustered to form local churches. In the light of this, how would the *offices* be structured? If they were even close to the way current cell group leadership is arranged, this illustration may explain the function of a church life that had no hierarchy. (At the very least, this attempt is a light year beyond the corruption the traditional church has made of the office!)

The Deacon serves the house group. Since an Elder (also called "Bishop") requires experience in the *developing* and *multiplying* of house groups, it would take about two years before he or she would be prepared to assume responsibility for several of them. Thus, Paul would rightly tell Timothy to appoint elders when returning to churches after an absence of a couple of years. Those to be appointed as Elders would be easily recognized after such a length of time. Note that in this interim no "Senior

Pastor" (to use a modern term) or "Elder" even existed. Until the house groups proliferated, there was no need for these workers. If such an office existed, Timothy would not have had the *freedom* to direct the internal affairs of the local church. Church planters in the book of Acts were circumspect about interfering in the churches after they were launched.

There is both biblical and extra-biblical evidence that some apostles, prophets, evangelists, and teachers were itinerant servants who travelled between the local churches. These titles refer to offices within church life. They *founded* churches, *taught* and *equipped* members, *transmitted* divine revelations, and *expounded* scripture. They were links between the house churches and their assembled local church structure and also between all the cities where churches existed.

This, then, is the "People Base Design" of the church as it is supposed to be. Contrast it now with the "Program Base Design" ("P.B.D.") which has insidiously crept as a deadly virus into all of today's church life.

Today's "Program Base Design" Church

Before I present these thoughts, I want to express my love and affection for the precious men and women who serve their Lord so faithfully in P.B.D. structures. Their love for Christ and their sacrificial service is not to be despised or ridiculed. They often labor seventy or eighty hours a week for their Lord and are sometimes scandalously underpaid. They are sincerely seeking to do the work of the Lord.

They are the victims of P.B.D. structures. It is an agonizing thing for a family trapped in church work to "start over" after spending years in a denominational or interdenominational system. Most are not in a position to even *consider* doing so.

In a sentence, the P.B.D. concept doesn't build *people* on the foundation of Christ; it only builds *programs*. The assumption is that the programs are necessary to build the people, but it just doesn't achieve this goal!

The first thing a P.B.D. church looks for are *Specialists* to direct the different programs of the church. Even the smallest group will seek for a *Pastor-Specialist* who can come and preach, teach, counsel, raise the budget, administer its spending, win the lost, and effectively manage the church schedule. He is not particularly seen as an "equipper of the saints for the work of ministry;" instead, he is The Minister. He does the things that professional clergymen do. He preaches, marries, buries, visits the sick in the hospitals, pays courtesy calls to the elderly, consults with the deacons or elders, and—if the church can afford it— supervises the staff. He is the primary victim of P.B.D. church life. He will move his family to new "church fields" on a regular basis, always seeking a more responsive group of church members to fulfill his desire to reach the lost.

Yet, while he desires to reach the lost, he doesn't have time to know many of them. Less than five out of a hundred P.B.D. pastors (or missionaries overseas) have as many as *three* gold plated, certified, hell-raising unbelievers numbered among their close friends. There isn't enough time in their busy week to *know* the unconverted. The entire congregation can thus assume that cultivating unreached persons is not a high priority for the Christian life, since their leader never produces a convert apart from his pulpit ministry. With such a model, they also busy themselves with church tasks.

The larger P.B.D. church will seek for other Specialists to work on the church staff. Typically, it is felt these people must come from *outside* the congregation. Thus, endless webs of "search committees" and "pulpit committees" scout out the best Specialists they can afford to hire. They arrive from Chicago or Memphis, Atlanta or Phoenix, move into their offices, and begin to develop their specialty.

For example, the Minister of Education will scour the church roll for those who can teach or serve administratively in a Sunday School department. He will faithfully fill vacancies with the best workers he can find and form classes to train new workers for the future growth he anticipates. These times of equipping focus on the needs of the *program,* not the needs of the unconverted community or the personal ministry of the trainee apart from the Sunday School.

The Minister of Music will find those who can sing, play instruments, or lead a children's choir. He, too, will offer *only* the training required to develop his specialty within the life of the church.

Other P.B.D. Specialists may include the Minister of Children, the Minister of Youth, the Minister of Singles, the Minister of Young Adults, the Minister of Median Adults, the Minister of Older Adults, the Business Manager, etc., etc. *In each case, they have a vertical vision of church life.*

Smaller churches fill these same Specialist positions with volunteers. These are the precious saints who have many stars in their crowns! Unlike full-time church staffers, they must juggle employment with their church work in a limited time frame. Sometimes their families suffer terribly because of the demands made on them by the church. Surveys of heavily involved volunteer church workers in P.B.D. structures show they burn out after two or three years. Furthermore, it's shocking to find a large number of them among the ranks of those who no longer regularly attend church.

With few or no exceptions, the Specialists involve no more than 15% of the total members as working volunteers. The balance of the members are expected to attend the many functions which have been arranged for them. In large churches, this may involve as many as one hundred meetings a month!

That brings up the next P.B.D. problem: *inactives* typically number from 40% to 50% of the church membership. In spite of the many meetings scheduled, simply being a passive participant loses its flavor after a time. Half of the inactives attend about once a month, and the other half don't come at all.

The mismatch of Christians with church tasks they perform is heart breaking. When the Program needs a warm body, people are enlisted regardless of their gifts (which are frequently ignored) or their abilities (which are frequently underutilized). Thousands more are not used at all—they are not deemed suitable for the vacancies to be filled. Few opportunities exist for the discovery of spiritual gifts. The work of the P.B.D. church doesn't need them very often or for very long at a time. The God-given calling of *every believer* to be involved in building up others in the body of Christ is never developed. This is true of the charismatic or Pentecostal groups as well as the Evangelicals.

Consider the inefficiency of the P.B.D. church: buildings stand empty except for a handful of hours a week; the Specialists service the members only to expand their specialty; only one-eighth of the members are involved in P.B.D. tasks; a massive group of hopeless inactives exists; and, last but not least, *the*

entire church has virtually no contact with the unreached community!

How can this be reconciled with the intention of Christ to "seek and to save that which was lost?" Jesus said in John 12:26, "Whoever serves me must follow me; and where I am, my servant also will be." Apart from a few contacts with the synagogues and the Temple, Jesus' life was spent among sinners. The One who reminded us that the sick have need of a physician simply cannot be pleased with the P.B.D. church that seldom ventures out of its church building to know or minister among the winebibbers and sinners. The reason this condition exists is that there are no Specialists in the church who are specifically hired to develop a "program" to minister to those who are poor, blind, imprisoned, and downcast—the specific tasks Jesus listed as His own job description. If the body of Christ is to be doing the tasks of Christ, the P.B.D. structure can be seen as not only inefficient, but *downright defective!*

Indeed, the "stranger evangelism" practiced by the P.B.D. church does more harm than good. The Monday night forays by the church into the community to invite people to return with them to attend church and accept Christ are devoid of even the *desire* to develop true friendships with those strangers visited. The fifteen minutes spent with those visited is often little more than an encouragement to attend the next public service.

The term used for the event is *"Prospect* Visitation." The term clearly reveals the value system of the P.B.D. church: people are viewed through the windows of the *programs:* "they are a *prospect* for our Sunday school class; he is a *good prospect* for our church—I happen to know he tithes." What is more demeaning or dehumanizing than turning a *person* into a *prospect?* When the *living stones* are turned into *programs,* the vocabulary also becomes demeaning.

Worst of all, life in the P.B.D. church does not provide the all-important *koinonia,* or "fellowship," needed to create true community, lifestyles where people build up one another. I recall a visit Ruth and I made to a small church in southern Indiana. I insisted on our being put into the Sunday School class for our age group. There were about fifteen of us in the class. The man who was serving as moderator said, "Folks, I ran into Bill Foster in the hardware store yesterday. He explained to me that he and Helen were divorcing, and he has moved out of their house. They talked it over and decided that neither one of them would feel comfortable coming back to our class under the circumstances. Each one is going to go elsewhere, and he asked me to tell you this so they wouldn't be embarrassed if either one bumped into you." After a few moments of stunned silence, one of the class said, "Why, I attended our class party in their home a month ago. I didn't know they were having problems. Did any of you know their marriage was in danger?" Everyone shook their heads "No." I asked, "How long were you folks together in this class with them?" The group had been together between three and four years—never becoming close enough to sense such a deep problem! The couple floated off into oblivion, sincerely wanting to be left alone as they went through their traumas.

There is literally no time or place in a P.B.D. church for people to become close to one another. The *programs* insulate members from each other. When they meet, it's in the neutral setting of the church building. Each encounter is carefully *programmed:* there's choir music to be rehearsed, a Bible lesson to be studied, a budget to be prepared. Bonding together in love and commitment isn't possible. *There's no community in the P.B.D. church structure.* Those who create it must do so in spite of the organization's schedule, and are subject to criticism for not being cooperative with the church program.

While all the preceding issues may be ignored by some, this issue of not living in true community is utterly unbiblical, totally indefensible, and tragically inexcusable! The P.B.D. removal of true community deeply grieves the Holy Spirit.

The "Parish Mentality"

Another problem with P.B.D. churches is their "parish mentality." A Baptist, Methodist, or other brand of church planter will enter a portion of a city and mark off a "church field." He recognizes the existence of "sister churches" (same brand) in neighboring districts, and considers their "church fields" out of bounds. Each "local church" sifts through its limited territory seeking for "like-us people" until most are finally drawn into the membership. Stagnation finally sets in. Recognition of the other brands (denominations) of churches also in the area is limited; such pastors barely know each other. They only cooperate when Billy Graham comes to town to hold a crusade. *None* of these churches pay much attention to the unchurched of the area at any time, even though it's obvious by counting noses on any given Sunday morning that 60-75% of the people in their parish areas are not attending anywhere.

The planting of new P.B.D. churches has become a serious problem. As long as churches are built upon a P.B.D., they will be forced to erect P.B.D. structures for them. You can't have one without the other! It now costs in excess of one million dollars to build a new church facility in many urban areas. As a result, many new subdivisions are devoid of churches.

The foolishness of this extravagance is revealed when one studies cell group church models. For example, the ICHTHUS Fellowship in London has vowed to never invest God's money in erecting a church plant. They are a beautiful example of the new style of church life, reaching the untouched on a daily basis.

This conviction isn't true of all cell group churches. Many of them have grown so large they cannot gather the local church together for celebrations in the small facilities available to them. Frequently, it becomes cheaper to build and own than to endlessly rent.

Dion Robert slept beside the desk of his office for years because the church had no space for his family to live. He preached seven times every Wednesday, Friday, and Sunday in a tiny, crowded room that might be used by 75 or 80 Westerners.

He packed 300 Ivorians into it! With 1,950 cell groups in Abidjan, he obviously needed an auditorium to assemble his people for celebrations. In that city about 80% are unemployed, making the costliness of construction a terrible burden. Many of us helped him with his financial need, and the cell group church now has a spartan "Temple" which might seat about two thousand Westerners, but seats six thousand people "African style." The cell groups built it with their own hands. As they received the money, they bought a few more bags of cement and reinforcing bars. It went up slowly, over a period of more than seven years, and is now complete. Dion Robert will soon need to preach seven times a Sunday in the new "Temple," for his congregation is multiplying the cells four times each year.

He will soon face the problem Yonggi Cho struggles with in Seoul: a need for even more space to use when the flock needs to be taught the word of God. The ten thousand seat auditorium was enlarged to twenty-five thousand, but it was still inadequate for the members to squeeze in to seven Sunday services. Cho has solved his current problem by adding a second 25,000 seat auditorium on the opposite shore of the Han River. Including the auxiliary auditoriums built into a high rise building next to the original sanctuary, he will now preach to over 70,000 people in each service. That's what can happen when churches have no "parish limits!"

In the pure cell group church, the growth of the congregation comes through the ministry of the cells, not just the "celestial funnel" of scintillating music and unique preaching. Cell group members travel to locations provided to be taught the word of God.

The Current "Lordship Evangelism" Controversy

At the present moment, a great controversy is raging among P.B.D. evangelicals over "Lordship Evangelism." The premise is that we are not telling people what salvation really involves. There should be more stress on the fact that one is not a Christian until he or she confesses Christ to be Lord over all dimensions of one's life. We are told we should insist on *total commitment* by every person claiming to be a believer. The controversy is a reaction to the cheap "easy believism" to be found in American churches. The suggestion is that people should be told *up front* that they can't be lukewarm Christians!

The debate is purportedly about authentic conversion and evangelistic preaching. It totally ignores the real problem which causes this "sit and soak" variety of church members. Such wimpy believers are the direct result of a church life that builds programs, not people, on the foundation of Christ. *As long as there are P.B.D. churches, there will be mediocre members.* They go together like ham and eggs! When a preacher presides over a P.B.D. church and allows 15% of the congregation to "fill positions" in his programs, he must admit that Lordship for them is simply oiling the machinery. While he comes out of his study after forty hours of preparation to deliver his sermon, he must realize he has failed to model the life of an involved Christian who sits down by wells to talk to women who have been married five times and now live in adultery. If he is not going to pay any attention to the equipping of the saints, what can he expect to have in the congregation? When 85% of the congregation who are not enlisted to work in the programs are herded from one meeting to another, and one sermon to another, the pastor should not be surprised when there are large numbers of mediocre Christians. Until he is willing to stop the P.B.D. virus, he has no right to chide the twaddlers in his sermons!

Dion Robert has no problem with "No Lord" church members. He actually prepares his messages from the feedback from the weekly cell servant reports. They indicate the spiritual and personal problems of people in the cells. He preaches on these subjects.

The cells meet to internalize the truths he presents. His preached word is briefly reviewed in their next meetings. If his sermon dealt with stealing, bitterness, or even adultery, the presider of the cell begins by asking each member in turn, "What is the state of your soul concerning this issue?" Each person frankly shares his or her condition. This is followed by the cell members building up one another, supporting one another, and helping one another through moments of weakness and sin. Week after week, this takes place in all the cells. "Lordship salvation" for a cell group church is not a theology to be debated by pastors and professors; *for the living stones, it's a lifestyle.*

In a cell group Ruth and I have attended for months, we

recently had a precious wife call the group to gather for a special session. As we sat around a kitchen table, she said, "I have called you together to confess my sins. I have sinned against my Lord, but that means I have also sinned against you who make up His body along with me." I shall never forget the power of Christ's presence in our midst that night! When we got into the car, I said to Ruth, "That's the closest we're ever going to get to the New Testament church. If we travelled in a time machine and went back two thousand years to go to church, it wouldn't have been much different from what we have just experienced!"

Straight ahead lies yesterday! The first century church has returned to us in a simple, straightforward format. It's composed of deeply committed people who form cell groups. For them, as for the early Christians, this is their "church," their "basic Christian community." They not only worship—they also minister to those who are poor, blind, imprisoned, and stepped on. They grow so fast that in the United States they can average multiplying into two groups twice a year—in Houston, every five and a half months, to be exact. They are God's solution to the decaying P.B.D. church problem. *They are where we go from here.*

I return to the disturbing point that has been made before in this book and will be repeated again and again. The cell group church lifestyle is too New Testament to be blended into a P.B.D. structure. It causes endless conflicts for those who attempt it.

The P.B.D. church competes within its own membership for people to fill the program positions. It's not unusual to find a truly dedicated worker who teaches a Sunday school class, serves on the official board, sings in the choir, and works on the finance committee as well. This person is assuredly a "pillar of the church." How do you think he or she will react when the suggestion is made that the church is now going to add on cell group life? Does this person have time to attend even one more "something" each week? Can the P.B.D. exist if all such people abandon their obligations to become relational, ministering, caring persons? Of course not.

Therefore, the pastor who attempts to insert cell group life into the P.B.D. can rightly expect the leaders of his church will not participate at all, or only passively. If the cells get off the ground, it will be done by involving those who now "sit and soak." It's mighty hard to get clinkers to burn after the fire has gone out.

They have gotten into the habit of doing nothing for so long that a major value change is required. I have prepared *Life Basic Training* as a small group module for such people, and it is quite effective—but should not be followed in a P.B.D. setting by forming a "second church," a cell group church.

We are not without experience in such matters. If the church forms a "right wing" and a "left wing," the result is *not* a Bird of Paradise! Pastors who have attempted to mix P.B.D. and cell groups have found themselves among the lists of the unemployed. The old leadership, still in power and tolerating this foreign object called "The Pastor" for a season, can be brutal when the "mere nothings" of the cell group movement begin to take hold.

Nor will the *Specialists* endorse a pattern of church life which threatens their careers and their programs. One pastor had a longing for many years to lead his church, mainly servicing those over fifty years of age, to transition into cells. Many of his staff members had served the church longer than he had and were almost unmanageable. When I was brought in to consult with the staff about the value of cell groups, the Minister of Education took me to his office. He bluntly said, "As long as I am in this position, I will fight the pastor, you, and this idea to the end. I have too much to do already, and this would fall on my shoulders to implement. I don't care *what* the pastor wants. I am solidly opposed to any new responsibilities around here."

The fact that the church, with over nine hundred members, had only seen converts among the children of church members for four years, meant nothing to him. The knowledge that a barbecue shop across the wide street from the church was a haven for crack selling didn't bother him at all. The awareness that the church was fast becoming a haven for the elderly was of no consequence to him. What *did* bother him was his own personal schedule and his unwillingness to win the world Christ died on the cross to redeem. He was the ultimate example of a Specialist gone to seed!

Perhaps there will be those who read this book who are not as old as I am and who still have enough youthful optimism to believe you can pour new wine into old wineskins. I no longer believe that. The hope of the church is in the formation of new wineskins. No matter how rich and tasty the wine may be, if it leaks out all over the ground, it has little value.

My friends in the "Fullness" and "Deeper Life" movements must, sooner or later, realize that they cannot bring the Lordship of Christ to folks who are nurtured in a Lordship of Programs structure. In this transitional period, some are convinced that we must simply create a hunger for God in individuals. To wrench them away from the importance of *living in community* in cells where they will discover their spiritual gifts is a great blunder. As my close friend Jack Taylor has stated, there is no better place under heaven for spiritual gifts to be properly developed than in a cell group. It is there, *and nowhere else,* that Christians can be taught to appreciate, desire, and exercise spiritual gifts. The cell group is the channel of power. It is the gateway to enter into the supernatural, the entrance to every believer discovering the power of God to heal, to deliver, and to provide growth. No matter how wonderful a theological position may seem, the heart of changing values is not theology but the practical application of it in experience. The valid church is only peripherally experienced in a P.B.D. setting. It requires the people of God to gather themselves as God intended before the setting for the experience will allow His fullness to flow.

Back in the 1970's, a pastor visiting our cell group experiment in Houston said to me, "One thing that bothers me is what is going to happen to the members of your church when they get a taste of this lifestyle and then move to another city. Will they be content to go back into traditional churches?" I answered, "I hope not!"

The power of culture is a strong magnet which draws people back into the kingdoms of this world. The P.B.D. church is more a worldly kingdom than a part of the Kingdom of God, providing personal significance and power, social life, and contacts to its members. It doesn't do a lot to equip them for warfare in heavenly places. So, for those who don't want to *accept* the Lordship of Christ, the church as we have known it is a safe haven.

For those who step into cell group church life, that's not an option. Every time the cell meets each person is to be a minister or a receiver of ministry. There's really no place to hide! As an Australian friend of mine in Sydney said to me, "When I came into this lifestyle, there was nothing more important to me than being *flat out* for God!"

A Study In Contrasts:
The New Testament and Today's Church

	THE NEW TESTAMENT CHURCH	THE CHURCH OF TODAY
LOCATION	Moved From House To House	Meets In Church Buildings
SIZE OF GROUPS	Small, Intimate Groups	Large, Impersonal Groups
ACTIVITIES	Daily Fellowship	Weekly Worship Services
SUPPORT SYSTEM	Building Up One Another	Problem? See The Pastor
RELATIONSHIPS	Intimate; Helping One Another	Remote; Little Transparency
DISCIPLING	"Mouth To Ear;" Modelling; Personal Values Shaped	Classes, Notebooks; Little Modelling; Values Not Shaped
PRIMARY TASKS OF LEADERS	Every Believer Equipped To Do The Work Of The Ministry	Directing The "Program Base Design"
PRAYER LIFE	Hours Daily; Heavy Emphasis	Individual Choice; Limited
PASTOR'S DUTY	Model The Life Of A Believer	Preach Good Sermons
EXPECTATIONS OF MEMBERS	Ministering To Others; Total Servanthood And Stewardship	Attendance; Tithing; Work In The "Programs"
PERSPECTIVE	Cell Groups The Focal Point	Congregation The Focal Point
KEY WORDS	"Go And Make Disciples"	"Come Grow With Us"
TEACHINGS	Apply The Scriptures To Needs And Relationships	Subscribe To The Distinctive Beliefs Of This Church
SPIRITUAL GIFTS	Regularly Exercised By All Believers To Build Up Others In The Cell Group Gatherings	Either Downplayed Or Often Used As A "Crowd-Pleaser" In Public Services
COMMITMENT	To Increase The Kingdom; Unity, Body Life	To Enlarge The Institution; Uniformity
EVALUATION TEST	"How You Serve"	"What You Know"
SOURCE FOR SECURING STAFF	Servant Workers Developed Within; Tested Before They Are Set Apart For Ministry	Trained, Professional Clergy

POOR LOST SHEEP: P.B.D. GROUPS

Theology breeds methodology! When methods are used without a proper theology, they become uncontrolled headaches. There must be a Biblically based foundation behind cell groups. For those launching a Cell Group Church, this is vitally important.

In the P.B.D. church, all sorts of cells have been tried. Prayer cells, Bible study cells, navel-gazing cells, closed cells (so we can "go deeper"), therapy cells—*all kinds of cells* have been started without a single thought to the theology behind them. Most of them have been ineffective, and some now think the "fad" of the cell group is passing away. *Not so!* We are simply seeing the self-destruction of small groups which have been built upon the sand instead of the Rock.

Dr. Robert Banks of Canberra, Australia, described some cells which are conceived and birthed with serious problems:

The Cell Of Self-Centeredness

The first of these is a cell which is not "owned" by *anyone*, let alone by the *entire group.* It is attended with a spirit of self-centeredness by its constituents: "I come to this group to be enriched by it. I don't have any commitment to it, or to the other people in it. Furthermore, when the group no longer meets my needs, I'll leave it. My only reason for attending it is for what I get out of it." The purpose of such a group might be for Bible study, for losing weight, or to get through a personal crisis. While it might continue for

"What's in this group for ME?"

some time, the average attender will drop out after a few weeks or months. This cell lacks a basic spirit of servanthood, so necessary for true Christian community to exist.

The Cell For Personal Enrichment

In this group, there is a sincere desire by the members to create a climate where personal growth can take place. They want to "peel off layers" to become totally transparent persons with each other, believing that in this openness they will come to new levels of spirituality and self-awareness. They mistakenly feel the only way to accomplish this is to create a *closed group*. Thus, they become alienated from all but themselves. In so doing, they limit the resources God might use to create new life in them.

"Us four, NO MORE!"

Such a group eventually ossifies. Whether it meets for "deep Bible study," for personal sharing, as a prayer group, or for some other reason, the seeds of demise are planted by the very way it has been structured.

This type of group also can be created unknowingly by a church that limits the membership of a cell to the formal membership of the church. Such a decision gives total license to the congregation to ignore the unbelievers around them, becoming closed to all but themselves. It has been tried over and over—and it has never, *ever* worked!

I recall a church that did this very thing a few years ago, changing their Wednesday prayer meeting in the sanctuary into groups meeting in homes. It was popular for a little while, but then boredom and ossification set in. The leadership eventually had to disband the groups entirely. Such a congregation will resist using *any* type of small group for a long, long time!

Theologically, this cell violates the basic New Testament teaching that maturity does not develop in a vacuum. To really have a *growth* group, the Christian community must be in touch with its environment, penetrating it like salt and yeast within dough. Quite often the insertion of just one new person into a group brings fresh insights to those already in it. Jesus warned us against becoming like the Pharisees, who kept to themselves and even refused to allow their *garments* to be touched by outsiders. Living things don't live very long in a vacuum. Thus, those who have experimented with this type of cell have had little success.

The Cell For Strengthening The "Witnesses"

Of all the models we have considered thus far, this one is most to be respected. It is composed of a group of Christians who sincerely desire to witness as a normal lifestyle. They see the office or the shop as a mission field. They are constantly sharing their faith with those who work around them. They face rejection and scorn, and often don't know what to do next in their ministry to unbelievers. These dear folks form a group to gain new strength for their battles. When they meet together, they bind wounds, praying for each other and for those they are seeking to bring to Christ.

Alas! Their theology has bred their methodology. They have not been helped to see that such a witnessing lifestyle does not work best. Does a hand, a foot, or an arm function apart from the other parts of the body? Can *one* person have *all* the spiritual gifts necessary to reach the lost?

Ours is a generation of "Lone Ranger Christians." It was not so in Jesus' generation. He *never* sent his disciples out one by one, but *two by two.* (We shall discover later why this is so important.)

Of a certainty, the members of this group are sharing their faith in a most valid manner. In the same way every root penetrates the soil around it, we must touch the people around us who need salvation. That's not the problem. The theological flaw is that these Christians meet together *alone,* and then go to witness *alone.* How wonderful it would be if they included *each other* in the relationships they establish with unbelievers, *and included unbelievers in their group life as well.* This group is close to reality, but still limited in its goal of winning the lost by not taking full advantage of the witness of God's people building up one another in a cell.

Perhaps you have already been thinking, "If they would make that change, they would become a *Share Group!*" Yes! That's what a "Share Group" does in the cell church. The group members would be in a position to "target" unbelievers they naturally meet. They would seek to draw them into their confidence and share next their fellowship of love and prayer. Of course, they would no longer meet with the same "private" agenda. They would meet to serve the unbelievers in their midst.

The "Football Team" Cell

This type of group has existed for years, often not even recognized as being a cell. It includes some of God's finest children! These may be teams of men who meet every Sunday afternoon and go to the jails to hold services for the inmates. Or, it may be a group of women who visit a home for the aged and brighten the lives of those who are shut-ins. Teens may "blitz" a football game, passing out tracts and witnessing to those in the stands. College students may descend on the beaches of a city during their Easter break, seeking to share their faith with beer-guzzling crowds who have come to find fun, not Christ. There are many times when the family of God may see the need to go as a *team* to share their faith.

While there are valid reasons to do this, the deficiency of this cell group's life is that there is no way to share the reality of "body life" with those being contacted. The evangelism used presents a *message*, but it does not offer a *community of love.*

And...saddest of all, we begin with the suggestion that the best we have to offer "them" will not be realized until we are dead. True...the "blessed hope" of the Christian is that we are *absent from the body, present with the Lord.* But, what about the interim? Why do we not offer them the joy of entering Christ's community *now?* More important, why do we remain apart from them except for our forays into their territories on specially promoted occasions?

Thus, the body of Christ exhibits itself once again as being separated from the world around it. Like a football team that goes to the huddle to work out a strategy, and then faces the other team on the scrimmage line, we come to "scrimmage" on special occasions with the crowds of unbelievers.

In Hong Kong, I participated in an evangelistic witness in front of an ancient Buddhist temple. The park was filled with men, mostly retired or drifting through life. A group from Australia joined us for the evening. They had come from their church to help win the Chinese. *The first thing the leadership did was to create a space for the Christians, separating them from the unbelievers.* This was done by stretching a yellow ribbon around chairs set far apart. The "Us-Them" philosophy was painfully evident.

To be sure, the crowd was so heavy that without some barrier there would have been no room for the street service to take place. I'm not criticizing the yellow ribbon as much as what happened next.

The Christians from "Down Under" had a great relationship with each other. They sang, clapped, prayed, and entered in with gusto—but they never blended with the men. Their lack of Cantonese must be taken into account, but the main problem was that they were so connected to each other there wasn't a deep interest in being connected to the crowd. Most stayed inside the yellow ribbon.

Sam, the man who led the service, was a part of those men. He had formerly slept on the streets, a heavy heroin user. Yellow ribbons meant nothing to him. He reached out with his heart, his voice, and God's power as he shared. When he began to speak words of knowledge that exactly pinpointed sin in the lives of some of the men, we literally saw a few run away in fear of God's power.

I'm not trying to be critical of the Australians; bless their hearts, they were doing all they *knew* to do! That's the problem with most of us: we don't *know any other way* to serve the Lord apart from what we have observed.

One church solved a part of this "Us-Them" problem by planting a ministry in the midst of a low income Spanish community, creating bedrooms as a "half way house" for men coming out of prison. These team members didn't just go out. They also brought in—and the communities of the poor and imprisoned had opportunity to share daily in the lifestyle of the family of God as they were joined to their cells.

Costly? Yes! It's a Sunday afternoon picnic to go to the jail service and then return alone to the church building for the evening service. It's *costly* to say, "Convict, come and live among us."

Have you heard of Jean Vanier? A graduate of the Royal Naval College with a Ph.D. in philosophy, he seemed to be a candidate for a university professor's position. In 1964, he founded l'Arche at Trosly-Breuil in the suburban area of Paris. They are now spread over the world. The Arche communities gather up people who are mentally handicapped. With fellow Christians—all of them highly educated—the deliberate choice of these Christians is to live in small groups with society's castoffs. In *Community and Growth,* Vanier writes,

> *Certainly we want to help them grow and reach the greatest independence possible. But before 'doing for them,' we want to 'be with them.' The particular suffering of the person who is mentally handicapped, as of all marginal people, is a feeling of being excluded, worthless and unloved. It is through everyday life in community and the love which must be incarnate in this, that handicapped people can begin to discover that they have a value, that they are loved and so loveable.*[1]

Something within us shrinks from the cross, from the faith that demands all, from the call to total commitment. In the cell group church, such issues must be settled by each incoming person. We must not *use* the body of Christ selfishly simply to get *our* needs met, nor can we *abuse* its witness by offering a limited ministry in Christ's name. The radical theology of the New Testament would say to those in the "Football Team" cells, "How can you serve the prisoner, the aged, the teen in the football stands, the beer-guzzling students at the beach, and do so in a way which will cause you to live with them, and for them to live with you?"

Obviously, God does not call all Christians to open a community for retarded persons. But He *does* call us all to open our groups and to be constantly involved with those who don't understand that we have more than a cognitive message to transmit; *we also have a lifestyle for them to receive!*

Here's a strong word, spoken with great conviction: the only type of small group which should limit its membership is a *clinical* one designed for therapy, supervised by professionals.

The "Bible Worm" Groups

Over the years of talking with Christian workers about cell groups, my concern about this type meets with the most resistance. I would first like to state for the reader that I am strongly committed to the "inerrantist" position, and have literally worn out at least a dozen Bibles in my lifetime. Don't consider what follows to be a downgrading of that precious book which God breathed into existence through men who wrote as the Spirit gave them utterance!

Let's attend a typical Bible Study group. It will probably be one of two types: a *true* Bible Study cell, or a *pseudo* Bible study cell.

In the first type, the group sits in a circle. The leader *(there must be a leader!)* follows an outline. Perhaps the church has purchased some of the slickly printed small group material that is so popular just now. Or, perhaps the outline has been typed or mimeographed by one of the church staff. A section of scripture or a topic is to be covered. A commentary may be used to throw light on the passages. The group then discusses the material, being cautioned by the leader not to "chase rabbits."

There are two problems with what is taking place. Too often, the group will "pool its mutual ignorance" about the passage. The leader may say, "Jim, read the next two verses." *(Jim reads them.)* "Who has an insight to share about these verses?" Since no one in the group has the gifts of teaching or putting deepest knowledge into words, speculative comments are often made. The evening is ended with prayer. Little light has been shed on the scripture by this method. Even worse, *true community* has not developed. All the participants have been insulated from each other by the Bible study itself. They go away strangers to one another.

I attended a group like this in Australia. The hostess sat to my left, obviously ill at ease. She requested the group to speak softly so her children would not be awakened. Her participation in the group was minimal. No one else seemed to sense she had a personal problem. Through the evening, I tried to draw her into the discussion, without much success. The time for prayer finally came, and I said, "I sense that you have a special need tonight. Can you share it with us?" Her eyes brimmed with tears: "I wrenched my back today. I have been sitting in this chair gritting my teeth because I am in pain. I just want to get this over with, so I can go to bed!" *The formal Bible study format had so limited our true relationships with one another that we were oblivious to her plight.* In a cell group, the most important ingredient should be *the people* in the circle...not study materials. Thus, one drawback of this first type of Bible study group is the way it insulates the members from each other.

The second problem occurs when there is a person in the group who *is* gifted to teach. The dynamics will now be those of a *large* group rather than a *small* group. Therefore, it is usually profitable to revise this cell to make it a *large gathering,* and let the teacher's gift be used with more people.

The most effective "Bible study" groups I have observed are the pseudo-Bible study cells. These don't really focus on the Bible; they use their group as an excuse to get together and share deeply. Usually these groups will begin with the reading of scripture, but the evening is spent in sharing. Those who attend such groups find them most meaningful and will speak with great conviction about the worth of their "Bible study" group—not knowing *it is actually a fellowship group.* There is, however, a missing ingredient to both of these types.

Why Did God Give Us The Bible To Study?

The answer is found in scriptures like these:

"All scripture is inspired by God and profitable for teaching, for reproof, for correction, for training in righteousness; that the man of God may be adequate, equipped for every good work." • 2 Timothy 3:16-17

The goal of all Bible study is to equip the Christian to serve! This verse tells us we are to be "made adequate," a Greek word *(artios)* which describes becoming *suitable, adapted for activity.* This same word also appears within *katartismon,* "building up," used in Ephesians 4:12, to describe the Body of Christ as becoming *effective ministers.*

In James 1:22-25, we are solemnly warned *against* coming to the Bible without a readiness to become "an effectual doer" of what we discover in its pages. Thus, Bible study groups which study the Bible for the sake of studying the Bible should be declared *unbiblical.* Unfortunately, few Bible study groups (or Sunday School classes) ever project themselves beyond their study into active servant ministries. This is why I have called these "Bible Worm" Groups.

> *"Husbands, love your wives, just as Christ also loved the church and gave Himself up for her; that He might sanctify her, having cleansed her by the washing of water with the word, that He might present to Himself the church in all her glory, having no spot or wrinkle or any such thing; but that she should be holy and blameless."*
> *• Ephesians 5:25-27*

This lovely passage describes our Lord Jesus Christ in the act of bathing His beloved. Through His death on the cross, He has created His Bride from the "Called-Out Ones." *These are to become one,* His "body." He will dwell within her, performing His redemptive ministry through her activity. Christ takes the cleansing "soap" of the scripture, adds His flowing, living waters, and cleanses her of all spots and wrinkles. The Bride of Christ is made glorious, holy, blameless!

The cleansing scripture is applied by Christ to the church. His motive is not to have a clean body to *display,* but to *use.* He is not willing for a single child of Adam to perish. His activity is to touch the poor, the captives, the blind, the downtrodden. It will be through His body this mission will be accomplished.

When we gather around the scripture, it should *always* be done expecting Christ to use it to cleanse and equip us for His work. Therefore, Bible study should focus far more on the *confirmation* of the Bride's life and task than on *information.*

Unfortunately, the study of the Bible seldom penetrates our value systems. It remains cognitive, focusing on knowledge and on a few "principles for living" we glean from it. Only when we meet with a deep sense of our life together as His Bride will we know how it makes us "one flesh," gloriously empowered to do His work in our world. *The proper use of the scripture will always be in its application to ministry.*

After thirty years of intimate participation in small groups within P.B.D. church life, I have come to the conviction that the all-important teaching of the scripture should be done by those who are gifted to do so. When the small group assembles, they should have *already* been taught the scriptures. Groups are for developing relationships and sharing experiences, not for cognitive input! The best cell group experiences I have ever had were when, after the teaching had taken place, a time of sharing from the depths of our spirits occurred. The application of the scripture, cutting like a two-edged sword, must be mingled with the flow of the *charismata,* the "grace gifts," provided by Christ for us to build up one another.

I know it's a long, long journey to what I am describing. But we must abandon the use of groups in Jesus' name on the level of the intellect and the emotions and move on to the level of the spiritual. At that level, the people of God discover and develop their gifts, making real all the theory they have absorbed in years of Bible study which did little to impact their value systems.

Again..."Theology Breeds Methodology"

In the following chapters, careful attention will be given to the importance of establishing each cell on solid principles, as well as on the foundation of Christ. When this is done, there is a radical departure in the understanding of cell group life from the models we have been examining.

One of the greatest struggles of those wishing to make the transition from P.B.D. church life to cell church life involves this shift in thinking: *the cell is the church, and the church is the cell.* It is the basic building block of the larger community called "local church." There must be no competition with it—none at all! Everything in the city-wide structure must exist *for* the cells, be operated *by* the cells, and must strengthen the *life* of the cells. As in the human body, the life of the church is *in the cells.*

Are people to be reached for Christ? It is done through cells. Are people to be built up in Him? It is to be done through cells. Are children to be nurtured? They are to be exposed from the start to the cell as normal church life. There are no *Specialists* and there are no *programs* in the cell group church. When Bible teachers share, they have in their heart that *all* listeners are ministers, and the word of God is spoken to equip them for their service. When praise music is sung, its purpose is to join the body to the Head in holy worship.

When prayer is used, it is not the intonation of a "holy man," but the mutual sharing of all present. For this reason, the Korean church has universally prayed aloud in unison for years. (It seems "strange" to Westerners for such a prayer pattern to be used, even though they see nothing "odd" about singing *A Mighty Fortress Is Our God* at the top of their lungs.) Half nights of prayer are common among cell group churches. On occasion, the cell itself may engage in this practice, or may join in with sister cells in the district for the activity.

Cell groups usually come to a time when they must multiply to remain viable. Six or seven people can become fourteen or fifteen in a short time. When that happens, it is mandatory for the cell to become two communities. Except for the most resistant cultures, this will happen in less than a year—often within six months.

When conducting a seminar on this topic, I am always asked: "How can you say that the work of the cell group is the building up of one another, and then add that they must multiply in six months?" This is a question asked by those who have not spent any time in the cell church! Those of us who have experience know that edification does not require a special set of *people,* but a special work of the *Holy Spirit* within the people.

There comes a time in the life of every group when each person "rewinds his tapes" and begins to replay them. For this reason, groups who remain together for long periods of time stagnate and ossify. My usual reply to the question is, "Those who insist that the quality of their group life is dependent upon the people in it are thinking carnally. In so thinking, we are not 'discerning the Body.' The richness of a cell group church is discovered when the group multiplies and the power of the Spirit's flow remains constant. We soon discover that while the faces have changed, God's power is still present to invade all the strongholds in people's lives and set them free."

It takes about three generations of cell group multiplication before the true life of the church is established. The "relearning curve" from a P.B.D. mind set is not easy. The pastor must resign his "Holy Man" lifestyle and learn to make tents, as did Paul. He must mix with the publicans and the sinners and learn how to bring God's power among their messed-up lives. The totally involved lay volunteer must get far enough away in time from the P.B.D. structure to no longer desire its leeks and garlic. When the transition has been made, there will be no desire to return to the old way.

Of course, none of this is a problem to those who have *not* been trapped inside the P.B.D. churches. The world is full of men and women who have experienced them and have withdrawn from them. Many of them are looking for transparency to go along with their faith, and are open to the cell group church.

From years of personal experiences, I can assure the reader that there are untold thousands in addition who have never *had* a contact with organized religion, and are sincerely searching for answers to why they were born. That's why the New Age movement has made such headway. People who will believe the lie Shirley MacLaine and others have peddled about reincarnation and the occult *must be desperate!*

The tragedy is that the New Agers are stealing the unreached who rightly belong to Christ, simply because we who are His children are fighting a shadow war inside our church buildings instead of storming the gates of hell.

The Lost Sheep And The Confused Shepherds

The P.B.D. church has not only spawned cell groups with problems, it has also generated amazing monstrosities when it comes to *administering* them. This was brought to my attention by someone, somewhere in the past as we sat in a restaurant late one night. I have no idea who first described the models set forth in this section, but I have seen all of them in operation! You will nod your head and smile as you review the possibilities of those who begin to use cells as gimmicks, knowing not what they do.

The Ivory Tower Model *(Pray and Hope)*

Those who seek to administer groups in this manner are usually preoccupied with other interests but desire the growth they have heard can be generated by having small groups in the church. The senior pastor of a large church often adopts this pattern. He turns the work of the cells over to a subordinate and never looks back. The poor staff member seeks to develop a deep commitment to a lifestyle the pastor shuns.

PASTOR

CELLS

IVORY TOWER
(Pray and Hope)

No amount of smiling endorsement of the cells by this pastor will compensate by his tacit "Don't do as I do...do as I say!"

Paul Yonggi Cho is adamant in his insistence that if a cell group is going to be effective, the leadership of the church must be participants. In all churches which have had effective cells, every single staff person—including the secretaries and the janitors—were involved.

Praying and hoping is not enough. The members of the congregation must be assured this is not another one of the projects which may pass away overnight. The Minister of Music and the choir must be involved, along with all others who serve on committees, etc. It's better not to begin at all if this is not possible.

The Umbrella Model
(Compete for Best Study Materials)

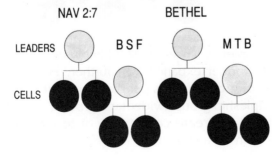

NAV 2:7   BETHEL

LEADERS   B S F   M T B

CELLS

This delightful model occurs when the vision of a church is foggy and its goals unknown. Different curriculums are introduced by staff or members who have become enamored by this or that discipleship or Bible study group pattern. Usually a desire to be polite to one another squashes any comments that this pattern will not be profitable. Thus, the congregation is split into varied interests, none of which create community. Groups which meet on a cognitive level for such courses will forfeit "body study," that powerful life in which the agenda is focused on the members and their ability to edify one another through the expression of their spiritual gifts.

A word of tribute must be included here for the ministry of Bible Study Fellowship. It has steadfastly refused to be under the mantle of any church structure and has quietly created cells that are extremely effective in providing community for Christians who are trapped in the P.B.D. structures. Only heaven will reveal the good this ministry has done in our day. It's a pity that American churches have not scrapped their entire structure to adopt the simple plan of BSF. I know of one Methodist woman who nearly dried up in her church. It was in BSF she met Christ, and through her the entire family became believers. I had the privilege of leading her husband to Christ over a spinach salad at his country club. This auto dealer is now one of my closest friends.

The Smorgasbord Model
(Shopping Cart Plan: offer everything except direction)

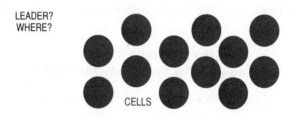

LEADER?
WHERE?

CELLS

One completely sincere pastor I know decided he would let the umbrella model expand even further. He created a large cafeteria line of groups for his people: prayer groups, Bible study groups, discipleship groups, videotape groups, etc. It kept people busy, but failed to *create community* or to reach people. Such "busy work" can kill a church!

The Terrorist Model
(Shoot down the Authority Figures)

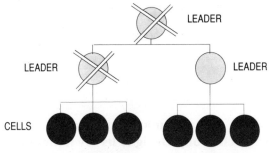

This little nightmare is the reason many pastors are dead set against any and all cell groups. Unless the small group happens to be a Sunday School class which meets on campus, they will not be allowed by him. This model only develops when there is not a proper spirit between leadership and laity. In all the years I pastored a cell group church there was never a single time when a rebellious group set out to become independent and assault the leadership. It rarely happens, and then only when communication patterns are poor.

The Junta Model
(Leadership Dissipated Among Equal Elders;
no one "in charge")

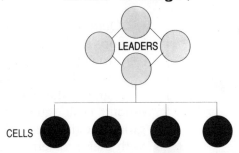

Junta models suffer badly from the weakest link in a chain of equal elders. All it takes is one neurotic who will hold out against everyone else to stalemate the church indefinitely. It sounds spiritual for all the leadership to be equal in vote and for the group to wait until there is total agreement, but the carnality residing in the best of us can create impossible situations! There *must* be one chair "where the buck stops."

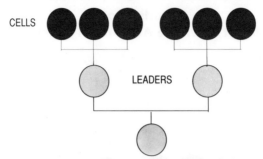

CELLS

LEADERS

The Skunkworks Model
(Each Group Designs Its Own Model)

In this inverted pyramid pattern, the pastor and other church leaders encourage each group to create its own lifestyles. From the "holy huddles" come the various activities which the groups will execute. Invariably, two or three strong personalities in each group make decisions for the rest. Thus, the "calling" of the group is not universal. As the weeks go by, the enthusiasm for the group task wanes. Those who were not really committed drop out first, often with scoldings from the more "spiritual." After a generation of this model, small groups may never be resurrected again.

The Jungle Model
(No Clear Lines of Assistance)

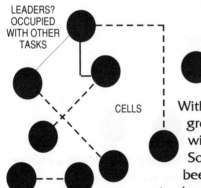

LEADERS?
OCCUPIED
WITH OTHER
TASKS

CELLS

Quite often this model develops slowly as groups grow and multiply. Instead of providing capable leadership to each group, the matter is ignored. Without clear guidance available, groups begin to cast about for help with their problems and questions. Soon leadership by default has been created. It is then impossible to create clear lines of assistance. Such glaring errors are a sign that the leadership of the Body did not plan for growth and was incapable of handling it when it came. Growth will be hindered and some will become frustrated and drop out of the groups.

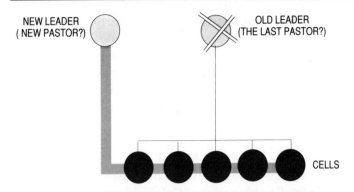

The Revised Utopian Plan Model
(Out with the old, in with the new;
"Hmmm...leadership is starting over...again!")

This takes place when a traditional church calls a new pastor or staff member. His egotism demands that what the previous leader did be discarded, and his "better plan" installed.

It is important to know that any attempt to develop a cell group church will require at least two to three years to take root. Actually, the explosive growth does not take place until the second or third generation of converts has matured enough to enter leadership positions. Churches who keep their pastors for long periods fare better than those who are constantly turning them over.

The Pyramid Plan
(Spend your time recruiting, not serving...)

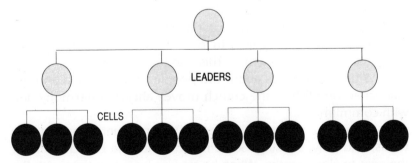

Those who are responsible for the cell groups *must* be involved in their ministries, not just their training. As cells develop, it is necessary for seasoned workers to become equippers of new cell group servants. These people must not be personally responsible for the life of a single group. It will be necessary for them to revolve among the cells they serve. If they do not faithfully do this, they will become "absentee landlords" of their groups. The first sign something is wrong *may* be when they dissolve!

The Ideal Model
(Led by the vision of the Senior Pastor:
Cells, Congregations, Celebrations)

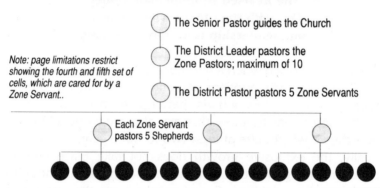

Note: page limitations restrict showing the fourth and fifth set of cells, which are cared for by a Zone Servant..

The Senior Pastor guides the Church

The District Leader pastors the Zone Pastors; maximum of 10

The District Pastor pastors 5 Zone Servants

Each Zone Servant pastors 5 Shepherds

This is the pattern followed by virtually all cell group churches. The interesting thing is that many of their pastors have never met, never compared notes. Each situation may vary with culture, the skill of the pastor to organize, and the spiritual strength of the congregation to reach out and invade Satan's territory.

The clear direction set for the church by the pastor is a mandate for the congregation to focus on one thing alone. As one cell group pastor said to me, "This one thing we do!"

With a clear focus about the people to be reached and the plan to accomplish it, the church moves ahead in harmony and with commitment.

Pastor Paul Yonggi Cho goes to Prayer Mountain once a year to fast and pray, seeking God's mandate for the church's life for the next twelve months. When he returns from that time with the Lord, the goals which are given to him are printed and framed. These framed statements are then hung on every wall of every church worker on the staff. All is in perfect focus, and everything done by every person is directed toward meeting that objective.

The basic difference between the first nine models and this final one is simply a clearly defined set of goals! As one Chinese pastor in Singapore said when the missionaries asked him what suggestions he had for their work: *"Have a goal, and help us to understand what it is!"* He then expressed the frustration of working with leaders who had never decided where they would end when they started out.

Cells, or "small groups," in the P.B.D. church are always tacked onto the existing structures. Thus, they are ineffective and poorly managed. Let's move on to view a better concept!

MY JOURNEY INTO THE CELL CHURCH

I want to share my own pilgrimage into the cell group church. Occasionally, I'll deliberately chase a rabbit in this chapter to help you understand things to follow. I'm praying as I write that the truth of the journey may motivate you to do something about your own...

For me, the journey started in 1965 as I turned thirty-six years of age. I had spent all my life living in parsonages: first my father's, then our own. I had preached in dozens of congregations during my education in Christian colleges and seminaries and years spent serving the ministry of Billy Graham. When I turned thirty-six I was absolutely, completely disgusted with traditional church structures that catered to self-needs and ignored the unchurched.

I could not understand why American churches universally suffered from stunted growth. Only a few dozen have been able to grow beyond 5,000 members, and only a couple of dozen have Sunday schools that are larger than 2,000. In the light of the population explosion, that seemed ridiculous. In the light of the book of Acts, it seemed intolerable!

What those statistics revealed was that America's churches stagnate and cease to reach the unreached people who exist all around them. I asked myself, "Why do churches quit growing? Why are half or more of their members inactive? *What in the world is wrong?*"

By then, I had already planted over a score of brand new churches in the Northeast. Ruthie, the boys, and I moved 4 times in 5 years, and I preached as many as 6 times every Sunday. In each new town, we started churches in the homes of a few believers. We grew rapidly as long as we met in that way. Everyone pitched in; everyone shared his excitement with friends over the newly forming church. Folks got converted regularly.

We would grow each church large enough to call a pastor and erect a "starter building." It puzzled me that, along with lovely new buildings and seminary graduates in the pulpits, nearly every one of those churches stagnated within a few years.

It is now 25 years later. Most of them have not added another 150 members since they were constituted! Only a few I know about have added to the original "starter buildings."

Next, I spent 5 years flying all over Texas as an evangelism consultant for the Texas Baptist Convention. I conducted endless evangelistic meetings foolishly advertised as "Revival Meetings," which unchurched folks boycotted en masse.

I preached to those I thought were the problem: "dead" church members who didn't care that the world was going to hell in a handbasket. We had altars full of folks weeping and asking the Lord to send a mighty harvest. The love offerings were great—but the harvesting profitability of these meetings was poor. Four months after each meeting, every church plodded along as it had done before, barely reflecting any fruit from our efforts.

Of the 4,500 churches our Division of Evangelism worked with, only a handful baptized as many as 100 people a year. Hundreds of them baptized absolutely no one, and repeated the awful statistic year after year! I asked myself, "How can this be?" It revealed that hundreds of preachers in the pulpits of those congregations never personally won a soul to Christ. *Could that be possible?*

I had hit upon my first real answer to one reason traditional church structures stagnate in America. As mentioned in Chapter Two, a majority of church workers don't have a single friend who might be described as a genuine unbeliever. They spend all their time insulated from the unchurched, working among church members. Their so-called "personal evangelism" consists of little more than sharing a well-memorized plan of salvation with total strangers on a visitation night, or preaching evangelistic sermons from behind insulated pulpits. Many of them only did the latter. Few of them had earned the sordid reputation of our Lord, who was criticized for being "a friend of winebibbers and sinners."

I deliberately broke with the pattern and began spending

the so-called "happy hours" in the Sportsman's Lounge near the Baptist Building in Dallas, talking to the beer-drinking unchurched. To my amazement, I discovered most of them had quit going to church years ago. They still believed in God, but they no longer believed in the traditional church. And they had no intention of going back!

They were quite vocal about the matter. Universally, they viewed the church as a set of programs which required buildings, meetings, and money. They resented this depersonalized church, where people never really got down to earth and opened up to each other, where they had to attend every activity or have a guilt trip laid on them in a sermon, and where the church collected money for its own projects but spent little helping hurting people within the community. Most of all, they resented the lavish buildings which were often used only a few hours a week. One said to me, "That church over there just spent millions for an auditorium which will be used no more than five hours a week. They also built a health club. It's paid for with tithed money from its membership, but they are now charging a monthly fee equal to what a *profit-making* health club charges! How can you justify that? How do they represent a Christ who deliberately lived simply? I believe in God, but I will never, never set foot in that church!"

Of course, his comment in a bar never reached the ears of the hundreds and hundreds of people who pack that auditorium on Sundays or the massive staff that keeps the machinery oiled. The lack of communication between those who *won't* come and those who *do* come to that facility is a great part of the problem.

So, here was the chasm. Christians were working their heads off inside insulated church buildings, believing they were doing "the work of the Lord." The people who needed their love never saw them at all. *How could we be so blind?* Was it not *obvious* the church was dying for lack of relationships with the unchurched?

The God of Abraham said to him, "I want you to let me guide you to a new location so we can become closer to one another." *Abraham was about to get a huge jolt!*

Jehovah didn't lead the patriarch to a tranquil garden where they might fellowship together in peace. He led him into the big middle of the vilest, most licentious, infant-sacrificing, Baal worshipping tribe in the Middle East and said, "Abraham, this is where I want you to live as you fellowship with me!"

How odd of God! No—how *typical* of the God who is "not willing that any should perish." He planted His worshiper among the captives, the hell-raisers who lived without anyone to witness of His love. While he didn't know it at the time, Abraham had just become a foreign missionary! He could have been the first mortal to capture the heartbeat of God and write the words later made famous by C. T. Studd:

> *"I do not wish to live*
> *'Neath sound of church or chapel bell;*
> *I want to run a rescue shop*
> *Within a yard of hell!"*

Certainly, our Lord Jesus Christ might *also* have penned that couplet. His life was dedicated to seeking and saving those who were lost.

· The traditional church fails the test! It endlessly preoccupies itself with its own routines. What it needs is to move its location from its buildings to the uncircumcised Philistine tribes a block or more away. It needs to so encounter God that it will have its name changed, as did Abram, who lived in the covenant relationship as Abraham, the man who received the very name of God into his own.

I was taught by my denomination that the Sunday School was our "Knight in Shining Armor," by which traditional churches would win America to Christ. Yet, when I examined the ten largest Sunday Schools in Texas—all with over 2,000 enrolled—I was stunned to discover they averaged fewer than eight adult *unbelievers* in actual attendance! *Who was kidding whom?*

Where did we come up with the idea that unconverted people are burning with desire to get all dressed up on Sunday morning instead of sleeping in, bursting with enthusiasm to drive to a church facility, and filled with an insatiable thirst for Bible study? After attending Sunday School for my adult age group in over a hundred churches, I was even more disgusted. The quality of the teaching in most classes was wretched.

I came to a conclusion. I now knew why churches didn't grow. Traditional churches were little insulated islands of Christians, who didn't even *try* to relate to the totally unchurched in the community. I discovered larger churches had actually hired one or more workers to go visit the visitors because the church members could not be persuaded to do so. Many pastors required their entire church staff to visit new people weekly since the lack of enthusiasm among the congregation to do so left few other options.

I did some serious statistical research next, using the annual reports in our state building and interviewing 300 pastors. Less than 1% of the salaried "pillars of the church" were investing *one hour a week* developing *personal* relationships with the huge masses of totally unchurched.

What about the memberships in the churches? Were they not in the marketplace all week long? Did *they* take advantage of the opportunities to share their faith? Let me share what I found out about them...

Tom Wolf, pastor of The Church on Brady in Los Angeles, showed me something I had never seen. The greek word *oikos,* translated "household," refers to people we relate to on a regular basis. We may *know* a hundred or more individuals, but we spend quality time (one hour a week of direct conversation, for example) with a limited number. When I took surveys among hundreds of church members who attended my seminars, I uncovered a shocking fact: the "world" of a typical Christian seldom contains more than eight or nine *oikos* people! Only a few had a *personal friendship* and spent *quality time* with hard core unbelievers. Most of the time, these unbelievers were relatives who had become impervious to further discussion about Jesus' claim of Lordship over them.

The depressing conclusion was this: *the typical church-goer relates to only five to eight people for at least one full hour per week per person, and half of those Christians cannot name a single unbeliever among their close friends.* Many of them have not even made a new acquaintance in the past twelve months. They live in little personal bubbles, having no interest in people who live and work close to them. When church members have no "root system" to make contact with unbelievers, they are powerless to be used to win others.

Even sadder, the rhetoric from the pulpit about the need to reach the lost for Christ falls on deaf ears. A proper theology breeds motivation for ministry. One pastor had a real gut-level discussion with his deacons about why not one of them had led a soul to Christ in the past year. He called me, shattered with their totally honest comments: to a man, their personal beliefs were that God would somehow take in the unbelievers even if they did not come to Him by way of the cross. He had a deacon board composed of *universalists*, although they publicly nodded their heads when he preached on eternity without Christ or the tragedy of living without hope. If churchgoers don't believe people need to meet Christ, their motivation to reach unbelievers is a *minus zero.*

Perhaps you are thinking, "Hey! Wait a minute! My church is really alive! We aren't like that. We're reaching others!" *Of course, you'll think that way.* If you didn't, you couldn't *exist* within the traditional church. Perhaps your church is "The Great Exception." But, where does your harvest *come* from? How many *unchurched* are represented in it? Is your growth your worst enemy, blinding you to the yet unreached all around you? Are you blind to the reality of those *ignored?*

I recall scores of conversations with pastors and education directors which went something like this:

> Me: *"You are showing significant growth. Have you eval-uated the source of your growth?"*
> He: *"We have so many visitors on Sundays we can't keep up with the load. As long as they keep coming and we keep visiting, that's all we have time to do!"*
> Me: *"But what about the nearly 70% in this city who never go to church? What are you doing to reach out to them?"*
> He: *"Well, we have a jail ministry on Sunday after-noons."*
> Me: *"How many do you have in your church family from that ministry?"*
> He: *"I don't really know. Perhaps none."*

Years later, after I had developed and proved a workable strategy to reach the unchurched, an Arkansas pastor spent hours with me discussing the need for a "root system" to penetrate the unchurched college students next to his university church. I shared with him the simple strategy of using cells called "Share

Groups." I suggested he develop varieties of them as contact points in the dorms. He went home with much excitement. A few weeks later, he called to say, "Ralph, I've aborted the idea. We can't seat all the people attending our two morning worship services. If we launch an aggressive outreach like Share Groups, it would only compound our seating problem. I have decided not to proceed." *Amazingly, He had limited the ministry of his church to the seating of his auditorium!*

I concluded that traditional church growth came mainly through the baptism of the member's children, transfers from other churches, or by a sickly and minimal evangelism harvest among people who actually visit worship services. Traditional churches, I discovered, have *absolutely no strategy for touching the unchurched.* I made up my mind to do something about it.

I began to spend sleepless nights in our Dallas home. The dead churches who had no flood of visitors ran a maintenance organization. The growing churches, usually located in newer housing areas, simply "visited the visitors." In both cases, the unchurched were unreached. There was no sign of this ever changing in the traditional church!

The sleepless nights were then filled with writing a strategy for an experimental church, a church which would find solutions to these problems. Soon, the document was 68 pages long. One day, Ruth and the boys sat me down and said, "Look! You've got to do more than walk the floor. If we need to, we'll all go to work to support the family needs. Let's go and do it!" That was all I needed. We began to pray about the location for the test, and God opened a door for us.

In 1969, a non-traditional church in Houston was formed with 38 courageous pioneers. We called ourselves "The People Who Care," and became a "Parable Church." Without knowing what we were doing, we stumbled into the patterns which were being used by other cell group churches we didn't know existed. We had no idea that a patched tent in a slum area of Seoul was housing another group who were also stumbling into the new patterns. Their pastor was sleeping behind the pulpit. *They* would become the largest local church in Christian history, now numbering over six hundred thousand members.

We would be used in a different way by the Holy Spirit. In twelve years' time, the People Who Care (West Memorial Baptist

Church) ministered to thousands of people. We would send over a score of couples to seminaries or to work with other Christian groups. Dozens more would go to strengthen weaker churches in the city around us. We touched a nation, and then a world, with our lifestyle and our books which shared our way of living and loving and reaching the lost. Hundreds of believers came to learn from us, and we interned up to fifteen workers during each of the summer months.

Without spending millions on fancy buildings, The People Who Care found themselves with a baptism ratio of one convert for every 4.5 church members from the very first year of their new lifestyle. Year after year, the ratio stayed the same. Traditional churches around us required up to forty-two members to produce one baptism after a year of "busy work" on their church campuses. At best, the Traditional Church ratio was twenty to one.

"Surely," we thought, "if we explain this strategy to reach the unchurched, traditional churches will adopt it!" As our congregation grew and grew, so did our vision of renewing traditional churches. Only time would reveal how impossible this is to do.

We formed home cell groups, where our unchurched friends were made to feel welcome. They loved these get-togethers! We made the rounds of all the taverns in our area and met unreached men and women. We held barbecues in our back yards and met unmet neighbors. Our wives joined bridge clubs as a contact point with women in the area. My high school sons hung out where teenagers bought drugs, and we started small groups with them. We even opened "The Giant Step," a ministry for prostitutes and pimps who were heroin addicts. Forty of us stayed with them by shifts, around the clock, in an old rented house, putting wet towels on their foreheads as they vomited their way through withdrawal. Later, we took them into our homes to show them how Christian families lived.

It was in 1971 that I recognized another serious flaw in the traditional church's evangelistic methods. They set too high a platform for evangelizing unbelievers. That platform was Bible study. If the unbeliever didn't want to study the Bible, they were ignored! That one single attitude of the church has deprived millions of people from receiving the Gospel.

Scripture teaches us a different pattern. In Athens, Paul gave us a model: for those who would not begin with Bible study, he quoted their pagan poets. He had the sense to know we must "become all things to all men, that by all means we might win some." He eventually brought some Athenians to the scriptures, but he did not start with them. He *worked up* to the scriptures. Cell Group churches recognize there is a way to reach the unchurched who refuse to enter into Bible study. It is by serving them at the point of their deepest need.

We discovered scores of folks who would not be caught *dead* in a Bible study but who were delighted to spend an evening talking with us. Slowly, we reached the people we called "The Outsiders." We brought them into our cells of love, to eventually face the power of the written word and finally to declare Christ as Lord.

We stumbled on "Target Group Evangelism" and formed the first evangelistic cells we had ever seen. Cal Wheeler started a group for kids with motorcycles, and Cal Thomas used his television contacts to start a breakfast group for politicians and business men. Bill and Betty Lottman formed a group for parents of retarded children. Soon there were over 20 target groups, each creating a root system to penetrate the unchurched people around us. We grew and grew, learning all the while, sharing our failures and our victories as God gave them to us.

When we baptized, each convert represented *months* of patient servanthood. In two years, we were 600. A large number had been unchurched persons before being touched by our cells.

The Associated Press covered our ministry. So did several magazines. Back then, we were convinced that the traditional church could be renewed. In 1973, Francis Schaeffer joined us for our first National Conference on the cell group church, where we explained our lifestyle to scores of pastors. What a rich time that was for us all!

In 1974, the church allowed me to go to Singapore and work on developing cell group churches there. While waiting for our visa, we took a temporary assignment in Saigon—just in time to see the nation fall to the swarming Viet Cong. Our time in Singapore was stormy. The mission there wasn't ready for innovation, and our presence as a "Change Agent" was resented from the first. In spite of their lack of cooperation, we were able to see 18 house churches planted by our Chinese brothers. It was my first taste of pure cell group life, and I carefully developed the equipping materials to make it work.

In our absence, a traditional pastor sought to restore old patterns to the Houston church. It fell apart; members scattered to the winds. When we left in June of 1973, there were over 600 people. When we returned to resume the pastorate in July of 1977, there were only 77 people left in the Sunday school. By 1980, we required two worship services, had a staff of 13, and once again had "Target Groups" up and running.

In 1979, the denomination asked us to test our pattern in 80 traditional churches. It flopped. The P.B.D. churches were not ready for change. I resigned my pulpit once again, determined to devote full time to discover what *more* could be done to help traditional churches get out of their shells. A precious friend loaned us $100,000 for the venture. We spent two more years revising our materials to make them more palatable to the denomination. Negotiations were renewed with its leadership to use the cell group evangelism strategy, and we came within *days* of signing a contract for me to work for them.

When the word leaked out about the new project, some denominational leaders were terribly threatened. They feared the competition of small groups might damage the profits from sales of Sunday school literature and the "stranger evangelism" materials developed for sale to all churches. In a stormy meeting, one executive said to me, "I won't allow another evangelism strategy to be offered to our churches. The one I have is all they need!"

In 1982, the hammer fell. The pressure was too great from the opposition. The denomination opted to sever all relations with Touch Ministries. My denomination slammed its doors to revision of the P.B.D., which might have opened its doors to the burgeoning mass of unreached persons in our society. After 20 years of seeking to bring "renewal" to the traditional church, our journey had come to a dead end.

Thus, when our work was done, the Holy Spirit gently ended the life of our parable church and years of my ministry, both committed to bringing renewal to our sister P.B.D. congregations.

After my resignation in 1980, the church again floundered. Pastors who followed didn't understand our motives for abandoning the traditional "large church" mold to become a "cell church." Members once again fell away.

Finally, West Memorial Baptist Church totally lost its original identity. It was dissolved on December 31, 1988. Both its constitution and incorporation were dissolved by a new pastor and a new membership that knew nothing about our original vision. The successor church, with a new name, a new theology, and some P.B.D. type cells, invested the massive profits from the sale of our property and developed its new "large church" lifestyle, complete with many programs, in another location. The dear pastor and his people are doing a fine work, using quite traditional concepts.

The original members are now scattered into dozens of ministries and scores of groups, and the original vision now exists only in our memories. We "old timers" still network, often talking on the telephone, visiting or writing, sharing what God is now doing because of what He did in the past. As one former staffer said to me, "We had no way of knowing it at the time, but *we were living in Camelot!*"

Afterglow: What's Left?

Much of what we learned pastoring in Houston and Singapore is readily applied to the new cell church structures. We have developed a twenty-week training program for cell group churches, giving them tools to reach the unchurched. We call it "Touch Basic Training." It's a part of an entire equipping structure which will be explained in later chapters of this book. It's the main thing that has come from those years of trying, learning, and preparing.

God has graciously permitted me to migrate out of P.B.D. circles into the new world of cell group churches. I am busier than I have ever been, more excited than ever before. I seldom return to preach in, or hold seminars for, P.B.D. churches. They will continue to reach a few, and the people in them are deeply loved by me. But their hopeless state depresses me every time I return to one of them.

My purpose for sharing all these details with you is for you to understand why people migrate from the traditional church to the cell group church. It's not the movement of sick neurotics; it is the migration of thirsty hearts. And it's not to imply that everyone is called to be a *part* of the migration. Most of those who have life investments in the traditional church probably will not do so. It's certainly not necessary to join a cell group church to be in the Lord's will. Christ is among *all* His churches, not just some of them. In Revelation, He stood among the Laodiceans and the Thyatirans, and He is among all the problemed churches today as well. But He *has* moved on to develop a younger Bride that is far more beautiful. There's a definite movement to report...a movement which will be significant through the end of this century.

In the chapters which follow, I am going to tell you about the world I live in at the present time. It's a world where cell group churches see from 20% to 100% growth every single year. I'm honored to be the Senior Associate Pastor of the Faith Community Baptist Church in Singapore, a partner to over four thousand who attend our weekly Celebration. Where do *you* go from here? Don't settle for less than the Holy Spirit will give!

If you are still thinking, "Where did you get the idea that 'bigger is better?' Those cell group megachurches are too large for any true Christian lifestyle to be lived out. Seas of people are not healthy."

My friend, that's not true! Anything that is *living* is *growing.* The cell group churches may contain thousands of members, but the only thing a person can "join" is a cell group that numbers no more than 15 persons. The building block of all living organisms is a cell. Anyway, cells don't *grow;* they *multiply* into more cells. Thus, the growth is composed of tiny "mini-churches," where there is a potential for more intimacy and transparency than one can ever find in a traditional church.

As exciting as the Singapore ministry is, I also have a burden for reaching the unchurched American. Because we are so stuck in the mire at the present time here, I fear that the wave of cell group churches, so developed overseas, may not happen in my lifetime. I'm working on the "unchurched church" for the unchurched people. We're calling it "Trilogy" because it sounds New Age and will seek to develop target groups among the Yuppies and others who will never, ever be impressed by the P.B.D. structures. They will be won to Christ and established in Shepherd Groups as their "Basic Christian Community." Like Uncle Sam, I'm looking for a "Few Good Men" who can raise their own support and come alongside to help. The unlimited potential for developing such a movement in America will extend it far beyond my few remaining years, and I truly believe some young Turks will share in the challenge of a new format for a new generation.

A Final Farewell To The P.B.D. Stage Of My Journey

Through the last 15 years, we have held dozens of seminars to show P.B.D. pastors how to begin home cell groups to reach unchurched persons. Over a hundred and ninety thousand dollars and twelve years went into creating the printed and videotaped training materials for use in the TOUCH strategy.

But I no longer encourage P.B.D. pastors to attempt to use it. Years were invested with them to verify over and over that they cannot effectively revise old P.B.D. structures. We have, in these past years, trained over eleven hundred pastors in three-day seminars. Seven denominations, including the Evangelical Free Church, endorsed the training program.

The results were discouraging. Many pastors frankly said at the end of the course that their church would never, *ever* be ready for this sort of ministry. Two hundred tried to install the ministry in their traditional churches and went into an irrecoverable stall. Approximately 75 churches actually formed cell groups for reaching the unchurched, some of which are in existence today.

One serious problem they all faced was the lack of time in their church schedules for outreach. A basic law of economics says, "If you spend ten dollars for a shirt, you can't spend it on a meal." And if you spend all of your time on the church campus keeping the machinery running, you can't spend all your time with unchurched friends. The stranglehold of existing programs choked out their potential ministry. The P.B.D. churches were unable to *stop* what they were doing, even though it didn't produce either conversions or Christians capable of *producing* conversions.

There were a handful of exceptions. A few churches pitched excess baggage overboard, established groups, and exploded in harvest growth. One church we worked with in Indiana grew to 125 groups, with a goal of 200 evangelism cell groups. Then *they* stagnated. They were trying to grow cell groups *and* Sunday School at the same time. While they continue to harvest many unbelievers, they don't experience growth as a cell group church does. They are trapped into dividing their energies and people into two directions. They compete with themselves!

An Oklahoma church has grown to 47 groups and baptizes many converts each week from the unchurched community. They are among a dozen or so I have observed who have effectively reached out from the stance of traditional church structures. Their gifted pastor and unique staff, plus an amazing congregation, made it happen. Unfortunately, there are few churches that can match their mix. That church is a bright spot left over from the years we attempted to renew the church.

However, most pastors faced such resistance to a new relational evangelism strategy by their church leadership that they never got it off the ground. By actual count, *twenty-one* of the seventy-five pastors who developed evangelistic Share groups have now been fired or were forced to resign by lay leaders who were totally threatened by the pastor's new outreach strategy. Their dismissals were *directly* related only to their attempts to revise the P.B.D. structures and their challenges to the memberships to get off the church campus and become involved in long-term faith sharing with their pagan neighbors.

In four of those situations, I flew in at my own expense to plead with church leaders to understand their pastor's motives. In every case, I was simply stunned by their feelings of fear toward accepting a new concept!

Two seemingly insurmountable problems face the transition of a traditional church into a cell group church. The first is a pastor who reigns over a churchly kingdom. In this situation, the clergyman is unwilling to assume his role as an equipper, unable to say, "Let them increase, even if I decrease!" Such a man will *never* release the laity to take over the priestly duties God has reserved for them.

The other problem is the church member who balks at the idea of becoming a responsible, ministering person. In many cases, personal significance and power is provided by holding an office in the church or a teaching task in the Sunday School. Impure motives for service have built many "power bases" for carnal people within church life. These church workers have no *intention* of entering into true servanthood. Those who "hire a holy man" to do the work of the church feel they have done their part when they drop their tithe into the offering plate.

The conflict can work either way: a pastor tries to move a

congregation that is unmovable and gets his head chopped off. Or, some inside a congregation press the pastor to let the laity begin to minister off the campus, and they get *their* heads chopped off.

Once a church has structured itself along certain patterns, it is virtually impossible to make any significant changes. Even something as simple as changing an Order of Service is liable to create strife.

As a child of the church, the fifth generation of clergymen, I sometimes feel black despair when I think of the dreadful mess the church is in. One Florida pastor of a large church listened as I shared the awesome conversion rates being seen by cell churches and finally concluded the conversation by saying, "I'm gonna dance with who brought me!" I said, "I don't understand." He answered, "I got to be pastor of this church by building a Sunday school. Why should I take a chance on a new idea?"

Why, indeed? Men who have "reached the top" of political power and affluence in their ministry seldom view the massive default of their own comfortable ministry, which may pack the pews and the offering plates while ignoring the 70% of the people who are not being touched by *one single thing they do.* Has not God called us to draw all men to Him? Is that not more important than "dancing with what brought me" to a fat income and being elected to ecclesiastical prominence? It is for this reason God is still taking the "mere nothings" Paul spoke about to create the cell group churches.

Why What I Attempted Didn't Work

Finally, in 1985, when that twenty-first pastor called me from California to tell me his three-year long struggle to develop relational church structures had ended in his forced resignation, I began to ask myself a serious question: *can new wine be put into old skins?* The answer is "No!"

Attempts at renewal don't work for one reason: our Lord told us over 2,000 years ago *it could not be done.* Every time we try to ignore His clear teaching, we fail. In retrospect, I could have saved myself 24 years of dreaming an impossible dream if I had taken His admonition literally. While I was trying to *renew,* He was shaping something *brand new.* That's what the rest of this book is about!

2

THEOLOGY

BREEDS

METHDOLOGY

5 COMMUNITY: THE REASON FOR CELLS

If we are to put cell groups in their proper place in church life, we must stop treating them like a "gimmick," an optional feature, or a way to find a "quick fix" for sagging attendance. Since theology breeds methodology, it will be valuable for us to shape a biblical view of the cell group church. We must begin by recognizing that the primary assignment in a cell group church is to develop "Basic Christian Communities."

Because community can occur most completely only in small groups, a cell group, numbering less than fifteen people, is all important. Essential elements of community include interpersonal commitments and a sense of belonging. Community takes place when there is a shared life, allowing common goals and commitments to develop between all of its members.

In *The Different Drum,* M. Scott Peck writes:

> *If we are to use the word [community] meaningfully we must restrict it to a group of individuals who have learned how to communicate honestly with each other, whose relationships go deeper than their masks of composure, and who have developed some significant commitment to "rejoice together, mourn together," and to "delight in each other, make others' conditions our own."*[1]

In the "kingdoms of this world" shaped by Satan, Christian community cannot exist. Only in the "Kingdom of God" can it be truly discovered. When Jesus went about announcing the "Gospel of the Kingdom," He was inviting fragmented humanity to enter into something it could not experience elsewhere.

As the extended family is the *oikos*[2] of society, so the cell group is the extended family, the basic building block, of the people of God. A large-group gathering of Christians (more than 15 persons) cannot provide the essential ingredients required for community. Nor will community develop if a small group meets fortnightly or monthly, or even just once a week. While the typical cell group will have a special time to be together weekly, there is a strong bond between the members who often spend time with one another between meetings. Couples may share an evening, ladies may go shopping, children may spend a night at the home of one of the other children in the group. They are family.

It is not possible to define community to someone who has never experienced it. Like falling head over heels in love, it must be experienced to be understood. Those who have been fortunate to enter into Kingdom relationships can never again be content with the shallowness of institutional church life.

Some years ago, I entered into a small group relationship with two other men. Hans was from Switzerland, working temporarily in Dallas. Erwin was a graphic artist. We began to meet together on Fridays for lunch. It was not long before I found myself looking forward to our times together, not really understanding why our weekly hour and a half meant so much to me. It was with these men I shared the deepest feelings of my soul, my longings to find a more authentic Christian life style. I didn't know it at the time, but we had formed a community. There were frequent telephone calls between our luncheons, and we edified one another with scripture verses, insights, and thoughts which came to us during our personal prayer times.

Twenty-seven years later, I have had many experiences with the power of community. Yet, I shall never forget the power of God which flowed between us back then. Hans has long ago returned to Zurich. Erwin went on to produce the Benjie movies. Because of their affirmations, I left the security of denominational ladder-climbing to enter a journey to find renewal for the church. God was good to me: I had actually found all there was to discover in that simple community with those two men.

Have you also discovered that the Gospel of the Kingdom is "among us?" Then, you will relish the thoughts that follow.

The Highest Life Form In The Universe

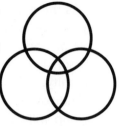

Why is God a Trinity? Most of us get bogged down just trying to understand it! The Athanasian Creed is our best source to grasp it:

> ...*we worship one God in Trinity, and Trinity in Unity; Neither confounding the Persons: nor dividing the Substance [Essence]. For there is one Person of the Father: another of the Son: and another of the Holy Ghost. But the Godhead of the Father, of the Son, and of the Holy Ghost, is all one: the Glory equal, the Majesty coeternal. Such as the Father is: such is the Son: and such is the Holy Ghost...*

Whew!

Even after we grasp this, the key question still remains: *why is God a Trinity?*

The Koran insists He is one! It is heresy, the Islamic firmly believes, to teach otherwise. Every time he genuflects in prayer, he rises with one finger raised: "He is one!"

Why is God not a *duality?* We are told that "God is love." Only two persons are required to give and receive love. Would two persons in the Godhead not have been enough? Obviously, the answer is "No," for God is a Trinity. A powerful truth emerges from this fact. Where there are three, there is—for the first time—community. There must be at least three before community can exist. God, by His very nature, has always lived in the richness which exists only in community.

John Samaan meditated upon this in a *Servants Among The Poor* newsletter:

> . . .*within God's very nature is a divine "rhythm" or pattern of continuous giving and receiving—not only love, but also glory, honor, life...each in its fullness. Think about it for a minute. God the Father loves and delights in the Son (Matt. 3:17), Jesus receives that love and pleases his Father as an obedient and loving Son (Jn. 8:29), and honors the Spirit (Matt. 12:31), while the*

Spirit glorifies both the Father and the Son (Jn 16:14). Each person in the Trinity loves, honors and glorifies the other and receives love and honor back from the others, because He is worthy. There is never any lack.[3]

It must be said with reverential awe: *He who is Eternal has always existed in the lifestyle of community*—with only one break in this continuity. That single exception occurred at Calvary. As Christ took the ugliness of our sin into Himself, He cried out, "My God! My God! Why have You forsaken Me?" The vileness of our sin, received into His sinless body, severed the eternal community of the Godhead! (The worst part about sin is that it *always* destroys community.)

What was it like for our Lord to experience separation from the Godhead? To know what Jesus experienced, we would have to enter into the perfect community of the Godhead. Unfortunately, our humanness precludes that for us.

Man Created For Community

In Genesis 1:26 God said, *"Let Us make man in Our image, according to Our likeness..."* An essential characteristic of love is its desire to enlarge community. Eden was not paradise because of its beauty but because it was the place of unbroken relationships. It was the place of giving and receiving, the continuous actions which take place wherever there is true community.

God knew the risks in carrying out His decision to create Adam with the freedom of choice. This freedom permitted Adam to enter into fellowship with the Triune One, but it also allowed him liberty to choose hate instead of love, disobedience instead of loyalty, selfishness rather than servanthood. Knowing the end from the beginning—and knowing what Adam would choose—God *still* made His decision. We begin to realize how much God treasures community as we consider His perilous commitment to allow man the liberty to decide things for himself. Community must always be a voluntary matter. We are never forced into it; it is something we desire.

Then, from Adam's side, God took a bride. Adam gave a rib and received a help mate. She was "bone of his bone, flesh of his flesh." Like him, she was formed to live in community. Their capacities were significantly different. Someone has said that God put a part of His nature in man, and another part in woman, so they would not be complete without one another.

With Adam, Eve could bring forth new life to share their intimacy in family relationships. No child could ever be born apart from physical union: there would be, for each baby, a father and a mother—and baby would make community. In God's plan, unbroken relationships were always to exist.

The Great Destroyer Of Community

Community was precisely what Satan attacked and hated. He succeeded in destroying all the potential relationships which might exist in Eden. God to man, man to wife, brother to brother—all were smashed to pieces!

Life after Eden quickly became a tragedy. Man's first knowledge of violent death became the ripened fruit of the ugly jealousy of a brother against a brother. Community among men was replaced by loneliness, fragmentation, and a tragic, needless grave.

In Genesis 4:16-24, we trace the line of the "God Rejecters." The genealogy cynically tells us how this family tree sought to gain personal significance. Enoch built a city; Jabal was a cattle rancher; Jubal was the first musician; Tubal-cain became an industrialist. We end with a crazed man shaking in fear, confessing he is a double murderer! Totally missing is any mention of community between these men and God, or with one another.

Satan's tactic was obvious. In each case, these men gained their significance from their personal achievements. At the same time, man discovered his deficiencies could be devastating to his self-image!

Then...Generations Of Men Who Lived In Community

In Genesis 4:25-5:24, we trace a parallel genealogy which also begins with Adam. Significant differences mark these generations from the one just presented, introduced by the comment in verse 26: *"Then men began to call upon the name of the Lord."*

Not one mention of personal achievements is recorded as these new men are described! The only thing we are told about them is that they chose to live in community with Jehovah. In contrast to the record of the previous family, the life span of each man is now carefully recorded. For those who live to gain personal significance, the length of their earthly life is of no consequence to God; for those whose life is spent in communion with Him, every day is precious.

Contrasted to his insane cousin Lamech, Genesis 5:24 reports that *"Enoch walked with God; and he was not, for God took him."* What a difference! Enoch's significance was not in what he did or did not do, but in his entering into communal fellowship with his heavenly Father. The lesson of the two genealogies sets a theme for the rest of scripture: the only "accomplishment" that makes man's earthly life worthwhile, or that will outlive him, is his fellowship with God.

Community In The Old Testament

Throughout the Old Testament, the theme of God and man entering into community is recurrent. With Abraham, with Moses, with Israel, with David, God offered intimacy as an alternative to estrangement.

Ruth's words become symbolic for those who cherish community:

> *"...for where you go, I will go, and where you lodge, I will lodge. Your people shall be my people, and your God, my God."*

Is it surprising that she is found in the genealogy of Jesus Christ?

As the self-centeredness of Israel reaches a crescendo, in Hosea 11:8 God weeps over their lack of communion with Him, as a parent agonizes over a child with bad values: *"How can I surrender you, O Israel?...My heart is turned over within Me..."*

Will Jehovah abandon the desire to live in community with His created ones? No! One after another, His prophets are given ecstatic visions of the future. Isaiah foresees a community where lions sleep with lambs and swords are beaten into plowshares. Jeremiah is promised that Israel will be restored to the land. Ezekiel envisions a glorious Temple in a kingdom of righteousness yet to come. In turn, prophets saw the end times when God and man will live together in intimacy and love.

Community In The New Testament

Then God comes to actually dwell among men! During the act of impregnating a virgin, God the Father declares His intention of penetrating the human race with His love. Unlike His presence among Israel as a cloud of smoke or fire, He will now become visible through His Son, drawing all men unto Him. Christ confronts Satan, even as did the first Adam—not in a garden, but in a desolate wilderness.

The activity of Satan through the centuries is designed to create prison cells which separate men from one another. The father of lies gave them the alluring name "Kingdoms Of This World." He brashly offered them to Jesus, who flatly rejected them. Christ will establish a kingdom not of this world! It will be a kingdom which unites men.

The Lord's "job description," provided by the Holy Spirit 742 years earlier in Isaiah's scroll, is an assignment to repair the horrid breaches in community caused by man's selfishness. To the poor, to the spit-upon, to the prisoners, to the blind, Christ will bring new hope and salvation.

He created community for His followers. From men who would normally never even *speak* to one another, Jesus shaped twelve disciples. A commando-like patriot rubbed shoulders with a quisling tax collector. Fishermen related to men who tilled land. What unlikely combinations!

He lived with them for three years, modelling a lifestyle of love and acceptance. These twelve men discovered that community can be a terrible place to mask limitations, egotism, ignorance, and jealousies. Try as hard as they could, they were unable to hide the selfishness within themselves. They manipulated Jesus to gain preeminence over one another, striving for significant positions in the "pecking order" of the little community. He saw through every one of their manipulations, and kept right on loving them. In true community, men look past warts and pimples to see the potential within one other.

Slowly, very slowly, these men recognized they must abandon their competitive lifestyles. The greatest among them would be the one who would become the servant of all. They discovered the essence of community is a sense of belonging: their true worth is not their reputation, but their readiness to give themselves unsparingly to the rest.

By living with twelve men, God in human flesh had made a clear statement of the way community develops. While thousands pressed him from every side, He chose to be with one cell of life. Indeed, existence lived apart from that cell had no value. He did not simply gather them once a week for a "discipleship class." He lived with them. They took trips, went fishing, visited Jerusalem, had cookouts by the sea. They camped in the mountains. They shared a common purse.

Of greatest importance, they had a purpose. If community is created without specific goals, there will soon be conflicts and the whole thing will collapse. In *Home for the Heart,* Bruno Bettleheim writes,

> *I am convinced community can flourish only if it exists for an aim outside itself. Community is viable if it is the outgrowth of a deep involvement in a purpose which is other than, or above, that of being a community.*[4]

Jesus was preparing them for His work. He did it without a great amount of teaching, choosing instead to let them watch as He modelled before them. Indeed, to the modern purveyor of discipleship materials, His pattern is perplexing! He barely *discussed* how to pray; instead, He took them to all-night seasons of prayer. Finally, some of the disciples said, "Jesus, don't you think it would be important for you to teach us how to pray? After all, John has taught his disciples about this subject."

Glancing over at them, He said, "Fine. Pray like this—" He gave them what we call "The Lord's Prayer," which took about one minute to recite. He might as well have concluded with a comment like, "Any questions?"

What a contrast this was to the hours and hours of praying He had modelled for them in the hills! Had they been wiser, they would have realized prayer is not *taught*—it's *caught.*

He delayed another important lesson about praying until they had returned from their first assignment. Jesus had sent them into Galilee to minister. After they returned, a man approached him with his son, explaining that the disciples who had come to his village failed to set the boy free from epilepsy. After Jesus healed the lad, the disciples asked: "Why couldn't we do that, Lord?"

Why had He not told them about that *before* they went out to minister? The reason is significant: when living in community, there are "teachable moments" which cannot be anticipated. Value systems are created in the context of *living*, not *studying*. This is one of the reasons values are always shaped faster in cell group than in impersonal P.B.D. structures. When one faces a crisis or wrestles with a sin, the group can respond immediately, rather than having to wait for a specially printed Sunday school lesson or a pastor's sermon to touch on the problem.

Jesus' Body On Earth

Christ first dwelled within the body shaped by the Father in the womb of Mary. His ministry then continued through the *new* Body, which replaced the first one. That new Body would have all the faculties and resources of a human body, plus all the eternal power and reality of the Godhead. Christ's indwelling spirit in the new Body would assure this would happen.

Matthew mentioned in 12:18 that Isaiah prophesied,

> *Behold, My Servant whom I have chosen; My Beloved in whom My soul is well-pleased; I will put My Spirit upon Him, and He shall proclaim justice to the Gentiles.*

The beginning of that ministry to the Gentiles was launched in a region where they were a distinct minority. The completion of His ministry would require Jesus to dwell in all the world throughout all generations, in every "kingdom" Satan would establish on the continents of the earth. He accomplished His task by creating His own Body from human bodies specially selected for this purpose. How simple was this task for the One who had spoken all things into existence by His Word!

Jesus personally named His new Body. He called it "the church" *(ecclesia)*, meaning "the called-out ones." These special treasures would be indwelled by Him. Through their bodies He would perform His ministry. All the supernatural power of the

Godhead would flow into and through them, even as rivers of water spring up from an artesian well.

He referred to the "called out ones" three times before His death. On the first occasion, He described them as a building under construction. He would be both the Foundation under it and the Builder of it:

> . . . Jesus . . . asked his disciples, "Who do people say the Son of Man is?" They replied, "Some say John the Baptist; others say Elijah; and still others, Jeremiah or one of the prophets." "But what about you?" he asked. "Who do you say I am?" Simon Peter answered, "You are the Christ, the Son of the living God." Jesus replied, "Blessed are you, Simon son of Jonah, for this was not revealed to you by man, but by my Father in heaven. And I tell you that you are Peter, and on this rock I will build my church, and the gates of Hades will not overcome it. I will give you the keys of the kingdom of heaven; whatever you bind on earth will be bound in heaven, and whatever you loose on earth will be loosed in heaven." [5]

His other two references clearly point to the church as an intimate *community* of people. He anticipates the friction which could only exist in settings where people are living together in close relationships:

> If your brother sins against you, go and show him his fault, just between the two of you. If he listens to you, you have won your brother over. But if he will not listen, take one or two others along, so that 'every matter may be established by the testimony of two or three witnesses.' If he refuses to listen to them, tell it to the church; and if he refuses to listen even to the church, treat him as you would a pagan or a tax collector. I tell you the truth, whatever you bind on earth will be bound in heaven, and whatever you loose on earth will be loosed in heaven. Again, I tell you that if two of you on earth agree about anything you ask for, it will be done for you by my Father in heaven. For where two or three come together in my name, there am I with them. [6]

For the *second time*, He has referred to the flow of power

between heaven and earth through the activity of the church. Is it conceivable that He will not demonstrate the same eternal power in His new Body that He demonstrated in His first one? *Of course not!* He will continue to transform the poor, the captives, the blind, and the downtrodden. Thus, *every member* of His new Body will participate in the divine power required for ministry.

Notice carefully: in this scripture, Jesus saw the church existing in communities as small as "two or three." Ponder the intimacy of personal relationships and the covenant commitments described by the procedures for handling conflict in this passage.[7]

Read the passage again: does it not verify the cell group concept of church life? M. Scott Peck rightly says,

> Currently the Church is not only not the Body of Christ, it is not even a body, a community. It must become a community before it can serve as the Body of Christ.[8]

One may well be justified in wondering whether our Lord saw the church as anything, *ever,* larger than a cell group capable of experiencing true community. He Himself could have created large group structures: He never did. It was enough to *address* five thousand; He chose to *live* with twelve. The basic building block of the Body which would be inhabited by Jesus would be composed of *cells,* not masses of people who do not experience community.

The Birth Of The Church

When was the church born? The common teaching is that it was birthed at Pentecost by the Holy Spirit's action. Not so! The discussion of the birth of His new Body must have occupied a large portion of His dialogue on the Mount of Transfiguration with Moses and Elijah. The full meaning of His death would involve giving birth to His new Body. From the side of the first Adam had come his bride; even so, the second Adam's bride would come from His riven side.

A woman delivering a child would never endure birth pains as extreme as our Lord's suffering to birth the church. His Body became a battleground between the forces of heaven and hell.

The only available link between a holy God and sinful men, He endured all which could be hurled against Him as Satan attempted to forever sever this connection. Jesus demonstrated for the church that "the gates of Hades will not overcome it." Satan became a defeated foe; Christ led captivity captive. When He cried, "It is finished!", the devil became a whimpering puppy, chained to the victory chariot of the King of Kings.

We must not detract from the crucifixion event by teaching His bride was birthed painlessly by the Holy Spirit in an upper room at the Feast of Pentecost. The whole point of Calvary is that filthy goblets cannot receive pure water until they have been cleansed. Jesus died to justify sinful men through His act of propitiation on the cross, to make them pure. The breaking of His body and the outpouring of His blood made peace with God possible for mankind, and it also made it possible for Him to indwell a pure, new Body. *He became the Head of His Body at the cross.*

The Beauty of the Lord's Supper

This is the very reason the Lord's Supper became precious to the cell groups from their very first gatherings. It was a constant reminder of the place and the cost of their birth and their life.

This ordinance has often become a trite, emotionless ritual in church life. In the patently absurd method of intinction, people kneel in rows at an altar. There is no awareness of community as people come and go from seats to the kneeling pads. In the congregational method, the closest thing to intimacy among participants is impersonally passing a tray down the row to the person on your right.

This ordinance was instituted in the upper room of a house with thirteen persons who had lived in community together. It was not meant to become a sacrament. It was not intended to be cut off from its meaning. It is the activity of a *community,* which means the activity of a cell group. Where is there any scriptural justification for its use in large clumps of Christians?

It was meant for use in *small groups* where there is community, where there is a sense of Christ as the Head. It takes the church back to its beginnings, reminding it over and over of the place and the costliness of its birth. It was, indeed, a unique "birthday party" as the early church shared it with one another.

In the early church it was a part of the Agape Feast held by the cells. In *Paul's Idea Of Community,* Dr. Robert Banks explains that each time a cell gathered, the common meal would begin with the breaking of the bread and close with the passing of the cup, a Passover tradition which had been carried on for centuries.[9] Thus, the "love feast" began and ended with a reminder that the life of this *ecclesia* began at the cross.

The Body Is A Battleground

If, in Christ's first body He suffered all that we suffer, it must be obvious that His new Body will also know suffering. The new Body, the church, is to be a battleground. The struggle between the forces of Christ and Satan will take place in it. "Onward, Christian Soldiers" sounded this note in earlier years. In contemporary praise music, the theme has been picked up in "God's got an army, marching through the land." We cannot recognize the validity of a church which insulates itself against conflict:

> Beloved, do not be surprised at the fiery ordeal among you, which comes upon you for your testing, as though some strange thing were happening to you; but to the degree that you share the sufferings of Christ, keep on rejoicing, so that also at the revelation of His glory, you may rejoice with exultation.[10]

The conflict is with Satan, who is determined to devour the Bride. One does not penetrate the kingdoms of this world without facing conflict. The good news we bring is that the greatest among us is the one who serves. Every world system teaches that's a *lie*, that the greatest is the one who sits at the head of the table. That conflicts! In fact, our good news "turns the world upside down!"

When the church fails to enter the conflict, battles rage within the lives of individuals who are captives of Beelzebub. When the church does not storm the gates of hell to release captives, their misery is our responsibility. One example of this is the way the church treats the "problem" of homosexuals by speaking hatefully of them from the pulpit, snubbing them if they attend services and freezing them out if they try to become active participants in the life of the church after conversion.

It is the task of the church to enter into conflict. That's done by *cell groups* in far greater depth than possible in large groups.

This was graphically illustrated in Abidjan, Cote d' Ivoire, at an Easter harvest retreat held by the massive cell group church, the Yopougon Baptist Church and Mission. Tens of thousands attended the retreat, among them more than 15,000 who would be converted. The West African culture is strongly dominated by witch doctors and the worship of demons. Thousands of women sacrifice a goat to a demon when desiring to become pregnant, pledging to dedicate the child to the evil spirit when it is born. Youngsters are taught to worship demons from their earliest childhood.

We were introduced to 100 teams who were prepared to minister to persons who might manifest demonic activity during the services. As we began to praise, unbelievers in the audience began to scream and writhe on the ground, overcome by the conflict between the demons living within them and the power of the Holy Spirit around them. The teams ran into the crowd and carried the demon possessed to an area reserved for ministry activity.

I observed those precious Christians as they worked with those possessed. Eighty percent of them had themselves been delivered. The tormented would roll back their eyeballs until only the whites could be seen. They would scream most tragically as demons within resisted the attempt to expel them.

How precious was the release experienced by those who had been screaming just hours before! As I saw these same people the next day, "clothed and in their right minds," I longed for the church worldwide to become engaged in the spiritual warfare that can heal adulterous lives and restore stormy marriages, heal diseases, and generally set people free!

As I recall those experiences, I realize that only small groups can deal with the problems in those lives. It took all five members of the group to assist the burdened person. These deliverance cells have become for me a symbol of what Christ wants His Body to be doing. The setting free of prisoners, the declaration of the Good News to the poor, the recovery of sight by the blind is a *team effort.*

Preparation For The Coming Of The Body

After His resurrection, He breathed on the disciples, telling them to receive the Holy Spirit:

> *Again Jesus said, "Peace be with you! As the Father has sent me, I am sending you." And with that he breathed on them and said, "Receive the Holy Spirit. If you forgive anyone his sins, they are forgiven; if you do not forgive them, they are not forgiven."* [11]

The word "As" in this passage is an essential connection between Jesus' mission on earth and their continuation of it. The disciples did not ask for the Spirit to be given to them; the act was Jesus' decision! He put His own life's breath into their bodies. They were thus linked to Him as the new Body He was to enter. Note that His focus in this scripture is related to the *mission,* not *personal sanctification.* Jesus had prayed in John 17 that they, along with all believers, should not be taken out of the world, but be protected from the evil one. He now *directly* connects their receiving of the Spirit to the harvesting of unforgiven sinners. The word "breathed" used here is not used in any other place in the New Testament and is identical to the word used in the Greek Septuagint in Genesis 2:7:

> *Even as God breathed into Adam's nostrils the breath of human life, so Christ breathed into them the life of His Spirit.*

When Jesus ascended to glory, He removed the human body He had inhabited since his birth in Bethlehem. He instructed 120 of his followers, including the eleven disciples, to await the baptism with the Holy Spirit. He would soon minister in the world through His *new* Body! He told them it would happen "in a few days."

Community In The Body Of Christ

Why did they have to wait? Could not the Holy Spirit have come upon them right away? No. Something had to happen first:

they had to become bonded into a community. Meanwhile, God's Spirit was patiently poised in the heavenlies, ready to give life to Christ's new Body.

These men and women shared their lives together for ten days in the upper room of a wealthy man's home. They didn't listen to sermons, nor did they organize Bible studies. There was no formal agenda. *They had each other;* their fellowship with one another was the essential ingredient of their time together. Their ten days of sharing together was God's way of helping *acquaintances* become a *family.* There could not be *church* until there was *community.*

We may surmise they would naturally form themselves into small groups during those ten days. That's what naturally happens any time 120 people gather, without formal structures, in one room. People must have moved from group to group as the days passed. They developed intimacy with all of the others as they spent those days together, sharing information about their lives, their families, and their contacts with Jesus. They also shared their pain, their heartaches, their problems. As they did so, they moved closer and closer to the goal Christ had for them: they were "in one accord."

I can imagine the disciples over in one corner, trying to piece together the truths Jesus had taught them. As new insights came to them, they probably called the whole group to hear what they were discovering. Perhaps Peter jumped to his feet shouting, "That's it! That's what He meant! How could we have been so blind?" The room would be silenced by his sudden outbreak, and he would excitedly tell them all what the disciples had just realized. Things of the Spirit blended into things of the Body and the soul as they ate, shared, and prayed together. A Sabbath would come and go as they were together. Some would go out to bring food back; others briefly ran necessary errands or perhaps cared for family needs. The focus in the room always remained on their life together. *(Was it in this setting that the first Agape Feasts took place, as they followed Jesus' instructions to "do this in remembrance of me"?)*

Day by day, an extended family was being shaped from diverse backgrounds. Their lifestyle, which would suddenly proliferate into 300 or more cell groups, was being learned in the same way Jesus had taught His disciples: by living together.

Power For Ministry

Then, it happened! As hundreds, even thousands, filled the streets for the Day of Pentecost, the clear sky resounded with the noise of a violent wind. How those on the outside responded to that noise we shall never know. Inside the upper room, we know exactly what took place. The same Shekinah Glory, which burned within a bush before Moses, now became tongues of fire which rested upon each person's head. The Glory entered their lives, and their spirits and words were under His control. Power for ministry had come to the Body of Christ.

John had forecast this event. He quotes Jesus as saying,

> *"I baptize you with water. But one more powerful than I will come, the thongs of whose sandals I am not worthy to untie. He will baptize you with the Holy Spirit and with fire."* 12

They had waited as instructed, and they had literally received power when the Holy Spirit came on them. Clearly, the empowering was in connection with their mission: *"you will be my witnesses in Jerusalem, and in all Judea and Samaria, and to the ends of the earth."*

They knew immediately the identity of the One who had entered into them. They knew—in the same way a sleeping husband knows the familiar footsteps of his wife in the darkness of the night. They had walked, talked, eaten and spoken with Christ, and they knew *He* had come back to live within them. They were the first to be able to say,

> And we, who with unveiled faces all reflect the Lord's glory, are being transformed into his likeness with ever-increasing glory, which comes from the Lord, who is the Spirit.13

As they mingled with the crowd, speaking with a power which translated their words into the languages of the hearers, they were the first to declare,

> God has chosen to make known among the Gentiles the glorious riches of this mystery, which is Christ in you, the hope of glory.14

As Peter explained, the Feast of Pentecost has not yet completed its fulfillment: it merely *began* to be fulfilled at that time. The pouring out of the Spirit triggered 3,000 conversions in a few hours. Not yet a day old, the church had grown to 25 times its original size. It was learning quickly that the Bride could not set goals to be met. Rather, it would become the agent of supernatural activity as Christ continued to perform His ministry.

Peter's proclamation called for a response to the manifestation of the spiritual power they had observed. He simply said, "This is that . . ." The first "evangelistic sermon" was little more than an explanation of God-sent power.

The Bride's Lifestyle

Without delay, the life of the Bride became structured as cell church life. No one had to organize it, write a handbook, or even create a system. The pattern was adopted by all, and within twenty-four hours it was in full bloom. There was no need to elect anyone, select anyone, or ordain anyone:

> *Those who accepted his message were baptized, and about three thousand were added to their number that day. They devoted themselves to the apostles' teaching and to the fellowship, to the breaking of bread and to prayer. Everyone was filled with awe, and many wonders and miraculous signs were done by the apostles. All the believers were together and had everything in common. Selling their possessions and goods, they gave to anyone as he had need. Every day they continued to meet together in the temple courts. They broke bread in their homes and ate together with glad and sincere hearts, praising God and enjoying the favor of all the people. And the Lord added to their number daily those who were being saved.*[15]

Salvation was definitely *not* a personal affair. Their priorities were to hear the apostles teach in the temple courts, and to fellowship, break bread (the Agape Feast), and pray, moving from house to house (Acts 5:42). They never stopped proclaiming Jesus as the Christ, and their meetings were always open to seekers and converts. Their love for each other was intense. Barnabas, from

Crete, ordered a parcel of land he owned back home to be sold, giving the funds to aid other believers.

A common concern for the needy caused the distribution of possessions and money to be channeled through the Apostles. This policy was intended to avoid the embarrassment of directly giving or receiving assistance from other members of the cell. At the same time, they learned that the Spirit would focus on the fact that though their Lord "was rich, yet for their sakes he became poor, so that they through His poverty might become rich." They gave out of love, not obligation. We can only imagine the impact this witness had upon unbelievers!

The pooling of funds before distribution also caused one of the first problems: the Greek widows complained that they were not getting a fair share of food. The apostles rightly delegated the problem to a group of seven men with Greek names. Gradually, as needed, structures were created.

Most important, Body life was composed of communities of cells, while miraculous acts continued to verify they had become the Body in which Jesus lived. They lived in and out of each other's homes, and became true families of faith. The division between the natural and the supernatural did not exist for them—nor was there a separation between the secular and the sacred. Theirs was not a weekly meeting to be attended; it was the life of a spiritual family, and involved them in each other's lives on a day to day basis.

Conclusion

In Acts, the gospel has to break out of hindering traditions. Its last verse says of Paul: *"Boldly and without hindrance he preached the kingdom of God and taught about the Lord Jesus Christ."* Nonscriptural traditions have always been the enemy of the church. Hindrances to the development of community today must also be rejected.

Cell churches are the only way that true community can be experienced by all Christians. It is not a "purist's dream" to suggest the church should structure itself around this truth. Rather, it is a return to a life style which has been bastardized by centuries of unbiblical, crusted traditions. The cell group is not just a *portion* of church life, to be clustered with a dozen other organizations. *It* is church life; and when it properly exists, all other competing structures are neither needed nor valid.

A community should not be primarily a grouping of shocktroops, commandoes or heroes, but a gathering of people who want to be a sign that it is possible for men to live together, love each other, celebrate and work [together] . . . A community is a sign that love is possible in a materialistic world where people so often either ignore or fight each other.

Christian communities cannot be outside society. They are not bolt-holes for the emotions, offering spiritual drugs to stave off the sadness of everyday life. They are not places where people can go to salve their consciences and retreat from reality into a world of dreams. They are places of resource, which are there to help people grow towards freedom, so that they can love as Jesus loves them. 'There is no greater love than to give one's life for one's friends.'

• Jean Vanier

ABOUT *OIKOS...*

To fully understand the importance of the cell group church, we must consider the word *oikos,* a biblical term that describes the basic building block of society. It appears throughout the Bible and refers to the *personal community* which exists for us all. It is translated into English as *house* or *household.* For example, in Acts 16: 31, Paul and Silas used it when they said, "Believe in the Lord Jesus, and you will be saved—you and your *household."*

Oikos: The World's Way Of Forming Cell Groups For All

The *oikoses* each of us lives within are not large. We may know several dozen, even several hundred, people, but quality time spent with others is extremely limited—and only those to whom we devote quality time can be said to be a part of our *oikos,* our *personal community.*

Each of us has a primary group which includes *some* of our relatives and *some* of our friends who relate to us through work, recreation, hobbies, and neighbors. These are the people we talk to, relate to, and share with, for at least a total of one hour per week.

It is most unusual to find a person who has as many as 20 people in his or her *oikos.* For many years, I have surveyed the sizes of the *oikoses* of those attending my seminars and classes. Christians usually average nine people, and a large percentage of them had not developed a single new *oikos* relationship in the past six months!

Life is made up of endless chains of *oikos* connections. Every person is already entwined in these relationships. If people are accepted into an *oikos,* they feel a security that does not exist when meeting a stranger.

In every culture of the world, the intimacy of *oikos* connections is considered to be sacred. The Chinese have a special word for close friendships, and such bonds are considered to be a sacred thing. In Argentina, I was shown a gourd and a metal tube with holes on one end of it for the drinking of *maté* tea. A most intimate *oikos* custom in their culture is sharing the *maté* by drinking from the same tube. Usually, the ceremony is limited to family members. The Argentine who explained this to me said, "Recently, I went to visit a friend who was sharing a gourd of *maté* with his wife and children. He paid me the highest honor by inviting me to participate."

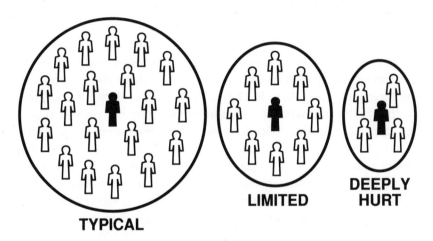

TYPICAL **LIMITED** **DEEPLY HURT**

Oikoses Vary With Emotional Strength

In *Pastor and Parish—A Systems Approach,* E. Mansell Pattison has examined this basic structure of human life in depth. He has sought to describe contemporary *oikos* relationships in psychological and sociological terms:

> I have found that the normal person has about twenty to thirty people in his or her psychosocial system . . . . There are typically about five or six people in each subgroup of family, relatives, friends, and work-recreation-church associates. About 60 percent of the people in this normal system interact with each other.

In contrast, neurotics have only ten to twelve people in their psychosocial systems. Their systems include people who may be dead or live far away . . . . Only about 30 percent of the system is interconnected. It is as if the neurotic, having a variety of individual relationships, is like the hub of a wheel having spokes that radiate outward but are not connected by a rim. Thus the neurotic has an impoverished psychosocial system.

For psychotics we get a third pattern. Here there are only four to five people in the system. The interpersonal relations are ambivalent and nonreciprocal. The system is 90 to 100 percent interconnected. The psychotic is caught in an exclusive nonpermeable small system that is binding, constructive, and destructive.[1]

Since the world began, men have always lived in *oikoses.* Every single culture, without exception, has them. The security of the individual is in the affirmation received by those who are significant in the *oikos.* In the earliest hours of childhood, the mother is the one who provides affirmation by her presence and her attention. As the child develops, this affirmation is received, or not received, by the other household members. Then the school teacher becomes a part of the *oikos,* and later it becomes the adolescent's *oikos* group which must approve him. In the workplace, affirmation is tied to promotions and raises in salary.

Each *oikos* becomes a part of a larger social structure, as we shall see in the next chapter. The important thing for us to grasp here is that every human being lives in a special, tiny world, often being forced to relate to people who are forced upon him or her by *oikos* structures. Today, the hurts of being thrust into a home where the mother is an alcoholic or the father is a daughter molester composes a significant ministry for cell group churches.

As you read this, consider the implications of this in your own life. Take a moment to write down the names of all the people you spend one full hour each week sharing with in a direct, person-to-person manner. (This hour can be accumulated a few minutes at a time, scattered over seven days, but it must be regular—and it must be face to face.)

Studies of American family life indicate that the typical daddy spends only *seven minutes a day* in direct communication with each of his children—a total of 49 minutes per week. That's not enough time to honestly include them in his *oikos*.

The overpowering impact of a limited few upon each of our lives must be considered. For example: who are the *significant others* in your own life, whose approval or disapproval is important to you? (I have counseled with those who are *still* trying to please a disapproving father, who has been dead for years.) Who do you fear may reject you, and who do you look to for affirmation? Meditating upon one's own *oikos* can bring great insights!

Christian Workers Have *Oikoses* Lacking Unbelievers

My own survey of this subject among Christian workers has revealed amazing facts. I am certain I have polled over 5,000 pastors, pastor's wives, church staff members, and missionaries in at least thirty countries. It is a rare thing to find those who are in "full time Christian work" who have unbelievers in their primary *oikos*.

Unless she is employed in the secular world, the wife of a Christian worker is least likely to have a *single contact* with the unchurched. Her *oikos* is filled only with church people. On one occasion in Oklahoma City, an educational director of a large Fort Worth church put his head in his hands and wept with embarrassment as he realized he had spent his entire career within the confines of church work. He could not remember having an *oikos* with an unbeliever in it since he graduated from a secular college.

Consider the unbeliever with a well established set of *oikos* connections, and the offer of the church visitor for him to become a Christian! Throughout this book, we shall return to that issue. It is critical to the matter of evangelism strategy. In a world of strangers, we ply our "soul winning" with little regard for the true nature of life for those we seek to reach.

Jesus Constantly Invaded Pagan *Oikoses*

While the church pulls people out of their *oikoses* and gives them membership in an organization which swallows them up, the New Testament reveals a different approach to people relationships. Jesus constantly did His work by invading *oikos* groups.

He knew there was no other way to share the gospel except to penetrate these small clusters of people. It is obvious that each *oikos* is based in a house, not an institutional building. Thus, the Lord spent his time going from one house to another.

In Luke 19:2-5, we see Jesus making contact with Zacchaeus. He says to him, "Zacchaeus, . . . I must stay at your house today." In Luke 7:36-38, we find Him in the *oikos* of a Pharisee who has invited Him to have dinner with him. While He reclines at the table, a prostitute comes and pours perfume on His feet. What amazing examples of *oikos* penetration!

In Matthew 8:14, He enters Peter's house and heals one of the *oikos* members living there. In Matthew 9:10, He eats dinner with His disciples and many tax collectors and sinners at Matthew's house. Again, he penetrates an *oikos;* in Matthew 9:23 as He enters the ruler's house and sees the flute players and the noisy crowd. In Matthew 17:25, Peter finds Him in a Capernaum house, where Jesus speaks to him about paying taxes. We read in Mark 3:20 that Jesus entered a house, and a crowd gathered, "so that he and his disciples were not even able to eat." In Mark 7:17, He enters a house where His disciples quiz Him about a parable. In Mark 7:24, He enters a house to be alone, only to be swamped by a crowd who learned where He was staying. In Mark 9:33, He is in a Capernaum house when He asks the disciples, "What were you arguing about on the road?"

The Early Church Penetrated *Oikoses,* Too!

In Acts 5:42 we read that the early church went from house to house. In Acts 8:3, when Saul wanted to destroy the church, he knew where to find the people of God. We are told, "Going from house to house, he dragged off men and women and put them in prison."

It is interesting to see in Acts 10 how the Holy Spirit arranged for Peter to get from the house of Simon the Tanner to the residence of Cornelius, where his conversion took place. The penetration of *oikoses* is the pattern for ministry in the first century.

Conversions are frequently recorded as sweeping an entire *oikos* into the Kingdom. In Acts 16, both Lydia and the jailer are converted along with the members of their *oikos.* The first act of

Lydia after her conversion was to invite Paul to stay at her house.

Rejection By One's *Oikos* For Becoming A Christian Is Painful

Jesus reminded us in Matthew 10:36 that following Him can be a costly decision: "a man's enemies will be the members of his own *oikos*.." Making a decision to follow Him can cause mayhem in relationships with primary people. This is why He said in Matthew 10:35, "For I have come to turn a man against his father, a daughter against her mother, a daughter-in-law against her mother-in-law . . ." In verse 37, he calls for a decision between the *oikos* and the Kingdom: "Anyone who loves his father or mother more than me is not worthy of me; anyone who loves his son or daughter more than me is not worthy of me . . ."

In Singapore today, there is a Zone Pastor Intern on the staff I work with who is from a Hindu home. After his commitment was made to follow Christ, the *oikos* descended on him with wrath. His uncle waited until he was present to say to his father, "Why do you allow your son to disgrace us all like this?" Another example in contemporary Southeast Asia is a young physician who followed the Lord at the price of his Muslim family declaring him dead and buried. *Oikoses* can be ruthless when one chooses another path for life.

Our Lord's Body Is Called An *"Oikos"*

However, there is a very special *oikos* for those who have faced the ultimate rejection. Hebrews 3:6 says, "But Christ is faithful as a son over God's *oikos*. And we are his *oikos*, if we hold on to our courage and the hope of which we boast." Consider these additional scriptures that speak of this truth, found in 1 Peter 4:17, 1 Timothy 3:15, Ephesians 2:19, and 1 Peter 2:5:

> *For it is time for judgment to begin with the oikos of God; and if it begins with us, what will the outcome be for those who do not obey the gospel of God?*

> *. . . if I am delayed, you will know how people ought to conduct themselves in God's oikos, which is the church of the living God, the pillar and foundation of the truth.*

Consequently, you are no longer foreigners and aliens, but fellow citizens with God's people and members of God's oikos . . .

. . . you also, like living stones, are being built into a spiritual oikos to be a holy priesthood, offering spiritual sacrifices acceptable to God through Jesus Christ.

The concept of *oikos* describing the church should make us recognize the significance of the cell as the Basic Christian Community. Scripture refers to the early Christians as members of this spiritual *oikos* by speaking of those who have come to faith by *family units*, rather than just by personal commitments:

Crispus, the synagogue ruler, and his entire oikos believed in the Lord . . . . Greet also the church that meets at their house . . . . Greet those who belong to the oikos of Aristobulus . . . . Greet those in the oikos of Narcissus who are in the Lord . . . . some from Chloe's oikos have informed me that there are quarrels among you . . . . Yes, I also baptized the oikos of Stephanas . . . . You know that the oikos of Stephanas were the first converts in Achaia . . . . Aquila and Priscilla greet you warmly in the Lord, and so does the church that meets at their oikos . . . . the saints send you greetings, especially those who belong to Caesar's oikos . . . . Give my greetings to . . . Nympha and the church in her oikos . . . . May the Lord show mercy to the oikos of Onesiphorus . . . . Greet Priscilla and Aquila and the oikos of Onesiphorus.[2]

Truly, the early church thought about the chains of *oikoses* to be won while they simultaneously rejoiced that God had formed them into Basic Christian Communities. For the church to live at *oikos* level was certainly God's plan, and assuredly the pattern which was followed until men's carnality got in the way.

Two Members Of The *Oikos* Family

Two concepts are shared in the scriptures which directly tie to our consideration of the church as *oikos*. The first of these words is *oikonomos*. This word appears in an *oikos* context in a comment made by Jesus in Matthew 24:45:

> Who then is the faithful and wise **oikonomos** [servant], whom the master has put in charge of the servants in his household to give them their food at the proper time?

The *oikonomos* was the servant in an *oikos* who was assigned the oversight of physical needs within the household. He had direct access to his master's funds and was responsible for providing physical necessities "at the proper time." In the early church, the *oikonomos* spirit invaded the cell groups, who shared their possessions as physical needs became known. The concept of "stewardship" as we know it today goes far astray from the spirit of the *oikonomos* in the house churches. (See my chapter in the *Shepherd's Guidebook*, entitled "Too Much Month At The End Of The Money.")

The second word is *oikodomeo*, discussed heavily in other parts of this guidebook. It shares similarities with its first cousin, *oikonomos*. Both are words directly related to the *oikos*, and both have a stewardship in mind in which God provides what His people need. However, *oikodomeo* does not deal with physical needs: it zeros in on spiritual necessities. Thus, the flow of spiritual gifts is emphasized in connection with its application.

In both cases, the heart of the Christian life is not related to a word for "Temple," or "Synagogue," or "Church Building." As the basic fabric of human life is embedded in the *oikos*, even so the life of the Body of Christ is to be *oikos* based.

In a later chapter, we shall consider the assignment of Jesus to penetrate unreached people through using the *oikos* principle. Let's move now to a consideration of the "kingdoms of this world" which embrace the *oikoses*.

7 PUTTING CELLS IN THE KINGDOMS

While developing an urban strategy in Brussels a few years ago, I discovered *A Gospel for the Cities* by Benjamin Tonna.[1] This Catholic scholar opened my eyes to the areas of *social systems* and *social structures* as he applied the concepts to church life. I took his chapters back to the scriptures and found a new awareness of why God is creating cell group church structures in today's urbanizing world.

In Matthew 4, Jesus is being tempted by Satan in the wilderness. In verses 8-9, the two are standing on a very high mountain, and Jesus is shown *"all the kingdoms of the world and their splendor."* Satan is proud of his kingdoms, and assumes they will also appeal to Jesus. He offers them all to Jesus if He will only bow down and worship him. (Imagine the importance Satan placed upon the Son of God bowing down before him! *He was willing to surrender all the kingdoms in exchange for being worshipped by Jesus.)*

Jesus didn't share Satan's value system. He knew something Satan didn't know about: the Kingdom of God was about to be established. He had come to invade the kingdoms of this world and to release their captives. He flatly refused the offer.

As we reflect on this encounter, we begin to realize that Satan intentionally created *kingdoms* for men which promise *"splendor"* as the carrot-on-a-stick, suspended one inch in front of their noses, tantalizing them to grasp it. Grandeur and magnificence was Beelzebub's great desire; why should not all men want it as much as he did?

Appealing to this basic desire within men to become significant, the evil one placed them in cells—*prison cells* called "kingdoms." It's the task of the church to set these captives free. There's a radical difference between the kingdoms created by Satan and the one Jesus came to plant among men. Grasping this difference helps us understand why the P.B.D. church will forever be ineffective in an urban world and why a new lifestyle for the church is necessary.

How Satan Created The "Kingdoms Of This World"

Satan launched each of his kingdoms by urging clans to understand the reasons for their existence and what the world around them signified. He then craftily manipulated their
conclusions, their "worldviews," defined by Kraft as the *"culturally structured assumptions, values, and commitments underlying a people's perception of REALITY."*[2] (We may also refer to worldview as their *basic belief system.)*

WORLDVIEW

Within every kingdom, people next built a *value system* on the foundation of their worldview. These enmeshed values encompassed all the events of life: conception, birth, puberty,
marriage, work ethic, wealth, power, death, and scores of other areas. These values permeated their daily life. With each thread woven into their values, the way to attain "splendor" was further spelled out. Without exception, "sitting at the head of the table" became a common goal in every separate kingdom.

VALUE SYSTEM

Exactly what was *considered* valuable varied from kingdom to kingdom. The discrepancies between these value systems kept kingdoms from merging, or even making it possible for people to easily transfer from one kingdom to another. Geography and language also separated people. Satan wanted to divide his blinded subjects forever, because, above all else, *he is the arch-enemy of community.*

When Kingdoms Clash

Malaysia is a classic example of what can happen when two kingdoms try to live together with different value systems. Malays are an easygoing, friendly, communal kingdom of people. They live in *kampongs* and wear *sarongs* made from a simple tube of cloth. Fish from the nearby sea, bananas, coconuts, and spices, along with noodle or rice based foods, make up their diet. Working day and night to store up gold is patently absurd to them. Having time to relax, be at home with family and visit friends, is considered to have great worth. They are a simple people, worshipping Allah and praying five times a day.

Enter now a kingdom of Chinese immigrants. These people have a different value system, and they place great worth in gaining personal wealth. They are not too interested in relaxing or visiting with others. They want to have expensively tailored clothes, fine homes, and many servants. They worship the ancestors, Buddha, and the scores of idols they brought with them from the "middle kingdom." In a relatively short period of time, they developed huge tin mines, amassed great wealth, and began to control the economic base of the nation.

Conflict was inevitable! The Malay's abhorrence of idols, the differences in values of all types, finally caused political crises. *Bumiputra* was passed by the Malay-dominated government to force the Chinese industrialists to surrender their power to Malays. The two cultures live today with deep cleavages between them. The kingdoms of this world do not possess the potential for developing *community.*

Satan is a devouring lion, a liar, and a thief. The deception with which he brainwashed the kingdom-founders totally eliminated their awareness of the living God. They chose to worship

RELIGIOUS STRUCTURES

snakes, animals, even chunks of carved wood or rock. They believed all kinds of spirits surrounded them. They "exchanged the truth of God for a lie." Not a single worldview in any of the kingdoms of this world left a place for Jehovah among their deities.[3]

Westerners are ignorant of the permeating power of world religions and the way they fill their adherents with fear. In an unforgettable historical novel about life in a Calcutta slum called "City of Joy," Dominique Lapierre explains:

> . . . these people lived in a state of osmosis with their deities. [Remember] the role these gods played in everyday life. Any intervention of fortune, good or bad: work, rain, hunger, a birth, a death—in fact everything was

ascribed to the gods . . . . No other people honours its gods and its prophets as fervently as does the population of Calcutta—despite the fact that the heavens often seem to have completely abandoned the city to its tragic destiny. Every day, or almost every day, the slum and other areas of the city resounded with the noise of some procession bearing witness to the mystical marriage of a people and its creator.[4]

Are the Western kingdoms any different? Only in the way the entrapped people act out their religious customs. Many church members in America and Britain *also* seek to manipulate their deity, cajoling God to heal or provide success in their business ventures, or to protect their family. They have used the God of the Christian religion to get what *they* want, often promising Him large tithes if He will make them successful and rich.

Distinct in the more developed nations is the worship of abstract things rather than carved idols. Many people bow at the shrines of their employer, their greed, or power to control wealth. They are just as pagan as Calcutta's idol worshipers, no matter how well they dress or how often they attend church. "Splendor" is always, in all cultures, the carrot-on-the-stick!

Each person entering a kingdom by birth must be taught how to properly *act out* the values. Teaching the behavior expected in the kingdom is important in child-raising. Parents

| ALL MUST |
| "ACT" RIGHT |

make comments to their children like, "We don't *act like that* in this family!" Discipline and the withholding of affirmation enforces the training of youngsters to act by the code of the kingdom.

Those entering kingdoms through marriage, adoption of a new religion, or both, must also be carefully tutored on how they should "act." They may be suspect for years to come by those who were *born* into the kingdom: "Is that person *really* one of us?"

Affirmation is a reward, and separation is a punishment, for not "acting right." This destructive behavior is found in all cultures. *Satan's great lie is that your significance depends solely on your performance.*[5] The gnawing fear of rejection—not only by

| REWARD & |
| PUNISHMENT |

the family unit but by the kingdom—creates prison bars far more powerful than steel! Satan has kept his subjects in his control by instilling them with *fear.*

While walking the beaches in Thailand, I came across a youth hostel run by the Catholic church. I sought to visit with an Irish nun and was quickly frozen out by her attitude. Finally I said, "Sister, in our lifetime can two people like us ever be friends?" She said to me, "In *my* lifetime, this is the first time I have ever talked face to face with a *Protestant!"*

Ours is a world where people live in prisons. Reaching others must be done with an understanding of what Satan has done to stop it from happening. I have often probed those who have converted to Christ from another faith. In many of these interviews, I discovered they were *expulsions* from their normal kingdom, searching for another kingdom where they might find significance. While this is certainly not true of all, it is a definite factor in studying the source of conversions.

Take the teenager, for example, who is drawn into drugs. She is gradually rejected by her parents and all others in her *oikos.* In limbo, she has two choices: live with other addicts, or find someone to take her in. She may marry to escape (thousands do), or she may search for the true significance for living. Christ *is* her answer, and we should rejoice to draw in the lost sheep. It's an important task for the people of God to find and affirm such persons—*but there are many, many more we will reach through the mighty power of God using the kingdom power and Jesus' strategy for the cell group church.*

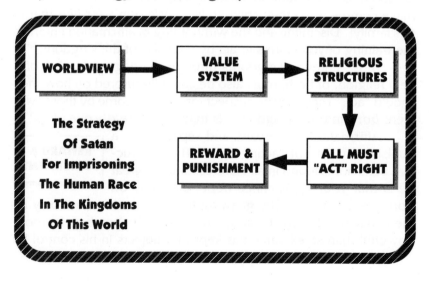

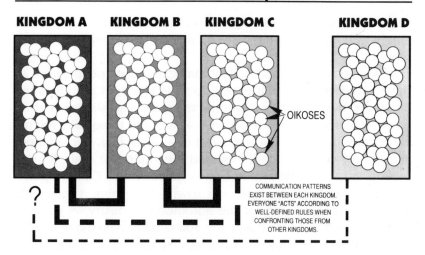

KINGDOM A   **KINGDOM B**   **KINGDOM C**   **KINGDOM D**

OIKOSES

COMMUNICATION PATTERNS
EXIST BETWEEN EACH KINGDOM.
EVERYONE "ACTS" ACCORDING TO
WELL-DEFINED RULES WHEN
CONFRONTING THOSE FROM
OTHER KINGDOMS.

Life In Rural Kingdoms

The diagram above shows people living in kingdoms in a small town. Life here is essentially rural and unsophisticated, providing few diversions for inhabitants. Note that each Kingdom contains many *oikos* groups of approximately 15 people.

In the diagram above, *Kingdom A* contains immigrants from Poland. They have brought their culture, their tastes for foods, and their religion with them. They moved near the small steel mill on the west side of town. All the Polish men work together there.

Kingdom B is a collection of Irish immigrants. They migrated in a stream from their homeland when starvation forced them to do so. They are farming in the area, raising corn and other vegetables. They share only their religion with the Polish but have created a new parish with a priest imported from Dublin.

Kingdom C is made up of Dutch settlers, sharing neither culture, food, nor religion with A or B. They are dairy farmers. The manure from their cattle wafts from the east side of town on some days, making their presence known to those living in the other kingdoms. They are staunch Reformed Church people, faithfully attending the church they erected near the town square.

These groups all send their children to the public school. The second generation from each kingdom has been drilled by the parents about the way Polish or Irish or German people *act* (there's that word again!) when meeting people from another kingdom. Each child dutifully follows the communication pattern taught at home, choosing close friends from the "right crowd" at school.

Events like a high school football game draw people from all three kingdoms, and while they do sit in kingdom groups in the bleachers, they shout for the home team and backslap each other when their sons have won a game. Peace and tranquillity reigns, except when a Polish girl is courted by a Dutch boy. Both of them are roundly censured until they end their innocent affair. It's not "acting right" for a Reformed boy to go out with a Catholic girl!

A new factory comes to town. It's going to provide specialized engineering for the automobile industry. A subdivision is erected to house the nearly 300 families who move in from many parts of the nation. Catholics in the new group find a warmer welcome in the Irish parish than the Polish and gradually assimilate into the church.

Many in the new subdivision are evangelical Christians. They erect a spartan building for worship in the middle of the subdivision. They form kingdom D. They are very active in their church life, and many quickly gain significance through elected positions. Many special Bible teachers come to visit them. Between work, family, and church, they have no time to meet neighbors.

When Pastor Brown pressed the new congregation to take a special "soul winning course," nearly everyone attended. They were shown how to use a small booklet to explain the "plan of salvation," and everyone memorized a brief presentation of how to accept Christ. At the end of the course, they went out two by two to knock on doors and "win the lost." Some were assigned to each of the three kingdoms. They used maps to find the streets.

Their visits were coolly received. Not much was known about this new Evangelical church by the Polish, the Irish, or the Dutch. Mrs. Zwilski listened attentively; but when pushed to pray, she thought, "What would my Polish friends think of me if I left our parish? I'm loved and respected there. I barely *know* these people. Would they even *accept* me as one of them?" *Slam!* The prison bars closed tightly around her, and the visitors left saddened by her lack of interest in the state of her soul.

After making three visits each, the hardy group of evangelists returned to report their results. A team that had visited their next door neighbors found a woman who was almost in tears. The adjustment to the new town and her husband's heavy work schedule had made her very lonely. Although she had been raised in a family that never attended church, she had been considering visiting one. She was most receptive and made a commitment to receive Christ. All rejoiced at the success of their training course.

The Evangelical congregation concluded that those in Kingdoms A, B, and C were not "under conviction" and that they would find their "Prospects" in their own area.

What Happens When A Kingdom "E" Person Appears?

The problem of how to "act" when meeting someone from a strange new kingdom can be a serious one. If no clear guidelines have been set down, one of three possibilities will be selected. The kingdom person can either *avoid, attack,* or *adapt.*

My Houston banker and I had a conflict over the Vietnamese that suddenly migrated into our area. Having lived and ministered among them in Saigon, I knew they were impeccable about meeting financial obligations; yet the banker refused to extend them credit. When he met the first one, his mind computed: "small, dark skinned, broken English, poorly dressed—like the *Mexican illegals* who walk in here asking for car loans." It took heavy pressure from our church before he agreed to make loans to our Vietnamese members. After a few months, he took me out for lunch in appreciation for changing his mind. Not a *single loan* made to these immigrants had defaulted. He just didn't know how to *"act"* when meeting people from a strange kingdom.

When pastoring "P.B.D. style," I often visited unbelievers on visitation night. All too often, as I went through scriptures to explain how they might become Christians, they would interrupt to say something absurd like, "You know, my mother's grandfather was a Methodist minister." *It irked me!* I was talking to them about *eternal life,* and they wanted to talk about their family tree. I would mumble, "How interesting!" and return to the gospel presentation.

I didn't understand what was going on in the other person's mind: "Have I ever known anyone like this guy? None of *my* kingdom friends 'act' like him. Here he sits with his Bible open, preaching to me. *Strange!* Wait a minute—my mother used to tell me about her grandfather, and how he used to read the Bible to her. Wow! I didn't think I had *any* sort of link to this guy—but I do!" In his excitement over his discovery, he interrupted me, certain I would be delighted to know that one of his ancestors had lived in *my* kingdom. I was too foolish to realize what was going on and offended him by not caring about his discovery!

Can A Church Become A "Kingdom Of This World?"

In the illustration about the new evangelical church that came to town, that's *exactly* what happened. It became a human kingdom, isolating its people from the other kingdoms. With an evangelical *worldview* and *value system,* the pastor and members taught their children and incoming people how to *act.* The *rewards* for "acting right" included being elected to the distinguished position of Deacon, or head of the Sunday school. Those who truly loved their Lord also loved the *affirmation* and *significance* they were given in Kingdom D. They lived insulated from the other kingdoms, all the time "doing the work of the Lord," blissfully unaware they were not doing His work at all.

Their foray into the other three kingdoms to evangelize didn't take their own kingdom life into account. Inviting those in other kingdoms to make a decision to accept the Lord involves converts facing the displeasure of their own *oikos,* and those in contiguous *oikoses,* and potential expulsion from their kingdom. Few converts will be made when people are required to change from one kingdom to another.

It's a brutal but true fact: *most churches have become just one more of the kingdoms of this world.* We shall not deny they have a proper theology, but their *ecclesiology* violates the clear teachings of our Lord, and Satan gleefully imprisons them in their own kingdom structure.

Kingdoms In The Urbanized World

Before we fully discuss that last statement, we must learn about a recent development in the history of man: the impact of *urbanization* on the kingdoms of this world. Let's imagine Mary has left the small town previously described. She's going to go to work in the city, 300 miles away. She has contacts with two other girls from her high school class who have found her a secretary's job. They have invited her to share their apartment. Being Polish, Mary feels a bit insecure about moving in with a Dutch and an Irish girl. That was only the beginning: in the office, one of the other secretaries is Jordanian and another is a black from Harlem. She quickly discovers her boss is a hard-swearing atheist. She is the only Catholic in the business.

Suddenly, all kingdom boxes have been mixed together for her! In her confusion, she decides to attend the local parish church. She gets up on Sunday morning (her roommates quit attending church long ago) and goes to mass. The priest seems to be unconcerned about personally knowing her, and the sanctuary has only a few dozen people in it. She goes away deeply disappointed, deciding not to return. Without her family to monitor her churchgoing, there's really no reason for her to do anything she *dislikes* doing.

She wanders through the quiet city streets, enjoying the sun and the sabbath lack of traffic. She crosses a boulevard—and suddenly everything has changed! She has entered an area that is no longer "middle class" like the district where she lives. She's in an elite section. Expensive cars are parked at the curbs, and apartments have uniformed doormen. She reads the names on the door plates of town houses: the Zwinkowskis live next to the Fields, and next to them are the O'Haras and the Al-Aqbars. Feeling she doesn't "belong" in this area, she retraces her steps. It was the last time she ever ventured into that district.

Like all city dwellers, she carves out a portion of the city that provides for her needs. Within a few months, a few blocks of the area where she lives and works becomes her habitat. The shopping mall, the theater, the local tavern where her age group congregates until midnight, and a few other locations have become the entire "city" for her.

She dates a young man who works in the shipping department where she works. She discovers he has used drugs to find the "ultimate reason" for living. She refuses his offer to "take a trip" with him. Another man comes into her life: after the third date, she discovers he's not really divorced. He still has a wife and three kids. She is disgusted by the news.

The city is making her suspicious of people. She withdraws more and more into a *restricted community* of people she feels she can trust. Loneliness becomes a large problem for her.

One of the other secretaries encourages her to "try astrology." She is also told about the Koran and the Book of Mormon. She investigates them all. Slowly, slowly, she begins to create her own private religion. It contains fragments of her Catholic faith, but also includes Eastern mysticism and concepts from the cults and the television preachers who talk to her about "prosperity truths" in their programs.

Wanting to expand her skills and earn more money, she decides to attend a community college and take computer courses. She meets a number of other young people who are also interested in computers, and she quickly forms friendships with them. After-class gatherings at a nearby lounge encase her in a group of eight people who enjoy serious conversations but also party a great deal. She finally moves in with one of them, a Jewish boy who offers her free rent if she will share his utilities and their food.

When he asks her to marry him, she struggles with what her family will say—but elopes anyway. She shrugs off the hostility she feels when she takes him to her town to visit: after all, she doesn't have to put up with her Polish relatives for very long before returning to the big city.

Urban Roles Are *Acquired;* Rural Roles Are *Assigned*

She had received her kingdom prison cell as a *child* from her parents. Her new prison cell was one *she* slowly developed in the context of the impersonal city. *That is the important difference between rural and urban structures.*

In her home town, relatives and other members of her Polish kingdom monitored her movements and urged her to live by the agreed-upon values. In the city, no one cared if she used drugs, stayed out all night, joined a Protestant church, or switched jobs. Emotional isolation and living without primary relationships are commonplace among city dwellers.[6]

How, then, do people in the city *find* relationships that are meaningful? They often find others with common interests or performing similar functions. Christians should understand this and take advantage of their opportunity to penetrate *oikoses* by targeting interests, needs, and responsive groups. Such persons exist in every sector of a major city.

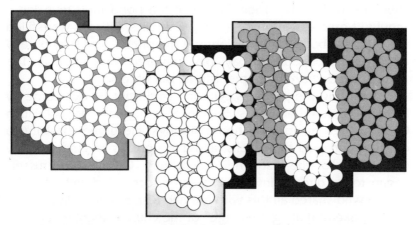

The Kaleidoscope of "Kingdoms" In The Urban Setting

In this illustration we see the urban culture. The boundary lines between kingdoms are confused. There may be an Italian section or a Mexican section, but the blur of people with different religions, foods, and values is unmistakable.

Old and new values swarm around urbanites. Every vice known to man has advocates. Subcultures for deviant groups produce disciples which must be tolerated. Homosexuals may live next door. One cannot trust neighbors who have never even been met. Thefts of homes and cars cause residents to live in fear behind locked doors and burglar alarms. Personal privacy is their only way to handle the chaos of an unharmonized society. "Privatized religion," as well as the rest of life, becomes a normal lifestyle. One's religious views are seldom revealed to others. They may have absurd logical contradictions, but they are never scrutinized for validity.

My urban strategy study of Brussels in 1982 caused me to see the loss of respect for the church which exists in the city. Of all the institutions of the community, the religious ones had the least impact. Since Catholicism claimed 95% of the population, I interviewed a delightful bishop who spoke frankly to me. He shared how Cardinal Suenin had come to direct the parishes of the city, distressed because only 2% of Catholics ever darkened the door of a church except for the "four seasons" of their lives: christenings, first communions, marriages, and burials. (At the time, there were only 300 Belgians attending Evangelical churches in the city!) Their survey of the population revealed a "couldn't care less" attitude among Catholics. Citizens were filled with stories about corruption among the priests, and they bitterly resented the pressure to pay, pay, pay into church coffers. The *institutional church* was prehistoric, out of touch.

Realizing the people's cynicism could not be overcome by building-centered activities, Suenin encouraged "Basic Christian Communities" to form in home settings. He urged the laity to develop and lead these cells, assigning priests to guide the lay leadership. For the first time in a century, Catholics in Brussels began to be directly involved in some form of church life. The bishop who shared all this with me had a special light in his eyes as he spoke of that "golden age" of the church when, in a city of 1,000,000 people, up to 5% of the parishioners became active.

For the first time, the people of Brussels had found *community* in their religion, and they flocked to it. In the estrangement of a European city where isolation was rampant, they had found something in religion that met their deepest need. To be sure, the attendance at formal services in the church buildings was only slightly impacted by these home meetings, but something important was finally happening in the church.

Sad to say, tradition won again! Suenin was replaced by a new cardinal, who set about to switch the direction of the cells away from Bible study, prayer, and sharing. He required all of the cells to get involved in projects related to social justice—*and the groups died away.*

Evangelicals in the city never did understand this resurgence in the formal church. If they had, they could have gleaned a large number of people who had once again been disappointed by the religion of their forefathers. To this day, Brussels remains one of the neediest mission fields in all the world.

What Is The Place Of The P.B.D. Church In The City?

How do church structures, shaped in the small town or rural area, fare in the city? *Very poorly.* They are out of step with this complex culture, often pastored by a man who himself has lived his life in a small town. He may have received limited orientation for his urban assignment. He is frustrated by the lack of effectiveness of his work. Programs which were so adequate in his town pastorates don't attract city dwellers.

While some metropolitan churches have tried to solve their problem by becoming "sanctuaries of safety" within the city, the problem of ministering in a diverse society of many languages, cultures, and value systems, is a serious one.

The P.B.D. church, which flourished so well in the simple structure of the small town, is in trouble. If it locates in an ethnic area, it might survive as in a village, servicing a special group. If, however, people of all languages and races mingle in the community around the church structure, the problems are immense. In a World Class City as many as 93 languages are spoken. As ethnics migrate into new areas, churches caught in their path lose their existing congregations and seem impotent to reach the new settlers. Churches dry up and blow away in these circumstances.

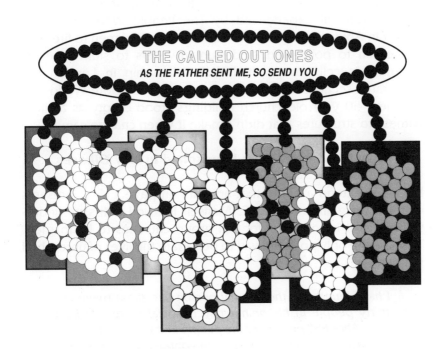

The Cell Group Church Is A Viable Urban Model

In many parts of the earth today, cities are being penetrated effectively by "Basic Christian Communities," the cell groups of churches which bury themselves *within* the kingdoms of this world. This is precisely what Jesus meant when He said,

> The kingdom of heaven is like yeast that a woman took and mixed into a large amount of flour until it worked all through the dough.[7]

Over and over again, scores and scores of times, I have observed and participated in the penetration of all the social structures of urban society through cell groups. In Dallas, Ruth and I chaperoned an Arab lad and a Jewess who had both found Christ in a cell group and who had fallen in love. In Houston, we saw homosexuals and an atheist school teacher face their need for Christ through a Share group determined to penetrate the unchurched. Cells with physicians, cells with politicians, cells with pimps, were all experienced by The People Who Care. Dion Robert in Abidjan, Ivory Coast, has networked firemen to firemen, policemen to policemen, and slum dwellers to slum dwellers through his cell groups. ICHTHUS Fellowship in London has penetrated sections of the city unreached since before World War 2, where 50 year old church buildings stood empty as a silent witness to structures that didn't make it when change came.

Unreached People Are Imprisoned In Tiny *Oikoses*

I want to extend a quote that appears on page 115. It presents extremely significant data. E. Mansell Pattison helps us understand why it is so crucial for cell group churches to be formed. They are the only possible way to penetrate the lives of unreached people:

> I have found that the normal person has about twenty to thirty people in his or her psychosocial system *[oikos]* . . . . About 60 percent of the people in this normal system interact with each other . . . . In contrast, neurotics have only ten to twelve people in their psychosocial systems. Their systems include people who may be dead or live far away . . . . Only 30 percent of the system is interconnected. It is as if the neurotic, having a variety of

individual relationships, is like the hub of a wheel having spokes that radiate outward but are not connected by a rim. Thus the neurotic has an impoverished psychosocial system.

For psychotics we get a third pattern. Here there are only four to five people in the system. The interpersonal relationships are ambivalent and nonreciprocal. The system is 90 to 100 percent interconnected. The psychotic is caught in an exclusive nonpermeable small system that is binding, constructive, and destructive.[8]

Think of it! The more a person is hurting, the more he or she needs Christ, the less possibility there is that the people of God will make contact!

Could anyone *not* believe Satan is the archenemy of community after knowing these things? He imprisons people in the small towns with one sort of kingdom prison and uses a far more deadly one in the cities. The more societies he can infest with isolation, the greater are his chances of losing people to the power of Christ. His isolation has made it extremely difficult to gain access to those who need salvation. Worst of all, his diabolical plot in isolating churches from their environments is working extremely well at the present time.

In the light of Pattison's comments, consider again our ministry as Christ's body: He is to be *in us*, preaching good news *through us* to the poor, proclaiming freedom for the prisoners and recovery of the sight for the blind, and releasing the oppressed. Every one of these hurting groups are so bound they cannot come to us. *In every single case mentioned in Luke 4:18, people helplessly wait for us to come to them.* There is no other way for them to be reached apart from our penetrating *oikoses* that are not "normal," where fragmentation of the social group has happened, and where hopelessness and loneliness reign in the kingdom.

In Singapore, we created Share groups to minister to those trapped in their isolation in the huge housing developments. We advertised groups for "Lonely People." We were surprised by the number who responded to our invitations, dropped in letter boxes. The first meeting of the first group took place in Toa Payoh housing estate on a Tuesday night. The fledgling Christian workers were overwhelmed by the instant, honest sharing of those who attended. On Thursday night, one of those who had come went to the top her 20 story block of flats, removed her shoes (a Chinese custom when entering a house or committing suicide) and threw herself over the parapet. The following Sunday afternoon when I went to train this team, I found them weeping. One of them said, "Oh, pastor Ralph! We came too late! We came too late!"

If the church is *ever* going to touch the very ones referred to in Luke 4:18, it *must* be done through cell groups! Not only can cells of Christians penetrate more deeply into neighborhoods, but the ministry which then follows requires the "surrogate family" atmosphere of the cell group.

Satan has done his cruelest work by shaping his kingdoms with the lie that *splendor* will be awarded to those who are loyal to him. Along with the search for significance comes alienation from others. Whether the pressure leads to drugs, alcohol, depression, or becoming a workaholic, lack of intimacy is always the result. We who have been called from darkness into light are their only hope. To do the work of our master, we must see the innate evil in church systems which bottle us up and limit our contact with the unreached ones.

⑧ GRACE GIFTS IN CELL GROUP LIFE

The Life Of The Flesh Is In The Blood

Cell group churches, the "body of Christ," are living organisms of the highest level. As such, we may consider the circulatory system which nourishes the human body.

Blood brings life-giving substances to all cells and excretes noxious wastes from them. It transports oxygen, protein, salts, and other chemical substances to various body parts, keeping them healthy. An adult male contains about five litres of blood. Some loss may take place without ill effects, but if too much is lost, death quickly follows. Cells cannot survive without the nourishment provided by blood.[1]

Blood is transported by a complex circulatory system of tubes which carry it to the cells, where it interchanges materials with them according to their needs.[2] For many years anatomists believed the arteries contained air, since after death the arteries are always found empty.[3] Only when there is life in the body does the blood constantly flow under pressure from the heart, doing its important work.

Gifts: The Spiritual Blood In Christ's Body

The God who created the human body has also made the body of Christ to survive through the work of "spiritual blood." This life-giving substance is called in I Corinthians 12:1 "the gifts of the Spirit." In the Greek, the term is *"the spirituals."* That term describes specific capacities flowing into the body cells through the channel—*the artery*—of the Holy Spirit.

The gifts of the Holy Spirit are not given because one has

become a super-spiritual person or because one has gained great Biblical knowledge. Gifts are not rewards! As the human body cannot live without fresh blood, so the believer and the cells made up of believers cannot exist for even a *second* without a constant flow of spiritual gifts. They are given to all at the moment of conversion, necessary for spiritual life to function. Thus, every new believer must be helped to understand and utilize spiritual gifts.

For those who insist that any one gift is universally poured out for all believers, it is important to know that Paul repeatedly expressed that the various spiritual gifts are *distributed* to the church. There is no scriptural validation for pressing a spiritual gift upon any Christian.

"The spirituals" are provided in order that the body of Christ may be used by Him to perform His work. The cell group church must become completely dependent on the Holy Spirit for all its service. Its life is in its *special blood.* Spiritual gifts transport the power required to perform a task and export from the cell noxious wastes. As in the human body, if the blood pressure gets too low the body becomes tired, passive, and powerless. The cells of Christ must never be viewed as social gatherings or cognitive groups which simply share emotional needs with some form of Bible study. They must function on the level of the Spirit, and that means *they must operate through the activity of spiritual gifts.*

The Service Gifts

Since all gifts are given to complete the work of Christ as He flows through us, the ones specifically mentioned in the scriptures should be understood. The booklet entitled *Spiritual Gifts Inventory* is designed to be used in helping a new Christian understand them.[4]

Among the eleven *service gifts* mentioned in scripture are:

THE FOUNDATION GIFTS

These two very basic gifts reveal the Christian's readiness to obey the Master and to enter into ministry:

1. The Gift of Service[5]
2. The Gift of Giving[6]

Serving has to do with using one's life to meet the needs of another person. The word is literally "table waiting." In the Greek, the word is *diakonia* —the source of the English word "deacon." In 1 Corinthians 16:15, the entire Stephanas family is described as having "laid themselves out to *serve* God's people."

Giving involves using one's possessions to meet the needs of someone else. The word describes a person quite deliberately parting with something in his possession, so that a change of ownership is produced. There is a note of *abandonment* in the act, like the Heave Offering in the Old Testament.

THE MINISTRY GIFTS

These three gifts are given in differing strengths to various members of the body and make it possible for us to function together to fulfill His calling:

3. The Gift of Helping Others In Distress[7]
4. The Gift of Faith[8]
5. The Gift of Discerning True Spirits from False[9]

Helping Others In Distress is a word meaning "to feel sympathy with the misery of another, especially such sympathy as manifests itself in act, less frequently in word." The use of this gift communicates—nonverbally—that God is on the throne! *Cheerfully* helping others in distress is a powerful spiritual gift!

Faith is a gift, according to Romans 12:3, which is given in varying measures to believers. Some are given a greater measure than others. We might call this gift the "spiritual eyes of the body." The retinas of the eyes of faith can discern heavenly realities before they become a part of earth's activity. There's *fore-knowledge* in the use of this gift. As the late Manley Beasley used to say, it's "Believing something *is* so, when it *isn't* so, because you *know* God will *make* it so."

Distinguishing True Spirits from False provides the protection of the Holy Spirit for the body, sensing and isolating the source of a foreign invasion by foreign spirits. It's a capacity that involves guarding others, protecting them in their naivete from the attacks of the evil one. It may be demonic attack which is involved, or it may be the discernment of a human spirit who is not under the Lordship of Christ and who can do irreparable harm to the unity of the cell. Jude warned in verse 12 about men who are *"hidden reefs in your love feasts when they feast with you without fear, caring for themselves."* Mature believers will have this discriminating gift for use in the family of God.

THE EQUIPPING GIFTS

Five of these are built upon the Gift of Leadership, an undergirding endowment for their use.

6. The Gift of Leadership[10]
7. The Gift of Prophecy[11]
8. The Gift of Teaching[12]
9. The Gift of Wise Speech[13]
10. The Gift of Putting Deepest Knowledge Into Words[14]
11. The Gift of the Counselor[15]

The Gift of Leadership is not an office—it's a spiritual gift. Those who are anointed by God to provide direction do so with an unction that is unmistakable. This is not a talent. It's a divine flow from Christ, selecting those He has ordained for guiding others. In the Old Testament, the example of David being anointed with oil for the work of serving as Israel's king is a lovely illustration of how God sets apart special people to flow with this gift. Hopefully, every Shepherd will possess a double portion of this "spiritual!"

The Gift of Prophecy is highly recommended by Paul in his discussion of the *charismata.* "Inspired utterance" is one translation for the Greek word *propheteia,* "prediction." It is to be used "for some useful purpose." When we were in Viet Nam as missionaries, there was a short-term worker who was causing a great deal of misery to all who were working with her. One of the women missionaries received a word from the Lord which revealed the worker was a lesbian. When confronted, the girl was shattered by the accuracy of the prophecy. It led to repentance and a search for help.

The Gift of Teaching requires a person to be constantly taught in turn by the Holy Spirit. Back in Numbers 3:1, the sons of Aaron are also referred to as the sons of Moses. The reason for this had to do with the importance of their teacher. Moses, their teacher, was considered to have *given them birth* through introducing them to the Law. So it is with the gifted one who imparts the revealed will of God and instructions which order the relationships between Christ and His body members.

The *Gift of Wise Speech* and *the Gift of Putting Deepest Knowledge Into Words* are very close to one another. Those who share deep truths and those with Spirit-given wisdom combine to provide guidance for younger believers. One provides truths, the other insights into how they apply to life situations.

The Gift of the Counselor is also called the "Gift of the Paraclete"—the "one called alongside to help." It uses the same root word used for the Holy Spirit. More than a psychological evaluator, this person is one who understands the deepest agonies in the life of another, suffers with others, and prays to the Lord about each problem.

All These Gifts Are For The Body To Exercise

All these gifts should be used in cell group life. The Foundation Gifts can be utilized by the new Christian almost from the day of conversion. Their use will lead to the maturity of Ministry Gifts. In turn, their use will develop believers to exercise the Equipping Gifts.

It cannot be emphasized too frequently that spiritual maturity is required for some gifts to be useful, but *all* Christians have gifts which can be used to build up others in the life of the body. It's very important that a great deal of emphasis be placed on the new Christian understanding and using spiritual gifts. If too much time erodes this process, the gifts will not be manifested and the work of Christ will not be done. Paul insisted that all spiritual gifts are simply an indication of the presence of Christ in the midst of His body.

The Sign Gifts

There are four *sign gifts* which may be useful in ministry:

1. Tongues[16]
2. Interpretation of Tongues[17]

3. Healings[18]
4. Miracles[19]

Tongues are divided by Paul in I Corinthians 14 into two categories.[20] First, the use of tongues with interpretation is a *public sign* which expresses Christ's attitude. It can be a *negative sign* of judgment for unbelievers who are present in the body life meeting, or it can bring a *positive sign* for the believers.[21] Second, it can be a *private prayer language.* [22]

Paul discouraged the use of public tongues as an activity which does not build up the body as strongly as does prophecy. At the same time, he indicated that he spoke in tongues more than anyone in the church in Corinth. His use was obviously in his private prayer, not in public.

Is this a contradiction in our premise that the gifts are primarily provided for the edification of others? Rather than a contradiction, it may be seen as the exception. For a full treatment of this entire subject, there is no better exposition than *Showing the Spirit* by Dr. D. A. Carson of Trinity Evangelical Divinity School.[23]

Interpretation of Tongues is to accompany every instance of the public use of tongues. As Carson writes,

> . . . the tongues-speaker, in consequence of edifying the church and the concomitant need for intelligible utter- ance in the church, should pray for another gift—the gift of interpretation.[24]

How the interpreter is to be identified in advance of the message in tongues is not specified in scripture. The comment in 1 Corinthians 14:27, *"let one interpret,"* does not necessarily mean there will be one who interprets all tongues messages, although some hold to that view.

The public use of *all* gifts remains constant: to build up the body. For a Christian community to receive valid prophecies or tongues with interpretation, as with any other gift manifestation, *they must be relevant to the needs of the people present.*

Healings and *Miracles* are God's special moments when He shows His grace and His power to bless us. There are special prerequisites for healings which are set forth in James 5:14-16 which involve the Elders as participants. In other instances, the prayer for healing may be a ministry of a cell or of an individual.

To repeat for emphasis, the primary use of these gifts remains the *building up of the body of Christ!* They are also used to demonstrate the reality of our Lord's body to unbelievers.

The Purpose Of Gifts

As discussed on page 41, spiritual gifts exist for *ministry,* not for personal enjoyment. Paul makes it clear in I Corinthians 14 that one can misuse and abuse gifts, turning them from their purpose to childish toys. The clearly stated purpose for the gifts is this:

> What then shall we say, brothers? When you come together, everyone has a hymn, or a word of instruction, a revelation, a tongue or an interpretation. All of these must be done for the strengthening of the church.[25]

Studying all Paul says about gifts in Romans 12, I Corinthians 12-14, and other scattered passages should make it clear that Christ intended for gifts to be the blood in the circulatory system of the body, flowing to cells for empowering and cleansing. From the *very moment of conversion,* every single believer is to be a channel of grace gifts to the body's members. Whether a convert's age is 15 or 75, spiritual gifts are given for the building up of the rest of the body of Christ and for ministry to a broken world. They must be taken from a Bible study topic to being literally applied in the cells.

The Cell Group Must Operate On The Level Of The Gifts

Not Just The Intellect
e. g., Bible Studies
"How does this apply to us?"

Not Just The Emotions
e. g., Begin With Our Needs
"How can we advise one another?"

The Gifts Of The Spirit
Life-giving power received; removal of noxious waste
"He who has an ear, let him hear what the Spirit says to the churches."

9 GIFTS BELONG IN CELL GROUPS

DEAR PAUL,

In 1 Corinthians 12:1 you wrote, *"Now about spiritual gifts, brothers, I do not want you to be ignorant."* Oh, Paul! If you were among us today you would be broken hearted by the ignorance of our generation about the proper use of spiritual gifts. If you were to journey through the churches you would discover believers have fallen into two ditches.

The ditch on one side contains those who *play down* the gifts, discouraging their use as "experience-centered." They're totally ignorant of their own special relationship to spiritual gifts—including the *elders!* They downplay everything except Bible study. They teach that any display of the power of God mentioned in the Bible is off limits for this age.

In the ditch on the other side are those who have become totally enamored with the *"sign gifts."* They exhibit certain gifts in public meetings, seldom or never exercising them for the purpose of building up the body. They ignore your warning that *"if the whole church comes together and everyone speaks in tongues, and some who do not understand or some unbelievers come in, will they not say that you are out of your mind?"*[1]

Those in *both* ditches have not yet grasped the importance of body life or the use of all the gifts in their proper setting. Sad to say, they are mortal enemies. Unity is impossible between them; sometimes merely being civil to each other is difficult.

Paul, neither group believes you were serious when you said, *"Since you are eager to have spiritual gifts, try to excel in gifts that build up the church."*[2] You see, our generation has made the church into a big blob of protoplasm that no longer has hands, feet, and inward parts. It just has a "membership list." I know you won't believe it, but they are actually divided about equally into "active" and "inactive" members. Worst of all, neither group pays much attention to the need for cells with true community. Therefore, they are puzzled by your comment that:

> *When you come together, everyone has a hymn, or a word of instruction, a revelation, a tongue or an inter-pretation. All of these must be done for the strengthening of the church*"3

They just can't figure out how *everyone* can participate as you have directed because their "coming together" takes place in large numbers of people who sit in rows, not in circles, and they barely communicate with one another. It should be obvious to them that their idea of "church" is erroneous, but it isn't clear at all.

Paul, take heart! The Spirit has been at work, and more and more cell group churches are emerging from the ashes of the first Reformation. Things are going to get better! America is a light year behind most other places in the world in this regard.

The stranglehold of a new style of church life called "Program Base Design" is a new method now being used. It bottles people up inside special buildings we now call "churches," and they are removed from authentic ministries to the unchurched. Since most Christians know little about "body life" or being equipped for ministry, they have ignored the gifts and their use. Remember us, Paul. We wish you were here to help us in this generation! If it were not for the letters you wrote, we wouldn't even know the mess we're in. Thank you for impacting us through them.

YOUR FAITHFUL SERVANT,
EPAPHRODITUS CCXXVII

How Can A *True* Church Exist And Ignore Spiritual Gifts?

A seminary professor I highly respect for the wonderful books he has written says flatly to his students, "Don't place emphasis on spiritual gifts in your teaching. You just stir up problems." His Evangelical orientation has made him wary of anything related to the subject. *Why do we fear what scripture clearly endorses?* How can we discharge the power of the written word while downgrading its teaching because we resent contemporaries who *abuse* gifts? This is what a friend calls "throwing out the baby with the bath water."

Charles Kraft has expressed my own feelings in his book *Christianity With Power:*

> *I want all that God has for us in this area, but in a balanced, reasonable way. The extremes in power ministry still bother me greatly. I have no desire to move toward these extremes. As I attempt to analyze my own experience, I see genuine growth in an area of legitimate Christian experience that I had previously not explored. "Why," I ask, "should this area be the exclusive preserve of Pentecostals and charismatics?" If—as I believe God has been showing me over the last seven years—spiritual power is the birthright of all Christians, why are we Evangelicals not appropriating this part of our inheritance?*[4]

In my book *This Gift Is Mine,* I took a hard line against those gifts that didn't fit my Evangelical background. I am delighted that the book is out of print because I no longer hold to the views I expressed in 1974. During these years I have lived in the cell group church, I now have no *question* that God provides *any* gift that people need to be built up or cleansed. *But I have a problem!* Let me tell you what it is...

Faking Gifts Isn't Necessary—Unless You're A Fake!

My heart is heavy as I pen these words, for I am thinking of the routines that have developed around the abuse of spiritual gifts in P.B.D. charismatic circles. A high percentage of these churches have *no cell groups.* Without cells, the display of spiritual gifts must take place in their public services. Frequently, these become a cheap sideshow of gifts being displayed without true ministry.

Always, *always,* these large impersonal settings cause the

gifts to be displayed as a part of scheduled events. Well established, worship patterns, duplicated over and over in these charismatic services, are routine. They are just another version of the Evangelical *"hymn, hymn, announcements, offering, choir, sermon, benediction"* pattern. *Ritual is ritual,* whether done with raised hands or with robes and candles, with overhead projectors or Baptist Hymnals. Spiritual gifts aren't designed to be ritualized.

In Brisbane, I visited the worship service of the largest church in town. They had developed a form of cell group life, and I wanted to study them. I was disappointed to discover they used the Charismatic worship pattern.

There came a prayer lull in the praise song time. Someone *had* to speak in tongues in the service; it was expected in every meeting. A woman near the front did so. After a brief moment of waiting for the interpretation to be given, the pastor went to the microphone and delivered a flowery translation, mostly quoting clearly recognized fragments from the Psalms and the prophets. An Australian friend whispered to me: "Every time I visit here, he's the only one who interprets tongues."

Soon after, I was chatting with another charismatic pastor. I asked him, "Why is it that most of the time the *pastor* is the one who interprets tongues in your public services? Are there no other gifted people who can do it?" He smiled sheepishly and said, "To be honest with you, I do the same thing in my church. You never know when some nut may embarrass you!" Such manipulation of spiritual gifts is unconscionable. When they are used out of context, Christian leadership must perpetrate a hoax that must deeply grieve the Holy Spirit.

The first time I was in a large group meeting where someone had a "word of prophecy," I was impressed by the story of a ship which had sails but no wind. A mighty wind arose, and the ship moved faster and faster toward its port. The wind was the Holy Spirit; the ship was the church; and a mighty movement was about to start. *I have heard the identical, or near-identical story spoken in a public meeting several times.* Who said it first? Who's copying someone else? Why?

I mentioned this matter to Viv Grigg, one of the most devout brothers I know, who currently ministers to the poor by living in a squalid Calcutta slum. We were eating together in Auckland at the time. He grimaced and said, "The men I know in New Zealand who are truly prophetic would never think of speaking out in a public meeting."

It's one thing to be in a small group where God is working and where people know each other so well they can't get away with faking their gifts, and another thing to be in these large meetings where "gifts" are manifested routinely to fit the program at just the right time. This perfunctory abuse of gifts is not right!

My deep respect for Yonggi Cho includes the way he conducts his multiple Sunday worship services. It's just about as formal as a Presbyterian church. While they recite the Apostle's Creed, no one manifests any spiritual gifts. Yet he is a leader among those who believe in their full use.

This is not to discredit in any way the work of the Holy Spirit in large assemblies. God can do anything He desires, regardless of the size of the group. It's the *faking* of the true manifestation of gifts that I point to in these remarks. At Faith Community Baptist Church in Singapore, the presence of God has been so powerful that people entering the auditorium have been swept to their knees in prayer before the meeting began. Many have been healed or have received other blessings because of the work of the Spirit in the Sunday celebrations. Authentic manifestations are most certainly taking place all over the world when the people of God truly worship. I rejoice over them! It's the *counterfeit* that bothers me a lot, and it bothers a lot of others as well.

Focusing On A *Few* Of The Gifts Isn't Good Enough

Among the charismatics there is excessive stress on a few of the spiritual gifts, including those which supposedly validate the recipient having attained a higher level of walking in the Spirit. Sadly, most of these folks ignore their need for manifesting the "service gifts" that God has given to the body. We shall never know until we get to glory whether Dorcas spoke in tongues, but we do know her use of the gifts of *helping others in distress* so endeared her to her body that our Lord raised her from the dead. There must be a balanced focus on *all* the gifts being used in edification.

The Cell: The Proper Setting For Using Spiritual Gifts

Every one of us arrives in the Kingdom "crippled inside." Living apart from God for years creates inner brokenness which must be mended. In addition, simply living in a fallen world of fallen men continues to damage us as we seek to live under His Lordship. The cell group exists as a community where the healing power of God is to be manifested.

Sharon (not her real name) had read about *The People Who Care* in Houston in a syndicated news article. She immediately packed her few belongings in a small trailer, hooked it up to her Volkswagen bug, and drove to Houston. Our family was eating dinner when she rang our bell. "Hi," she said. "I was up in Denver and I read about your church. I decided to come down and be a part of it." We invited her to share our meal and found her a place to stay.

This attractive young woman had arrived in a lot of emotional and spiritual pain, and she required a lot of healing. We often found ourselves at the end of all our formal training and experience as we sought to help her. Again and again Ruth and I would agonize in prayer over her. God had sent her for a special purpose. Without her severe need, we would not have moved so quickly beyond our resources to discover the power of Christ flowing through us, ministering to her in a way we could never accomplish.

She impacted *our* lives as much as we impacted *hers.* Her life story would have made a granite statue weep! Seeing her slowly healed and delivered was one blessing, but it was accompanied by a *second* one. At the same time we were caring for her, she was building up others in our group, learning how to use her spiritual gifts. It was high drama!

She had become a part of the *reciprocal ministry* that takes place when cell group members build up each other through exercising spiritual gifts. We were learning to *receive* grace through others as we learned to *be* channels of grace. This is the power of the church as cells. The healers are those who are also healed.

When we begin a life together in which all are equipped for ministry, the most effective growth always takes place in an environment where we are called upon to *give* as well as to *receive,* to *heal* as well as to *be healed.*

How does Christ desire for us to be healed? Are we to find our healing *independently,* going to Him all alone? While that happens, it's not His primary plan for us. Instead, He gives gifts of healings to His body. Spiritual gifts are related to the body and its needs.

Christ Touches Me Through You

Our Lord could have chosen to minister to each one of us apart from others, but He chose one or more persons to become agents of gifts that would minister to us. This requires participants in the cell group church to use spiritual gifts in all phases of ministry to build up one another.

Are we to live as mutual cripples who cling to one another? No! As discussed in Chapter 2, we are to build up one another *oikodomeo* through the divine flow of spiritual gifts. As we do so, growth takes place both in the life of the giver and the life of the receiver. There is one form of growth we experience as the agent of *charismata* and another form as we benefit from them. In all cases, the flow of spiritual gifts is required.

My strong objection to turning cell group gatherings into Bible studies is that they replace the time when a *reciprocal relationship* in the Christian community should take place with another cognitive activity. When the cells meet it should be for edification, not teaching.

Of course, there must be strong Biblical teaching *before* the cells meet. The cells must operate under the authority of scripture *previously received,* but the gatherings must be for *edification.* Those who gather under the *shadow* of scripture will be guided by what they have previously learned. They now meet with the intention that *"Nobody should seek his own good, but the good of others."*[5] Instead of another cognitive-based session, the gifts must flow between body members.

Gifts Don't Come From Inner Storage Batteries

There are different kinds of gifts, but the same Spirit. There are different kinds of service, but the same Lord. There are different kinds of working, but the same God works all of them in all men.[6]

How are spiritual gifts discovered by the believer? Has God latently stored up supernatural power within us as a flashlight battery stores up electric energy? No! Spiritual gifts are not stored up, ready for a special occasion to be taken out and utilized. Instead, they are like an electric current that must flow from a *source* to a *need*. If the believer is not attached to both Christ, the *source*, and another person with a *need*, there's little likelihood the gift will be manifested. Spiritual gifts are the "energizings" that *service* the work of God where a need exists. Thus, in the cell group each need of a body member is a valid reason for the gifts to flow.

As a result, the *needs* in the life of a person will call forth the spiritual gifts that are necessary for Christ to meet the problem area. In references to gifts throughout the New Testament, the emphasis is on their *activity, not the gifts themselves.*

To isolate spiritual gifts from their tasks is to create a serious problem. This was the problem in the Corinthian church. They had lost a sense of community, and as a result their participation in the *agape* feasts was a farce and a disgrace. At the same time the gifts were no longer being used for building up one another. They became privately used toys practiced by individuals for personal edification. 1 Corinthians 11 to 14 is a continuous discussion of the misuse of the gifts. We may outline the section as follows:

1. You have lost any sense of community, and you have no love for one another: 11:17-22.
2. Your observation of the Lord's supper is done in an unworthy manner because you do not recognize the importance of body life: 11:23-34.
3. Your use of spiritual gifts does not recognize the importance of honoring other body members: 12:1-31.
4. Love is the heart and soul of body life, causing the gifts to flow in the proper context: 13:1-13.
5. Spiritual gifts have one primary use: the edification of the other body members, and all are to focus on their ministry to others through the use of the charismata: 14:1-40.

What could be clearer? Spiritual gifts, wrenched from the place of the cell group—the only form of church life which makes it possible for *every person* to participate—are usually used in an inappropriate manner. Yet, even in the popular small group movements of today this fact is missed. *Away with the study booklets, the discipleship leaflets, the Bible study guides! Let the church be the church at its best, doing its work of edification through the manifestation of spiritual gifts.*

False Motives For Receiving Spiritual Gifts

What are the proper motives for a believer to receive spiritual gifts? If it is to attract affirmation or receive rewards, the motives are not proper and the gifts will not flow.

One who is close to me was taken to a meeting and pressured to "loosen his spirit" and receive a particular spiritual gift considered necessary for all believers. As the group gathered around him to pray he would receive the gift, he felt most uncomfortable. He decided he would receive anything the *Lord* had for him, but he wouldn't fake anything! He didn't "get the gift." The group ended their time with him shaking their heads and muttering, "He just isn't ready to go all the way with the Holy Spirit."

Thousands of people have "received their gift" because of such group pressure and a desire to be accepted as a fully endorsed member of their charismatic peer group. Since gifts can be counterfeited, this motive propels many people to have an experience which validates them as "authentic" before their friends. At the same time, they are cheated from knowing the glorious reality of Christ's power flowing through them for the building up of others. *This is evil!*

Those who pressure others to receive a gift are forgetting some important scriptures. Let's consider some of them: *"We have different gifts, according to the grace given us."*[7] One term for gifts in the Greek is *charisma,* which comes from a verb *charizomai,* "to grant as a favor, gratuitously pardon; rescue." This word is used by Paul, clearly set in the context of being used to build up the body:

> *Just as each of us has one body with many members, and these members do not all have the same function, so in Christ we who are many form one body, and each member belongs to all the others. We have different gifts, according to the grace given us.*[8]

While this can be interpreted to mean *"each person has a gift different from all the other members of the body,"* it is could also refer to *one person* displaying *different gifts,* according to the *charismata* needed for the occasion.

In 1 Corinthians 12:4-6, the emphasis is again on the differences in the gifts. In this passage, we see the gifts automatically leading the recipient to be appropriate to the occasion:

> *There are different kinds of gifts, but the same Spirit. There are different kinds of service, but the same Lord. There are different kinds of working, but the same God works all of them in all men.*[9]

The place of the gifts must be seen in the context of their use: *"All these are the work of one and the same Spirit, and he gives them to each one, just as he determines."*[10]

The emphasis is on the *action,* not the receiving of the gift. Peter wrote pointedly about the use of gifts:

> *Each one should use whatever gift he has received to serve others, faithfully administering God's grace in its various forms.*[11]

Once again, the emphasis is on the *action.* In addition, there is not a definite article with the word "gift" in this verse: *"each as he has received gift"* is the literal rendering. Thus, when spiritual gifts are seen in the context of their use in the cell group for the building up of the body, their manifestation will always be related to the *situation.*

Once Again, With Feeling: Gifts And Usage Are Inseparable!

> *Now to each one the manifestation of the Spirit is given for the common good. To one there is given through the Spirit the message of wisdom, to another the message of knowledge by means of the same Spirit, to another faith by the same Spirit, to another gifts of healing by that one Spirit, to another miraculous powers, to another prophecy, to another distinguishing between spirits, to another speaking in different kinds of tongues, and to still another the interpretation of tongues.*[12]

Is it not obvious that God is flowing into the cell group all the spiritual gifts required for carrying out the ministry of edification? Paul points out they are a part of body life:

> And in the church God has appointed . . . those having gifts of healing, those able to help others, those with gifts of administration, and those speaking in different kinds of tongues.[13]

He then points out that not all will have the same gifts: *"Do all have gifts of healing? Do all speak in tongues? Do all interpret?"*[14] The answer is an obvious "No." *Not all* have these gifts—only those who have been selected by the Spirit to be a channel of grace through their use.

Then he adds: *". . . eagerly desire spiritual gifts, especially the gift of prophecy."*[15] The "eager desire" for a gift, in this case the gift of prophecy, is a manifestation of a desire to have what will build up a brother or sister in the group. It speaks of a readiness to be a servant. There is no reason at all to think Paul is suggesting we get a gift for the sake of having it. Such a thought flies in the face of the close connection between the *gift* and the *need.* As with all other gifts, prophecy is a *working gift.*

The writer of Hebrews confirms that the gifts of the Holy Spirit are distributed according to the will of God.[16] We are free to express our willingness to *be* used, but the Spirit decides *when* and *where* we are to serve Christ. In this context, we may remember that we may *dedicate* our lives for His use, but our Lord alone *consecrates,* sets us apart, for the work. Good news: He turns none away except those who are full of themselves.

The Motive For The Use Of Our Gifts Is Love

Paul paused in the middle of his discussion of spiritual gifts in 1 Corinthians 12 and 14 to discourse at length about the motive for them: *love.* If Christians seek the manifestation of gifts for any other reason, they will fall into error.

In a prayer time in Indiana, a black brother in a wheelchair asked for prayer for his healing. His was a heartbreaking story. He was born deaf. A smart aleck behind the wheel of a racing automobile saw this man walking toward the road. He said to his companion, "Let's scare that guy!" Sounding a horn which was not heard, he started to sideswipe him, expecting he would leap out of the way. Instead, he hit him and severed his spine.

Deaf and paraplegic, our brother in Christ requested we pray for his healing—no small task! As we knelt and prayed, one young man cried out in agony, "Oh, God! He's my *brother!*" The pure love which was manifested in the group was overwhelming. It should always be so when gifts are manifested.

Over and over, the writers of the New Testament focus on the activity of the body as flowing from love. Desiring the best for another person in all situations is easier talked about than performed—particularly when you are locked into a small group where that person's eccentric behavior is obnoxious to all concerned.

D. A Carson comments on 1 Corinthians 13:1:

> *This value judgment is meant to be shocking. Part of its power is that Paul does not merely say that under this condition . . . it is not the gift of tongues that is only a resounding gong or a clanging cymbal, but I, myself . . . . as if my action of speaking in tongues without love has left a permanent effect on me that has diminished my value and transformed me into something I should not be.*[17]

In referring to 1 Corinthians 13:2 he says,

> *Again, however, Paul's conclusion is even more shat-tering: not only are the spiritual gifts exercised without love of no value, but, says Paul, "I am nothing"— "spiritually a cipher."*[18]

Ponder the cell group implications of these verses:

> *Instead, speaking the truth in **love,** we will in all things grow up into him who is the Head, that is, Christ. From him the whole body, joined and held together by every supporting ligament, grows and builds itself up in **love,** as each part does its work.*[19]

> *Follow the way of **love** and eagerly desire spiritual gifts . . .* [20]

*Above all, **love** each other deeply, because **love** covers
over a multitude of sins.[21]
And let us consider how we may spur one another on
toward **love** and good deeds.[22]*

*May the Lord make your **love** increase and overflow for
each other and for everyone else, just as ours does for
you.[23]*

*We ought always to thank God for you, brothers, and
rightly so, because your faith is growing more and more,
and the **love** every one of you has for each other is
increasing.[24]*

*Do everything in **love**.[25]*

*Since you are eager to have spiritual gifts, try to excel in
gifts that build up the church.[26]*

Susan (not her real name) was barely a teenager when she
came into our group. Her slight retardation caused the public
schools to promote her from one grade to the next without much
concern for her future. She stayed with us in our cells for several
years. Her lack of sensitivity caused her to make wisecracks when
others were sharing deeply, and her laugh rattled windows.

For a few months she was passed from group to group, with
a sigh of relief made by cells who no longer had to put up with her.
She then entered a cell with some believers who felt God had a
special plan for her in spite of her handicap. For the first time in her
life, she was frankly confronted with her unacceptable areas of
behavior. The group *loved her.* The meetings began to manifest
helping gifts toward her. One of the men said, "Susan, when you
are in the group you keep your eye on me. Since you don't know
when your behavior is out of line, I'm going to help you. If you see
me pull on my right ear, you will know you need to stop what you
are doing. You won't be embarrassed, and you'll learn to recognize how others see you." Some of the women took her aside and
talked frankly to her as well about personal matters, but always in
great love.

Susan's social adjustment developed more in a few months
with that group than she had been able to do in a lifetime of being

passed around among unloving people. The cell group rejoiced when she was hired by a fast food restaurant. She kept that job for many years. She was a tribute to those who served her with their spiritual gifts. Love had brought her to a new awareness of what she *could* be, and Christ built her up through His body.

Love, Plus Gifts, Equals Church Life

Living the Christian life apart from the relationships which are built in community is a dangerous thing to do. For eighteen years I conducted a daily talk show on the radio. Hundreds of letters poured in during that time, nearly all asking for prayer, nearly all written by believers. The reason they reached out to a voice that became a part of their lives each morning was because they had no one else they felt they could talk to about their hurts. When they would call, I would ask: "Have you talked to your Sunday school teacher or your pastor about this matter?" Over and over they would say, "I can't. They barely know me. I feel I would be a bother to them."

How would you place these things on your priority list?
- God
- Family
- Church
- Work

Dion Robert, pastor in Abidjan, Ivory Coast, points out that the Biblical priority for these items is:
- Church
- Family
- Work

He explains, "God is not a separate priority. He is in all we do. He is in His Son, and the church is Christ's body. Christians who put the church behind their family make a grave mistake. The home cannot be Christian until it is *within the life of the cell.* It is only then that the family lives in a place of love, of nurture, of edification. It is when the church is supreme to all else that the family and the work situations are benefitted by the power of spiritual gifts."

Knowing the divine pattern provides access to Christ in a special way. He flows through other body members to meet my needs, and He flows through me to build up other body members. When one has experienced it, there's no desire to turn back!

10 THE HOLY SPIRIT IN THE CELL GROUP

We have already seen that the primary purpose of spiritual gifts is the building up, or edifying, of believers by other believers. Each member is responsible for applying spiritual gifts to edify others. Moreover, *every single believer* is to be active in this ministry.[1] There are no exceptions.

Therefore, the work of the Holy Spirit in the life of the believer begins to take on a pattern. First, we were sealed by Him.[2] We were simultaneously baptized by Him both into Christ and also the Body of Christ.[3] He is the provider of spiritual gifts to each believer for the common good.[4] He further directs the use of these gifts when the group assembles in such a powerful way that the observing unbeliever declares "God is certainly among you."[5]

The Cell Group Is The Believer's Gateway Into Gifts

The personal use of spiritual gifts in the cell is the believer's gateway into the supernatural world. In that realm, warfare occurs.[6] In that world, spiritual gifts serve as the entrance for the believer to discover *how* God heals, delivers, and causes growth in believers.

There is no better place for spiritual gifts to be developed than in cell groups. All necessary conditions are present for the gifts to be received and used for edification. Needs present in the lives of the believers and the small size of the group make it possible for all present to exercise gifts for building up one another in the Spirit. The modelling of the proper use of gifts can protect new believers from absurd excesses.

Members should be taught to appreciate, desire, exercise, and receive the benefits of spiritual gifts. Through using them, they can learn how to become the channels of God's power. This makes the activity of the Holy Spirit very personal to members of cells. Members must experience both the power of gifts flowing through them to edify others and the personal edification received from others who exercise them.

There is grave danger present when a cell is unplugged from the work of the Holy Spirit and the use of spiritual gifts. It has no alternative except to become a religious social club, which soon ossifies and diverts its activity to other tasks. As a result, no building up takes place in the cell. Soon, this tragic condition will occur:

> *For everyone who partakes only of milk is not accustomed to the word of righteousness, for he is a babe. But solid food is for the mature, who because of practice have their senses trained to discern good and evil.*[7]

How Learning To Edify Changed A Group

When an Auckland church asked me to help them prepare for cell group life, I had just been taught by the Spirit the truths about *oikodomeo*. The pastor took me to work with a small Bible study group that had been in existence for several years. We were invited by the hostess to come early and share the evening meal with her family. With much embarrassment, she apologized for the absence of her husband. She explained he owned a construction company and often worked late.

When the group arrived, I spent a few minutes teaching them about the importance of learning how to build up one another using spiritual gifts. Since they had been together for a very long time as a Bible study group, I assumed they knew each other intimately. With that knowledge, they were to ask the Holy Spirit to guide them into a ministry of edification. I asked them to pick a place to be alone and pray, to prepare themselves to edify others in the group.

As we returned to our circle, the sun was setting and the missing husband arrived. With a brief greeting to the group, he went to shower and change clothes. About fifteen minutes later, he joined us.

Meanwhile, I suggested that we let the Spirit guide us into our season of edification. No one spoke a word! To get the ball rolling, I turned to the man on my left—a church leader and a strong Christian—and said, "Would you like to be the first to share?" He was petrified! He said, "I have never heard or seen anyone do this, and I'd like for someone else to begin."

One lady read us her "life verse" from the scripture. Another read a brief passage from the Psalms. Of course, *any* scripture one would read would *edify*—but it didn't seem to meet any special need in the lives of those in the circle.

With a sinking heart, I realized this was about to be a fiasco! I chided myself for believing that their many meetings spent intellectualizing about scripture had caused them to know each other on a spiritual level. That was my mistake: before one can build up someone else, there must be an understanding of spiritual needs. *They neither knew how to edify, nor what needs were present.*

I turned the meeting over to the pastor, suggesting we might have a season of prayer before we dismissed. He asked, "Does anyone have a special problem we might pray for?" The hostess said, "I do. I've had a rash all over my body for months. Fever blisters are on my lips. You can see the rash on my arms and neck. My whole body is like that. I've seen dermatologists who have given me creams and pills, but nothing makes any difference. I'd like you to pray for me."

She moved her chair to the center of the room. We all gathered around her. *What would happen now? Would we politely pray for her healing and move on to the next prayer request?*

Then the Spirit came. A word of knowledge was given. Quietly, the pastor said, "I sense in my heart the Lord is telling me your problem is the result of great anger. Perhaps it's something you wish to share with us . . ."

She was silent for a few moments, and began to weep softly. "Yes, that could be. *I am so angry at my husband!* He promises us he'll be home for dinner, but night after night we eat without him. I put his food in the fridge, and usually I'm asleep before he comes home to eat it. He's broken his promises to me over and over, and I feel I am a widow as I raise our children."

There was an awareness that a special word had come from the Lord through one of the members that had surfaced a problem that *several years* of small group meetings had never revealed. Who could speak with the husband blushing red with embarrassment?

One of the men cleared his throat and spoke to the husband: "You know, I nearly lost my family doing the same thing you are doing now. In fact, my wife had packed her things to leave me. I felt I was the best husband and father possible because I worked day and night to give them nice things. The Holy Spirit had to deal severely with me. I came to realize that the very thing I was *working for* was about to go up in smoke. If it did, what would my past or future work be worth? It was then that Paul's writings to Timothy and Titus began to show me I would never be God's man until I managed my own household well. I had one of the most profound spiritual experiences of my life. Our marriage and our home have radically changed since the day I put my family after God and ahead of my workaholic lifestyle."

Several others then shared. Scriptures were quoted. Some spoke special words using the gift of wise speech. The Spirit of God had taken control, and *oikodomeo* had begun to operate.

The husband fell to his knees and wept, his face buried in his wife's lap. He prayed first—a personal prayer of confession and repentance. The group prayed along with him. The man who had shared his own personal experience laid his hand on his friend as he prayed for him.

Then our prayer time moved to his dear wife. It seemed all were now praying at once, no one desiring to "wait his turn." We all lost track of time. *The Lord had invaded His Body, and the gateway into the supernatural world had been crossed by us all.*

That's not the end of the story. The following Sunday morning, I was sitting on the front row in the church auditorium, looking over my sermon notes. Through a large plate glass window, I could see this group talking in the parking lot area. A few minutes later, they stood in a circle around me. Our cell group hostess drew back the flowing sleeves of her dress and said, "Ralph, look! No rash! No rash anywhere on my body!" Then, with deep love in her eyes, she said, "My husband wants to say something to you." He said, "Ralph, I've cut back my workday to eight hours. I took the kids to the zoo yesterday. We have a new home. I'll never be the same. God did a deep work in my heart in our cell group."

Once Caught, No Escape!

I want you to imagine the radical change which took place in the lives of those in that group from that day onwards! Once a cell group has stepped into the supernatural world, it can't ever be the same again. It's like going to school for the first time, or having your first baby: you can't ever go back and be what you were before the event. A holy boldness invades a group after it has seen the power of spiritual gifts working in its midst. They become aware that their battle is not against flesh and blood, but against principalities and powers of the air. Every experience of knowing God's mighty power, instead of just reading about it in the scriptures, moves the group deeper into warfare and ministry.

For many years as a pastor of a P.B.D. church I taught that Jesus' words in John 16:13 simply referred to the light the Spirit would give to the believer as he sought to study scripture. That passage says the Spirit will guide us into all the truth. My teaching wasn't error—it just didn't go far enough. The Holy Spirit doesn't limit His guidance only to cognitive truths. *He also guides us into the application of those truths.* Without the application, what is the significance of the scripture?

Spiritual gifts are to be *used,* not studied, and the Holy Spirit is the source of their use. Guiding us into their application means He must be active and present wherever, and whenever, they are used. A cell group experiencing their use will be guided into truth that cannot be discovered in any other way. Thus, the agenda for a cell group must be formed around His right to revise it at any time He chooses to do so.

Needs Precede The Use Of Gifts

The work of the Spirit is always attached to needs. Jesus tied it together when He said in Luke 4:18, *"The Spirit of the Lord is upon me . . ."* By the Spirit the needs of the poor, the captives, the blind, and the downtrodden would be met. Thus, in a cell group it is important for the needs to surface so the gifts can be used to build up.

In Samuel Wesley's account of the religious society begun in Epworth, in the Isle of Axholm, Lincolnshire, February 1, 1701-2, the following statements are given:

I. Every week at set hours, when 2, 3, or more do meet together for this Intent, First to pray to God; Secondly, to read the Holy Scriptures, and discourse upon Religious Matters for their mutual Edification; And Thirdly, to deliberate about the Edification of our neighbour, and the promoting it.

II. Those that do thus meet together, are above all things sollicitous about the Salvation of their neighbour, yea they make it their business to be Christians not only in name but in deed: Least they should strive rashly to pull out the Mote from the Eies of others, not observing the Beam in their own; and lest while they preach to others themselves should become castaways.

III. For this Reason they do not admit every body promiscuously, but if any one desires to be of their Society, it must be done by the Consent of all; and therefore his Piety ought to be known to all, lest a little Leven should spoil the whole Lump, For they take it for Granted that things will then fall out well, when each of them shall be of that mind, as that it may be affirm'd upon good Grounds that This is Emanuel that dwells through Faith, of the power of God, in the Heart of every One, as in his Temple.

IIII. Nor do they allow that the number of their members should encrease too much, lest this Religious design should fall with its own weight, or at least be marr'd. Therefore when they have twelve Members they admitt no more. But if God shall stir up more, two shall desire the same Edification with them, they seperate [sic] two Members from them, to form a new Society with those that desire it, till that also grow's up to the number of Twelve, and so another new Society be form'd out of it.[8]

In our modern culture it seems legalistic, even cult-like, to enter into such a covenant relationship. Nevertheless, the focus of Wesley's group members was on becoming responsible to, and accountable for, one another. The very stress placed in this document on edification and being concerned about the beam in one's own eye gives us assurance the groups operated on principles of loving compassion, not legalism.

In *The Rules of the Band Societies Drawn Up December 25, 1738,* the following statements serve to affirm the transparency of the groups. (It should be noted that all bands were made up of one sex only. In America, we have often found much more openness when men and women meet separately.)

> The design of our meeting is, to obey that command of God, "Confess your faults one to another, and pray one for another, that ye may be healed."
>
> To this end, we intend,—
>
> 1. To meet once a week, at the least.
> 2. To come punctually at the hour appointed, without some extraordinary reason.
> 3. To begin (those of us who are present) exactly at the hour, with singing or prayer.
> 4. To speak each of us in order, freely and plainly, the true state of our souls, with the faults we have committed in thought, word, or deed, and the temptations we have felt, since our last meeting.
> 5. To end every meeting with prayer, suited to the state of each person present.
> 6. To desire some person among us to speak his own state first, and then to ask the rest, in order, as many searching questions as may be, concerning their state, sins, and temptations.
>
> Some of the questions proposed to every one before he is admitted among us may be to this effect:—
>
> 1. Have you the forgiveness of your sins?
> 2. Have you peace with God through our Lord Jesus Christ?
> 3. Have you the witness of God's Spirit with your spirit, that you are a child of God?
> 4. Is the love of God shed abroad in your heart?
> 5. Has no sin, inward or outward, dominion over you?

6. *Do you desire to be told of your faults?*
7. *Do you desire to be told of your faults, and that plain and home?*
8. *Do you desire that every one of us should tell you, from time to time, whatsoever is in his heart concerning you?*
9. *Consider! Do you desire that we should tell you whatsoever we think, whatsoever we fear, whatsoever we hear, concerning you?*
10. *Do you desire that, in doing this, we should come as close as possible, that we should cut to the quick, and search your heart to the bottom?*
11. *Is it your desire and design to be on this, and all other occasions, entirely open, so as to speak everything that is in your heart without exception, without disguise, and without reserve?*

Any of the preceding questions may be asked as often as occasion offers; the [five] following at every meeting:—

1. *What known sin have you committed since our last meeting?*
2. *What temptations have you met with?*
3. *How were you delivered?*
4. *What have you thought, said, or done, of which you doubt whether it be sin or not?*[9]

The pattern of Dion Robert in Abidjan, Ivory Coast, is a valuable one to consider. From his cells he receives weekly reports about deep spiritual needs within the huge cell church membership. In each sermon he deals with the most prevalent of the spiritual needs reported. His messages are strong teachings from the scriptures, designed to guide members to personal victory. A testimony from a cell group member may accompany his message, demonstrating how victory came from the Lord to overcome sin or doubt.

Then, the cells meet. The cell pastor reads a brief passage of scripture, often quoting the actual text of Pastor Dion, makes three or four minutes of remarks, and then systematically asks the group members: *"What is the state of your soul concerning this sin or situation?"* After this first cycle there comes the opportunity for the gifts of the Spirit to flow and edification to occur. One shares who has experienced personal victory; another is trapped in the problem. Here is still another person who has never faced the problem, who listens carefully and builds strength and insights which will be a future protection from this snare of Satan. One feels constrained to pray for another; a commitment is made to "be there" for a member should the temptation be faced during the next week.

A woman, trapped in a liaison with a married man who was supporting her, was offered a place to live by another woman in her cell. All agreed to help her as she sought to get her life back on a Godly foundation.

A child was ill; the group gathered around the sleeping baby and prayed for his healing. A person weak in her faith was encouraged, and another resisting the clear leadership of the Spirit was admonished about the danger of doing so.

Thus, the Spirit causes those in cell groups to experience His mighty work—*performed through the body members.*

The Holy Spirit Guides Cells Into Ministry

Over the Easter season in 1988, cell groups from the ICHTHUS Fellowship in London joined hands to plant a new cell in Woolwich. This district had been the site of munitions manufacturing for generations. During the Battle of Waterloo, for example, all the men in both armies fought with identical arms manufactured in the arsenal in Woolwich. It was a prime target of the Germans during World War 2; they virtually bombed it into oblivion. After the war, it became a site for low cost government housing.

Imagine the demonic powers that had controlled that district for generations without being challenged! How pleased the soldiers of Satan must have been while factories created implements of death. No Christian witness had succeeded in gaining a foothold in Woolwich. Since 1947, no church had been established among the people.

So it was that cell groups, located on either side of Greenwich, had decided to invade this domain of darkness. I attended a prayer meeting held in a Baptist church which had been "loaned" to the ICHTHUS Fellowship after being closed for many years. The refurbished, rent-free space now serves as the site for their Greenwich congregation. After prayer and training we drove a short distance to the edge of Woolwich. For the first time in my life, I learned how to sing "war songs" to the principalities of the air. We sang of our invasion with a firmness gained from our season of prayer. Never before had I been more conscious of the battle we face when taking territory from Satan. In my mind flashed the words of Abraham Kuyper, "There is no sphere of life over which Christ does not say, *"Mine!"*

On that Saturday morning, a light snow was falling as we gathered in the center of the outdoor mall. The ICHTHUS Christians are battle-seasoned veterans; that fact became obvious as we stood in a group, singing and giving testimonies of their changed lives. I was impressed by their transparent confessions of wicked living and how Christ had brought new life. Spiritually blind residents ignored or ridiculed the hardy band, not even slowing down as they passed us.

Our orders were clearly given back at the church: as God lays a certain person on your heart, break out of the group and talk to him or her. My "tap on the shoulder" from the Spirit led me to a man standing in front of a shoe store. He was one of only a half dozen who had finally stopped to listen to the testimonies. I said, "I'm a Yank from Houston. We're about the same age. Were you in the war?" "Yes," he responded. "I fought and was wounded." He opened his overcoat and showed me the well-worn insignia of his decoration. He openly shared his life's story. His wife had died. He had been living near many friends on the other side of London in a government housing development when a stroke put him in a hospital for several months. When he recovered, he was assigned by the housing board to live in a Woolwich flat. He was without contacts, lonely, and a bit frightened. He asked, "Could you tell from my speech I had a stroke?" "No," I said. "You speak well at present. May I ask you if anyone has ever discussed Jesus Christ's reason for dying on the cross with you?" "Haven't been to church since I was a tiny lad," he said. He quickly responded to my invitation to join me in a nearby pub, where we shared from my New Testament the story of Jesus.

Three hours later, he had prayed to receive Christ and became one of the charter members of the first cell in Woolwich. The next Sunday, seven people made professions of faith in the first Woolwich gathering! God had greatly blessed our efforts.

Ministry Involves Spiritual Warfare

The first Reformation began with a man who had no illusions about the battle zones. Martin Luther's verse from *A Mighty Fortress Is Our God* makes this plain:

> *And though this world, with devils filled,*
> *Should threaten to undo us,*
> *We will not fear, for God hath willed*
> *His truth to triumph through us.*
> *The prince of darkness grim—*
> *We tremble not for him;*
> *His rage we can endure,*
> *For lo! his doom is sure,*
> *One little word shall fell him.*
> *That word above all earthly powers—*
> *No thanks to them—abideth;*
> *The Spirit and the gift are ours*
> *Through Him who with us sideth . . .*

Even so, the second Reformation is being launched with an awareness of the battlegrounds to be faced today. The rise of the occult, Satan worship, and the New Age movement has caused America and Britain to be as full of demonic activity as Africa or Asia.

John described the first level of maturity after becoming a spiritual *"little children"* as *"young men, who have mastered the evil one."*[10] It's crucial that new Christians are equipped to do battle very soon after conversion. John's comment makes it important for *all* believers to mature in this area, not just some of them. However, this must not be taught through feelings and fervency of emotion. That cannot create a solid foundation for warfare. Objective doctrinal truth, keyed into the teaching of inspired scripture, must be the source for the believer's battles.

The Arrival Kit for New Christians is a deliberate updating of my earlier work which focuses on the scriptural foundations for converts in a cell group church. It is necessary to help "little children" learn scriptural truth related to mastering the evil one. Particularly those who manifest the gift of Discerning True and False Spirits will be of much greater worth if they are well grounded in the scriptures as well as in experiences with them.

Ministry: The Result Of The Spirit's Control

Flowing with spiritual gifts which have been exercised to build up body members, the people of God will reach out to rescue those who perish in their lostness. Every cell group which has experienced the Holy Spirit's anointing will *automatically* reach out to others. It is a blight on the family of God to have a Basic Christian Community which occupies itself *with* itself.

One of the consuming drives of the physical body is the desire to reproduce. In the same way, the healthy body of Christ will be restless until it becomes a part of the army which invades Satan's domain. "God's got an army, marching off to war," is more than a praise song. It's a philosophy of life for a cell group!

Always, *always,* the measuring stick for the health of a cell should not be how much they pray or study the Bible, but *how much they minister.* In the case of the Abidjan church, Dion Robert's Zone Pastors do not permit more than a two week period of stagnancy before they step in and ask the Shepherd, "What's wrong in your group?" Yonggi Cho told how he does the same thing with Zone Pastors. If a zone does not show conversions for a couple of weeks, he says to the pastor in charge, "You go up to Prayer Mountain and fast and pray until God shows you your problem. Something is wrong spiritually, or the cells would be reaching out!"

With such a spirit, the cell group churches can grow at a rate which far exceeds what traditional churches can expect. Wearing the "full armor of God" is intended for *soldiers,* not *sitters!*

11 THE LISTENING ROOM

I want to begin this chapter with a confession. On the last page of *The Four Loves,* C. S. Lewis wrote,

> *Those like myself whose imagination far exceeds their obedience are subject to a just penalty: we easily imagine conditions far higher than any we have really reached. If we describe what we have imagined we may make others, and make ourselves, believe that we have really been there.*[1]

I confess that where I am going to take you in this chapter is a model of cell church life I have never *fully* experienced myself. There have been times, though, when it happened without being anticipated. In those precious, unforgettable serendipities where gifts flowed and edification took place, I felt as though I were caught up, as Paul, into the heavens—not as far as the *third* one, but much higher than the *first* one! And I also confess that *I feel cheated.* Before I die, I want to know the full reality of body life as described in scripture. *Of this I am certain: for those who won't settle for less, all we shall describe is possible.*

A Japanese Garden

While touring Japan, an American preacher was invited to the home of a pastor for a meal. His host showed him a beautifully manicured garden behind his house.

He had constructed a small room in the middle of the greenery, barely large enough to seat two people. It had a *tatami* floor, a sloped roof, and a single door. On the floor was an open

Bible. Above the door, written in Japanese, was a small sign. Said the pastor, "That sign tells how I use this place. Can you guess what it says?"

The American replied, "Is this where you prepare your sermons?" "No," the pastor replied; "This is my *Listening Room."*

Before spiritual gifts can be properly manifested in cell groups for building up one another, believers must have a *Listening Room* and must know how to hear the voice of God. The physical location is not as significant as the event. The believer must not only *talk* to the Lord Jesus in prayer, but also *hear* from Him in the process. Christ must *provide* edification before the believer can *use* it. Otherwise, the "building up" in the cell meeting is nothing more than the activity of the flesh.

The point is crucial: one must *hear* God before *speaking* for Him. Strengthening, encouraging, and comforting one another in the cell group is to be done as each person becomes a direct agent of Christ's grace. The Holy Spirit's ministry in every participant is the source of the gifts we bring to one another.

When believers *hear God,* a *revelation* is given. While some evangelicals vociferously object to there being any further revelation beyond the canon of scriptures, these same people are frequently heard to say, "The Lord has showed me that..." or, "I feel definitely led by the Lord to..." In each of these instances, their words reveal that they *do* have a Listening Room where God speaks in a deeply personal way to their need. Like all believers, they find direction in the scripture and also direct guidance from the Lord. If this were not true, the place of prayer and meditation would be ruled out by them as having no value.

Among other groups, things are not so cloudy. "Words of knowledge," as they are popularly called, are often manifested. (It's too bad the term has been so abused that many now recoil from any person who uses it.)

Sometimes these "words of knowledge" are so unfocused that the cynic remains genuinely skeptical. D. A. Carson tells of a pastor who called for a member of the audience named "Bill," who "had a backache," to come forward for healing. When no one responded, he became more insistent that the person identify himself. Finally, a student stood up with a backache, but said that his name was "Mike." Carson writes,

"Close enough," the speaker judged, and proceeded with the "healing." Such nonsense ought to be dismissed for what it is.[2]

Once again, my own reaction to such aberrations is that the use of spiritual gifts in large crowds is radically different than when exercised in a cell group, where people know each other so well that someone would say, *"Come off it, George! Who are you trying to impress?"* It behooves those conducting public meetings to be *absolutely certain* their word from the Lord is authentic before declaring it to the audience.[3]

On other occasions, words given in the Listening Room are so powerfully correct they cannot be contested by any skeptic. When Les Scarborough was told by a godly wife in his church that he was about to enter the most difficult six months of his ministry, he listened prayerfully to her words. She shared that the Lord had given her an awareness that it would involve another church that would go through severe satanic attack. Exactly as her word of knowledge indicated, he was asked by a nearby church to advise them about a deep problem. That church was actually destroyed in the weeks that followed, and the membership disbanded. Such special guidance from the Lord cannot be scoffed at.

Such personal revelations from Christ must not be seen to challenge the finality of the Bible as the ultimate revelation of God's truth. Spirit-prompted guidance does not threaten the infallible canon of scripture. Obviously, such direction will always be in harmony with what the Bible teaches.

The book of Acts is packed with instances of personal revelation. In Acts 10, Peter sees a vision while on a tanner's rooftop which leads to the conversion of Cornelius, who has also received direct guidance from God to send for Peter. In the life of Paul, many instances show the place of special revelation as he planted churches. In Acts 16:9, for example, he is called to Macedonia through seeing a vision of a man of Macedonia standing and begging him, "Come over to Macedonia and help us."

The Burning Question: Is This A Normal Experience For All?

There are so many dear believers who, in a desire to be accepted by their peers, engage in the use of tongues, prophecies, and visions, that are extraordinarily trite. These fleshly counterfeits are seldom examined as directed in I Corinthians 14:29. *(In large meetings of Christians, it is also impossible to do so!)* Nevertheless, we are called back to the reality of a cell group life where a special lifestyle is carefully outlined. Let your mind imagine a house meeting in the first century, depicted by Paul in these words:

> *What then shall we say, brothers? When you come together, everyone has a hymn, or a word of instruction, a revelation, a tongue or an interpretation. All of these must be done for the strengthening of the church. If anyone speaks in a tongue, two—or at the most three—should speak, one at a time, and someone must interpret. If there is no interpreter, the speaker should keep quiet in the church and speak to himself and God. Two or three prophets should speak, and the others should weigh carefully what is said. And if a revelation comes to someone who is sitting down, the first speaker should stop. For you can all prophesy in turn so that everyone may be instructed and encouraged. The spirits of prophets are subject to the control of prophets. For God is not a God of disorder but of peace.[4]*

This is not a "typical" modern small group Bible study! The thrust of the passage causes us to realize the focus is on the active flow of the Holy Spirit through each person for the edification of the rest. It presupposes a deep personal knowledge of the needs of others, and time spent in the *Listening Room* in preparation for the gathering. It also indicates some *had come* prepared, while others received an *unanticipated word* from the Lord in the meeting. Whenever this occurred, Paul instructed the group to accept such interruptions as a special activity of the Spirit.

The concept of the *Listening Room* flows throughout the cell meeting. All are sensitive to what the Spirit wishes to do, and all are receptive to His message to the church.

It must be recognized that Paul stressed the underlying motive for these gatherings was to be *mutual love,* and not a *love for the sensational.* Those who participate are those who have learned to take up their cross daily and to live the crucified life of a servant. They do not desire to attract attention to themselves or their gifts, but rather to edify others.

Is this too "far out" for our age? Shall we relegate this scripture passage to ancient history and see it as inappropriate for today?

No! In a very special way, those who discover the church is not a P.B.D. structure must see the church as powerful yeast within bread or blinding light within darkness. The church is the Kingdom of Christ which functions within the kingdoms of this world (see illustration on page 127). It should not be expected to function either on the *natural* plane of the world or the *semi-supernatural* plane of the P.B.D. church. As the resident Body of Christ on earth, it has its own lifestyle. It exists to edify its members, to penetrate Satan's kingdoms, and to bring the power of Christ into direct encounter with the power of Satan.

Such A Gathering Requires People With "Listening Rooms"

Consider the spirit of those who gather together for such a cell group. Each one present has spent time in the Listening Room, communing with Christ and meditating with deep love on the other members of this special family. The writer of Hebrews captures the spirit of it all:

> And let us consider how we may spur one another on toward love and good deeds. Let us not give up meeting together, as some are in the habit of doing, but let us encourage one another—and all the more as you see the Day approaching. If we deliberately keep on sinning after we have received the knowledge of the truth, no sacrifice for sins is left, but only a fearful expectation of judgment and of raging fire that will consume the enemies of God.[5]

The assembly's motive is clearly stated in the first phrase: *"to spur one another on toward love and good deeds."* The last sentence in this passage speaks of accountability to Christ. If truth is rejected, there is nothing left but judgment.

With their cell group in mind, members go to their private places, their *Listening Rooms.* Edification is inescapably supernatural. For believers to be channels for edification, they must first be in touch with the Source.

What pastor has not experienced the direct connection

between time spent before the Throne and the anointing of the sermon when preached? *So it must be for every saint of God.* Listening precedes ministry for us, even as it did for our Lord. His nights of prayer prepared him for his days of ministering to others. Personal seasons with the Lord in prayer and contemplation open up the channels of edification.

Elizabeth O'Connor describes the experience of prayer as preparation for ministry:

> . . . *community is not programmed into an evening, but becomes possible only when there are those who have done the essential, preliminary, inward work of prayer . . . . When the work of prayer has been done, we can see and hear in each other what otherwise comes to us distorted or is entirely blotted out. We do not have the same need to be confirmed by others or to find a place for ourselves in the scheme of things. Prayer frees us to be for the other person. It is preparation for the event of community.*[6]

An attorney who participated in an Anchorchurch group in Fort Worth, Texas, said to me: "I begin to prepare myself for the next gathering of our cell at the close of each meeting. The longer I stay in the group, the more time I need alone with the Lord contemplating what He wishes to do through me for the others. My prayer life has taken on a new dimension as I have learned how to intercede and to hear the Lord speak to me about how I should minister to others in the group."

Many keep a little diary to use in the personal *Listening Room,* containing the names of all who have ever attended their group. Prayer times can then focus on what God has already done with and through others in the cell and on strongholds already invaded and overcome. In addition, specific needs which have been shared can be targeted for intercession and listening. Keeping in contact with others in the cell between meetings is almost automatic if such intercession is taking place. Often a word from the Lord comes to make contact *right away* with a person; such guidance should be readily obeyed. Doing things that show mutual love for one another may include remembering birthdays, anniversaries, etc.

In addition, these personal times should focus on seeking

the very best from the Lord for each member of the cell. Lifting up the other members to experience the highest possibilities of Christian experience is worthy of extended intercession.

Praying about sin in the life of a fellow cell member is an entry into the battleground where Satan has strongholds. Such a sin should be seen as a reproach upon each cell member, and all should bear the sorrow as if it were personally committed. What does Christ want to do about it? What spiritual gift does He want to flow to restore a fallen brother?

Above all, one result of time in the *Listening Room* should be a resolve to point the way by personal obedience. Paul wrote in 1 Corinthians 11:1, *"Follow my example, as I follow the example of Christ."*

In addition, time listening to the Lord should include seeking ways to let the cell share in one's own life needs, including doubts and burdens, dreams and aspirations. The closer people come to one another in love and understanding, the clearer all personal faults are seen. In this way, edification becomes a mutual ministry.

Prepared People Create Powerful Cell Group Meetings

As each member performs this spiritual "homework" in preparation for the cell meeting, the work of the Holy Spirit prepares each person to be a channel for spiritual gifts to flow, and also to be the receiver of edification. There will be a topic for the meeting, but edification will be its *purpose*. Writes Elizabeth O'Connor,

> *Contemplative prayer is communion with a sphere that is beyond the world we know, but that communion makes possible an authentic, healing community in the here and now into which people can come and be renewed and find out what it is they are supposed to be doing . . . . it is about being commissioned. It is going some place because one is sent, and then it is being a contemplative person in that place until one knows or is told what to do next. Much of our unease comes from not knowing where we are supposed to be . . . . Whatever our path, we do not feel right inside. The same dilemma is evident in the church's corporate life . . . . she is engaged without having been sent.*[7]

Gifts Flow In Precious interaction

In 1 Corinthians 12:7, Paul says, *"Now to each one the manifestation of the Spirit is given for the common good."* D. A. Carson points out that this verse and the ones that follow do not exalt one gift more than any other. Their application to *life needs within the Body* is the issue, not the exaltation of gifts seeming to be more significant.[8]

Here is a couple with a heavy financial debt: *the message of wisdom* is manifested. In another case, a person is struggling with a significant decision to be made soon: *the message of knowledge* is manifested. For another family, deep despair over a son on drugs has overwhelmed them: through the Body, *the gift of faith* is given for them. The parents are enabled to trust God to bring about his salvation.

The *gifts of healings* may be a focal point on another occasion. Countless illustrations document the way this grace gift has brought joy to cells that have seen God restore the sick through prayer alone.

Discerning between true and false spirits is needed more and more; demonic manifestations have become commonplace. Those who have tampered with the occult in the past are rampant in today's society. Bringing them freedom from their oppression calls for this gift to be exercised in the cell group from time to time. Our Zone Pastors in Singapore are frequently called by a cell group to assist them in an idol burning service for a family they have recently brought to Christ. Stephen Khong has prepared an expository message he uses on such occasions, helping the converts understand their new life and the power of the Christ who has come to indwell them.

The gift of support is mentioned in 1 Corinthians 12:28. I recall a teen-age cell group who took up an offering for the abandoned mother of one of their recent converts. The Internal Revenue Service was about to confiscate their furniture for back taxes the errant husband had never paid. After their meeting, the group taped an envelope filled with small bills to her front door, rang the doorbell, and hid in the bushes. As she opened the envelope, she must have heard a cough in the darkness. She called out with a quivering voice, "Thank you, whoever you are!" It was through that event she followed her son into personal faith in Christ.

Also in the same verse is the *gift of direction,* which uses a Greek word primarily used for piloting or steering of a ship. It's a powerful gift which is needed by the Shepherd and Intern, among others, for the building up of the Body.

Paul summarizes the manifestation of these gifts by saying in 1 Corinthians 12:11-12,

> *All these are the work of one and the same Spirit, and he gives them to each one, just as he determines. The body is a unit, though it is made up of many parts; and though all its parts are many, they form one body. So it is with Christ.*

It has amazed me that book after book, commentary after commentary, ignores the transparent teaching of scripture about the manifestation of these gifts as the focus of Body life in cell groups. It is the result of minds entrapped by centuries-old traditional thought patterns. No matter how much Greek or Hebrew a scholar knows, he still writes in terms of his church being a large group, gathering on a campus with buildings used for worship or Bible study. It's reflected in page after page of his writings.

Why can't he realize that? If spiritual gifts are to be manifested by every believer for the building up of the Body, what possible form can the church take except the cell group, the Basic Christian Community?

In the same way, the 36 books in my library on prayer never even *touch* the concept of the *Listening Room* as a part of a corporate lifestyle to prepare a believer for ministering the gifts. Nothing I can find has been written to prepare believers for the edifying event so beautifully described by Paul in 1 Corinthians 14:26-33. It is obvious that, to him, this was a normative event for church life.

Applying spiritual gifts for edification is a lost truth in our generation! While controversy rages over the least of all the gifts, the thrust of this fourteenth chapter is buried and forgotten. We neither edify one another, nor witness to unbelievers by doing so, as depicted in verses 24 and 25. This is reason enough for us to focus more earnestly on the importance of listening to God for His direction for the Body of Christ. *Lord, bring on the Second Reformation!*

12 CHILDREN IN CELL CHURCHES

(Note: this chapter was contributed by Dr. Lorna Jenkins of Auckland, New Zealand, lightly edited by the author.)

The Context And Conditions For Children's Learning As Discovered In The Bible

In the Old Testament, children are viewed within a group of people, most often their primary family. God's plan in creation was not just that *man* should not be alone, but that *children* should not be alone, either. A child enters the world in the midst of a ready-made group of people on whom he is dependent. *The child's physical and spiritual welfare is the prime responsibility of the family which brought him into being.*

The Hebrew family was not an isolated unit. It was part of a larger community, the tribe, which was in turn part of a still larger unit, the chosen people of God. The network of community reached out from the child to the boundaries of the nation.

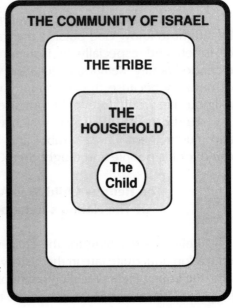

THE COMMUNITY OF ISRAEL

THE TRIBE

THE HOUSEHOLD

The Child

The Hebrews did not see the child as the chance result of a physical human act. They regarded children as a gift from God, the sign of God's favor.[1] God knew each child from the time of its conception and his life was planned out ahead of time.[2]

When a child entered the world he belonged to God first, especially in the case of the firstborn.[3] The responsibility for the spiritual nurture of the child lay squarely in the context of the family, with the father having the duty of teacher and leader.[4] In Deuteronomy, the command to the family is to remember and teach.[5] The family is the context in which to retell the deliverance from Egypt and the greatness of God.[6]

The family was not alone in this enterprise. In a real sense, the individual saw much of his personality as being involved in the corporate personality of the nation. The individual's life was linked directly with the life of his ancestors and with the life of his living contemporaries. When the individual sinned, Israel sinned.[7] When the nation sinned, there was guilt upon every individual.[8] Israel could be described as

> . . . a group of persons whose lives were so bound up together, in what must be called a physical unity, that they could be treated as parts of one common life.[9]

With this understanding, it was impossible that a child could be taught to know God outside the framework of the community of Israel, and especially in isolation from his immediate and extended family. Religious education was the responsibility of the community because the community was the arena in which the religious life would forever be practised.

Furthermore, the way in which a father cared for his children and taught them was a symbol and illustration of the way God cared for his people and taught them.[10]

The Hebrew Child Was A Living Picture
Of The Nation's Relationship To God

Religious teaching for the child was not a matter of formal education until quite late in the history of the nation. From an early age, the young Hebrew child was involved in the daily and weekly prayers of his family. He watched the preparation and observance

THE COMMUNITY OF ISRAEL

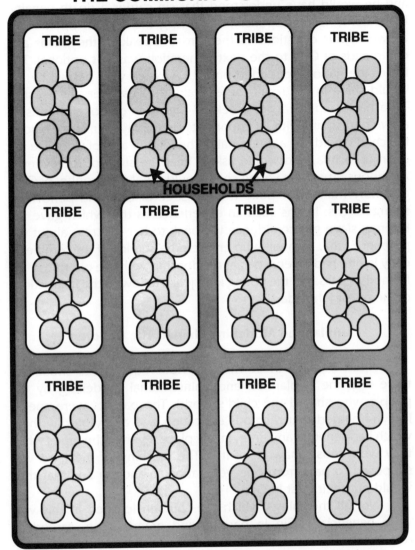

THE IMPACT OF THE COMMUNITY OF ISRAEL ON THE CHILD

- Modelling Of Daily Life
- Passovers And Festivals
- Rituals And Sacrifices
- Commandments
- Sabbath
- Celebration Of Events (Births, Entering Adulthood, etc.)
- Hearing The Law
- Drama And Signs (Prophets)
- Prayer, Witness

of the Sabbath. He witnessed the sacrificial patterns of his family, and he would have understood that sin carries a death penalty. His parents were responsible for living the faith in open view, answering his questions as they arose. Speaking the words and commands of God to the next generation was not optional. The life of the nation depended on it.[11] As each year passed by, he would share in the round of festivals, the Passover, the Feast of Tabernacles, the Feast of Weeks,[12] not as an onlooker, but as an active participant with an important role to play.[13] In some places, the child would see a memorial of the mighty acts of God, like the cairn of Joshua, and would ask to hear the story of the event.[14] At various times, the young child would meet the prophet of God, or a holy man who spoke the message of God and performed strange signs. It was such an experience as this which gave the Hebrew slave girl confidence to speak to her mistress about the prophet Elisha. Samuel, who entered the service of the temple so early in life, had a very special relationship with the old priest, Eli. In another passage, the young king Joash followed the instructions of the priest Jehoiada.[15]

Unplanned Modelling Shaped The Children

Apart from all these more obvious educational situations, there was the unplanned and unintentional modelling by the people who shared the child's world. The parents were specifically reminded that religious education was a day-by-day thing which happened at any time, in any place, even at the times when they were most unaware of it.[16] The teaching of the Lord was supposed to pass from one generation to another so "that they would put their trust in God."[17]

Not all the things which the children learned in this way were beneficial.[18] Sin in parents and grandparents carried its results into the lives of children to the third and fourth generation.[19] At times the children had to be protected from the idolatrous practices of their parents.[20]

Children Were Not Identified With The Nation's Sin

Yet, God did not always consider that the children were identified with the nation's sin. When the people of Israel refused to enter the Promised Land out of fear, God forbade all except the children to enter. The people had claimed that their fear was on behalf of their children, but ironically God transferred their inheritance to the children.[21]

Much later in Israel's history the prophet Ezekiel condemned this idea of community guilt. The righteous son should not die for the sin of the guilty father.[22] This suggests the New Testament idea that each person must find forgiveness for his own sin, but it does not invalidate the community nature of the child's nurture. Perhaps the most encouraging aspect of the Old Testament view of the child was the affirmation that he was capable of spiritual understanding and that his praise was acceptable to God.[23] God called the child, Samuel, and revealed his word to him.[24] Curiously, Samuel as a child is described in very similar terms to Jesus as a child.

> And the boy Samuel continued to grow in stature and in favor with the Lord and with men. [25]

Others who were called to be prophets from their birth were Samson and John the Baptist.[26] Apart from the book of Deuteronomy, Proverbs is the book which says most about the education of children. Once again the responsibility for training the child lies with the parents.[27] The father's authority over the child was closely allied with the authority of the Lord.[28] Probably the key verse for the nurture of children is in Proverbs 22:6:

> Train a child in the way he should go, and when he is old he will not turn from it.

This is not a promise that the children of godly parents will always turn out well. But it does suggest that the training a child receives does profoundly affect his later life.

The Childhood Of Jesus

Probably the best example we have of the nurture of a Jewish child is the early life of Jesus. Even the sketchy evidence we have reveals the pattern of a godly Jewish household. After His miraculous entry into the world, God chose to provide Him with a family to guard Him and train Him. Even before His birth, His extended family relationships were strong.[29] Jesus was the oldest in His family, and probably carried the responsibility for His younger brothers and sisters from an early age. He participated in all the Jewish rituals[30] and began His worship in the temple festivals from the age of twelve. We know that He was a part of an interacting community, because when He was absent during the return journey from Jerusalem it was three days before His parents missed him. Like many close-knit communities, they would have assumed that He was in the care of other adult friends.

Like *all* children, Jesus loved to asked questions; unlike *some* children, He listened to the answers. He felt completely at ease in the presence of adults, even learned theologians. By the age of twelve, He already had a strong sense of relationship with God as His Father.[31] His life was also characterized by obedience. I do not think we should regard this pattern as exceptional. It is still possible for a child to grow up in a community of faith, to be mature (as a child) and obedient, and to have a relationship with God from an early age.

The Gospels do not record many direct encounters between Jesus and children, but some information can be inferred. It is certain that Jesus had close contacts with younger children in His home and community. He could describe their games, including playing as though they were attending weddings or funerals.[32] Perhaps He had even played with them.

He was sensitive to the needs of children. He knew they could be afflicted with demons or disease like any adult, and He healed them.[33] When He raised Jairus' daughter from the dead, He was most gentle and sensitive as He brought her back to life—like a mother waking her child in the morning.[34]

Jesus' teachings were not so boring that children could not appreciate them. At least one small boy appears to have followed Jesus all day, even forgetting to eat his lunch. The story method which Jesus so often used was intergenerational. A child might be able to perceive the point as quickly as the adults, sometimes even faster.

Children were never far from Jesus during His public ministry. When Jesus called a little child and placed him in the midst of the disciples, He did not need to search for one. He smiled, beckoned, and the child came. When He was at the busiest point of His ministry, Jesus gave the children His priority time and became angry when the disciples tried to exclude them. Like many adults today, they had assumed that Jesus did not have time to waste on children.[35] Jesus was glad to receive the praise of children even when some adults wanted to silence them.[36] (Children typically praise noisily and without suitable discretion.)

Jesus reveals the attitude of God towards children in a variety of contexts. He sees their relationship with their father as a model of the relationship between God and man.[37] He believes that God can reveal truth to a simple child which is hidden from their more learned and sophisticated elders.[38] He is so identified with children that to welcome a child in His name is the same as welcoming Him personally.[39] Conversely, the person who causes a child to turn away from God may as well destroy himself as face the terrible anger of the Lord.[40]

We have tended to lightly apply this verse to non-Christian parents or atheistic schoolteachers. We should not forget that many children have been turned from God by Christians who have acted in a harsh or insensitive manner towards them, or by Sunday Schools which have bored and insulated the children against the dynamic of the faith.

Children have special access to God in that their angels represent them before God. For this reason, no one should despise or overlook children.[41] God does not want any child to perish.[42] This surely says something about God's attitude to children who die before they are capable of making a responsible choice.

A child has something to offer God. It seems ironic that when the disciples were unable to meet the needs of the hungry multitude, a small boy was able to offer all that he had.[43] Jesus quoted the Psalms to remind the priests that praise from children was perfectly proper and acceptable.

Probably the most difficult area of Jesus' theology of children was their place in the Kingdom of Heaven. Jesus reminded His disciples that the citizens of the Kingdom must be like children in their nature.[44] This does not mean that childhood is a specially sanctified time of life. Jesus was a realist and did not romanticize childhood. It does mean that certain characteristics of childhood should also be characteristic of the Kingdom citizen.

A child has to receive the Kingdom by trust. He has nothing of his own that he can offer to buy his way in. He cannot earn his right to anything. The Kingdom is given to him freely.

The child is also a model for humility in Kingdom living. A child lives essentially in a state of total dependence on others. The only appropriate return he can make to his parents is obedience. Trusting and obeying is his required way of life. Later, adults imagine they have grown beyond that stage into independence and personal decision-making.

This does not mean, of course, that a child cannot be aggressive or self-centered. It does mean that in our society a child is without personal power and authority. His significant adults assert their authority over him, and many children attempt to resist that authority. In contrast, the child of God accepts his earthly father's authority, is secure within it, and uses it as his proper guideline.

This is an illustration of the nature of authority which Jesus envisaged within the church. Jesus would not accept a dominating, hierarchical system of authority. In fact, He expressly forbade it.[45] The authority of the Kingdom belongs to the Father. All citizens of the Kingdom have the role of servants or children, powerless in their own right, with their own authority being derived solely from their relationship and likeness to their father.[46]

There is one further indirect comment from Jesus on the nature of children's education. When the rich young man wanted to follow Him, he could claim perfectly honestly that he had obeyed the commandments of God from his earliest years.[47] However, he had missed the heart of the matter! His religious education had not altered his attitudes towards his possessions and his stewardship of them. Today, many children who have been well taught within our churches have also not seen the relationship of their Christian education to significant aspects of their lives. There has been no dynamic transformation.

Children, then, have a unique place in the Father's Kingdom. They are under His special care and are under His protection. Jesus identifies Himself with them and takes into Himself the attitudes with which people treat them.

Perhaps the most significant phrase in passages related to children reflects the place Jesus gives to them. He takes a child and places him "in the midst."

That's where children belong—in the midst of the learning community of God. They have two reasons for being there. First, they will learn best if they are in the midst of a vital community of faith. Second, the community needs to see the children visibly in their midst as a reminder of the nature of the Kingdom and their own attitude within it. The child is a living visual aid to the whole church.

The Child In The Early Church

In the history of the early church, children are notably absent from the scene. We can only infer the place of the children in the events which occurred. In Peter's first Pentecost sermon the promise of the Holy Spirit is extended to the children and descendents of the present generation of people.[48] The reference to household evangelism and baptism also seems to include children within the household, though we cannot be certain of the level of children's participation.[49]

The description of the nature of the church at that time gives a clearer picture of what children must have experienced. Churches met in homes for the most part, small homes where

children must have witnessed what went on. They saw the believers meeting together often, sharing their goods with those in need. They must have heard the prayer meetings and watched the miracles which were performed. They must have been acutely aware of both the goodness of God through the merciful ministry of people like Dorcas,[50] and of His power, through the judgment of Ananias and

THE COMMUNITY OF FAITH

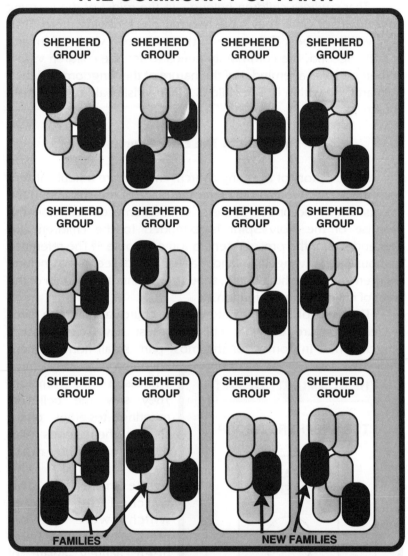

THE IMPACT OF THE COMMUNITY OF FAITH ON THE CHILD

- Modelling Of Daily Life
- Festivals
- Rituals
- Scripture
- Worship
- Celebration Of Events (Births, Entering Adulthood, etc.)
- Fellowship, Other Children
- Power Encounters, Healings
- Prayer, Witness

Sapphira. They were probably present at the shared meals and saw the believers remembering the Lord's death. Much of their learning must have come through *being there,* witnessing the life of the church first hand.

For some, there was an even more immediate learning experience. Some children were orphaned or saw their parents imprisoned because of their faith. They must have come under the immediate care of the Christian community.

For some children the influence of their family was crucial, even if one of the parents was an unbeliever as in Timothy's case.[51] Paul covers that point in 1 Corinthians 7:14, when he argues that the presence of a Christian partner in a marriage has a covering effect both on the other partner and on the children of the marriage. Paul's teaching on the stable family relationship is at the core of his view of the church as a community. The family is vitally linked with the church and the relationships in the church are based on the family model.[52] Children have a Christian duty to obey their parents, but the new element of the family relationship is the responsibility of fathers to treat their children with respect and not provoke them unnecessarily.[53] This must have sounded strange in a society where the power of fathers over their families was absolute, even to the point of life and death. The overall impression of the New Testament evidence is that children basically learned their faith from their parents, with whom they had a special Godly relationship. That teaching was, however, reinforced by the sharing of the family in the life of the Christian community. The children saw the words of their parents being lived out in the lives of people they knew best. They had a first hand experience of the power of God and the cost of discipleship. They knew that, for *their* family, being a Christian was not a nominal allegiance, but a serious daily risk to which all their adult friends were wholeheartedly committed. Half-hearted Christians can never inspire a lifetime faith in their children!

Conclusions

The Old Testament and the New Testament concepts of child nurture show remarkable similarities which are diagrammed in the illustrations included in this chapter. The cellular structure seems to have particular strength in holding the families together within the overall community. This framework is better than a hierarchical structure where the whole weight of responsibility rests on the family alone. In the cell structure, there is mutual support and understanding, with one cell reinforcing the pattern of another cell. A partial or shattered family can be sustained within the whole community with supplementary help from other families. The one additional element in the New Testament illustration of the church is the possibility of outreach as *families* reach out to *other families* who are not in the faith.

The following principles seem basic to the Biblical view of children's ministry:

1. God intends children to be taught and nurtured within the family setting.
2. The immediate family is supported and surrounded by the extended family and the community of faith.
3. Children are capable of spiritual understanding, and can offer acceptable praise and service to God.
4. Children are needed in the church community as a challenge and an example of some basic elements of kingdom living.
5. Children learn best through first hand experience and participation. Merely teaching children the right ideas is not enough. The goal is that their lives should be transformed as they become followers of Jesus.
6. The ultimate goal is full maturity in Christ.[54]
7. The present goal is maturity at the level of the child's development and understanding.

3

THE STRUCTURE

OF A

CELL GROUP

CHURCH

Overview of a Cell Group Church

The Cell: The "Basic Christian Community"

THE CELL (SHEPHERD GROUP)

The **CELL** is the "Basic Christian Community." The Church is formed from them and is the sum of them. Cells never grow larger than 15 people and multiply as they reach this figure. There are no other activities which exist in competition with the cells. Everything in the church is an extension of them and flows from their combined strength.

Two Types: One For Nurture, Another For Outreach

SHEPHERD GROUP → SHARE GROUP

In this section we shall learn about two types of cells. The first is called a *"Shepherd group."* It's the "Basic Christian Community," the place where edification takes place as members care for one another, using spiritual gifts and support systems. Each Shepherd group is "on mission." It is constantly in touch with the unreached, constantly ministering to them.

Since many unbelievers will not respond to public meetings or home groups as spiritually intense as a Shepherd group, a second type of cell is formed called a *"Share group."* It is formed using three or four mature Shepherd group members. See it as an evangelism extension of the Shepherd group, a "subcommunity." It meets separately from the Shepherd group for a single purpose: it connects believers to hardened unbelievers who care little about spiritual matters. In these gatherings, the power of Christ within believers impacts the unbelievers. Their interest in Christ comes alive as they are quickened by the Holy Spirit. Some are led into a one-to-one Bible study with team members. As these come to Christ, they are brought into the life of the Shepherd group.

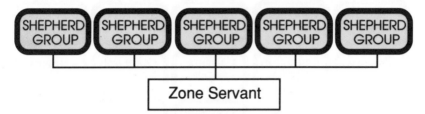

Approximately five Shepherd groups are clustered and guided by an unpaid worker called a "Zone Servant." He or she will be appointed to this task only after serving effectively as a Shepherd of one or two groups.

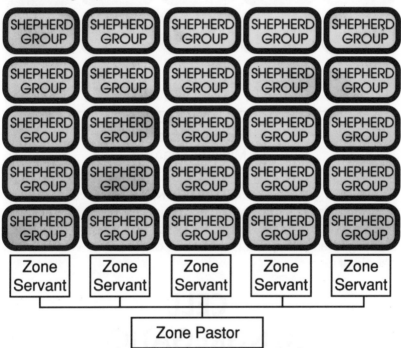

25 Shepherd groups then become a **CONGREGATION.** They typically form on a regional basis. They cluster for some equipping or evangelism events, and in some cell group churches also meet together for worship. Congregations are activated by the cells and guided by their members. It's important to rethink your understanding of "Congregation." It is only used for the *clustering* of cells, not for the *controlling* of them.

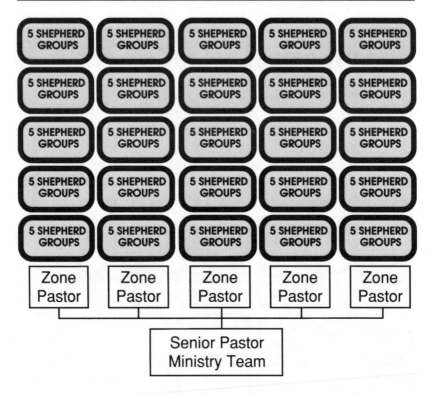

A third gathering, the **CELEBRATION**, is a mass meeting in which all the cells gather for public witness, praise, preaching, and teaching. This city-wide meeting is used for praise and worship, solid Bible teaching, evangelism, and is a vital part of the public witness of the people of God.

CELL
CONGREGATION
CELEBRATION

These are the three "C's" of cell group life. Now, let's look at each one in depth in the next chapter. Refer to these pages again if you wish to get the overview in mind.

13 CELL, CONGREGATION, AND CELEBRATION

There are three words beginning with "C" which summarize the Cell Group Church: *Cells, Congregations, and Celebrations.* The most important of the three is the Cell. For those who are conditioned to think of the *Congregation* as the focal point of church life, this will require radical adjustments.

CELLS

Cells are the basic building block of all life forms. Following Biblical patterns, the cell is also the basic life form of the church. Participation in these new churches takes place by joining a cell. The "one another" passages of the New Testament come alive as believers literally obey the pattern of Acts 2:42-46. They move from house to house on a regular basis. They break bread together, sometimes reverting to the original pattern for the Lord's Supper, where the broken bread introduced the Love Feast, and the passing of the wine completed it.

The cell's fellowship often includes the voluntary sharing of assets, even as was done in the early church. This is best done by the givers remaining as anonymous as possible, channeling the gifts for those in need through the Zone Pastor.

And, the cells *pray*—not polite little tritenesses, but by reaching toward heaven and bringing divine power into the needs of people in the room. Half nights of prayer are often cycled into the lifestyle of cells. Seasoned veterans of cell group life have seen God work in many ways and in many lives and delight in opportunities to pray for others. Intercession, deliverance, and other ministries often call for prevailing prayer by cell members.

This diagram shows the people who will typically be found in a Shepherd group, not because it is so formed but because experience has shown it works out this way. If you were to attend a Shepherd group for the first time, you would be able to identify the people belonging to each category.

SHEPHERD SERVANT		SHEPHERD INTERN
COMMITTED SERVANTS Can be equipped to penetrate the unchurched and care for others in the flock	**UNDEVELOPED BELIEVERS** Can be equipped to harvest seeking unbelievers and care for others in the flock	**BABY CHRISTIANS HURTING PERSONS** Can be nurtured, healed, and led to move into ministry

We Are Going To Refer To Cells As "Shepherd groups."

The Shepherd group is the cell where people are nurtured, equipped to serve, and where members build up (edify) one another. It forms a community where believers are called to be accountable to each other, and where they can be totally transparent with one another.

Because the Cell meets all the basic needs of the believer, it replaces the many "programs" that go on inside the traditional church. A Cell Group church has no Sunday School, Training Hour, Visitation Night, Midweek Prayer Service, or *any* of the other formal services which comprise other church calendars. In place of this, each Cell becomes a true community, an "extended family unit" for Christians. A pure cell group church sees no need for other programs. Its basic needs are met in the Shepherd groups. Adding further activities to its life dissipates the focus of believers and becomes counterproductive.

There are limits to the activity within a Shepherd group. While it may begin its sessions with a brief time of praise and worship, that is not its primary purpose. While it will use the Bible freely in its lifestyle, it is not a place for Bible Study. These needs are fulfilled at a different level in the life of the church, as we shall see in the paragraphs which follow. Thus, it is not necessary for the

Shepherd to be a great Bible teacher, or even a strong communicator. Instead, the Shepherd must have a love for the flock and a desire to minister to their needs. He or she serves on a *pastoral level,* caring for the needs of the sheep. The primary activity of the Shepherd group is *edification,* building up one another. This joint ministry of all is directed by the Holy Spirit, built upon scriptural teaching already received in an assembly of the cells meeting together in a Congregation or Celebration assembly.

In contrast, the traditional church collects people into classrooms in a church facility. Nearly always, members are insulated from closeness by involvement in a study of some sort, or a rehearsal, or a lecture, or a project. There are few times when members simply gather to belong to each other. They assemble to *do* something. Thus, people never really become close, and seldom visit in each other's homes. Their prayers are sincere, but they seldom expect immediate answers as they tarry together.

Cells Provide True Community

At one time, all people lived in family groupings. We now live among neighbors we barely know, where there are all sorts of beliefs, habits, and attitudes. In the cell group church, a strong focus is placed upon the development of relationships. People become responsible for, and to, each other. They sing, *"Bind us together, Lord! Bind us together with cords than cannot be broken; bind us together with love."* There is a deep-as-life sense of belonging to one another in the cell group church. That only exists when the group is small enough for intimacy to happen. All realize they are not there simply for themselves or their own sanctification, but for others who have parched hearts.

I am not talking about the creation of psychological therapy groups! The cell group church's point of reference is not on the emotional level, but upon the spiritual level. These people serve one another, edifying each other.

In contrast, the traditional church collects its members by rows in an auditorium or classroom. They sing the same song, put their money in the same plate, take notes on the same sermon. Their Bible study classes bring a sense of friendship, but not to a depth where the class becomes aware that Bill and Betty have a marriage in "white water." There are limited ways for each person to share spiritual gifts with others. Often, if the members of a traditional church create small groups for prayer or discipleship, they close the group to new people. The people who gather in them are there to receive, not to reach out. This is not true in a cell group church. Each cell knows it should multiply in a certain length of time. In Houston, for example, the cells should multiply in 22 weeks. In Abidjan, the time for multiplication is closer to 12 weeks! (One of the reasons is that 80% of Ivorians are unemployed, giving them many hours a day to focus on their cell group ministries.)

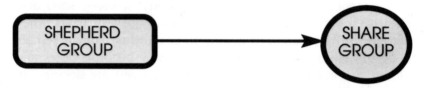

Share Group Cells Communicate The Gospel

Most significantly, the cell group church realizes they not only *share* the Gospel—they are the *living demonstration* of it! For them, "church" is never, never a word to use in referring to a building or activities which are held within it. The *believers* are the church, the beautiful Bride, the Body that lives in unity, the Living Stones, the holy and royal Priests. The Gospel is embodied *within them,* not programs, services, or edifices. Thus, their cell groups are never, ever closed meetings.

To more effectively communicate the message of Christ's Lordship, a "sub-cell" of the cell group is formed, called a *Share group.* In a later chapter, the structure of this subgroup will be explained in depth. Its purpose is to become a point of contact with "hard core" unbelievers who are totally unresponsive to gatherings of believers. The topics in a Share group focus on the needs, problems, interests, hobbies, or inclinations of unbelievers. The Christians in the Share group cell meet these persons on their own "turf," and on their own terms. I have seen a Jewess and an Arab student drawn to Christ by the same group at the same time. I have seen homosexuals face their lifestyle in a Share group, and a lovely "Yuppie" with a razor-sharp mind confess her faith as she sat on the hearth of a fireplace in a group. Share groups work!

More frequently than not, unbelievers will migrate from

these sub-cells to the Shepherd group itself. This is a result of a simple Biblical concept taken literally: *every single child of God is a minister, and every one has a ministry!* Thus, all speak for God, and as a community they speak in a special way for Him through their community lifestyle.

Their evangelism is shaped by I Corinthians 14:24-25, which explains how harvesting is supposed to happen: when an unbeliever attends a cell group and witnesses the presence of the Holy Spirit among the group,

> . . . *he is convicted by all, he is called to account by all; the secrets of his heart are disclosed; and so he will fall on his face and worship God, declaring that God is certainly among you.*

A Shepherd group had first-time visitors from a Share group. They were not yet believers, but had developed a hunger to know more about Jesus. One was a Jewish woman, the other a man who, unlike the rest who came informally, was wearing a suit and tie. He was a banker with a Catholic background and had not attended a church in years. The group shared a common meal. One of the men briefly presented some powerful truths he had gleaned from his Bible study. A single woman parent had brought along her tape player with a background tape for "Surely the presence of the Lord is in this place," which she sang to the group. Her voice broke with emotion as she sang, and all were filled with a sense of Christ's presence.

The group took some time to get acquainted with the man in the suit, and he with them, by sharing the "Quaker Questions."[1] He shared that he had recently received a note from his wife telling him she had walked out of their marriage. *He was hurting!*

A lovely young wife shared with him how she felt when her father walked out of his marriage when she was only 16. She told how she and her mother's relationship with Christ had brought strength to them during that time. He felt Christ's edification coming to him through her. The Shepherd suggested the group cluster around the man and pray for God to bring him a deeper sense of His presence. Several prayed for him.

The cell then discussed another couple, not present that night. The husband had called. Their Chevrolet had blown an engine. It was his eighth week job-hunting, and they didn't have the money to fix it. He explained his wife was hurting too badly to attend the Shepherd group. Someone suggested those present take up an offering for them. Checkbooks appeared, and a few moments later the total was counted: $765. The group gleefully planned how they would surreptitiously deposit their checks to the couple's account, so they would not know who had given the money.

A twenty-five year old single had to make a decision about buying a house or remaining in his apartment. Some of the older ones asked some penetrating questions about his monthly budget. No one advised him, but he began to see that the choice to purchase a house at that time was unwise. He thanked the group for helping him. His own father had died a year earlier, and he shared how he missed being able to talk over things like this with him.

At the close of an hour and a half of such sharing, the group broke into pairs to pray. The Intern sat on carpeted stairs with the unbeliever, where they could talk uninterrupted. He said, "Shall we both pray, or shall I pray for both of us?" The unbeliever said, "I have another suggestion. Would you pray for me? I was deeply moved when the group prayed for me. But, I don't know how to pray for myself. And, for the first time in my life, I think I know why people get so close to God. I want to get close to Him. Pray I will learn how to share with Him."

The Intern probed more deeply. The man lacked all under-standing of the basic truths of the gospel. God, Jesus, Man, Sin, the Cross, the Exchanged Life—these were all unknowns to him. He needed much more than a 20-minute presentation of the plan of salvation. He needed to share what he already understood, and the Intern needed to know what he was distorting when he used Christian words.

He was worth more to Christ than the reciting of a short speech. The men needed an entire evening alone together to really settle his decision for Christ. He agreed to set aside the next night for this purpose. They shared a meal to begin the discussion. It continued for several hours.

Do you understand? The evangelism "method" in that meeting was the presence of the Lord, operating through His Bride! He was *"convicted by all; called to account by all; the secrets of his heart were poured out;"* and he almost literally fell on his face as the men prayed together on those steps. He had discovered God was certainly among the people in the cell!

Once you have experienced such body life, it's agony to go back into a stuffy auditorium where strangers share a formal service, and no one even whispers a greeting to those seated around them.

How Do Cell Group Churches Differ From House Churches?

There is a distinct difference between the house church and cell group movements. House Churches tend to collect a community of 15-25 people who meet together on a weekly basis. Usually, each House Church stands alone. While they may be in touch with nearby House Churches, they usually do not recognize any further structure beyond themselves.

There are tens of thousands of House Churches around the world. Because there is no possible way to study them, there is no one pattern to describe them. Most of the time they grow slowly. Often they may not grow larger than their original number for years, having no aggressive evangelistic activity. They do not become a true movement of *church expansion.* Perhaps it is fair to say that some simply do not possess a vision for aggressively reaching the unevangelized, either in their own communities or abroad. It would also be unfair to say that's true of them all!

Many of Christ's finest people are to be found within the house church movement. One of their most celebrated writers is Dr. Robert Banks of Canberra, Australia, who has written several important books. He and his wife Julia have authored *The Home Church,* an absolute treasure of information about house churches.[2]

In contrast, the cell group church recognizes a larger structure for church life. An assembly composed of cells which have networked under a common leader and ministry team is the norm. A good way to describe the cell group church is to think of a human body. It is composed of many cells, but no one cell would ever consider existing apart from the rest. There are links of love between all the cells in the church. Further, each one lives under the authority of a structure which services their needs and provides strong equippers to help them. Thus, the cell group church is a movement of God's people, always reaching out, always intent on drawing in the unconverted, always concerned about the equipping of every single member to function under Christ's Lordship.

Congregations

EQUIPPING EVENTS
"Getaways" combining fellowship and Bible study taught by gifted men or women.

SPECIAL EVANGELISTIC ACTIVITIES
Banquets, Parties, Films, Proclamations, Speakers, Open Air Events, Planting New Cells.

WORSHIP AND PRAISE
Public Meetings, led by Shepherd Groups Singing, Testimonies, Children's Activties, Messages by Ministry Team Leadership.

COMMUNITY PROJECTS
Caring for Aged, Rap Sessions for Teens on Drugs, Assisting Families in Crisis, etc.

CHRISTIAN ACTION
Challenging Local Anti-Christian Ordinances, Working Against Pornography, etc.

Cells usually grow from 7 or 8 persons to 12 or 15 in 4 to 6 months. They then multiply into two cells. As the number of cells increase, the spiritual gifts of the body are called forth. Those who have the gift of teaching are discovered. Those who have the gift of "telling forth" are recognized.

The cells begin to form regional congregations, which seldom number more than 175 people. From within them, teachers and prophets come forth to share the Word and exhort, train and encourage. Thus, as the cells grow, many small congregations will be formed. However, they *do not* replace the cells as the most significant part of church life. For example, one never *joins* a congregation; the only available link to its ministry is to join a *cell*.

In some cell churches, the congregations have praise

sessions. Large-group interaction takes place here. The congregation may set aside a half night of prayer, or sometimes several days for prayer or for teaching or training. Here the elder is one among equals, but loved and respected for the spiritual maturity which provides direction for younger servants.

I earlier referred to the cell church in St. Marys District, just west of Sydney. Les Scarborough has seen a few cells grow to several congregations of cells in 5 years. He meets every Tuesday night with the elders and their wives who care for the cells in each congregation. I have attended some of those unforgettable gatherings. This dear pastor has multiplied himself sevenfold. He is greatly loved by the men who preach to those little flocks under his loving direction.

In contrast, the P.B.D. church finds it difficult to permit those within the membership to exercise pastoral gifts for fear the pastor's prestige might be undermined. Often the pastor jealously guards the office he holds, withholding significant preaching or teaching roles from the general membership.

Later we will look at the superstructure which exists to service the Cells, the Congregations, and the Celebration, and we will be introduced to a "Zone Pastor." He often is a man gifted in the areas of counseling, administration, and evangelism, but not in preaching or teaching. He is usually assigned to a Congregation of cells and ministers among them. In no sense of the word does he become the "Senior Pastor" of the area cells and Congregation he serves. His ministry is people-oriented, not pulpit-oriented.

The role of the Congregation varies widely in cell group churches around the world. Faith Community Baptist Church has gathered its membership for a Celebration, with weakly developed Congregations. ICHTHUS Fellowship in London and St. Marys Baptist Church in Sydney are examples of strongly developed Congregations. As I have studied these, it would seem that the vision of the pastors shapes the direction more than any other one factor.

Since all cell group churches are truly *movements* that have no geographical limitations, Congregations are needed as the years go by. Dion Robert has made good use of them for those who live too far away to conveniently travel to the main buildings. So has Yonggi Cho, who has auditoriums miles away from Yoido Island, where he is viewed by closed circuit television.

Celebration Life

PRAISE EVENTS
Led by Praise Team

SPECIAL EVANGELISTIC ACTIVITIES
Special Speakers
Concerts, Special Events
Banquets

WITNESS OF THE WORD
Teaching by Pastor(s)
Focus on Truths Needed by the Body

WITNESS OF THE BODY
Testimonies of God's Power and Grace
Public Baptism, Dedication of Babies

WITNESS OF SPIRIT'S ACTIVITY
Invitations for Salvation, Healing, Deliverance
Ministry of Prayer

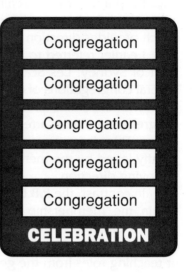

Finally, there are regular occasions when the cells gather for a demonstration of their life together in a giant Celebration. These are "events," not services, and their length is of no consequence. They may last 2 or even 3 hours, with a break for refreshments.

Music focuses upon worship of the Godhead. There is much singing, often blending traditional hymns with scripture songs. Slides or an overhead projector may display the words of songs; in some groups, hymnals are seldom used. Sometimes there is no song leader: the focal point is music projected on a screen. The room is charged with joy. A full hour of such praise time is not unusual.

Different traditions select different types of music. For example, in Dr. Cho's church the music is quite "Presbyterian." Nearly all of the selections are traditional hymns. On my last visit, the robed choir sang a beautiful selection from the Messiah. The audience recites the Apostle's Creed—most unusual for an Assemblies of God church.

Testimonies may be shared. Scriptures may be read responsively. The service may include public baptism of converts. An hour (and if *I* am teaching, longer!) of solid Bible teaching will always be included, often with the overhead projector used again. Scores of visitors may be present. At the close, the speaker (usually the senior pastor or elder) will invite those who wish to accept the Lord as Savior, or who have a special need, to raise their hands. In the place of an invitation to come forward, sometimes small groups of members encircle those who have raised their hands and minister to them. The hall then becomes one massive counseling room.

Most cell group churches must expand to two, four, even seven Celebration services to minister to all the people. Rented facilities like ballrooms of hotels are often used, but eventually there is no facility in the city large enough to hold the people. By then, the numbers of members and the depth of their commitment makes it possible to pay cash for the construction of a facility to be used for these meetings, all-night prayer services, special equipping events, etc.

Why Not Just Divide Into Smaller Units?

This is a frequently asked question in my seminars on cell group churches. The answer comes quickly when you examine the state of "parish churches" developed by denominations. They all believe the same doctrines and practice church life in lock-step with each other. Yet, their growth is erratic. It is caused by the different styles of leadership. The pastor of one church likes to counsel and does not teach very well. Another pastor is evangelistic, but does not feed the sheep. A third pastor is just downright *lazy,* while a fourth cannot manage well. A personnel director once told me that only a few people have an "automatic starter button" when they get up in the morning; most of the human race does better when they are supervised.

An effective cell group church must be a *team effort.* In nearly all of them I have visited, they have another important ingredient: a truly *anointed* leader. Many pastors are good administrators and preachers, but they don't have an anointing, a God-given *vision* that causes others to catch fire and burn for Christ in a special way.

When there is an anointed leader and a committed Ministry Team serving with him, honoring Paul's combination of Pastor-Teacher, Evangelist, Prophet, and Apostle, there is much room for others to serve within the structures that form. Small churches which never grow larger than 250-300 simply lack the depth of vision and leadership that a city-wide or regional cell group church can have.

There is room in *any* city for more than one cell group movement, however. On one occasion I was visiting with Dr. Cho in his office in Seoul and he said to me, "I have been studying our Zone Pastors. I have two of them that I am going to sponsor to begin a work like ours. I will give them 5,000 members and $50,000 to begin their work. I know them well enough to know they can successfully carry out our pattern." *As a professor of church planting, that made my mouth water!*

14 MORE ABOUT SHEPHERD GROUPS

Cell group churches worldwide use many terms for their cells. Dale Galloway's New Hope Community Church in Portland, Oregon, calls his "Tender Loving Care Groups." The name is awkwardly long, but it zeros in on the spirit of love and nurture which exists in each cell sponsored by that fine community of faith. Yonggi Cho speaks of his "Cell Groups." Lawrence Khong in Singapore adopted the term "Growth Groups." In Cali, Colombia, the San Fernando Baptist Church selected *"Grupos de Amor."* It really doesn't matter what they are called, as long as some thought is given to the way the description will be perceived by outsiders.

I have chosen to use the term "Shepherd Groups" in the guidebook I have written for cell servants. The main objection I usually hear to this term is that it isn't *urban* enough. One person commented, "What does anyone today know about *sheep?*" Of course, none of the *other* names mentioned above are particularly urban, either. My choice was made because the term is deeply rooted in scripture. It makes sense to use it if one is looking for a *theological* base for a name. In 1 Peter 5:1-4, the apostle wrote:

> To the elders among you, I appeal as a fellow elder, a witness of Christ's sufferings and one who also will share in the glory to be revealed: Be **shepherds of God's flock** that is under your care, serving as overseers—not because you must, but because you are willing, as God wants you to be; not greedy for money, but eager to serve; not lording it over those entrusted to you, but being examples to the flock. And when the **Chief Shepherd** appears, you will receive the crown of glory that will never fade away.

The name has a solid relationship to many, many scriptures, which are reviewed in the first chapter of the *Shepherd's Guidebook* to emphasize that the pastoral role is not just *leadership,* but *servanthood.*

The New Webster's Dictionary gives this definition:

> Shep·herd, n.: . . . one who exercises spiritual care over a community; a pastor or minister.

Choose whatever name you like for your cells, except "Care Group." (Ugh! More about that in a later chapter.) "A rose by any other name..."

Whatever the terminology, there are some very important principles which should not be ignored:

1. The attendance should never grow larger than 15 persons.
2. They should begin with three to eight persons.
3. They should always multiply when they reach 15 persons.[1]
4. They should meet *weekly,* never *biweekly.*
5. They should be recognized as the Basic Christian Community of the church.
6. They should understand they are under authority, a part of a greater vision, and will be given assistance every step of the way by a vitally concerned pastoral team.

Shepherds Are Pastors Of A Flock

A good shepherd is a *revealer,* not a teacher. Shepherds must be enablers, facilitators. They may or may not be effective teachers, counselors, or evangelists, but they must be lovers. They share their lives with transparency with those in their group, praying always that Christ will be formed in a new way within each life. They see three tasks as their primary assignments:

1. Each cell member should learn to exercise spiritual gifts.
2. Each cell member should be led to have a servant heart, edifying others through the exercising of spiritual gifts.
3. Each cell member should be equipped to minister to unbelievers, and personally experience bringing them to personal faith in Jesus Christ as Lord.

Shepherds Guide Each Person On His Or Her Journey

I have written the *Journey Guide* for the Shepherd and the Shepherd Intern to use with all incoming members. It helps each believer chart the equipping steps needed for the journey into ministry and outreach. In the first year, the track makes it possible for the Bible to be surveyed from cover to cover and outreach to be experienced on two levels. (This is further explained in following chapters).

The family of Christ functions best when each Christian is led by someone who has walked a few steps ahead and at the same time is caring for others who are a few steps behind. It's a chain of caring. Thus, "discipleship" is replaced by "apprenticeship," as each cell member is responsible *to* someone and also *for* someone. This chain of caring extends all the way from the Father, through the Son, to the Shepherds. It then extends through the cell members to the newest believer.

It's pretty clear, isn't it, that being a Shepherd is not for the half-committed! It's a lifestyle of servanthood. It involves staying in close contact with the Lord and with the flock.

A good Shepherd doesn't ever drive the sheep. Instead, he lovingly leads them:

> *He chose David his servant and took him from the sheep pens; from tending the sheep he brought him to be the shepherd of his people Jacob, of Israel his inheritance. And David shepherded them with integrity of heart; with skillful hands he led them.*[1]

Some Christian groups look for "task oriented" personalities, who are then enlisted as cell leaders because they have a particular skill or ability to fill a particular job. Thus, most attention is given to finding the "talented." Without exception, every single Christian is gifted by the Holy Spirit and is expected to exercise spiritual gifts. There is no "hierarchy" among God's people. As we will see, this includes the children.

From time to time, a flock will include people who have severely damaged personalities. In some churches, they are passed along unhelped from one group to the next. That's not God's way! A Shepherd group should pray over these problemed persons, asking God to help them become more than they now are. This may require special time with them, or perhaps a loving confrontation about their conduct. We shy away from such people...to their detriment.

The Three Spiritual Levels In A Shepherd Group

Consider the three levels in the Shepherd Group as seen by John:

> I write to you, dear children, because your sins have been forgiven on account of his name. I write to you, fathers, because you have known him who is from the beginning. I write to you, young men, because you have overcome the evil one. I write to you, dear children, because you have known the Father. I write to you, fathers, because you have known him who is from the beginning. I write to you, young men, because you are strong, and the word of God lives in you, and you have overcome the evil one.[2]

It's important to have a proper mixture of the levels of spiritual maturity when forming groups. To be an effective community, there should be "children," "young men," and "fathers." Note the levels of spiritual maturity in these three groups:

1. **Level One: Children—New Believers, Problemed Persons**
   The *Children* know forgiveness of sins, and know the Father...not with the deeper knowledge the fathers have of Him, but with a simple, childlike trust. These are represented by the first level in the diagram: New Believers and Problemed Persons.

2. **Level Two: Young Men—Visitation Team**
   The *Young Men* have overcome the evil one by their knowledge of the word of God. They are no longer tricked by the lies and accusations of Satan, who is described as the "accuser of the brethren." They can do battle with experienced eyes, knowing how he will attack. These are represented by the second level in the diagram: Teams of Visitors.

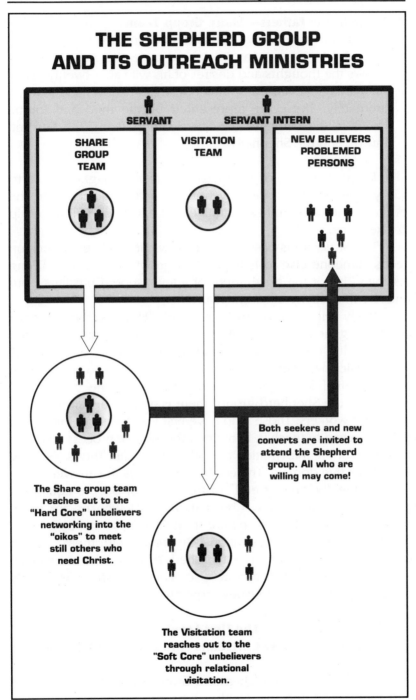

THE SHEPHERD GROUP
AND ITS OUTREACH MINISTRIES

SERVANT   SERVANT INTERN

SHARE GROUP TEAM

VISITATION TEAM

NEW BELIEVERS PROBLEMED PERSONS

The Share group team reaches out to the "Hard Core" unbelievers networking into the "oikos" to meet still others who need Christ.

Both seekers and new converts are invited to attend the Shepherd group. All who are willing may come!

The Visitation team reaches out to the "Soft Core" unbelievers through relational visitation.

3. Level Three: Fathers—Share Group Team

The *Fathers* truly know God, and function knowing whatever is bound in heaven can be bound on earth. As a husband knows the thoughts and desires of his wife after twenty years of marriage, even so spiritual "Fathers" know God's ways intimately. These are represented by the third and fourth levels in the diagram: the Share Group Team, the Servant Intern, and the Shepherd.

These divisions, or levels, shown in this diagram are artificially inserted. They are only used to help you recognize the levels of spiritual maturity suggested for effective apprenticeship to take place.

This structure is based on the conviction that every person needs someone else to help spiritual growth to occur. "Making disciples" is not the assignment of a few "super-Christians," but must be the activity of *all* Christians.

Many cell group pastors have said, "How are the other cell churches generating enough leaders to keep up with their growth?" It's not possible to use the traditional "discipleship" model which has been generated in the United States and achieve this objective! However, by using the "each one equip one" pattern of the Shepherd group, there is a rapid development of equipped workers. Those who have first learned something, and then have had to teach it, know that this double process solidifies the grasp of the information as nothing else can. This is also true in the affective domain. The equipping chain is the answer!

At the "beginning end" of that chain of *people equipping people* is the brand new Christian. These newborns are to be treated as babes who "crave pure spiritual milk, so that by it (they) may grow up in (their) salvation." Beginning with them, a chain of caring for one another is established. Anyone who has walked a few steps ahead of someone else can share what has already been learned, and the journeys continue.

The First Level:
Working With New Christians And Problemed Persons

The first level in the Shepherd Group includes new believers and problemed persons. Neither type can become involved in

They helped every one his neighbor
and everyone said to his brother,
"Be of good courage!"
• Isaiah 41:6

ministry until after they are nurtured and matured.

Each new believer is assigned to someone in the group who will help him become established in his walk with Christ. The Arrival Kit for New Christians helps this take place.[3] Over a period of eleven weeks, a new believer can usually mature enough to move into the middle division.

Problemed persons need the nurture of the entire group, but should be given special care by the Servant Intern. One type of person will be going through *a temporary period of crisis,* such as the death of a loved one, a divorce, loss of employment, etc. Like someone who has influenza, these persons must be temporarily helped until recovery takes place. They can then move into the middle level.

A second type in this first division is the *chronically problemed person.* These individuals are often "tolerated" until it is time for them to be "passed on" to someone else. Some are limited by their personality characteristics, and others never mature because people tend to avoid them. Their personalities are often anti-social. Sometimes they constantly say tactless things. In the *Shepherd's Guidebook* there are suggestions about how they can be helped.

The Second Level: Working With "Type A" People

Developing "Young Men" at the second level requires giving them experience. One characteristic of being immature is impatience. When children want something, they are not able to wait. They want it—now! This is also true with younger Christians who have not yet learned how to wait. It is best to give immature Christians a ministry which will produce quick results.

To do this, the Shepherd group helps them to minister to "Type A" unbelievers— persons who are totally open to the gospel and to the church. These persons have visited Celebration Services and have asked to be visited. The names have been passed on to the Shepherd Group for further contact and ministry, perhaps because of age, geographical location, etc.

These contacts provide experience in meeting people, sharing in their needs, and inviting them to become a part of the Shepherd Group. If they are not yet Christians, it is often because no one has explained to them how they can receive Christ as Lord and Savior.

Knocking On Doors, Opening Hearts has been written to equip those who will participate in this ministry. The course expects the one being discipled to actually make visits with his or her sponsor. Thus, it provides "on the job training" for those who are doing this for the first time.

The Third Level: Working With Type "B" People

"Fathers" are equipped by involving them with the hard to reach. The Type "B" unbelievers are not searching for Jesus Christ and show no interest in Bible study or other Christian activities. Only mature Christians able to patiently minister can reach them. Like a mother with child, this "Special Forces" team must carry the burden of Type "B" unbelievers tor many months before seeing them born again. Deliverance may be required as well.

This equipping is achieved by forming a *second* small group called a "Share Group." As shown on page 213, the Share Group meets *separately* from the Shepherd Group. These mature Christians will have two group meetings to attend weekly: their Shepherd Group and their Share Group. Each week, this Share Group team will move from house to house, involving "hard core" unbelievers in discussions chosen to bring them closer to accepting Christ as Lord and Savior. *(More on this in the next chapter.)*

The commitment of time required to meet with *both* the Shepherd Group and the Share Group is significant. Only mature Christians who have "put away lesser things" can devote themselves to this dedicated life style.

Experience has shown that once a Christian has entered into Share Group ministry, he rapidly matures in the Lord. He will be thrust into new levels of faith which make possible God's further calling to become a Shepherd.

TOUCH Basic Training has been written to equip these "green berets" of God's army. The team conducts a Share Group between each equipping session. The course is twenty weeks in length and is always taken by teams, not by individuals. Five days of daily devotionals reinforce the experiences provided in the weekly training times. Once again, "on-the-job training" guarantees maximum effectiveness.

When It's Time To Multiply

In all probability, in about six months a Shepherd Group will have grown to fifteen members, and it will be necessary to multiply it into two cells. At that time, the Servant Intern must be capable of shepherding half the group. From the very first week the cell meets, the Intern should be preparing for this time.

The pattern for this is found in 2 Timothy 2:2:

> *And the things you have heard me say in the presence of many witnesses entrust to reliable men who will also be qualified to teach others.*

Consider the pattern of sharing which is described by Paul. His equipping was seldom if ever done using a "one on one" pattern. He refers to the "many witnesses" present as he worked with Timothy. Both Jesus and Paul discipled men in small groups, rather than "one-by-one." Thus, the Servant Intern is equipped in the presence of the entire Shepherd Group. In this way, the members observe how the Shepherd equips the Intern. Since each of them is also developing someone, the Shepherd will be modelling how it is done.

The most ineffective way of developing your Servant Intern is by using one of the many discipleship courses available. Christianity in America, Australia, New Zealand, and Britain is saturated with notebooks, study guides, and lesson plans. Those who have spent months using this pattern of discipleship usually end up having good *devotions,* but few people have actually developed the capacity to shepherd others. The reason is obvious: *shepherding is not taught; it's caught.* That's why Paul wrote,

> ...*our gospel came to you not simply with words, but also with power, with the Holy Spirit and with deep conviction. You know how we lived among you for your sake. You became imitators of us and of the Lord; in spite of severe suffering, you welcomed the message with the joy given by the Holy Spirit. And so you became a model to all the believers in Macedonia and Achaia.*[4]

Here's the pattern for apprenticing, taken from the *Shepherd's Guidebook*:

1. Your Intern watches you.
2. You explain what you did, and why you did it.
3. You observe as your apprentice does the same thing.
4. You objectively explain strengths and weaknesses you have observed.
5. You provide remedial activity to strengthen the weaknesses.
6. You turn the task over to the Intern.
7. You withdraw, using "benign neglect" as your strategy.
8. You closely monitor as your apprentice disciples a new Intern.
9. You remain a close friend, now treating your Intern as your equal.

How Do You Measure Spiritual Growth?

Measuring maturity is tricky! I have two grandchildren who live in California. We get to see them two or three times a year. When they come bouncing into the house, the first sign of change we observe is their physical growth. Grandma says, "Ruthie! You have grown three inches!" Little Ruthie beams with pride—as though she had personally triumphed over being smaller! We notice she no longer throws food on the floor. Mother lets her feed herself. She asks to go to the bathroom. Marvelous!

After a few hours with my grandson, I think: "Nathan's vocabulary has grown. He's writing new words, and he's also learning new facts. His little mind has grown."

At the close of a meal my son says to them, "Let's recite our scripture verses for Maw Maw and Paw Paw." I listen as they speak the memorized words, rejoicing that spiritual foundations have been laid within them.

Then they get tired. Ruthie screams like a banshee when Nathan takes her favorite toy. He changes his cherubic facial expression, and glowers with selfishness. She throws another toy at him. Oh, dear! They are, indeed, still immature babies. I take Nathan to my office and say, "Nathan, you are a big boy now. Why do you still steal Ruthie's toys? You are too old to act like that."

He looks at me in stony silence. My mature words are not in his childish vocabulary; I am wasting my breath on him. Sadly, I realize such conversations between us are years away...

How do we measure maturity in these children? By knowing where they were, by seeing where they are, and by discerning where they must develop.

These same guidelines apply to those in the cell group. Where have they been? Are they responsible for their own lives, or are they controlled by circumstances? Do they know who they are in God? Do the decisions and choices they make reveal a God-centered value system? Are their jokes reflecting carnal aspersions to sexuality? Do they pray "on command," not at all, or with an appetite for fellowship with the Father? Edification is unique for all persons. It will be based on *where they have been, and where they are.*

Being Mature Is Measured By Being Responsible

The extent of a person's spiritual maturity is the extent of the commitment he or she has to Kingdom activity. This way of measuring maturity is most important. The Shepherd's assignment can be reduced to one simple statement: *encourage flock members to be totally responsible for properly exercising their spiritual gifts.*

Traditional church life robs the believer of being responsible. The pastor does all the Bible study for the congregation, and shares his findings in the auditorium. The Christian is never exposed to Biblical content in its entirety, never encouraged to purchase a basic set of books for personal research and study. When the believer has problems, he is given advice about what to do. If he has an illness, someone comes to pray at the hospital bedside. If a friend needs to accept Jesus, an appointment is made for him with the pastor.

Dealing With Strongholds

The weapons we fight with are not the weapons of the world. On the contrary, they have divine power to demolish strongholds. We demolish arguments and every pretension that sets itself up against the knowledge of God, and we take captive every thought to make it obedient to Christ.[5]

The word for "stronghold" used in this passage describes a well established, strongly defended fortress. It guards the entrance to a territory or to a trade route.

Strongholds are the enemy of growth. With the Intern, the Shepherd will want to find private times with individual members to deal with strongholds. These times are crucial to the deliverance of Christians who have spent years wandering in the swamps of immaturity and defeat.

The use of the *Journey Guide* provides a perfect environment to discuss these areas of defeat in the life of the believer. It should be used as quickly as possible when a new member joins the group. A vital part of the journey is challenging fortresses!

Daily Relationships And Shepherd Group Size

A Shepherd Group has a formal weekly gathering, but its life is actually embedded in the daily relationships and mutual sharing of life which is made possible by its existence. For that reason, its size simply must not exceed fifteen persons, but that's not the critical factor. More important is participation. There must be an adequate involvement of all the members in the life of the group. When the community grows larger than fifteen, this becomes difficult.

The Shepherd Group is a Christian community. Jesus Christ has formed these living cells, and He is truly their Head. Perhaps you have experienced, or have observed, small groups in the church that sprang up quickly and disappeared just as rapidly. The reason? There was no true community: no renewal of persons, no ministry, no sacrificial love for others. These groups were simply *meetings,* regularly gathering on Sunday or Wednesday nights to "do their thing." Sometimes they piously revelled in their spirituality while ignoring the need-filled people around them. No room was made for the cross.

"Kinning"—As In *"Kinfolks"*

"Kinning" is creating true Christian community, where people become "Kinfolks" to one another. The cell must be a place where one is always welcome, no matter what stupid decision has been made in the past or the present. It's a place where crotchety, disagreeable, thankless old sinners are welcomed and challenged to be free from their inner strongholds. Praise and worship shape the cell's personality. The Lord's Supper, prayer, the Word of God, are vital to its lifestyle. It is *missionary,* reaching out to others until it must multiply and become two cells.

As people gather to form the group, there's no fixed pattern for how they will adjust to community life. All must start from where they are. Some will have had prior experiences of living and working together in the spirit of community, while others will find the entire experience a brand new lifestyle. Those who have never been a part of a warm family, who have lived lives of self-sufficiency for many years, or who have been betrayed in trust relationships, will need special encouragement.

"Kinning" takes many forms—as many as there are individual personalities. People cannot be developed by others; they must develop themselves. All others can do is provide the environment for this to take place. That's why it's important for the Shepherd to quickly provide specific tasks and ministries for all who are entering the cell group. Remember—becoming *mature* means becoming *responsible.* A person who is being useful is feeling worthwhile. Those who are simply expected to "be present" will soon fade away.

Like a marriage, after the honeymoon the group will have to work hard if the relationships are to be successful. The gold, silver, and precious stones in a Shepherd Group will not be found sitting on the surface. To discover them, there must be the digging out of deep spiritual relationships.

Shepherd Groups Multiply!

Only stagnation and spiritual bankruptcy can keep Shepherd Groups from growing! They will multiply, as we have said repeatedly, in about six months of time. As they do, Satan's domain has been penetrated and Christ has claimed His rightful ownership once again!

You are urged to read the *Shepherd's Guidebook* in conjunction with this chapter. Large blocks of this material have been reproduced from it, but there is much, much more in it for you to discover!

---

15 THE DYNAMICS OF SHEPHERD GROUPS

Architect Eugene Seow is one of scores of men who have caught a vision as he served as a Shepherd in a cell group. Even as I write this, he is winding down his professional practice to join us on the staff of the Faith Community Baptist Church.

After months of experience in shepherding groups and seeing them multiply, he was made responsible for the equipping of incoming Shepherds. As he reflected on the challenge of imparting his experience, his architectural training took over. He developed charts that make the dynamics of Shepherd group life clearer than I have ever seen them described. I joyfully share a series of charts with you, edited from his work, which show the pitfalls of not properly guiding the groups in their sessions together.

A lack of preparation for the Shepherd group meeting is inexcuseable! Each segment must be prayerfully, carefully developed using the concepts presented in this chapter. As Eugene Seow said to me, "If one cell group session ends at a low mood level, some will not desire to return. The Shepherd will pay a price for this, and will have to work doubly hard in the next meeting to build up the group again."

Mr. Seow has developed both a "Micro" and "Macro" look at the life of a cell. His Micro chart presents the actual Shepherd group meeting; the Macro charts describe the stages the group goes through from the time of launching until it is ready to multiply. We are going to dissect the primary charts as we explain how things *should* go, and present charts which explain what will happen if things are *not* done properly. There truly is a skill in being a Shepherd—a skill which is *caught,* not *taught.*

Like anything else worthwhile in life, there is a "learning curve" before a person becomes effective in leading a Shepherd group. While Shepherd skills are developing, the preparation time required is greater than it will be when they are mastered. Shepherds who come to group meetings fully equipped in spirit and in mind will bless everyone involved. *God honors preparation!* In spite of the time required to develop into an effective facilitator, the true Shepherd will rejoice to see lives changed through his or her ministry to the cell.

Keeping a diary of the dynamics in the meetings and what happened during the weeks is extremely helpful in solving problem areas. These notes can be shared with the Zone Servant, who can give helpful counsel.

In a few months, what seemed awkward at the first will be mastered. Then the Shepherd can concentrate on the *ministry* side of his or her work without worrying about how to use the tools. In the beginning stages of launching a cell group church, it's important for the leadership to have previous experience in small

WHAT IS THE AGENDA FOR A SHEPHERD GROUP MEETING?

This is thoroughly covered in the *Shepherd's Guidebook.*

It also contains examples of how meetings should be conducted.

It also shows the stages in Shepherd group life which are depicted in the graphs which follow.

Order one from us today!

group dynamics. While it's possible to read books on the subject, there's no substitute for experiencing the group process. Those who have done so will tell you that groups build to a peak as the session goes on. In the case of a Shepherd group, there are four important stages:

The first is called the "Ice Breaker Stage." It has two parts to it. First, light refreshments should always *precede* the launching of the group meeting. As people arrive, this provides an informal gathering point. When all have arrived, chit-chat ends as the Shepherd calls the group to be seated. He uses a question which is totally non-threatening. My favorite can be used week after week: "Share the most important thing that has happened to you since we last met." It's important that *all* present participate in this, guaranteeing there will be no silent people in the group.

The second is the "Worship Stage." After relationships have been established between those present, there must be a bonding between the Body and the Head. It takes some skill and experience to create an effective worship period in a cell group. This is a topic so important it deserves a separate book! You will notice on the graphs which follow that the group hits its highest peak as Christ enters their midst in all His glory.

The third is the "Edification Stage." The group focuses on the needs of those present, and/or the special work Christ wishes to do in and through the group. While scripture is a vital part of this period, it must be stressed that the focus is on using the Bible as a tool, not the focal point. *The people present are the focal point.* The manifestation of spiritual gifts which build up the members present is vital, as is total participation.

The fourth is the "Share The Vision Stage." This will *always* focus the attention of the group on their calling, the vision of the cell group church, and their ministry to unbelievers. As the first graph shows, this should be the highest point of bonding in the entire session. If people leave with a vision, they will feel Christ has been in their midst in a very special way.

Let's look at the graphs, described by Mr. Seow as "prescriptive, not descriptive." By helping the Shepherd anticipate both the macro and micro stages, problems may be avoided. They are designed to help in the planning for effective meetings and the effective multiplication of the Shepherd group.

FIGURE 1

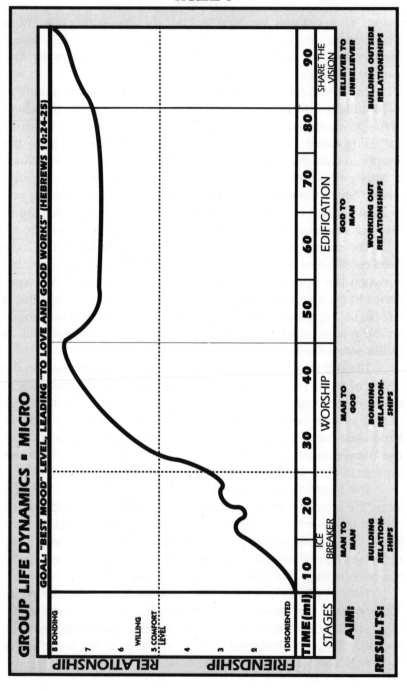

THE MICRO LOOK

A Shepherd group session will pass through several stages, as indicated on this chart. This is an example of a perfectly guided session.

The goal of the meeting is taken from Hebrews 10:24-25, which encourages the people of God to arouse fellow believers to love and active goodness, encouraging each other. The aim is to *build relationships,* not just to conduct a meeting by following a purposeless agenda. To be prepared for this task, there are two key steps which must precede the period of edification.

The first stage is called the "Ice Breaker" time. It's a time for folks to feel comfortable together, to "shift gears" from whatever has been occupying their thoughts. It's a time of saying, "I'm here for you, and I accept that you're here for me."

After the relationships between those present have been established, it's time for the group to come into the presence of their King and worship him. Bonding the group to Christ is crucial for the time of edification which follows. "Man to Man," then "Man to God" are two phrases which will help you remember the pattern. Note the time frames set forth. The vertical lines which are dotted indicate the *flexibility* of these two time frames.

When the group has been bonded with one another and with Christ, the level of edification can begin. To end the meeting on a high note, Mr. Seow recommends that the SHARE THE VISION segment of the agenda be placed at the very close. (Prayer, of course, has been a vital part of the edification period.)

His experience as a Shepherd verifies for him the importance of leaving the cell on the thoughts related to reaching out. He developed a barbecue every six weeks for his cell—a time for them to bring seekers or other unbelievers to be introduced to community. Such special events, along with the visitation ministry and the Share group ministry, are the focus of the final period,. As the chart shows, the meeting ends on the very highest level, and people are looking forward to their next get-together even as the present one ends.

FIGURE 2

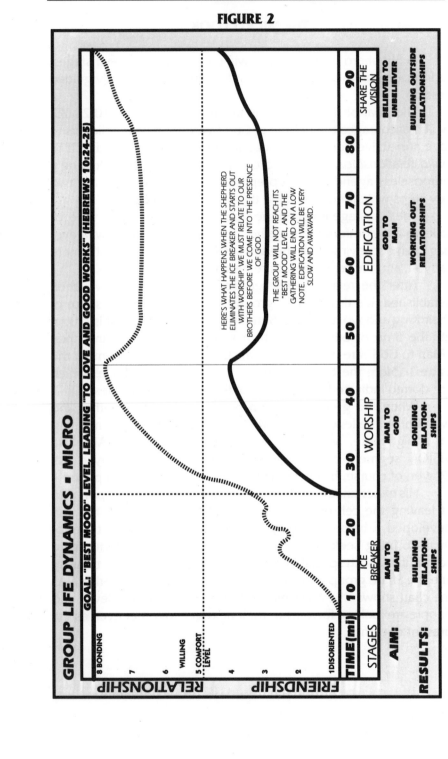

FIGURE 3

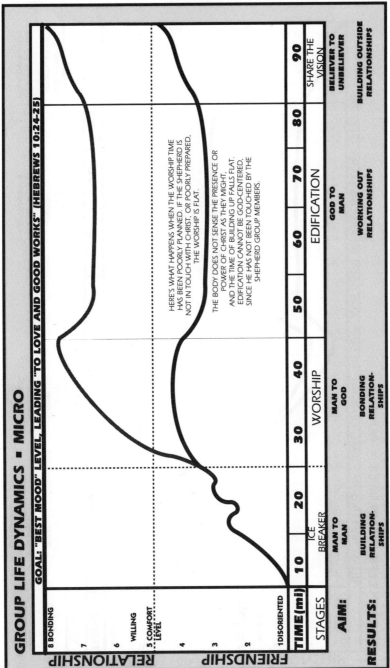

FIGURE 4

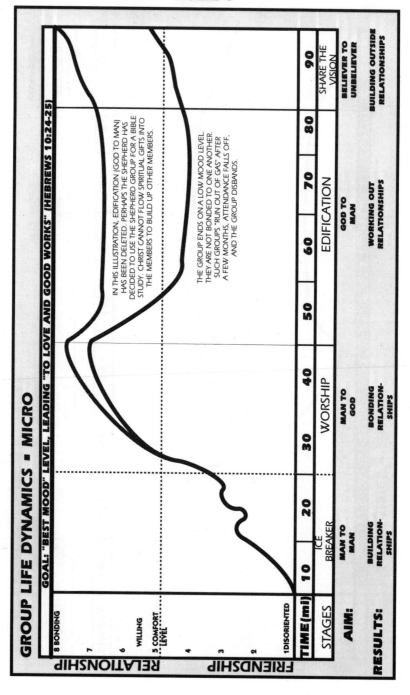

GROUP LIFE DYNAMICS ▪ MICRO

GOAL: "BEST MOOD" LEVEL, LEADING "TO LOVE AND GOOD WORKS" (HEBREWS 10:24-25)

IN THIS ILLUSTRATION, EDIFICATION (GOD TO MAN) HAS BEEN DELETED. PERHAPS THE SHEPHERD HAS DECIDED TO USE THE SHEPHERD GROUP FOR A BIBLE STUDY. CHRIST CANNOT FLOW 'SPIRITUAL GIFTS' INTO THE MEMBERS TO BUILD UP OTHER MEMBERS.

THE GROUP ENDS ON A LOW MOOD LEVEL. THEY ARE NOT BONDED TO ONE ANOTHER. SUCH GROUPS "RUN OUT OF GAS" AFTER A FEW MONTHS, ATTENDANCE FALLS OFF, AND THE GROUP DISBANDS.

TIME (mi)	10	20	30	40	50	60	70	80	90
STAGES	ICE BREAKER		WORSHIP		EDIFICATION				SHARE THE VISION
AIM:	MAN TO MAN		MAN TO GOD		GOD TO MAN				BELIEVER TO UNBELIEVER
RESULTS:	BUILDING RELATION-SHIPS		BONDING RELATION-SHIPS		WORKING OUT RELATIONSHIPS				BUILDING OUTSIDE RELATIONSHIPS

RELATIONSHIP

8 BONDING
7
6 WILLING
5 COMFORT LEVEL
4
3
2
1 DISORIENTED

FRIENDSHIP

FIGURE 5

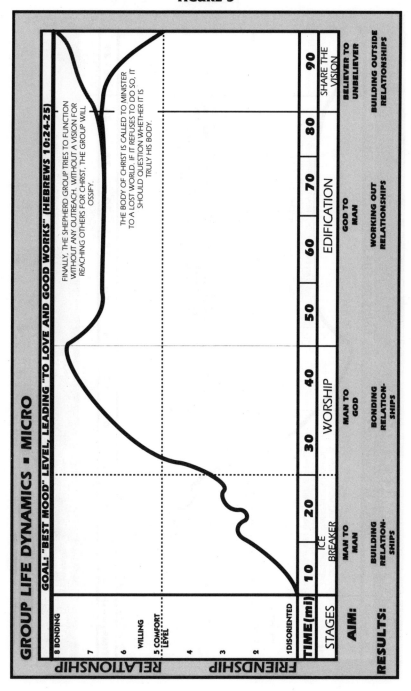

FIGURE 6

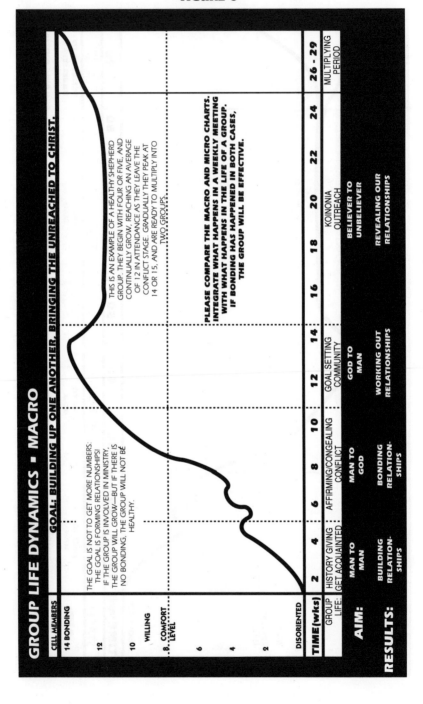

GROUP LIFE DYNAMICS - MACRO

GOAL: BUILDING UP ONE ANOTHER, BRINGING THE UNREACHED TO CHRIST.

THE GOAL IS NOT TO GET MORE NUMBERS! THE GOAL IS FORMING RELATIONSHIPS! IF THE GROUP IS INVOLVED IN MINISTRY, THE GROUP WILL GROW—BUT IF THERE IS NO BONDING, THE GROUP WILL NOT BE HEALTHY.

THIS IS AN EXAMPLE OF A HEALTHY SHEPHERD GROUP. THEY BEGIN WITH FOUR OR FIVE, AND CONTINUALLY GROW, REACHING AN AVERAGE OF 12 IN ATTENDANCE AS THEY LEAVE THE CONFLICT STAGE. GRADUALLY THEY PEAK AT 14 OR 15, AND ARE READY TO MULTIPLY INTO TWO GROUPS.

PLEASE COMPARE THE MACRO AND MICRO CHARTS. INTEGRATE WHAT HAPPENS IN A WEEKLY MEETING WITH WHAT HAPPENS IN THE LIFE OF A GROUP. IF BONDING HAS HAPPENED IN BOTH CASES, THE GROUP WILL BE EFFECTIVE.

TIME(wks):	2	4	6	8	10	12	14	16	18	20	22	24	26 - 29
GROUP LIFE:	HISTORY GIVING GET ACQUAINTED		AFFIRMING/CONGEALING CONFLICT			GOAL SETTING COMMUNITY			KOINONIA OUTREACH				MULTIPLYING PERIOD
AIM:	MAN TO MAN		MAN TO GOD			GOD TO MAN			BELIEVER TO UNBELIEVER				
RESULTS:	BUILDING RELATION-SHIPS		BONDING RELATION-SHIPS			WORKING OUT RELATIONSHIPS			REVEALING OUR RELATIONSHIPS				

CELL MEMBERS: 14 BONDING, 12, 10 WILLING, 8 COMFORT LEVEL, 6, 4, 2, DISORIENTED

THE MACRO LOOK

The Macro charts provide signs to *look out for,* and *goals to move toward* as the weeks progress. In each case, the signs are indications of *relationships* being established and *community* being formed. There are five stages to the development of a Shepherd group from birth to multiplication.

A healthy Shepherd Group should multiply in about six months in the United States. It will vary with the hardness of the soil being penetrated, of course, and with the experience of the team leadership.

In this first graph, the left bar shows the number of cell members who are attending. Often the number of people who have attended one or more times may be double this figure. All should be contacted by phone each week, whether they are attending regularly or not. Note that there's a lot of "coming and going" in the first eight weeks. People decide whether they are in their "comfort zone" during this period of time. Gradually, the group stabilizes.

At the end of ten or twelve weeks, the group will have passed through the Affirming/Congealing/Conflict Stage and will move into the period of living in love together. This introduces the deep times of building up one another, with spiritual gifts exercised in a special manner.

It is at this time the cell seriously begins to reach out to unbelievers. The visitation team and the Share Group team are engrossed in their ministries, and growth is solidified as new people are brought into the "mix" of a stabilized community. The harvest replaces those who were earlier a part of the group but dropped out for one reason or another. These dropouts may be the result of a job change, moving to a new area, a death or serious illness in the family, etc. Although such persons do not now show on the attendance chart shown here, they may be considered a part of the ministry of the cell if they have not moved far away.

Shepherd Interns must be ready to guide half the group when it is multiplied in six months. This position is so important that no group should ever be launched without *both* a Shepherd and a Shepherd Intern from the very beginning.

FIGURE 7

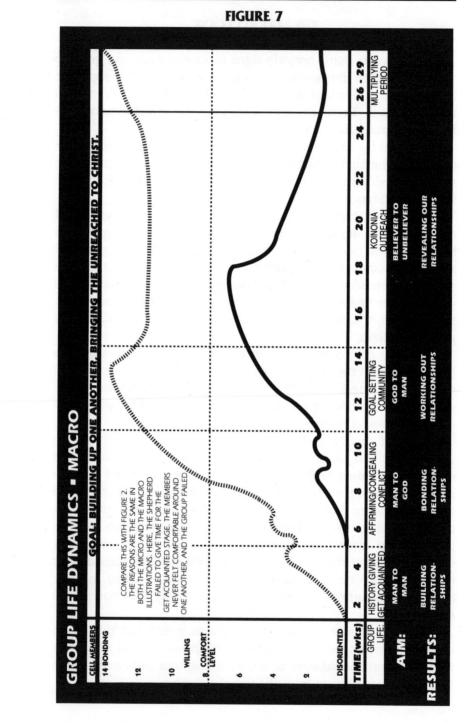

FIGURE 8

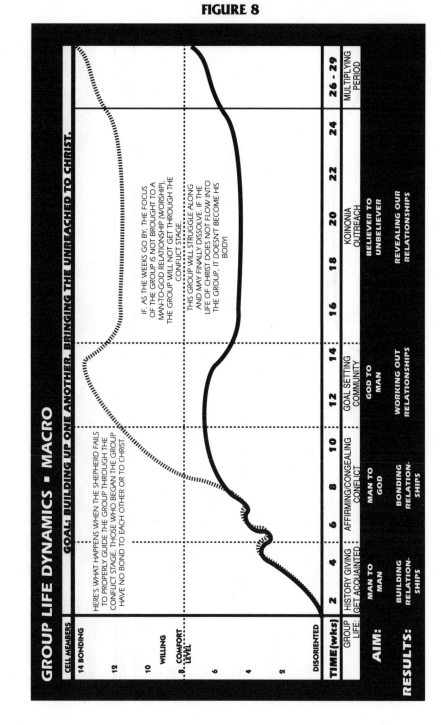

GROUP LIFE DYNAMICS – MACRO

GOAL: BUILDING UP ONE ANOTHER, BRINGING THE UNREACHED TO CHRIST.

CELL MEMBERS

14 BONDING

12

WILLING

10

8 COMFORT LEVEL

6

4

2

DISORIENTED

HERE'S WHAT HAPPENS WHEN THE SHEPHERD FAILS TO PROPERLY GUIDE THE GROUP THROUGH THE CONFLICT STAGE. THOSE WHO BEGAN THE GROUP HAVE NO BOND TO EACH OTHER OR TO CHRIST.

IF, AS THE WEEKS GO BY, THE FOCUS OF THE GROUP IS NOT BROUGHT TO A MAN-TO-GOD RELATIONSHIP (WORSHIP), THE GROUP WILL NOT GET THROUGH THE CONFLICT STAGE.

THIS GROUP WILL STRUGGLE ALONG AND MAY FINALLY DISSOLVE. IF THE LIFE OF CHRIST DOES NOT FLOW INTO THE GROUP, IT DOESN'T BECOME HIS BODY!

TIME [wks]	2	4	6	8	10	12	14	16	18	20	22	24	26 – 29
GROUP LIFE:	HISTORY GIVING GET ACQUAINTED		AFFIRMING/CONGEALING CONFLICT			GOAL SETTING COMMUNITY			KOINONIA OUTREACH				MULTIPLYING PERIOD
AIM:	MAN TO MAN		MAN TO GOD			GOD TO MAN			BELIEVER TO UNBELIEVER				
RESULTS:	BUILDING RELATION- SHIPS		BONDING RELATION- SHIPS			WORKING OUT RELATIONSHIPS			REVEALING OUR RELATIONSHIPS				

FIGURE 9

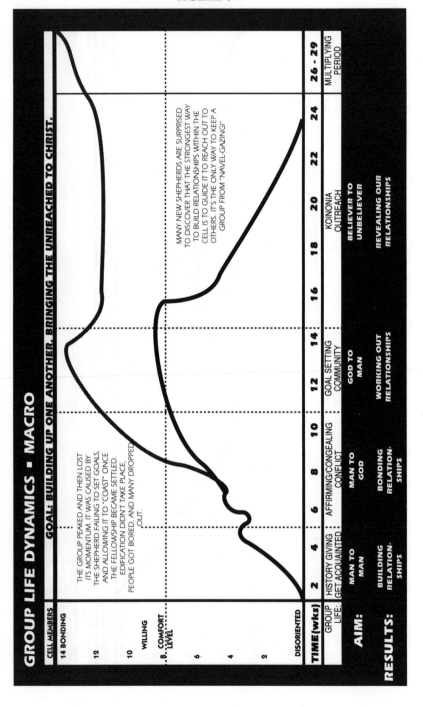

FIGURE 10

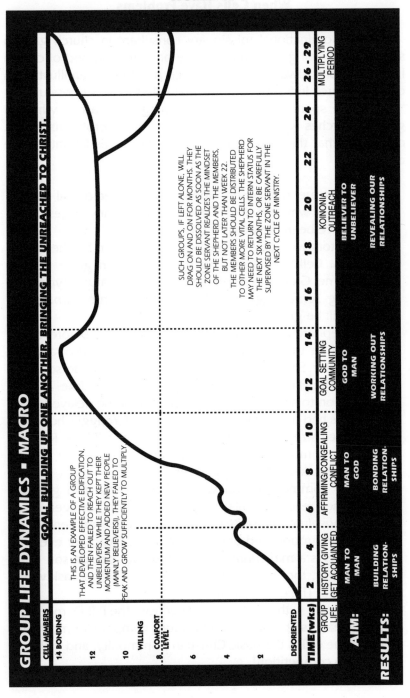

When Cells Have Problems

A denominational missionary consultant in church growth said to me, "Cell group churches are only one method of church life. They don't always work." He then pointed out an illustration of a cell church in South America that failed to be successful.

I have spent many years examining the reasons why cell group churches grow, and why they have problems. I am convinced that the reasons behind the difficulties fall into these categories:

1. The cells are not based upon a solid theological under- standing of why they exist. This is why so many pages of this book have been devoted to this area.
2. The pastors who develop cells are using them for the wrong motives. Cells developed to make a church grow will fail every time! Growth is never a goal—it's the natural byproduct of *doing something right!* Where there's true *community,* there will be growth.
3. The Shepherds were not properly equipped before being released for their ministry. The six month period of appren- ticeship for Shepherd Interns is critical. If the person isn't going to be effective, it will show up during that time, and the promotion to serving as a Shepherd should be delayed.
4. The cells had no zeal for the lost. Many of Yonggi Cho's cells *triple* their size through people won to Christ. If Dion Robert's cells go a month without a conversion, there are serious questions asked about its lifestyle.
5. A most common reason why cell churches stop growing when they reach 25 cells is that no attention has been given to the *absolute necessity* of providing one Zone Servant for every five groups, and one full time Zone Pastor for every 25 cells. This is a *maximum* case load for any one person. It's a major error, too, to assign a Zone Pastor another task within church life. The cells will suffer!
6. Competition with cell life leaks over from the P.B.D. mentality of the leadership. Other organizations compete for member's time. The cell is the Basic Christian Community, and it should have no competition!

16 CELL EVANGELISM EXPLAINED

As the illustration on page 213 indicates, reaching out to the unbeliever is as important to the life of the effective Shepherd group as is edification. No true discipleship or spiritual growth will occur among Christians who are not involved in ministry to a broken world.

Since the Christian life is *caught,* not *taught,* imagine the impact made in an environment where even the newest Christians are reaching out to others. In a traditional church, it's quite difficult for a newcomer to actually observe others involved in evangelism. In a cell group, the focus is placed on personal growth with a *motive*—winning the lost!

The form of evangelism which is used is significantly different from contemporary styles of faith-sharing. It is important to grasp the contrast before proceeding further with our study of the cell church.

True Cell Group Churches Avoid
Impersonal Evangelism Patterns

I have already shared my deep concern about the evangelism strategy within traditional church structures. Think about this fact: evangelism methods have changed very little in the last half-century. Denominations known for being evangelistic (many are not, of course!) report steadily declining harvests. *How long do we keep on doing what doesn't work before we admit we have a problem?*

In my book *Future Church,* Os Guiness reminds us of an old Chinese proverb: "Never ask a fish what water is like." If you want to understand the limitation of evangelism methods used in traditional churches, don't talk to an evangelist or the instructors of commercially sold evangelism programs! *Talk to the unreached pagan.* Get out of the fishbowl and talk to those the traditional church has not touched. You will learn an important fact quickly: *the evangelism strategy of the traditional church is totally out of sync with our society.* It continues to assume everyone in America has a belief system similar to that held by we evangelicals.

Consider the problems we cause by the non-relational, insensitive use of personal evangelism methods now being used. A popular lead-in question demonstrates the issue clearly: "If you were to die today, and God were to say, 'Why should I let you into my heaven?' what would your answer be?"

I'm not critical of that question; I frequently use it myself. It's appropriate to use it with the *"like us" people*—the folks who will come on Sunday mornings to traditional church services. I sometimes use it with a stranger on an airplane. As have others, I have also seen strangers come to accept Christ on the spot. But always, *always,* I use that question *only* when I am sure I am speaking to a searching heart who is versed in Bible truths and open to God's good news.

It is the height of absurdity to assume that all *unchurched* people find that question relevant.

If you were to die today..."

Tens of thousands of unbelievers do not *believe* in a life after death. The question assumes too much!

If you were to die today...and God..."

What does this person think when you say the word "God?" Alcoholics Anonymous has recognized for years the wide variations in the way the word "God" is used in America. They skirt the problem by referring to Him as "your higher power, however you choose to define him." I strongly disagree with their approach as a Christian. Man doesn't have the freedom to define "God" by personal choice. However, in a pluralistic society *my* definition of God is *not necessarily held by others.* We are kidding ourselves when we use the word "God" and think every listener will define Him as Jehovah, our loving Father who has sent His son to redeem us from our sin.

I was in a Share group with a number of students attending the University of South Carolina. Among them was a Japanese girl who had just arrived in the United States. We were sharing the "Quaker Questions" as an Ice Breaker. The final question asks, "When did God become more than a word to you?" She couldn't comprehend the question. A fine Japanese Christian in the group slipped into their mother tongue and explained what the question was asking. I shall never forget her response! She closed her eyes, shook her head to the right, waving her hand to the left. It was her way of saying, "I have nothing in my frame of reference on this subject."

...and God...were to say..."

Say?" God talks to mortals? To us, God is personal; He talks to us. Millions understand God as an impersonal force within an impersonal universe. The idea that He is relational is not believed by them.

...why should I let you into my heaven?"

Theological assumptions: there is a heaven, there is a hell, there is a judgment. I tell you from years of dialogue with unchurched unbelievers that thousands of them do not share *any* of those assumptions, particularly that there is a final judgment and an eternal hell.

I repeat: I am in full agreement with using that question with those who are living *within a Christian orientation,* and certainly with anyone at all who is searching for peace and is open to listen. But the idiocy of using it with the secular person who does not share our Christian orientation ought to be obvious. To talk to a stranger *you* do not know, about a God and a Christ *he* does not know, and to think that 20 minutes of memorized explanations without prior discussion will trigger a desire in that person to become a believer, is patently absurd.

Would you agree to *marry* someone in that manner? Is not committing your life both now and forever even more important? Or, would you even commit yourself in advance to a *lifelong friendship* with a stranger? Then, why do we think disoriented unbelievers will respond in great masses to this approach? Nevertheless, this technique remains the primary "formal pattern" of evangelism in traditional churches. It continues because we absurdly hold the false assumption that all uncon- verted persons believe as we do.

As long as we remain in the traditional church and seek to evangelize only the "like us" people, this method presents little problem. However, the cell group churches are committed to *touching the unchurched,* and they have a *big* problem in using this technique!

What About Life BEFORE Death?

Have you ever wondered why the first question to the unbeliever has to jump from the here-and-now to life after death? *Why* does our offer of the Gospel have to start with life after death? *It is because what we have to offer the new convert in this life is a bit embarrassing to us.* That's not really true *if* the Bride of Christ is what it ought to be.

Jesus' focus was on the *here,* not just the *hereafter.* His concern was for those who are *now* poor, blind, imprisoned, and trampled upon. If we are His body to perform His work, His power should be flowing through us to *make this life new, right now!*

Look at the back page of any of the evangelism booklets or tracts. *After* the prayer of commitment on the inside back cover, *then* they suggest the convert find a good Bible-teaching church and join it. It seems we are a bit embarrassed at what we have to recommend to them between the moment of conversion and the Second Coming. Where Body life doesn't exist, the church is not a part of the Gospel message: it's a tack-on.

A Pure Church Has A Purer Evangelistic Message

In the Cell Group church, we have the rich treasure of the life of Christ being embodied in the here-and-now. So precious is it that one man in our congregation in Houston used to regularly fly in from California or New York to meet with his cell, returning the next morning to the tasks he left unfinished. Thus, the offer of salvation for the Cell Group evangelist is: *"How would you like to experience the down payment of what Christ has reserved for you in eternity? You can begin to do so...right now! You can enter the Kingdom of God's love and discover what His family is like this very minute. It's awesome!"*

A proper church life opens dimensions of evangelism not known in traditional church structures. The opportunity to first know an unbeliever in depth opens the way for the message of Christ to be inserted as a *value,* not just a piece of information. Bit by bit in the Share group and in personal times together, the unbeliever begins to comprehend the joy of a life in Christ. He or she begins to question the Christian about spiritual truth, and the flow of reality begins. It continues through both discussion and observation.

One of my favorite phrases to use in the last stages as an unbeliever comes to Christ is to ask, "Bill, knowing all you have come to know about the life in Christ, and considering all you have already come to accept as true, is it possible for you to turn around and walk away from Him?" One dear Jewish convert told me he felt like I had struck him in the chest when I asked that question. He thought for a moment and said, "When you put it that way, I see I am caught and there is no escape."

Instead of giving him a "canned presentation," I asked him, "Okay. Let's start with God. What do you believe about Him?" As we worked our way conversationally through all the Biblical truths which are foundational to a conversion experience, we continued to dialogue. This was not the time for a lecture. It was a time for us to struggle together to find the pieces which were and which were not in place in his understanding.

When we finished, we found we had journeyed together to the Cross. I said, "Marvin, your last steps must be taken on your own. I will pray as you approach your Lord and exchange your present life for His eternal one. He will now indwell you, and His Holy Spirit will baptize you into His Body. When you return from the Cross, we will no longer be friends. We will eternally be blood brothers!"

Two General Classes Of Unbelievers

Scriptures refer to *"those who are far away, and those who are near."*[1] Unbelievers who are "far away" have no comprehension of the gospel message. Unbelievers who are "near" are aware of the truth about God as shared in scripture, and will be found filling out guest cards in the Celebrations or Congregations. They are two distinct groups, and must be ministered to in distinctly different ways. Their prior knowledge, or lack of it, is the key to classifying them in one of these two categories. For example, an unbeliever may say, "I believe all people who are sincere will make it to heaven. Buddhists, Baptists, *everyone.*"

The following description is quoted from *Knocking On Doors, Opening Hearts,* the equipping manual to train those in the Shepherd group who are learning to work with the "Soft Core" unbelievers:

Two types of unbelievers: that's right—two types! Later, we'll subdivide them again into three stages of Type "A's" and two stages of Type "B's." First, let's learn about "A" and "B" types...

Type "A" Unbelievers: The "Like Us" People, Easily Reached

1. They have attended a Celebration or Congregation meeting, and have been referred to you because they signed a visitor's card.
2. They already believe in God, accept the Bible, understand that Jesus is the Son of God, and have some awareness of scripture facts (like Christ's death on the cross).
3. They may already have a church membership somewhere, but are inactive—perhaps have been so for years.
4. They are searching for something, and have come to our congregation in their search.
5. They may not have all the "pieces of the puzzle" in place as far as Christian knowledge is concerned.
6. Bible Study, and explaining the plan of Salvation, are appropriate activities to share with them.

...these people are reached through visitation!

Type "B" Unbelievers: "Hidden" People, Needing Cultivation

1. They seldom attend church; have no desire to do so.
2. They may not believe in God, do not accept the Bible, do not understand Jesus is the Son of God, and have very little awareness of scripture truths.
3. They have no active church membership.
4. They are not searching for the Lord's purpose for their lives, and have no intention of visiting church activities.
5. They have very few of the "pieces of the puzzle" in place as far as Christian knowledge is concerned.
6. Bible Study or discussing the plan of Salvation aren't appro-

priate activities to do with them at the start. There must first be a time of developing relationships—exposing them to the reality of the living Christ in our own lives.

...these people are reached through Share groups!

This Pyramid Further Illustrates Type "A" and Type "B"

Those at the Type "A" levels are open to the message we have to share. A special NIV New Testament has been prepared to provide a "programmed learning" tool for one-on-one Bible study that "fills in the blanks" for the unbeliever. It is used by the person who has visited him or her, and has developed a personal relationship as the foundation for close sharing. At the top of the pyramid, the person is ready to make a commitment, and the cell group member is trained to help in this wonderful moment.

The progress toward Christ is much slower with Type "B" unbelievers. Patience and continued ministry through Share group life will bring many out of their spiritual blindness into the reality of Christ's love.

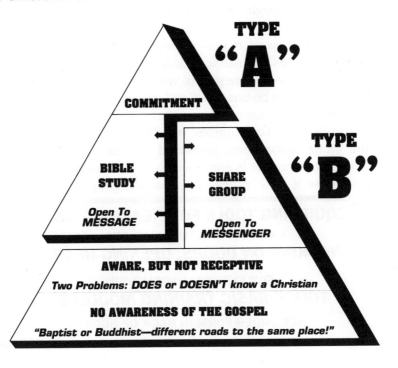

While there are many evangelistic patterns in the world of traditional churches, 99% of them focus solely on Type "A" people. This is logical: they are the only type who invade the private world of the Christians. Over 20 years of writing, testing, rewriting, and revising have been invested in the *Touch Ministries Seminar* and *Touch Basic Training* equipping materials. Along with *Knocking On Doors, Opening Hearts,* they fully prepare a Christian to minister at all five levels found among unbelievers. It is possible, through the application of this equipping in the cell, to fully train a new believer in a year's time to sow, cultivate, and harvest. This is not done through classes taught by pastors, but by the members of the cell learning and then sharing what they have learned with other cell members. The pattern must be a tight combination of *participating* together in ministry, and *studying* the affective materials of the courses.

The *"Oikos"* Family Of Words

Three words which belong to the *Oikos* family are helpful to the cell group trainee in evangelism. The first is the mother word, *Oikos.* It's the key to making contacts naturally, evangelizing those who are brought into our lives through the people we know.

The second word is our old friend *Oikodomeo,* "building up," which requires the manifestation of spiritual gifts. It is a most powerful witness in a Share group, where three Christians actually form *community* to be observed and entered by unbelievers.

The third word has been stressed by Tom Wolf, pastor of the Church on Brady in Los Angeles, in a Touch videotape segment. It's the word *Oikonomos,* translated "steward." It refers to a household servant who is entrusted with his master's wealth. He is to dispense it as a "proper ration at the proper time" to the

---

EQUIPPING TOOLS FOR REACHING OUT

• FOR TYPE "A" UNBELIEVERS:

KNOCKING ON DOORS, OPENING HEARTS

• FOR TYPE "B" UNBELIEVERS

TOUCH BASIC TRAINING MODULES

SEE ORDER FORM IN BACK OF BOOK

members of the *Oikos,* based on their needs. The Christian learns there are different "rations" for those at the five levels of the pyramid. Knowing that evangelism involves sharing the message of the cross is critical; knowing *when* to share it is also important. These details are carefully woven into the equipping materials provided for the cell group to use in the development of their outreach ministries.

These two tasks dominate the Shepherd group life, and give a common task to all in the body of Christ. This common vision—reaching the lost and equipping believers for that task—provides the continuity between all the cell groups. It avoids the danger of the common direction being dissipated as different cells use different approaches to their lifestyles. There should never, ever, be a "skunkworks" community of cells, where each one does what is right in the sight of his own eyes.

"Target Groups" Reach Different Segments

However, the targeting of unbelievers will cause many Share groups to take different approaches to their ministries. "Target groups" divide into two types: those which attract unbelievers who are in crisis or struggling with deep problems, and those who are open to a relationship based on a common interest. There must be a balance between the sponsorship of these types. If this is not done, a church may collect a large group of broken people who will create a "Mash Unit" out of the cell.[2]

I have seen cells go overboard in attracting really sick people, only to be overwhelmed by needs which exceeded the capacities of the members. In addition, I have some personal battle scars from pouring hours into broken lives who were finally healed—and then "left our hospital group" to go to a church of "normal people." I'll never forget one woman schoolteacher who came to us out of an illicit relationship with a married man. Her daughter was into drugs and sex, and she was a basket case. After months of being together in the same cell, she suddenly joined a large church with a spiffy single's group—and never even bothered to say "Goodbye!" I went to see her and asked why she had dropped us like that. She said, "Ralph, I knew you guys wanted me to be healed, and leaving the group was my last step in that direction. I love you all very much, and now I can belong to a group where *everyone* is healthy." That happened years ago, and caused us to rethink our whole approach.

For that reason, a Shepherd group should not have more than a couple of people who are in *serious crisis*. The Shepherd must guide the evangelism ministry of the Share group in this matter, carefully evaluating the spiritual strength of the team before encouraging them to work with emotionally fragmented target groups.

As I write this book, Faith Community Baptist Church is preparing to launch a number of target groups, relating to marriage, preparation for marriage, tennis, photography, hiking, lonely people, preparation for entering military training, personality development, and many more. These are the "root systems" which penetrate the world of the unbelievers. Share groups can focus in any direction the members desire by making these "touch points" in the community.

During the life of *The People Who Care*, we had over 20 different target groups. They included a Share group for parents of retarded children, a group for teens who drove motorcycles, "H O P E" (Helping Others Practice English), another for divorcees, etc. Twice a year we had a "Touch Fair" on Sunday morning. Each cell would set up a booth explaining their target ministry, encouraging new cells to join them in their outreach. The fair was complete with pizza and activities for our children. The atmosphere of reaching out permeated the entire church, and the target groups were a key to this spirit.[3]

In 1987, Houston's job market collapsed with a resounding thud! Rich and poor found themselves unemployed, and more than one person committed suicide. As the economy plunged and thousands of homes were foreclosed, I developed "LIFT groups." Using the *CARPOOL* radio audience, I collected 119 unemployed listeners in a hall provided gratis by a local hotel and trained them. Free television and newspaper coverage got the word out to the city, and within a month we had *over one thousand* people involved in the 10-week target group ministry. Scores were won to Christ and channeled into nearby churches.

The opportunities to penetrate the lost world are *endless!* Each cell can find its target, and growth will be automatic. Try it: our Lord will be delighted!

The *Oikos* Strategy

A Type "A" unbeliever comes to a Celebration. A cell member, using *Knocking On Doors, Opening Hearts,* has been trained to make contact on behalf of the cell. A special relationship develops between the visitor and the visited. In the proper way, a *friend* asks a *friend* about his relationship with the Lord. The person shares that the issue has never been settled. Using John 3:16 and a simple drawing done on the back of a place mat in a restaurant, a two way discussion takes place about the meaning of becoming a believer. The seeker fully realizes what it means to declare Christ as Lord, and then accepts Christ. He begins immediately to mature through attending the Shepherd group.

The family of this new convert, along with friends and business contacts, is his *oikos.* The cell member who brought him to Christ meets most of them, introduced by the new convert and therefore accepted into the "inner circle" of their group. Following the principle of Luke 10:1-7, they search for others who are looking for the peace Christ brings. An *oikos* network of conversions begins.

The *"Oikos* Strategy" is built upon some important concepts Jesus gave the seventy-two disciples before He sent them into Perea in Luke 10:1-9. Let's examine it point by point:

> *After this the Lord appointed seventy-two others and sent them two by two ahead of him to every town and place where he was about to go. He told them, 'The harvest is plentiful, but the workers are few. Ask the Lord of the harvest, therefore, to send out workers into his harvest field."*

Thirty-six teams of two are going to penetrate an area ignored by the religious leaders in Jerusalem. When each pair met a local person, there would be three—the starting place for *community.*

Our Lord doesn't paint a rosy picture. He says,

> *Go! I am sending you out like lambs among wolves. Do not take a purse or bag or sandals; and do not greet anyone on the road.*

"Lambs among wolves?" That's a sure way to get ripped to pieces—unless you are certain the Shepherd is there to protect you! They need neither money nor clothes nor extra shoes. They are to depend totally on the Shepherd for both protection and survival.

Can you imagine what such total dedication does to a servant of the Lord? Can you imagine what such commitment meant to those in Perea who would meet these people?

> When you enter an *oikos*, first say, *"Peace to this oikos."* If a man of peace is there, your peace will rest on him; if not, it will return to you.

Here's the strategy. They are to journey into a new territory where they have no previous contacts. They are to find a person who will bring them into his *oikos*.

They are to specialize in penetrating *oikoses!* No suggestion is made of their doing "personal evangelism." Stress is to be placed upon this point: their peace is to be offered not just to the *first* person they meet who belongs to this *oikos*, but to *every person* within it. They are "fishing" for a special type of person, called "a man of peace."

I. Howard Marshall explains these details:

> . . . the word 'peace' is no longer an empty formality but refers to the peace which is associated with the coming of the salvation of God . . . . Luke speaks of the presence in it of a 'son of peace' . . . . A 'son of peace' is an example of an idiom found in Classical and Hellenistic Greek . . . . The saying does not refer to finding a house in which there are already disciples, but to offering salvation to those who are willing to receive it . . . Such a person will receive the blessing offered to him.[4]

Oikos chain conversions happen all the time. In the same way that the *oikos* can attack the new believer, there are many more occasions when the opposite takes place. I have observed these networks of conversions through my years of pastoring. First, a wife or a child is converted, then others of the family, and finally the husband. In Singapore, I am always fascinated to talk with first-generation converts about the spread of the gospel into their family tree. From criticism or stubborn persecution, scores have told me of their persistence until other family members also came to know Christ.

This harvest principle must not be longer ignored! The initial contact with *anyone* should first be seen as a credential to meet an *oikos* of people, to live in their community of life, and to find the key person who is willing to receive the peace of salvation. Thus, cell group outreach is always to be seen as coming *from* the household of faith *to* those households who live in despair. For that reason, penetration is to be done by *at least two* believers from the Shepherd group. Together, they model the love and fellowship which binds them together through their *oikodomeo* experiences they have had in the previous weeks. It's *literally* bringing the Kingdom of Christ into the kingdoms of Satan.

> *Stay in that house, eating and drinking whatever they give you, for the worker deserves his wages. Do not move around from house to house [oikos to oikos]. When you enter a town and are welcomed, eat what is set before you. Heal the sick who are there and tell them, "The kingdom of God is near you."*

The lifestyle of the believer is set for us in this passage. As Type "A" unbelievers are contacted, the penetration should deliberately be to all the *oikos* group.

The Same Pattern Works With Type "B" Unbelievers

Without faith bridges to cross over into an *oikos,* there must be another step before the hard core unbeliever will be responsive. Such people are intensely driven by their own desires, and are best reached by "scratching where they itch." This is where the Share Group has proved to be powerfully effective.

Short-term, 10 week group encounters place the unbeliever in a cell of three believers. The size of the Share group is limited to nine persons. Thus, there are two unbelievers for every believer in the group. *Touch Basic Training* shows how the target group contact is to be used to penetrate the *oikoses* of these two persons. Those who have taken this ministry seriously have discovered, over and over, that the "man of peace" is seldom the original person who comes to the group sessions. If the team focuses only on the six unbelievers they enlist for their Share group, the harvest will be lost! They are taught two terms in their training: "In Visits" (visiting in the *oikos),* and "Out Visits" (inviting people out of these *oikoses* to enter *their* home for a meal, taking them to a birthday party for a Shepherd group member, etc.)

Great impact is made by the "Out Visits." I recall an Italian lad who played with my son in Westchester, Pennsylvania years ago, when we were church planting. He always showed up in time to enjoy our evening dessert, so I taught him to read the Bible with us and share in our circle of prayer. Then, Ruth and I got acquainted with his parents. They were pure Type "B" pagans, totally out of touch with anything related to faith or religion. We shared a lovely meal together. When it was over, I handed the Bible to their child and asked him to read. We then invited them to listen along as we had our evening circle of prayer. When it was completed, the boys popped out of their seats and ran to play. I noticed the woman was wiping her eyes. In a moment she said, "That's the first time in my life I ever heard one of my children pray!"

Such relational *oikos* activities can penetrate the toughest hearts with the good news that "there's more!"

The World *Oikos* Principle

Using the little diagram on the facing page, write in your own name at the top. Then, list four or five members of your own personal *oikos* in the space shown for them. Next, think about the *oikoses* of your family or friends you have chosen. Is it not obvious that *you already know something about each one?*

God has designed a simple pattern to network each member of the Shepherd group to an enormous number of people! The only "skill" it takes is a desire to be friendly, to care about others, and to limit the evenings spent watching TV so there is time for people who need your interest and your love.

Shepherd groups who have such people in them find it easy to multiply in a hurry! Seldom will such a group take more than six months to expand into two groups in America. It's faster in Abidjan—multiplication in about three months, and slower in London—a tough place to minister. *Anywhere you go, there will be a "man of peace" if you search for him!*

A JOURNEY INTO YOUR OWN "WORLD *OIKOS*"

WRITE YOUR FIRST NAME HERE:

NOW, WRITE THE FIRST NAMES OF FOUR MEMBERS OF YOUR OWN *OIKOS* (FOR EXAMPLE, YOUR BROTHER, YOUR SPOUSE, YOUR SON, YOUR BOSS) IN THE SPACES TO THE RIGHT:

THEN, WRITE THE FIRST NAMES OF ONE PERSON YOU KNOW IN EACH OF THEIR *OIKOSES*. (FOR EXAMPLE, YOUR BROTHER'S WIFE, YOUR SPOUSE'S BEST FRIEND, YOUR SON'S BEST FRIEND, ETC.) IN THE SPACES TO THE RIGHT:

FINALLY, CIRCLE THE NAMES OF ALL THOSE WHO ARE UNBELIEVERS.

ARE THEY TYPE "A" OR TYPE "B" UNBELIEVERS?
IN A SHEPHERD GROUP USING THE TOUCH TRAINING MATERIALS,
WITHIN THE FIRST YEAR OF A NEW CONVERT'S LIFE,
THIS PENETRATION OF *OIKOS* CONTACTS MUST BECOME A WAY OF LIFE.

HAVE YOU OBSERVED THIS PATTERN?

Conversions often "travel" within *oikos* relation-ships. List below the names of people you know who came to Christ because the gospel moved through their *oikos*. (For example, a woman wins her friend to Christ; her friend wins her older sister, who in turn wins her husband, etc.)

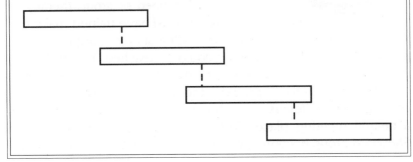

17 ALL ABOUT SHARE GROUPS

A Bird's Eye View Of "Share Groups"

The word *SHARE* is taken from I Thessalonians 2:8 (RSV):

So, being affectionately desirous of you, we were ready to **share** *with you not only the gospel of God but also our own selves, because you have become very dear to us.*

While Paul wrote this to a specific group of believers, the verse accurately describes the ministry of believers to those who need their Lord. The word itself stands for "Sharing His Answer Regarding Everything."

Please, *please* don't change this name to "Care Group!" If you do, you will destroy the evangelistic impact of the cell. To an unbeliever, there is a great difference between attending a group that *shares* (equality is inferred) and one that *cares* (being "cared for" infers someone is better off than you are, or you are in need of group therapy). I have discovered many I have trained make this shift ignorantly, not realizing that such a simple thing as a name change can cut off people who could be reached. We must train ourselves to *think* like unbelievers think if we are to *reach* them.

SHARE GROUPS provide the contact between the unchurched and believers, using homes of Share group members as a neutral meeting place. Three or four mature members of a Shepherd group become the Body of Christ as a Share group team is formed. As group members reach out, the group grows—both numerically and spiritually. Unbelievers become interested in the Gospel, leading to in-depth Bible study to explain the plan of salvation to them at a later time. Share groups are a special arm of evangelism, reaching out from the Shepherd group to the hardest groups to reach—the totally unchurched persons who have been ignored by the P.B.D. churches.

Facts About Share Groups

- They provide an informal, non-threatening time where unbelievers can experience sharing and Christian truth.
- They provide an atmosphere of trust, where people can truly be themselves without being rejected and condemned. Gradually, deep and abiding personal relationships develop between believers and unbelievers.
- They provide a setting where individuals can work through their problems with the help and love of the others in the group. Solutions based on the scriptures are ultimately found.
- They provide a special structure for Share group team members to learn how their spiritual gifts work together.
- They strongly emphasize the importance of prayer as the source of power and harvest.
- They are never a closed group, but are always seeking to grow through reaching out. "Body Life" is its method for sharing Christ's love and offer of salvation.
- They meet any time during the week. Each group sets its own schedule.
- Topics are relational, and apply to the "sting of sin" found among unbelievers. (Example: "Loneliness: What is it, and when do you experience it?")
- They may incorporate a "pre-believer's Bible Study," The Way Home, used either on a one-to-one or a group basis.
- They meet at any time during the week. Each group sets its own schedule.
- They can be age grouped (e.g., high school, over 35 singles), mixed groups (singles and couples), or special groups ("Live Long and Like It").
- They move weekly from house to house. Thus, everyone hosts the group from time to time.

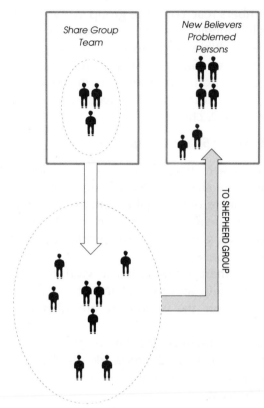

In this illustration, we see a small team, three or at the most four, meeting together for prayer and training (square box) once a week. They then meet in their homes (round box) with unbelievers who are not open to Bible study (lighter figures). Soon the relationships deepen, and Bible study is developed on a one-to-one basis.

Either just before, or as soon as, a person has accepted Jesus as Lord, a new group is formed—the Shepherd group. Nurture now takes place as the original team forms the new cell with the first fruits of their ministry.

The cell group church will focus on reaching out to others through the Share group. The fellowship, prayer, and encouragement needed by the team members in the early stages is provided as they meet for their weekly equipping times. Working with unbelievers is the best way to keep the Shepherd group from becoming an ingrown toenail!

Oikos Penetration Is Critical

The *Touch Ministries Seminar* and *Touch Basic Training* materials have been designed to help with this type of development, but it must be learned in real life—not in a classroom. The focus of this training is the penetration of *oikos* people.

The *Touch Ministries Seminar* is five hours long. It is designed to introduce the philosophy behind Share group ministry, and familiarize the trainee with the difference between traditional evangelism and cell group strategy. It uses a workbook and has video segments which are used in the equipping. The Seminar should be provided to the Share group teams, not just to individuals. At the end of the five hours, the team will be prepared sufficiently to launch its ministry.

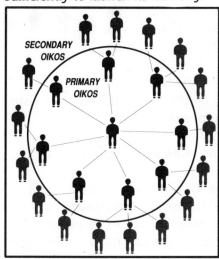

In the Touch Ministries Seminar, each person makes a list of all the people he or she talks to for a total of one hour in seven days. These are the basic members of the *oikos* for that individual. The list is classified by those who are not believers, and by those who are. This list becomes the primary mission field for each person. Then, the names of those who are in the secondary *oikos* structure are developed.

Obviously, each team member will have an entrance to these people through the members of their own *oikos*. Many people are surprised to discover that they actually have natural connections with as many as one hundred individuals. These people should be the first to be reached and brought into the Share group.

The formation of the team in this five hour seminar is followed by a break in the training. Before the launching of the Touch Basic Training units, the team must form the Share group. Sometimes as much as a month will elapse while they are developing the relationships required to form the group. The equipper should be heavily involved in supervising the untrained team members during this time, doing whatever is necessary to be sure each person has one or two people who will join the group. I usually spend time individually with each team member, and meet with them weekly for prayer and strategy planning. Because this is a new type of ministry, nothing can substitute for a seasoned equipper who has already done such a ministry.

A Share Group Usually Lasts 10 Weeks

In the Touch Basic Training material, the team learns that the length of the Share group is usually brief—10 weeks on the average. The purpose is to develop a relationship with people who have no interest in spiritual things (Type "B"), and meet the people in their *oikos*. A ratio of one team member to two unbelievers should never be changed. That "case load" makes it possible for quality time to be spent with each unbeliever and his or her *oikos* family. "In visits" and "out visits" are possible when the ratio is kept small.

Next, "Target Groups" Can Be Developed

After there has been time for the team to learn about the Share group cycle and how the ministry is conducted with *oikos* contacts, a second strategy for penetrating can be presented. It should never, ever be used first of all with new trainees. They need to learn about penetrating *oikoses* and conducting the Share group with friends before the second strategy is attempted. I have often explained the two strategies by comparing the difference between serving the Lord in your homeland, and serving Him in a foreign country as a missionary. If you can't do the first effectively, it's doubtful you will be successful in a strange new culture.

The second strategy is called *targeting*. In this case, people who are strangers, but who share common interests, needs, or problems are gathered for a Share group.

For example, Ruth and I joined hands with two Godly divorcees to begin a group for women who had been recently divorced. Since such women are often financially limited, we assumed they would all read the local "For Sale Or Will Buy" bulletin board in the supermarkets. We stuck a card on several of them which read, "Recently Divorced? Need A Lift? Join Our Group! It's Free. Call 497-2420." We had so many responses, we had a waiting list of women who wanted to join us. We shall never forget the wonderful moments we had as we watched total strangers grow close to us, and become open to know the Christ who lived within us.

Another group I have personally targeted since seminary days in New Orleans are the men who frequent neighborhood bars. They always go to the same one about the same time of the day. I have made contacts with many families by first meeting a man in this way, then inviting him to have lunch with me. Gradually, the relationship would grow.

Cal Thomas, the journalist, worked with me as we targeted key men in the Houston professional world. His wife made the best breakfasts in town, and we always had a house full of lawyers, judges, and public officials for those early morning men's Share groups.

One of the specialists in this type of group is Dale Galloway at New Hope Community Church in Portland, Oregon. He has come through his own personal pain to know the great value of such groups. He has about 96 different categories for targeting! The groups he offers include:

- Mr. & Mrs.
- Mothers of Excellence
- Self-Esteem
- Building Remarriage
- Grief Recovery
- New Life Victorious
- New Hope Seniors
- Overcoming Sorrow
- Total Healing
- WOW (Women of Worth)
- Separation Survival
- Divorce Recovery

The best way to decide what groups to offer is to talk to the Share group trainees as they are working with the *oikos* contacts in the first phase of their training. Their hurts or interests or background will often trigger enthusiasm for a special target group. For example, Eugene Seow in Singapore has formed a Share group entitled, "Cooking for Diabetics." He was packed for the first session!

MATERIALS TO HELP YOU GET STARTED:
- A five hour *Touch Ministries Seminar,* to help you launch the Share Groups.
- The *Touch Basic Training Manual* and the *Facilitator's Guide,* along with 6 hours of *Videotapes,* to provide weekly equipping sessions for each Share Group team.
- TOUCH Seminars, provided upon request for groups of 40 or more organized by you in your area.

(SEE ORDER FORM IN BACK OF THIS BOOK)

TRILOGY Groups And The Hard Core Pagans

As I complete this book, I am excited about an experiment we are going to launch in Houston, and then hopefully in many other places. We're calling this experiment "TRILOGY Groups."

Sounds "New Age," doesn't it? It's intended to target people who are completely turned off by religion. As we saw in Chapter 1, there are more and more people like this. In Texas, the New Age movement is growing many, many times faster than churches. In fact, a recent survey revealed that a surprising number of new adherents are simultaneously attending churches in the mainline Protestant stream.

It's my conviction that a lot of reachable people are turned off by a religious connection when they are offered a group. Therefore, we're going to create a movement that is very clearly grounded on the Bible, "Share groups" that will be sponsored by well-trained believers who will penetrate *oikoses* and seek those who are searching for peace. TRILOGY groups sound neutral, and give believers opportunity to interact with those who would never, ever respond to a group which is obviously church sponsored.

The "trilogy" includes three types of groups. The first is for hurting people. Many of Galloway's topics will be appropriate for these folks. With alcoholism, substance abuse, and depression all on the rise, there will be no end to the possibilities for TRILOGY group formation. Groups for the unemployed (LIFT groups) always provide an opening for relationships to be developed between people who are out of work and unable to find a new job.

The second type of group is for people who are not in crisis. These will focus on areas like jogging, photography, cooking, computers, how to study more effectively, etc. There are thousands of "Yuppies" in Houston and any other major city who have a good job and are bored to tears. In the past, we have snagged homosexuals, atheist school teachers, and many other segments of society that usually rebel against groups with a religious flavor.

In the place of Celebrations, a very "churchy" event, we are going to substitute "Getaways." The contemporary culture has encouraged people to get out of town for the weekends. The freeway near my home is jammed with people getting away on Friday evenings—for a distance of 200 miles! Corporations take their executives on getaways, where skiing, golf, tennis, fishing, or hunting is mixed in with seminars and lectures related to the work place. *We are going to flow with this cultural activity.* Living together in community for a couple of days and a night is very much in tune with the theology of the cell group church.

The third type of group, of course, will be the Shepherd group. When conversions occur, those who have been turned off by traditional religion will be introduced to a new life form for the people of God. Thus, in this movement, the end goal is the establishment of new believers who are equipped and sent out to form new TRILOGY groups (Share groups) and penetrate even more deeply the millions of people who are being ignored by churchianity.

Some day, I'll write a book about TRILOGY. First, we must develop the pattern. As God provides people who want to intern with us, we will seek to equip others to share in the outreach to the unreached.

Actually, the idea isn't new. The Faith Community Baptist Church in Singapore has a separate ministry which feeds its cells. Lawrence Khong took the name "TOUCH" from me, and now has many ministries for outreach under that name. The TOUCH Singers have held concerts which have been attended by thousands. The follow-up by the cells of these musicals has brought many people into TOUCH groups, which are very similar to TRILOGY.

18 WHAT ABOUT FINANCES?

*Note: you are encouraged to read the chapter entitled "Too Much Month At The End Of The Money" in the **Shepherd's Guidebook** in conjunction with this chapter.*

Can you imagine a Body of Christ where nearly everyone is an *oikonomos* (steward)? Cell group churches approximate that to a much greater extent than do P.B.D. churches. It's quite easy to understand how that happens: where the person has come to terms with the Lordship of Christ and sees his or her role as part of a vision, stewardship is no longer a fund-raising word. It's a way of life.

To finally come to terms with the fact that everything *inside* my skin, and everything *outside* my skin, *everything I am* is the property of my Lord, is to settle the place He takes in my assets. This needs to be taught in such a way that it isn't connected to the institutional needs for another building or something of the sort.

The responsibility of the *oikonomos* to provide "proper rations at the proper time" is the key principle to be stressed over and over. As the *Shepherd's Guidebook* explains, we're dealing with an *oikos* concept. Those in Acts 2:42-46 generously cared for one another's needs because they were all in one accord.

A video segment used in the *Touch Ministries Seminar* focuses on this important truth. So does the material produced in the *Life Basic Training* small group series. It must be inserted over and over into the life of the cell church—in Shepherd group meetings, in sermons, in personal conversations.

When the believer realizes that becoming a Christian has made him or her a bondslave of Christ, nothing will ever be the same again. The issue is *total ownership* of our lives by Christ.

The exciting side of the entire issue is found in this trilogy:

> *It is the task of a servant to obey his Master.*
> *It is the obligation of the Master to provide all his*
> *servant requires.*
> *Therefore, that servant must never live in fear his*
> *supply will run out.*

I often use the illustration of the master who told his servant to build him a house. The servant went to his wife and said, "How much money do we have in the bank? The master has told me to build him a house."

The wife replied, "Wait a minute! Did he tell you to draw out your resources to do it?"

"Well, no. He really didn't."

"Then you march right back to him and get the money from *him!*"

It's a great day when the people of God realize that a poor household servant who lives in the mansion of a millionaire wears better clothes, eats better food, and enjoys life more than ever possible if he were left to his own resources.

If an *oikonomos* sees one in the *oikos* with a need, and if that servant has received the Father's assets in order to *meet* that need, there will be again a condition in the church like that described in Acts 4:32-35:

> And the multitude of those who believed were of one heart
> and soul; and not one of them claimed that anything
> belonging to him was his own; but all things were common
> property to them. And with great power the apostles were
> giving witness to the resurrection of the Lord Jesus, and
> abundant grace was upon them all. For there was not a
> needy person among them, for all who were owners of land
> or houses would sell them and bring the proceeds of the
> sales, and lay them at the apostles' feet; and they would be
> distributed to each, as any had need.

Learning to live this way cannot be done apart from life in a community where believers have stepped into that faith walk. Rather than the "preacher getting off on money again," the issue of dollars is best left alone, and teaching about Lordship stressed.

Scrutiny of cell churches reveals they usually grow quite large before investing in a Celebration Center. It's inevitable that one will be needed. Nearly all of them I have visited can't find an auditorium in the city which will hold all the members. However, by the time they do build or buy a place, they are large enough that the payment is usually made in cash.

When And Where Are The Offerings Taken?

This varies widely among the cell churches. Personally, I like Dr. Cho's plan. Each cell group member is given envelopes for the offering. The amount inside is marked on the envelope. They are turned in during the cell meeting. After being totalled by two persons, the separate envelopes are placed in a larger one. This envelope is then brought by the Cell Leader to the next worship service attended. Under the main auditorium there is a wall with pigeonhole boxes, where these envelopes are dropped. I have been deeply moved as I have watched one Cell Leader after another approach their pigeonhole in the wall, put the envelope to their heart and passionately pray for its use, and then drop it in a slot.

In addition, offerings are taken at every public service held. On one occasion I got in the way of the ushers after they had collected the offering from 25,000 people in the auditorium. They were using containers on wheels to roll the gifts into the counting room! Churches like this one seldom make special appeals for funds. When you have nearly 600,000 people serving as *oiko-nomos* servants, there is no need to beg!

What Does The Budget Of A Cell Church Look Like?

In order to explain this, let's look at an illustration of how the funds must be utilized. First and foremost, the investment must be in staff workers. There must be one paid Zone Pastor for every 250 people, representing approximately 25 cells and five divisions of cells conducted by volunteer Zone Shepherds. Their gifts must also provide for secretaries, office space, rental of Celebration facilities, the music staff, etc.

THE CELL GROUP: LARGE CHURCH STAFF		
CELLS	**CONGREGATIONS**	**CELEBRATIONS**
S E N I O R　P A S T O R		
MINISTER OF CELL GROUPS	**MINISTER OF CONGREGATIONS**	**MINISTER OF CELEBRATIONS**
	DISTRICT LEADERS 1:25 District Pastors	**CHOIRS**
		PRAISE LEADERS
	DISTRICT PASTORS 1:25 Zone Servants	**DRAMA TEAMS**
		ORCHESTRAS
		ETC.
ZONE SERVANTS 1:5 Cells	*In the District, a mature cell church will develop and use these gifted cell members:*	Those serving in this category are all involved in cell group life. Belonging to a cell is basic. Those who are musical are some of the most effective cell group members. Some cell churches organize their musicians by cells, others leave them in geographical cells.
ZONE SERVANT INTERNS		
SHEPHERD 1:15 Maximum	**EQUIPPERS** **TEACHERS** **COUNSELORS** **EVANGELISTS** **PREACHERS**	
SHEPHERD GROUP INTERN		
SHARE GROUP TEAMS 3 People: Minimum	This is a model of a cell church with a Senior Pastor. Some cell churches use a team approach with a Leadership Staff, but there is always a key man who can be identified as the leader. Staff positions appearing in the shaded areas are paid positions. All others are volunteers. The number of people supervised is given as a ratio figure.	

Using numbers in a book like this is not wise, so I'm going to do it using "Units" (U), which will represent currency in whatever nation this book is studied. Factor the units into the proper proportion for your currency, and see if it works out:

1. Income provided by Shepherd groups:

Average number of persons in one Shepherd group: 10
Number of households represented: 5
Annual support from each household: .... U   3,000
Average annual support of the church
from one Shepherd group: .... U   15,000
Average annual support from
one District of 25 Shepherd groups: .... U 375,000

2. Expenditure of income provided by Shepherd groups:
(Please note: everyone in ministry is paid the same amount.)

Salary, Leadership Team (2 couples).................................... U   60,000
Salary, first Zone Pastor .... U   30,000
Salaries, two secretaries .... U   36,000
Rent, office... U   24,000
Cost of Celebrations, including rent .... U   95,000
Cost of equipping materials.. U   9,000
Cost of retreats or "getaways" .... U   19,000
Additional expenses, unspecified, including
  missions, care of members, etc... U 102,000
Average annual expenditure by cell group church .... U 375,000

It is obvious that with the second Zone the addition of one more Zone Pastor, plus a musician or two to be responsible for the Celebrations, and another secretary or two leaves a significant surplus is left for missions, the opening of a training school, and the creation of additional "root systems" to penetrate the community of unchurched people.

Actually, the only cell church in the world I have perused where money was a significant problem is Dion Robert's work in Abidjan. In that case, 80% of the members are unemployed! The principles remain the same, but he certainly deserves support from wealthier areas of the world.

19 CHILDREN'S CELL GROUPS

This chapter is slightly edited to be appropriate for American readers. It is adapted from Dr. Lorna Jenkins' dissertation for her D.Min. degree at Columbia Biblical Seminary and Graduate School of Missions. It's published here with her permission.

Children Need Small Groups Of Their Own

When we consider the impact of small groups on large renewal churches around the world, it seems strange that small group strategy has not been applied to their ministry to children. With a few exceptions, there has been a reluctance to carry the benefits of small groups into the younger age range. Possibly people believe that children are not yet mature enough to interact well in group situations. Evidence suggests otherwise. Furthermore, the breakdown of so many families in our society means that children have a need for intimacy which can be met in few other places than in a small group.

> *The family fabric is no longer adequate to contain and support all the life of the child, no more than it can contain and support the life of adults. The child, noticing life outside the family, reaches out to become part of other life forms and fabrics. The lives and fabrics of other people offer new possibilities to the child/youth, new supports, new responses to one's subjectivity.* [1]

Parents who are struggling with the economic pressures of survival are often working long hours and suffering perpetual fatigue. Children are often more familiar with the people on the television screen than they are with their own parents. Mobility and urbanization has removed families from small local communities into city apartments or housing districts where isolation from the community is the rule. Even in upper class housing areas, families tend to retreat behind gates with security systems to protect themselves from unwanted social contact. The practice of bringing friends home to play is now being regarded as a risk in many quarters, and therefore not to be encouraged.

Because children know so few adults whom they can trust with their secrets, they often seek help from their own peers when they have serious problems. This is especially so if the parents happen to be part of the problem. Children offer playground counsel to each other which is usually lacking in experience, information and mature judgment. Often there is a conspiracy of silence among the children against the adult world. To break silence by telling an adult is to break faith with the child's peers. That is why a crisis can develop among children or in a particular child's life, while the parents or caregivers remain totally unaware of the problem. At the same time, friends at school often know all about it.

Children need a group to belong to, preferably a group where there is a trusted significant adult who can offer love, support, and acceptance while being alert for the warning signals of incipient trouble. In churches where small groups are the basic growing units for the adult congregation, the children need the same context for growth, a place to find peer acceptance within their spiritual family.

Do They Not *Already* Have Small Groups?

It can be claimed that children already meet in small groups in the church when they attend Sunday School. They do indeed meet in small groups, graded according to age and with a teacher/leader to guide them. The difference is one of attitude and style, rather than obvious structural differences. A good Sunday School teacher can create a small group within a class. The same effect can also be achieved in a neighborhood Bible club, or with more difficulty, a Vacation Bible School. Yet in most cases it does not happen—not because teachers do not want to meet the relational needs of their children, but usually because they are unaware of the children's life experiences and do not have time to discuss them.

In a small group, the acknowledged purpose of the group is to help each member grow into Christian maturity through the help and support of others. The aim is transformation, a life which is marked by daily obedience and communication with God, a desire to participate in worship, a willingness to discover gifts of service and be trained in them, effectiveness in prayer, open and unashamed witness to Jesus Christ, an ability to relate to others in trust and encouragement and a sense of life calling, in either secular or full-time Christian ministry. Profession of faith is not enough. The transformed Christian life cannot be taught in a series of lessons. It comes into reality through God's power in the lives of others.

A group of children who are walking together in the Christian way have a profound effect upon each other. They do not all have to be the same age. By witnessing the growing maturity of the best models in the group, there is mutual encouragement to strive after similar attitudes.[2] For example, a younger child watches the actions of an older child. While not fully understanding the behavior, the *attitude* expressed is added to his world view almost by osmosis. It is accepted long before the reasons for the action are understood.

The Nature Of Children's Small Groups

Children's small groups in the cell church should be designed to fulfil all the functions of adult small groups, but they will also have characteristics special to children. The people who lead them will be *group leaders* more than *teachers,* and they will shape their ministry on the model of kinship.

The *climate* of the group makes group interaction possible. Learning takes place not just from instruction but through the relationships, the personalities, and the interaction of the participants. Children may belong to a number of different groups within their life experience. Participation in a children's cell group enhances the ability to interact positively in other contexts. It also gives them a point of reference to evaluate secular groups they have joined.

The Climate Of A Children's Small Group

The climate of a cell group which is most conducive to positive learning and interaction is that of a family. In a family there is not continual "sweetness and light," but there is a commitment to each other to live together and work out problems which arise. A family context is not sheltered and unrealistic. It is a place in which there has to be give-and-take, in which there is limitation of rights, concern for others, and security in the midst of struggles. A child returns to his family to lick his wounds and express his anger and hurt; then, he takes courage from his family members to go out and try again. In the family the child encounters real struggles and grief, real frustration, real hurts and forgiveness.

So also in a children's cell group: there needs to be an atmosphere of love and acceptance so children know they are among friends. They need to know it is all right for them to try things and fail, and that they will be encouraged and not criticized. When they know that the group will not be judging them harshly, it is possible for them to risk doing things which they would not otherwise attempt. It is a good climate for creativity and experimentation.

Ideally, a children's group atmosphere should be free from fear, a place where it is safe to ask questions, where it is acceptable to introduce new ideas. This is not an easy atmosphere to create. Children can be devastatingly frank and critical of ideas they do not understand—especially if they disagree with them. The adult leader has the responsibility of allowing *both* sides to be fully heard and understood. The children need to learn to respect a person even if they don't understand his ideas, and to be merciful in judgment.

The atmosphere of competition within society is opposed to such a climate of acceptance. In the schools, competition is regarded as a desirable incentive to motivate children to greater efforts. While this does work, it also acts in reverse. Some children feel they will *never* be able to succeed, and they lose heart. Often they feel resentment against children who succeed and children who win. At the same time, those who excel feel an undue superiority over children who fail. The relationships become rivalries instead of friendships.[3] The winners have to maintain their status at all costs, and losers must withdraw or find less acceptable ways of winning attention.

> *The Bible does give us a picture of a race. The race of life. But the aim is not to beat my brother who runs next to me. It's not that kind of race! I'm not out to show myself better or stronger in any way. Why encourage children to think more strongly this way than they already do? Why [encumber] some with false pride and handicap others with a false sense of failure?*[4]

The atmosphere of a children's cell group is informal and relational. Workers who were trying to evaluate their own group practice described the mood they were striving for in these terms: it is like "talking with a good friend," or "having a group of friends together," or "being honest with the kids."[5]

> *You know at camp where you sit around the fire and just talk? It's more like that ... it's having a cup of coffee with somebody and talking for a while about something that really matters to you . . . having a group of friends together —not in your home—but it is like your home.* [6]

Conversation among friends implies some sort of equality. Many adults are inarticulate in the presence of children, or they converse in an artificial or patronizing way. Adults who are going to converse naturally with children need to yield some of their superior status and experience. They must take seriously what the children are saying and create an atmosphere of mutual respect. The only way to learn this skill is to watch children and talk with them as much as possible. The secret is in talking *with* them, not *to* them.[7] An adult who talks *to* them approaches them from a position of superiority and strength. The person who talks *with* children expects the "give and take" of normal conversation from a position of equality.[8] For this reason, it is helpful to be on the same eye level with a child. In that posture, it is much harder to be patronizing.

If we ignore the children's contributions to a discussion or conversation, we are signalling that we do not consider they have much to offer.[9]

> *Children quickly perceive that adults disregard their opin-*
> *ions and comments and feelings and they learn to keep their*
> *thoughts and ideas to themselves.*[10]

Eventually they adopt the same attitudes as adults, and reject their own ideas and insights as unimportant. That is why it is important for children to interact with other children as well as with adult leaders. In a reciprocal relationship where two or more children can talk on a basis of equality, they are able to initiate relationships and explore their understandings of each other. They begin to learn mutual respect and the need to take other people's opinions into account.[11] If there is a conflict, they need to restore harmony and find a way for both sides to compromise without loss of face. Children learn how to adapt their behavior to the expectations of the group.

If, on the other hand, the major relationship in the group is from a superior adult to inferior children, the children tend to become passive, to allow the adult to be the problem-solver and submit their thinking to the voice of authority.

A children's cell group should be a place where positive comparisons can be made. Children become interested in the lives and experiences of other children. When they see the way other children react to problems and difficulties, it influences their own reactions.[12] They discover that other children are trying to cope with the similar learning and growing processes, or perhaps have just passed through them. The experience of another child is far more relevant than the childhood experience of an adult. *He* may be interested in what happened in the "old days," but every child knows the world is a different place today. Adults drag from the attic of the past stories of how they dealt with childhood conflicts, but these do not offer relevant solutions. Only another child can fully know the pressures and problems which face children today. Thus, under adult supervision, children can give good support and counsel to another child, especially if the child is a little younger.

> *A child's friendships are important influences in his social*
> *development...Fears and apprehensions diminish in size*
> *when it is discovered that other persons have them too. A*
> *friend may share skills and abilities that make the child more*
> *acceptable both to himself and to his peers.*[13]

Skills And Functions Of Children In Small Groups

One of the basic components of being accepted in a children's cell group is the need to acknowledge that other people have rights and deserve sympathy. This is a considerable step in maturity for a child, especially one who has never before had to seriously consider the rights of others. If one child tries to dominate the group or to override the will of the majority, the children will be quick and ruthless in enforcing fair play. Sometimes the adult/leader will need to suggest leniency and understanding. These qualities do not come naturally to a child.

Another required skill is the ability to listen. The cell can only operate if the members are prepared to hear what the others are saying and try to understand it. With encouragement, children can even perceive nonverbal communication and respond sensitively to it. In this situation the leader acts more as a facilitator—hearing, responding, interpreting, refereeing, clarifying. If the leader is the dominant speaker, this kind of talking and listening cannot take place. Even the most sensitive leaders talk far more than they think they do and tend to offer solutions, rather than help the children discover them for themselves.

Disagreements in the group are not a disaster. Often the children enjoy a heated debate and have no hard feelings afterward. Ideally a child should feel free to offer an alternative opinion without fear of ridicule. Again, this may be an area for the leader to be the peacemaker. If there are never any disagreements in the group, it may mean the children are not asking their serious questions. Children are quick to know that some questions cause embarrassment or disapproval from the leader. These are the questions they suppress.

> If we listen to children and young people, we soon find that they are asking profound questions. They may not be able to articulate them in polished language, but the questions are there. If we do not let them ask them of us, they will ask them of each other, but if the group is permissive, the members do not need to wait until the meeting is over and they are by themselves. If the members feel that the adult leader accepts and understands them, the important questions start flowing.[14]

I had a vivid example of this recently when I was visiting another church. A group of eight-year-olds gathered round me, and when they discovered that they could talk with me safely, they began to bring out their questions. In the course of fifteen minutes we discussed the omnipresence of God and the nature of Jesus' resurrection body. They asked how we could know that the creation story is true when no one was there to witness it and write it down.[15] These children had been in Sunday School all their lives, but they were glad to form a spontaneous group around an adult who would listen to their questions.

Virgil Foster suggests five functions for children's groups.[16] They should be places of companionship, where children can share jokes, whisper secrets and work together on projects and games. They should be a testing ground for group behavior. The patterns of behavior which have worked very well at home or in other contexts may not work in a children's group. Children can learn to widen their relational skills. A small group is a source of information as children pool their knowledge, both accurate and inaccurate. An adult/leader is needed to help them sort out the difference. It is a forum in which new values and standards are learned. Children have a rigid sense of fair play and they formulate very strict rules about the conduct of a group.

A group also helps to bridge gaps between different groups of children—gender gaps, racial gaps, socio-economic gaps, religious and educational gaps. In a cell group, many prejudices can be broken down so that children can enter adult life without necessarily carrying their traditional cultural bias.

The Role Of Leaders In Small Groups

The Leader As Kin

The leader of a small group is characterized by an *attitude* rather than a *technique*. Instead of saying, "How can I teach this lesson?" she will say, "How would I treat these children if they were my own family?" It is a role of kinship rather than teacher/pupil.

> As long as teachers and learners perceive themselves to be in school, they will not develop the kind of relationship or the kinds of sharing which are important for discipling.[17]

Strikingly it seems that when we adopted from our culture the formal school approach to nurture, we in fact, set up the conditions under which discipling and growth in likeness are least likely to take place.[18]

This view is supported by Laura Lewis, who made a recent study on the memories church teachers had of Sunday School and their attitudes toward the children they teach.[19] In almost every case their best memories of Sunday School came from a teacher who cared for them. In relating to the children they are now leading, their ideal is to recreate that friendly family image.

I want to try and give those children the same kind of pleasant memories . . . that is the kind of teacher I want to be . . . the person who can give someone pleasant memories and let them know they have a special friend. It is a community tie which is there forever. [20]

I try to answer their questions like I would if it were a child of mine. I tell them as a parent. I might say,"Look, it is like taking a long walk with your grandchildren—answering their questions and telling them some of the things you have learned.[21]

They really do become part of you. They are your kids. You don't have to think of them as anyone else's when you've got them in your classroom. . . It's kind of condensed into one hour a week but it's really more than that too . . . You want to hear about the rest of what they are doing from them or from their parents or from their friends. They are important. [22]

So (my goal) would be for children to explore freely without ever feeling that they are in a "I lecture and you listen" format which they get Monday through Friday and don't need in Sunday School. [23]

The home and family is still the prime context in which affective learning can take place—where attitudes, behavior, and values are created. Since Christian nurture has a large affective component, the family is likely to be the best model for trans-formative education. A cell group best reflects that model.

This does not mean that no *cognitive* learning takes place in the home. In some homes, intellectual stimulation is very high. Reading and questioning are encouraged, but learning in a home does not take the form of lessons. It arises out of the normal material of life. It is pursued out of curiosity, not out of a desire for good grades. The information takes the form of a story, or a shared experience. There is a spontaneous sharing of personal needs.

Even so, in a children's cell group the Bible instruction will be secondary to the relationships. The relationships become the necessary background for the Biblical teaching—the context in which learning is possible.[24]

> *Admittedly most of the Biblical concepts that have been isolated, organized and expressed by adults are difficult to understand. Nevertheless it is possible to make them clear if the experiences of children are used to illustrate the meaning of the Bible message.*[25]

In the family context, the teaching material is wide, varied and interesting. Children may be hearing a story at the same moment as they are learning to handle a watch with care. Prayer is mixed with value judgments about what to pray for. Inter-personal relationships are worked out in doing the household chores. No one can exactly say when a lesson was learned, but the growth into maturity is observable. There is no need to teach everything on a subject in one day. The matter will come up again, and the previous teaching will be recalled.

This model for the cell group requires different attitudes and skills from the teacher. The kinship role does not happen auto-matically. It is built out of trust and caring. The leader has authority that arises from respect, friendship and a desire to please; it does *not* come from status and position.

Just as in a family, the learning experiences are unstructured. A cell group for children will contain an interplay of songs, stories, conversation, questions, physical activity, discovery, thought and prayer, with the affective and the cognitive domains thoroughly mixed up. However, this does not mean the leader has not planned a schedule of activities. It *does* mean the leader will know the children's needs sufficiently well to be able plan the group time to meet those needs. It also means that the leader must be flexible enough to change direction if a particular need arises unexpectedly. He will not be upset if the plan does not work out on a particular day.

The Leader As Information Source

Though the group may be growing in its personal relationships, the element of cognitive learning should not be omitted. In fact, for elementary school children this can be one of the attractive things about the group. Children love getting new information, provided it relates to the things they want to know.

> *The constant repetition of the same or similar stories makes children's ministry boring and creates a pressure on the teachers to get children's attention to listen to what they've heard before.*[26]

A child feels great joy when he discovers a new truth for himself. He gets even greater joy when he can translate that truth into action. When a leader wants to deal with a topic she should ask herself, "What are the questions the children are wanting to know about this?" They may be questions which have already arisen in the group.

I encountered an example of the need for relevance in teaching material a few weeks ago in New Zealand. The topic for the day was "Prayer" and the material explained to the eleven-year-olds that prayer means talking to God and expecting him to answer. The lesson also said that there are a variety of styles of praying: thanking, confessing, requesting. The children were bored. Most of them knew from nursery class that God was supposed to answer prayer, and that when you pray you use words like, "Thank you" and "I'm sorry," and "Please bless..." The group came alive when I started a discussion on "Why God does answer some people's prayers and not others?" and, "Is it fair to pray for your team to win?", and, "What if two people pray opposite prayers? Does prayer really make any difference?" It is far more important to touch the right questions in the children's thinking than to get the right answers filled in on the activity sheet.

The Leader As Interpreter

To be an interpreter, the leader must know the children's situations well enough to assess which issues are crucial at the moment. That cannot happen in a formal situation. It is more important for the leader to hear the children talk and be sensitive to their needs than for the leader to talk. The conversation in the group needs to be supported by individual contacts outside the cell meeting. The leader, like a good brother or sister, will care to find out what is going on in the child's world.

All through the week, the children are caught in the harsh realities of daily life. Some of their experiences will have been joyful, some hard, and some simply confusing. Many times the child will misunderstand the events which took place, or a comment which was overheard, or a reaction from another person. Often an idea which has been heard will be embroidered by his/her imagination until it becomes a monstrosity or a terror. Sometimes a child will assume blame where he is totally innocent. It is common for a child to say that "Daddy left home because I was naughty," when the real conflict was between the two parents. In the safety of the cell group, such things can be discussed. The child needs trusted adults and older children to hear his fears and uncertainties, and to correct the distorted impressions which he may otherwise carry into adult life.

Frequently, a child receives conflicting signals from the things he is told and the things he sees adults do. He generally observes the actions without understanding the reasons for them.

Interpretation of our experiences is one of the major functions of the church, and for children it is essential. They are surrounded by contradictory messages from people whom they think are authoritative. Their parents say one thing, and the school teacher may often say something which is contradictory. Their sports coach has one set of values, and their grandparents another. The television personalities affirm a lifestyle which is based on blatant self-centeredness, and the comic books tell them that winning will justify anything. If the church offers just one more dissident voice to the clamor around them, the children become even more confused. The cell group should be the place where the varying voices of the world are examined, interpreted, and judged. A child should know that his church friends *also* live in the world, that they face the same problems, and can make sense of them. The Christian's faith is the touchstone for all other viewpoints, against which they stand or fall.[27]

This ministry of interpretation cannot take place in a formal atmosphere where the child cannot express his bewilderment and confusion.

The Bible cannot be applied to the problems of childhood if the leader does not know what the problems of the child are. Most adults only guess at what childhood is like now. It has changed radically since most of us were children. Children are dealing with sophisticated issues which are much too big for their understanding and experience. If the children are meeting belief systems which are destructive to the Christian faith, there is all the more reason to talk about them and reveal the flaws, rather than shelter the children from them.

> Christian educators concerned about nurturing a faith which will endure assault, are therefore best advised to introduce belief threatening material within a supportive context for examining it.[28]

The Leader As Model

The growth of children within the group does not depend entirely on the interaction of the group or the interpretative function of the leader. Children also learn to identify with an admired leader and to try to be like him. A great deal of research has tried to discover whether it is possible to transfer likeness from person to person.[29] While the process through which this transformation occurs is not fully documented, there is no doubt that it happens.

Modelling, according to Richards, is not just imitation.[30] He see it as an identification in which,

> . . . a person believes himself to be like another person in some respects, experiences the other's successes and defeats as his own, and consciously or unconsciously models his behavior after him . . . The fact that there is emotional involvement with the other person distinguishes identification from mere imitation.[31]

Lawrence Kohlberg makes the distinction in this way:

(1) In identification the total role is learned, with the self modeling many aspects of the model (not just overt actions).
(2) Identification is based on a strong emotional tie to the model.[32]

This is simply giving an academic rationale to the experience of Henrietta Mears who said, "First I learned to love my teacher. Then I learned to love my teacher's God."[33]

The importance of good modelling is that it has such an all-pervasive influence on the child. The life of faith is caught through human contact. It is not taught like a lesson. It is organic in that it invades every aspect of life.

Modelling touches various aspects of human lives: knowledge, emotions, values, behavior. However consistency is the vital ingredient that bonds them. Only as the learner sees the Christian faith exemplified in all aspects of life, will change be effected in his/her own life.[34]

If this is true, then the child needs contact with the adult outside of the immediate group. That is why leadership of a children's cell group cannot be seen as a once a week activity. The leader will want to cheer on the sidelines when the child is playing a sport, or acting in the school play. He may invite the child to come and see him/her play a sport. Or, they may organize a picnic or a camp-fire together. The children always want to visit in the home of the leader. They want to know what kind of bed the leader sleeps in, what kind of food he/she eats. Does he have a pet? Where does he go to work? What games does he play? The children need to be able to put the leader into a context so that they can understand the real person.

The leader will also want to find a context for the children in the group through visiting their homes and getting to know the other members of the family. Such visits should never be seen as a substitute for personal individual contact with the child. Every child in the group needs some time when he/she can see the leader. It may be a trip to MacDonald's, or an ice cream cone in the park, or a fishing trip. It is a time when the child feels special and is receiving the leader's undivided attention.

Sadly, in this bent society it is unwise for the leader to be entirely alone with the child in such meetings. Another adult nearby, or an open, populated location are essential to avoid the suspicion of illicit dealings with the child.

The leader is not the only person who can become a model to the child. In groups of my own, I have found great value in inviting guests of all ages and backgrounds to talk with the children. Suddenly these anonymous figures in the church become real people who become good supporting or alternative models of the Christian faith. The children discover that this kind of Christian is not isolated to their leader or parents, but he/she is part of a larger Christian community.

Skills For Leading A Small Group

Acceptance

Probably the most important skill which group leaders require is the ability to show open acceptance of the children. In a recent training group I was leading, I demonstrated some of the skills of small group leadership. In the evaluation, one of the observers commented, "You were 'buttering them up' all the time."

He was right, but I would have said that I was affirming and accepting their participation in the group. The knowledge that the leader will accept their ideas and contributions not only encourages the children to talk freely, but it helps them clarify their thinking. The leader can take an immature comment, repeat it and rephrase it, helping the group to build upon it until it becomes a very appropriate insight.

> *Accepting ideas help children dare to think out loud. It provides freedom to ask questions or express ideas enabling children to expand their concepts. A climate of openness encourages honest conversation about ways of dealing with disappointments, personal hurts and crises in daily life.*[35]

Children are so quick to recognize implied rejection. If they are made to feel foolish before the others, they will withdraw into silence or into bad behavior. They must find their significance somewhere. We should never imagine that our words mean nothing to a child. They may call their friends names and say they are stupid. They may even call themselves stupid. But if a significant adult (a parent or leader) says it, they fear it must be true.[36] Thus, the child receives a self-fulfilling prophecy that he is lazy or slow or disruptive or unacceptable to others.

Many children have already learned the pain of failure in the school system. They know that there are things which they cannot do as well as other children, and often they are afraid to risk having another try. Children's cell leaders need to create situations in which a child can succeed or at least gain self respect from a good attempt. Children in a cell group should not be asked to do things which are well beyond their capability. Forcing a child to read aloud before others may be an agony to him. Asking for detailed Bible information may be an encouragement only to those children who already have a solid grounding in the Bible. For other children it is proof that they are unacceptable.

Some children who cannot excel in intellectual areas may be skilled in artistic or physical areas. Every child has his place of greater ability. One retarded child I knew had a natural ear for music and played the organ quite acceptably without instruction. The leader needs to become sensitive to the strengths and weaknesses of the child and to highlight the things a child can do well.

When a child says "I can't do it," he is really inviting help and reassurance. He is saying, "I'm afraid I'll do it wrong." At this point the leader can agree that the task is not easy, but they can work on it together. By talking about it and outlining the first steps, the child can gain the confidence to try. For instance, a child who cannot do a forward roll needs to learn how to crouch down and make himself small first. A child who cannot draw a picture needs to imagine the picture in his mind first. As each step of the task is conquered, there is a sense of wanting to go further. Another child can be helpful at such times by going through the actions slowly with the beginner and showing him how it is done. This is one of the benefits of having some older children in the group who do not see themselves as rivals.

While the leader needs these skills of acceptance and understanding, there is also a need for control and arbitration. Inevitably there will be conflict in the group at some time.

Conflict Resolution

Children do not usually conceal their feelings or opinions. Conflict is as natural to them as breathing, but they expect it to be resolved. The leader often acts as referee, ensuring there is fair play and that one child is not oppressed or rejected by others. Conflict often arises from the sense of competition which is endemic among children. Schools and sports teams use competition to spur the children on to greater efforts. Unfortunately, the reverse side of healthy competition is aggression and domination. The opposition must be crushed! In a group, the competitive spirit destroys the atmosphere of trust. Winning implies the seeking of personal aggrandizement and the failure of others.

Achievement is not a matter of competition. It is possible for everyone to achieve at some level, and in fact that is the Biblical picture of competition. When Paul says, "I press toward the mark for the prize of the high calling of God in Christ Jesus," he is not saying that he wants to defeat all the other Christians in the race by coming first. He is urging them to join him in reaching the same mark and the same prize.

The leader should not reject the presence of conflict. To deny the conflict or to forbid it will only drive it underground and the trust level of the group will suffer. What does not get resolved in the group will be fought out on the way home, or on the playground. It is much better to talk about the disagreement within the group, seeking the help of the group to resolve it and giving some ideas about how harmony can be restored with honor on both sides. The cell leader is there, not so much as judge but as counsel for the defence. He interprets the viewpoint of each side so that the children can understand the problem and begin to deal with it. He can also lighten the atmosphere by provoking good-humoured laughter.

The thing I like most about Miss Forman is that when things get sorta uptight in our classroom, she laughs with us and everything is O.K. again.[37]

In talking with children, especially boys, it is clear that one of the most desirable qualities in an adult is that they should be "funny," which is their interpretation of a friendly, laughing, warm personality. Girls tend to use the word "kind" when talking of a favourite adult.

Perception

The leader needs to be able to "read" the signals, verbal and non-verbal, which a child is sending. An excellent discussion of the giving and receiving of messages during relationships is set out in David Johnson's book, *Reaching Out: Interpersonal Effectiveness and Self-Actualization.* He also includes some useful training exercises. However, he is largely dealing with adults. When children communicate, while most of the same elements are there, there are some additional dimensions. Children have a basic desire to please, or at least gain attention. This means that they will carefully gauge what the desired response will be and elicit it to the best of their ability. Sometimes it becomes just a trigger response, without serious thought or intention. The level of the response is often a fair estimate of the depth of the trust relationship between the child and the leader. Children quickly get signals when they are trespassing into areas where their leaders do not want them to go.

Recently I observed a class of six-year olds learning the Christmas story. One small boy asked the question, "Are angels real?" His teacher replied swiftly, "Well, they're in the Bible, so they must be." But that wasn't really answering the child's question. Basically, the child was wanting to know why we don't *see* angels today, and what an angel would look like if we *did* see one. Are they "story book" real, or common-every-day real? The child was left with the impression that the teacher did not want to talk about it, and probably did not know. This sows the seeds for later rejection of the Christian faith.

Children can be honest and be deceivers at the same time. They will come out with honest statements which we adults have learned to politely avoid. They face facts such as age and death, often with a cheerful pragmatism. At the same time, they may live double lives—one life around their parents and church friends and another one with their friends at school or on the street. It is a kind of self-protection to keep one part of life separate from another part so acceptance can be received from both. That is why parents are so often amazed when part of the "other life" of their child becomes briefly visible. When a child does not want to talk about his life outside the home, it is a way of saying, "I don't want you to invade my other life. You might embarrass me." If we put too much pressure on a child at this point, we can provoke angry confrontation or a wall of silence.

A group leader is more likely to be able to win the child's confidence, allowing him/her to talk in a non-threatening atmosphere. Because he does not live with the child every day, he may be able to sense the stress points, the silences, the non-verbal signs of misery, suppressed excitement or antagonism, which are part of a child's experience.

Keeping Confidences

There is a question about whether a children's cell leader should keep the things he hears privileged, as totally confidential. An adult who breaks trust with a child will never regain that trust. It is a final betrayal. Yet, there are some who justly say that parents should be told all that affects their child. In broad terms, this may be true, but there needs to be a degree of wisdom in handling the confidences of a child. It is not fair to run to parents with stories of every minor misdemeanor their child is involved in, especially if the parent is likely to over react. It is not fair to tell funny stories about the child's "cute" sayings for the amusement of adults. We should not report back to parents every ill-judged or hasty criticism their child makes about them. However, there are situations which are so serious that the parents and/or pastor needs to know for the child's own protection. Sometimes the parents themselves are part of the problem.

In any case, the child needs to know in advance that the leader intends to make certain facts known. They can discuss together the need for it, about the possible reaction, about the support the leader will give to the child, and about how much needs to be told. In some situations, this can be a relief to a child in that it removes from him the responsibility of deciding to tell or not to tell. The unforgivable part of breaking confidence with a child is in not letting him know what is happening.

The Shape Of A Children's Cell Group

The basic elements of a cell group will be wider than the average Sunday school program. Food always plays a part in fellowship. It creates a relaxed atmosphere where conversation seems natural. It can fit anywhere into the program, but it needs to be presented in a controlled manner with the children assisting in the preparation and the serving. If it is just handed out by the leader, each child will try to grab a greater share for himself. Preparing and sharing food together is a universal bond of friendship. It is also a chance for children to learn about being fair and courteous to others.

The Covenant

For children, the existence of a covenant is probably easier to accept than it is for many adults. They are growing towards the age when rules are very important and must be observed. In their own gangs they form their own "covenants," which they strictly enforce. Children long to be part of such a gang, and within the gang they find acceptance and identity through learning to keep the expectations of the group.

In a child's normal peer groups, a major pleasure of being part of a gang is that others should be excluded. It is a recognition of status and the excluded children are seen to be the "enemy," to be tricked and circumvented. The children's cell group runs counter to this tendency. The mood should be inclusive. This will not come naturally to the children, but the policy needs to be constantly demonstrated and encouraged by the leader.

The formation of the covenant, therefore, while it is a joint effort with the children, needs the guidance and help of the leader. If the leader produces it alone, the children will not "own" it. If the children create it, it is likely to be inadequate because of their inability to empathize with other children. The covenant may include such areas as attendance, sharing, keeping confidences, taking turns, dealing with obstructive behavior, praying for each other, and caring for each other.

The covenant, once it has been agreed to by the children, can be of great assistance in discipline. The leader is not solely in charge of discipline. A breach of the covenant can be drawn to the attention of the group, and the whole group can decide the best thing to do. Often the leader will find herself arguing for leniency. Often the older children will temper the rash judgments of the younger ones. Children can understand the need for discipline and accept it, if they know it is considered fair by their peers.

When the leader encourages and models care for each child, the other children are sensitive to observe and copy. There is no better way to demonstrate the love of God than through the spontaneous love we show to children.[38]

Size and Place

If a true bond of relationship is to be built within the group the accent has to be kept on the word "small." Eight children is a good number to be led by two people—one leader and one trainee. As the group grows to about twelve or fourteen, there should be preparation for multiplication. This is often painful for both children and leaders. Groups may meet as subgroups in the same location for a while, and share some joint outings. Finally, the break becomes actual and each leader needs to look for a new intern. The mixed ages of the group generally makes the division easier. Each group should have children of differing ages, but it is usually unwise to separate very close friends. Often, children do not want to divide at all.

If the group becomes larger and larger, the intimacy is lost and it becomes too risky for the children to share in the group. It is possible to have more than one group when the cells meet— sort of a "mini-congregation." The children spend some time in the larger group, and some time in their cell groups. The danger is that the cell group may be lost in the larger group. It is easier for adults, especially if there is a shortage of leaders, to combine the cells and deal with them as a unit. However, as soon as this happens the worker's personal relationship with each child is lost.

The room in which a small group meets should not look like a classroom. Ideally, the living room of a home is a good location.

If one is not available, the room used should be made to *look* like a living room.[39] Cushions on the floor are better than chairs: they bring leaders and children to a state of equality. A low table for food or games is also useful. Often it is better to remove shoes at the door. If the group is being held in a home, the rules of behavior are those of the host household. Children need to learn that everyone must respect the rules of another home. If the cell meeting room is in a church or hall, the children can take pleasure in preparing it and making up their own rules for caring for it.

Flexibility

A cell group structure does not always have to be limited to one weekly get-together per week. One set of cell groups might meet on Sunday morning, while another group could meet after school or on an early evening. Some may be church building based, and some may be neighborhood based. Each grouping may have different purposes, but the underlying philosophy can be the same.

In a survey carried out among some of the Anglican churches in England, these were some of the groups reported by the churches: Sunday teaching groups, mid-week teaching groups, uniformed groups, Saturday children's clubs, choirs, toddler's groups, and play groups. To these could be added after-school clubs for latch-key children, tuition groups, hobby groups, music or drama groups, and planning for worship groups. The task or the time of the group is far less important than the relationships shaped in the group. Some groups can be long term, and others organized for a short term function, such as a play or a musical.

Children's cell groups can also be adjuncts of adult home groups. After a time of being together with the adults, the children go off to their own cell group.

Reporting In

There needs to be adequate time for the children to report in on the events of the week. A few cursory questions at the beginning is not enough. Other members of the group may want to comment or explain or sympathize. Such a discussion may trigger a discussion of an important idea, which may become the vital theme for that day. In God's good providence, the prepared story for the day may have some relevance for the problem under discussion. If it does not, the leader may need to change the story or abandon it. The aim of the group is to meet the need of the children, not to review the facts of a given Bible story. Often a simple verse of Scripture that can be remembered may be the best therapy for a distressed child.

The continual monitoring of the experience of childhood is only possible in a regular small group, where children are free to tell others of their problems. There can be follow-up and re-enforcement during the next week. Of course, this kind of activity can and does take place in a Christian home, but too often it doesn't.

Storytelling

The Bible needs to have an important place in the group, not as an exercise in reading, but as a resource where truth can be discovered. An illustrated Bible may take pride of place, but it needs to be in a place where the children can reach it and learn to use it. There can be more than one story in any group session. One may be a Bible story and another a story from daily life. The children always love to hear something from the leader's past, or the leader may help the children make a story about some event from their own lives. Missionary stories or animal stories can catch their imagination. A serial story may challenge them to read a book they would not otherwise open.

Children can help in the telling of the story. Most children who have been in the church from childhood know most of the facts of the popular Bible stories by the time they are ten, or even younger. Either the leader has to find a new twist to the story, or she can get the children to tell the story back to her with different children adding details and giving color.

The leader's task, then, is to find the aspect of the story which is relevant to the questions the children are asking at that point in their experience. This can be done through relational questions such as, "Do you think it was fair that..." "What would you have done if...?" "How do you think he might have felt...?" "How could they have done this better?"

The other kinds of questions which need to be asked are the ones which support historicity. "Do you think this really happened?" "Where did it happen?" "Do you think it could happen today?" "How do we know about these people?"

The discussions which arise from these two styles of questions are far more important than working through an activity sheet. Generally, activity sheets are there to reinforce the lesson, but not to develop or to apply the story. They do not encourage children to continue talking about the group material after they have left the room.

Again, the atmosphere of the story telling will be based on the family model, not the school model. The group gathers round to hear a story. They may wriggle or contribute, or interrupt or get lost in their imagination.

It should not have the mood which says, "I hope you're listening. You'll be tested on this." The story may be specially chosen by one or more members of the group, or it may arise from an event in the life of the group. When the children are involved in the story, either through experience or through helping in the telling, the meaning of the story seeps into their lives. It is not a way of amusing them. It is part of the Great Story which God tells to us.

Prayer

Prayer is also an activity which children find fairly natural in their early years. If God is real, then children are able to speak to him. If Jesus is alive, then He should be present to hear their prayers. There is often some confusion about who they are praying to, God or Jesus. In fact, they pray to both interchangeably, and it does not seem to matter. Children are very natural when they talk to God in their early years. They confide their secrets to him and they make their own comments on the events of their world. They seriously believe that God does answer prayer, and they get excited when he does. Prayer for others seems to be a spontaneous reaction of concern, if the child has discovered the praying habit.

> *Children tend to pray more spontaneously in response to feelings—fear, anxiety, loneliness. Prayer becomes more altruistic as children become aware of the needs of others.*[40]

This spontaneity in prayer is a delightful facet of childhood.

It is lost very quickly as the children learn and copy adults modes of prayer. If the leader performs the official prayers, children perceive that prayer should be formal, with a special kind of phraseology, so they become afraid to try.

They might get the words wrong. At this point the emphasis is on "the words" of the prayer rather than "the heart" of the prayer. If the older children can help model praying and the leader can learn to pray spontaneously and in simple words, the child will also be encouraged to try.

Children get keen on prayer when they can observe that God takes notice of children's prayers. If the group keeps a prayer diary, the topics for prayer can be recorded as they occur. Later, the children will be excited to read through and check the prayers which have been answered so far. It is also a good time for discussing why God has not answered some prayers yet.

The most effective kind of praying in the group will be when the children pray for each other out of a deep concern for problems. This sharing of concern will ensure that children keep in touch between meetings to find out how things are going. The knowledge that he is not on his own is infinitely precious to a troubled child.[41]

Ministry

In the cell group, the children can plan ministry projects for the whole group or for individuals within the group. The group may plan a visit to a retirement home, or make a banner for the Celebration. They may pray for the adults in the church and send cards to sick adults or children. They may prepare some music or a Bible reading for the Congregation or Celebration meeting, or some of their number may help greet people at the door. They may prepare a report of their activities for a sharing time in the Congregation service. Or, they may introduce a worship idea to the adult cell group. In one church, I saw the children prepare a basket of flowers to welcome a new baby being brought to the church for the first time. Another excellent activity is to invite adults or teenagers from the church to visit the group so that they can get acquainted. Both sides benefit. It should include special people like missionaries or church leaders, but also some ordinary people—especially the elderly.

Sometimes two or three children in the group may join to

befriend another child and invite him to the group. The whole group can work on making newcomers feel welcome. An individual may be appointed to be a special friend to a lonely child or a new child, until he/she feels comfortable in the group.

Inviting other children to come to the cell in order to gain a reward is an inferior way of winning children. Christian children soon learn how to manipulate the system, and the children who are invited quickly discover the invitation came not out of friendship, but out of self-interest. The children also need to know that they can invite children from outside their own age group. This is one of the great benefits of a mixed-age cell group. A child who is of a different age can come with his friend or brother or sister. The bond which already exists between them can be strengthened by their membership in the same group.

Mixed Age Groups

This is one of the hardest areas for traditional teachers to accept. We have been trained to believe that children always learn best within their own grade, but people have questioned this. In his plan for families, God planned that children would be mixed in ages.

Children in the same group share the same tensions, problems and needs to achieve. They want to prove that they are as good as the others, if not better.[42] Older children, however, are not threatened by younger children. They know they are more mature, and they can be generous in helping someone younger. They get genuine pleasure from watching the achievements of the smaller children. The younger children also are not worried by the skills of the older ones. They know they will grow up to be able to do those things, and they will try to copy what they can.[43] Because they admire and want to copy older children, they will often listen to them more readily than they would an adult.[44] In commenting on the schools where this mixed age concept has been practised, Maria Montessori comments,

> It is hard to believe how deep this atmosphere of protection and admiration becomes in practice. Finally the children come to know one another's characters and to have a reciprocal feeling for each other's worth."[45]

In such a group, discipline becomes easy, since the older children have a sense of responsibility for the younger ones and the younger children will respect the word of the older children. Generally, there needs to be at least a two year age gap for this dynamic to work, but it can work right down into the lowest age levels. A five year old will assist and take responsibility for a three year old, and will grow in maturity through the experience.[46]

The secular world perpetuates the concept of age segregation among children. Children are often grouped on a very arbitrary age basis, making the unwarranted assumption that children of the same age will have the same intellectual and relational maturity.

Children themselves perceive this distinction and they often exclude children from their play because of very minor age differences. Zick Rubin reports a fight involving three children.

> *"We're all big guys and he's little. We're four and we can beat him up."*
> *"Uh,uh" Caleb objects, "I'm three and three quarters."*
> *"I was told you're almost four," Ricky coolly answers. "When you're going to be four, I'm going to be five and you can't beat me up."*[47]

This does not mean that children should not have friends of the same age, but mixed age groups can supplement those friendships in a valuable way. Children's cell groups may be one of the few places in society where children can learn to relate to others outside their own graded world.

Singing And Worship

Worship in a family is a special experience. It is when the family expresses their dependence on God and their commitment to Him that faith blossoms.

It is not always formal and structured. It can take place around a meal table or around the fire, on Sundays or on a weekday. It can be spontaneous or planned, but the consistent feature is that it involves the whole family.

It is also true that many Christian families find it hard to worship together. There is a great guilt about the fact. They need help in making worship meaningful and natural, and a cell group can help people learn some of the skills.

A children's small group worship can also be both structured and spontaneous. A formal singing time at the beginning seems to be less effective in Australia and New Zealand. Boys have decided that it is not "cool" to sing, so they ignore the whole attempt. Girls try to sing, but they are distracted by the boys who are amusing themselves in their own way. Boys *do* still enjoy percussion and instruments.

Some groups have found it better to avoid formal singing, and simply to play lively Christian music in the background at appropriate moments. After a while the children sing along.

Worship should not just be identified with singing. Worship takes place whenever the group responds to God in a situation. It can take place in the midst of an activity, during a prayer time, in the middle of the story. The aim of the leader should be to turn the thoughts of the group towards God at any moment when it seems appropriate—just as a father would do in his family.

Activities

The range of activities which are appropriate in a children's cell group is limited only by the leader's imagination. Almost anything which is part of family life in a home can also be part of cell group life. Games, active and passive, hobbies, skills, walks, investigation of ideas, combined activities such as music groups or drama, can be used. The bookshops are overflowing with the creative ideas of skilled children's leaders. The real difference with a children's cell group is not so much in the *activities,* but more in the attitude and climate in which they are done.

Special events in the group require celebration. The birth of a baby brother or sister, the conversion or baptism of one of the group, a family wedding, a graduation can be celebrated. Death also needs to be recognized by the group, with a time for grieving and for group sympathy.

These events are occasions for talk and explanations. Why has this happened? How can we respond to it? Where is God in all this? How will it change our lives?

My son felt real grief at the marriages of his brother and sister. Suddenly he was alone. It was a time for ministry to him.

A leader will be sensitive to such events with more than just a card through the mail. It is a potential learning experience for the whole group, a chance for the group to express solidarity and love for one of its members. In New Zealand it is often the custom for the members of a small group to come forward and give a special blessing to one of their members who is being baptized. Then they all stand close to the pool to watch, and to greet the person as they come out of the water.

Training Leadership

The greatest problem in beginning groups for children in the life of the cell church is the recruiting and training of leadership. Many Sunday School teachers have been enculturated into an activity which is based on a school model and which takes place only on Sunday mornings.

They feel safe with that, because it is the pattern they grew up with and it can be fitted into an already busy program. Children's ministry in the cell group model requires time, concern, openness and great energy. It is a call of God to children.

Existing teachers will often have some difficulty in re-arranging their thinking to fit the cell group concept. It is easy to fall back into the old habits of teacher domination. Mothers who know the family concept best are often good group leaders, and if a couple can be recruited, that is probably the best of all. Elderly active people have much to give to the children, and older Christian teenagers can form good role models. They are especially good at the area of children's discipleship because they have just walked the same way themselves. They are the desired models for many children. Late teenage men seem to have some special bonds with very young children.

It is hard to expect a parent to act as a cell group leader to his own child. Often he/she is too overwhelmed by their own relationship with the child to be effective.

All leaders need to understand the concepts of the cell group. If they are participating in an adult small group in the church, the relationship will be easier for them to comprehend. Their own group may become prayer partners for them in this ministry.

The cell group has to be a place of trust, and winning that

trust is the first goal of every leader. Trust is won through getting to know another person in a variety of situations. The child is able to test the validity of the person's words by scrutinizing the reality of their lives. That is why a cell group is important. People reveal themselves more easily, and get to know each other personally.

It is also very important that each child gets the opportunity to talk with the leader individually at some time.[48] To know that his leader has come to the school play or the big match means more to a child than he can express.

During some interviews with children of different age levels, I asked them these questions:[49] "Mostly, your teachers say the same sorts of things your parents say. But if the teacher does say something different from your parents, who would you believe?"

Among the younger children the answer predictably was "Mummy and Daddy." Among the older children, all but one child said that they would need to find some *other* adult they could ask, or some *other* book, to find out who was right. This was a surprise to me. It indicates the independence of mind which the schools are encouraging. If a child has a good cell group leader, he will be the kind of person the child could ask to discuss the matter. This role of support to the family may be comparatively new, but it is vital in the Christian growth of the child.

In preparing for the group session, the leader needs a mental picture of all the children, filling up her memory about them as she knows them better. As she pictures them, she can pray for them by name. She needs to ask herself, "What are the needs of these children this week?"

She may prepare the cell group time with those needs in mind, but with the consciousness that if another need arises during the group activities she may feel free to abandon her prepared program.

Visuals are good, but should not be used in the instructional mode. They should be utilized more like an adult friend who pulls out something interesting to show to a child.

The best way to train people for the leadership of a children's small group is to have them experience one. It is good to have an intern leader present in the group to learn techniques and to build his own trust level. The skills of relating to children do not come out of a teacher training session.

20 "HE SET A CHILD IN THE MIDST"

This chapter is written by Lorna R. Jenkins, lightly edited.

A Short Story

Don's small group was going well. Even his wife Margaret said so. They'd started out with seven people: Tom and Ruby, Ken and Molly, and Roy. They'd all been cautious to start with, because they didn't know each other very well. But over several months they'd learned to trust each other, to be honest, yet supportive of each other. They'd also been joined by Bill and Carrie who brought along their friend, Chris. Chris became a Christian on the fourth night he was there.

One night Carrie said,

"Our baby sitter told us she was quitting tonight. I don't know how we'll get on next week. Could we pray about that?"

Then Bill added rather shyly,

"Actually we were wondering if we could bring the boys *with* us on Sunday nights. They just sit home and watch television, and to be honest we'd like them to get to know the group. We've had so much blessing ourselves! It doesn't seem right that Tim and Garth shouldn't share it, too."

No one spoke for a moment. Then Don asked,

"Do you think the two boys would really enjoy this type of meeting, Bill?"

"I think they might. They only know you from church. They really don't know what great people you are. I think it'd be good for them to get to know some enthusiastic Christian adults apart from ourselves. Besides, Tom, you're a bit of a hero to Garth. He follows every soccer match you play in. You could have a very good influence on him."

"I'd like to, Bill, but don't you think he'd get rather bored during the sharing time? I mean, listening to us talking about how we're coping as Christians?"

Tom was looking uncertain.

Suddenly, Chris plunged into the conversation:

"You know, I think we underrate kids and their problems. I mean, some of the hang-ups you guys have been helping me sort out dated right back to when I was at school. I didn't have *anyone* I could talk to. There didn't seem to be a single adult who cared."

"But I really don't think we could be as open in sharing if there were children present," suggested Molly. "It's not that I'm against your children, Bill, but children as a class really don't know how to keep confidences."

"That's a valid point," said Ruby, "but I'd really like to include those kids. They're great little guys. How would it be if we spent some time with the children present, and then when the adults wanted to talk together in more depth I could take the boys to another room and have some special activity with them. Then, we could come together for a final prayer."

"I wouldn't mind taking a turn on that," offered Chris. "I like kids."

Ken had been waiting to say something, and at last he found a break in the conversation.

"The one thing I fear is that the nature of the group might change too much," he began. "One of the main things I've appreciated about this group is that we can sit together and talk things over sensibly like adults. I mean, we can deal with some of the *really tough* questions."

'If you want to talk about the tough questions, Ken, you ought to talk to Tim," said Bill. "He comes up with some real lulus. I often don't know how to answer him. I'd appreciate the group's help in sorting out some of his questions, for my sake as well as for his. Besides, sometimes I think we get a bit too bogged down in the serious side of life. We could probably do more singing, include some stories, maybe even tell them some of the stories from our past. A bit of drama could be fun, for us I mean, as well as the kids."

At this point, Carrie dug Bill in the ribs.

"Don't push it, dear," she whispered. "Maybe it'd be better if we just advertised for another babysitter."

Don intervened: "Now just hold on, Carrie. We haven't said 'No' yet. We're just trying to think through the implications. Maybe God is challenging us through you to consider something we'd never have thought of on our own."

Margaret had been quietly thinking.

"It'd be nice to have Tim and Garth here," she said, "and even if Tom and Ruby brought their little Stephanie, she could probably sleep in a bedroom. But, suppose we get more couples with more children? Wouldn't they rather dominate the group? Wouldn't the mothers and fathers be on edge trying to see that they behave?"

"Wow," exclaimed Ruby. "I've just had a great idea. If God ever gave us *that* many children, we could spend some of our group time together and then have a special children's small group at our place just across the street. I mean, a *real* cell group with the children sharing with each other and praying for each other and everything. I bet we could do it."

"Well, if we get more children, that could be a great way of handling them, Ruby," said Don. "Would we handle it like a Sunday school and get some lesson materials?"

"I haven't had time to think it through yet," answered Ruby. "I guess we might need *some* sort of framework, but the important thing is that it should be a proper small group, just like we have. The other advantage would be that when we have group picnics or social outings, the children would already know each other, and know us too."

"I wouldn't mind kicking a ball around with them," said Tom.

"Well," said Don, "we've talked about it. What do you think we should do about it? Should we invite Tim and Garth to join us on Sunday nights?"

"I think Bill or Don should explain to them first what the group is all about and what we all agree to as group members," suggested Molly.

"That's good, Molly," said Don. "They need to understand our covenant just like anyone else who joins us. But of course, if they're going to *keep* the covenant they will need to pray for us just as we pray for them. That means they need to be present when we share prayer needs."

"That reminds me of something I've been meaning to suggest anyway," broke in Carrie. "Why can't we have a prayer diary where we record our prayer needs and check them off when God answers them? The boys would learn a lot from that."

"Good idea, Carrie. Suppose you buy a book and get us started. If this thing works out, you might even get Tim to help you later on."

"O.K. So when are the children going to be with us, and when are they not?" asked Ken.

"Well, Don's already suggested the prayer sharing time, and maybe the time when we report in on what God's been doing during the week," answered Ruby. "And we could sing together. I liked Bill's story and drama ideas, though we wouldn't do it every week."

"Could the children follow the same theme that we talk about?" asked Chris. "I mean, introduce the theme while the children are there and let them ask questions if they want to, and then we divide up and handle the idea at our own levels."

"I don't see why that wouldn't work," said Don. "We could try it.

"I'd like to take a turn for Ruby sometimes," said Tom, giving her a squeeze.

"So would I," said Margaret and Bill simultaneously.

"Well, I'm not going to offer," said Ken. "I'm really not good with children. I don't know what to say to them."

"That's O.K.," said Bill. "All the same, I guess my boys could learn something from the way you handle the Scriptures."

"Well, I'm happy to try this out," said Molly, "on one condition—no—*two,* actually. First, I think we ought to have some agreed signal so that if any adult felt the discussion was getting too, well, 'heavy' for the children, Ruby could quietly take them elsewhere. Secondly, I think we should have one night occasionally when there are no children."

"That's fair enough," Bill replied. "But just now and then we might have a special children's night when we concentrate on the children and let *them* choose our activities."

"Is everyone happy then?" asked Don.

There was a circle of nods.

"Just one thing," mentioned Tom. "Suppose we have new people come into the group who are not Christians? Could we handle the children *then?*"

Margaret smiled. "Suppose they had children they needed to bring along?"

Don opened his Bible to the next chapter in Matthew, chapter 18. He read,

> *"At that time the disciples came to Jesus and asked, "Who is the greatest in the kingdom of heaven? He called a little child and had him stand among them. And he said, "I tell you the truth, unless you change and become like little children, you will never enter the kingdom of heaven. Therefore whoever humbles himself like this child is the greatest in the kingdom of heaven. And whoever welcomes a little child like this in my name, welcomes me..."*

Children And Small Groups

Considering the way cell groups have multiplied and enriched the lives of adults, it seems strange that children seem to have been largely excluded. Some groups have made valiant attempts to include the children, but they have problems. Other cell churches have tried to stick with Sunday school and youth groups as being the tried and true way of dealing with children.

Too often parents who appreciate a cell group style church feel obliged to return to a traditional church at the time when their children start school. They feel they have a responsibility to provide Christian teaching for their children. They feel this responsibility even more keenly when their children become teenagers.

Nevertheless, there is no reason why children should not learn and grow through a cell structure church. Indeed, their learning experiences are likely to be more varied and vital among a small group of totally committed Christians. They will see prayers answered. They will see people's lives being changed. They will hear reports of God's actions, and they will know and respect adult Christians apart from their parents. They will have a community where they can ask questions, and have their life experiences interpreted in the light of the Bible.

Some parents feel uneasy if their child is the only one in an age group. This uneasiness arises from the fallacy that children can only learn and make friends among their own age group. We *believe* this, even though our own families disprove it to us every day.

Children often choose their friends from another age group. My son, aged eight, had a best friend aged eleven. While they were separated at school, at home they spent all their time together. Older children often take pleasure in being helpers and guides to younger children, and they can be effective in that ministry. Children also like to relate to another trusted adult apart from their parents.

Every Child Needs An Adult Friend

Having children in groups requires at least one person who likes children and has some creativity. If your group has no one like that, ask God to provide you with someone with those gifts.

The following section lists some suggestions which have been tried by various small groups. Since each group is different, you may have to select appropriate activities, or think up some of your own.

The Need for a Policy

Any cell group or church which hopes to minister success-fully to children needs to have thought out and prayed about a policy. If children are to be regarded as an integral part of the church community, people need to understand where the youngsters belong, and what responsibility adult members have for them.

There is some difference of opinion among Christians about how children fit into the community of faith. Some would say they become members upon baptism. When baptism takes place in infancy, their membership is based on the faith-pledge taken by their parents. They are in the community to be loved and nurtured until they make a faith-pledge of their own. Others, who practice believer's baptism, see the children as "pre-Christians," sinners who are not held accountable for their sin until they are able to make a conscious choice to follow Christ. In either case, the nurturing of the children is seen as being primarily the responsibility of parents, but within the context of a loving and active community of saints. If the parents in the cell group church have a picture of what kind of Christians they hope their children will be, it will be much easier for them to work toward that expectation.

These Are Some Steps To Help You Form A Policy

1. Ask the parents to share the Christian characteristics they would like to see in their children's lives. Cover areas such as witnessing, serving, prayer, Bible knowledge, missionary vision, giving, and social justice.
2. Discover what the Bible says about children within the Christian community.
3. Let the cell members ask the parents what sort of support they would appreciate from the group, and how they could share in nurturing the children.
4. Try to work out the role of adults, other than parents, towards the children in the Shepherd group.
5. Talk about practical ways for the group to minister to the children, and ways the children can minister to the group.
6. Discuss ways the group can adopt acceptable norms of behavior for the children within the group. Can other group members exercise any restraint on the children?
7. How can the group benefit from having the children within the group, and still allow time for the adults to have particular times of sharing?
8. How can the teenagers be both integrated and retain their sense of independence?
9. When you have come up with a possible policy, talk to the elementary school children about it, explaining what it means and asking for suggestions.
10. Ask teenagers what their reaction to the policy is. Request that they also speak on behalf of smaller children they know in the cell group, voicing what they might say if they were older.
11. Ask the adults to consider any additions or changes the children and teenagers may have suggested.

12. Have a meeting with everyone present in which the policy is explained and accepted by the group. Make it a gala occasion with celebration and love shown among all age groups. Include inter-generational activities and food.

A policy should not be regarded as unchangeable, but it *does* provide a framework for the cell groups. The process should be surrounded by prayer and loving concern for each of the little ones.

The Shepherd group will also need to seek out those who have spiritual and creative gifts for planning children's ministries, and ask for assistance. All cell group members can be helpers from time to time.

Children In Intergenerational Groups

There are three major settings in which all the generations of a group are together: the regular group meeting (which includes worship), the special event, and the social activity. All of these are learning and growing experiences that will be important to the lives of children.

Children In The Weekly Shepherd Group

When children attend the regular group meeting, it is important to determine how long they should be there, whether they should be present on all occasions, and what part they should have in the proceedings. One group in Australia has adopted the pattern that on two weekly meetings of the month the children should be present in a regular group and share whenever they can, but without special emphasis placed on their presence. When they are tired or have homework, they are free to leave the group. One week in the month is Children's Night, and the group concentrates on them, with all adults joining in the activities. Another night in the month is a child-free night, when parents arrange for baby sitters. Other groups prefer to have the children present every time, but to divide into sub-groups for part of the evening.

What Do We Do With the Children?

The Basic Rule: don't try to entertain them. Children today are overwhelmed with high quality entertainment. Their standards are high and the boredom toleration point is low. If you focus the group on entertaining the children, the session is likely to succeed with no one.

Do involve them. Children like doing what the adults do. The trouble is that adults often do such boring things—even for grownups! There are so many things that adults and children *can* do together, where genuine relationships can be formed. Consider these:

1. *Eating.*

   A meal is a cohesive action among people. It is a place of trust and acceptance. Children who eat with adults learn adult patterns of eating behavior. Older children, teens or other adults can assist the little ones to give their mothers a rest. It is no accident that in both the Old and New Testaments the central act of worship was in the form of a meal. At meal time, children can learn to serve others.

2. *Praying.*

   Long, rambly, irrelevant prayers makes most children "switch off." Most adults do, too! Yet, children can and do pray with a fervor and faith that few adults can match. They pray about the things that seem important to them —like the health of the cat, and the success of the school team. When we talk to children about genuine needs and listen to their needs too, the children will pray briefly and earnestly. A prayer diary which records answers to prayer is an excellent idea. It produces a sense of wonder and praise when we see God in action.

3. *Worship.*

   It is amazing how children sense the awe of being in the presence of God. If worship and praise is genuine, they will be able to *appreciate* it even when they cannot *comprehend* it. Themes in worship make it easier for children to understand what is happening. Physical actions help them to praise God with their bodies. Objects such as banners, nature objects, posters, and photographs, help to focus the worship.

Music, rhythm, poetry, verse speaking, sacred movements, all enrich the quality of the worship to make it more explicit for children. Children can contribute to the worship not just to entertain the adults, but to make genuine offerings of praise. They may use their physical, musical, and artistic skills with joyful exuberance.

4. *Story telling.*

    This is one of the oldest intergenerational activities of all. Television is simply a story telling device for all ages. It replaces the professional community storyteller. In a group, there are many individual stories to be told. Older generations tell of life as they knew it. Younger people tell of life as they see it. There are the stories about families, the local community, and the history of the nation. There are stories of the church in history, and the church all around the world. Most of all, there is the Great Story—the story of God reaching out to people, and the way people respond. The Bible is full of stories. Jesus used them constantly. Do not just confine yourselves the the parts which we call "narrative" with the children. There is hardly a passage of Scripture that cannot be told as a story.

5. *Sharing.*

    Sharing is a kind of story telling. People tell the story of what has been happening to them during the past week. "Sharing" takes place when cell members are listening and sharing an experience with a person, helping him to understand it and deal with it. Since there is often joy or pain involved in the experience, the group also shares the *feelings* of the person. Children can participate in this process. They need to be able to share what happens to them, too, and have some trustworthy adults help them interpret it. They also like to know what happens in the lives of adults. They can be surprisingly sensitive. Of course, there are some things which should not be shared while children are present. The Shepherd and members can delay some sharing until the children have left.

6. *Drama.*

    Drama is nothing more than a game of "Let's Pretend." It may be retelling a story, explaining a problem (in a role play), demonstrating a challenging idea (in a skit), expressing a feeling (in a mime). Drama requires all kinds of participants and children can participate with adults on equal terms. It doesn't have to be formal and rehearsed, though sometimes it's a challenge to produce a polished performance with children. Often, however, enjoyable drama is spontaneous, without scripts or scenery, with makeshift props, and with plenty of improvisation. A practice run just to keep everybody on track is followed immediately by "the performance." Mistakes and side comments are the rule. The opportunity for learning is great.

Festivals and Ceremonies

The Lord's Supper and Baptism

Most Shepherd groups like to celebrate the Lord's Supper. Children respond well when they are present. They understand that this is a special meal, and often they long to be part of it. They know it is a way of expressing love to Jesus. It is hard to say when a child is ready to share the Lord's Supper. Scripture is silent on the issue. Some people like their children to participate very early, as part of the family faith. Some like to wait until the children understand the meaning of the symbols and have expressed their faith and love for Jesus. Often partaking of Lord's Supper is a kind of "rite of passage" into meaningful membership in the life of the church.

Children understand and value Lord's Supper more than many people think. When I was ten, there was a serious epidemic of poliomyelitis in New Zealand, and children were not allowed to meet in groups. Therefore, the public school and Sunday schools were closed, and no children were permitted to attend church for five months. During that time, I missed being part of the church community. The thing I missed most was participating in the Lord's Supper. I began to celebrate Lord's Supper on my own at home, using orange juice and bread. In my mind I was not playing: *I was worshipping.*

Children also like to participate when a person is baptized. They like to know who the person is and what is happening. If the person is a member of the Shepherd group, they like to participate in the baptism in some way. In one church I attended which practiced believer's baptism, the members of the home group would gather round the baptismal pool and give messages of love and encouragement. The group leader assisted with the baptism. The group sang afterwards. Children loved being a part of this. It made a lasting impression on their own commitment.

Group And Family Celebrations

There are many causes for spontaneous festivals in the life of a Shepherd group community. Of course there are religious festivals, like Christmas and Easter, but in a Shepherd group there are also family festivals, birthdays, new babies, graduations, examination or sports successes—in fact, *any* kinds of personal achievements. There can be festivals for age groups, festivals for occupations, festivals of the land, or festivals of the seasons. They are all good reasons to praise God, and children delight in making them into special events. Even death is a time for a ceremony. It is part of the grieving process, which children also share.

Games and Activities

Many children's games can be adapted for use in the life of the Shepherd group. Singing games, word games, action games, and paper games can all be used to teach the children along with the adults. Modelling activities using things such as modelling clay, pipe cleaners, or paper folding and tearing, are intergenerational in their appeal and sometimes can reveal feelings or Biblical truth. *Objects* can also become symbols for ideas. One cell group gave each family an apple, and asked how the apple reminded them of God. The children came up with some of the most profound of all the statements given.

Some groups find that games are too disruptive to their overall aims. They need to be used with discretion, but if they form part of an overall theme and the Shepherd shows sensitivity, they can add variety and richness to group life.

Children in the Social Setting

Most Shepherd groups have occasions when they gather just for friendship and enjoyment. It may be a picnic or barbeque, a fishing trip, a bush walk, a weekend camp, or attending a sports event. Children usually participate in such occasions according to their age, but they may not enjoy the outings unless they already know the other families who participate. If relationships are already bonded, the social events have a deeper joy. It is also easier to include new families if the children know each other first, and are happy to welcome the newcomers. Some kinds of social events are special to children. For instance, a sleepover at the home of another Shepherd group family helps them to see another Christian family in their natural setting. Going fishing or seeing a ball game with the men or teenagers in the group may be wonderful experiences for the children of a solo mother.

Special Events

Sometimes the whole group can plan for a special event. It may be a play or concert to be presented to the Congregation. It may be a visit to a retirement village. It may be a children's Christmas party, or attending a minifair in the community. This is a wonderful opportunity for adults and children to work together. There are always tasks where children can be involved. Their enthusiasm encourages everybody—even when they make mistakes. It takes some patience to involve children. We all think we can do it better ourselves, but children need to be servants too. They need to know that God appreciates and honors their ministry.

Children's Shepherd Groups

When children have their own Shepherd groups, many elements in the adult groups should still be present. A covenant, for instance, is a useful way of establishing the expectations and behavior patterns of the group. If children accepted a set of rules as being fair and worthwhile, they will try to make sure they are obeyed.

Adult leaders of a children's Shepherd group should not be seen as teachers. They are *friends,* trusted by the children to plan for the group sessions. If there are teens in the group, they can be seen as leader apprentices, serving the younger children. In fact, *any* older children can be given responsibility in assisting the younger ones. That is their natural family function.

Groups need a *pattern,* so the children know what to expect. This provides security. They also need *variety,* so that a new thing happens quite often. This provides excitement. The most important ingredients in a children's group are trust and affection. The children need to know that this is a place where they *belong*, where grownups will listen and understand. This trust atmosphere is not just the responsibility of the leaders. Every child in the group needs to learn that he or she has a part in helping others.

Here is a format of a possible group meeting. It can be widely adapted to the needs of Shepherd groups:

Model Of A Small Group For Children

Setting:

The group might sit on the floor on cushions. Have food set out on a low table perhaps on individual plates. Ask some "children" to serve it to the others.

Sharing:

While they are eating, the leader can begin to ask about the events of the week. If there have been any answers to prayer from the last week, check them off in the prayer diary and give thanks for them. Some children may have questions to ask, or problems to raise. Others may be able to make suggestions, or pray for the person. Questions do not have to be answered immediately. If the matter is serious, arrange to meet privately with the child. Allow time for celebration and congratulation for any achievement.

Praise:

Using a guitar or autoharp or similar instrument (even a ukelele), sing songs which are suggested by the sharing. You might ask, "What could be a good song to sing in that situation?" Lead from one song to the next, with sentences of praise. The children can look up psalms to find praise verses. Make sure to include some action!

Story telling:

Get everyone comfortable, and tell the Bible story in a lively, imaginative way, or get them to tell the story back to you with suitable questions and comments. If the scripture was not a narrative passage, create a story around the theme. At the end, ask if anyone can think of a similar story that happened to them. If they can't, think up one from your own experience, or from someone you know.

Discussion:

First of all, make sure the children have understood the story and the point of it. Ask questions which will encourage the children to think about how the story relates to what happened to them in the past week. Do not use questions the children know have preset answers. The questions should encourage the discovery of both facts and feelings. If they are having problems finding answers, put them in pairs to search the passage or to discuss the question. Refer back to the questions which arose during the sharing time, so that they are included.

Activity:

Children need a means of expressing outwardly the ideas they have been thinking about. This can be accomplished through using art, music, drama, dance, poetry, and crafts. Means of expression are as wide as the imagination, and can include wood crafts, cooking, puppetry, modelling, science experiments, surveys, gardening, and animal care. Don't try to complete a project every week. Children like to finish work properly. When it is completed, show that you value it. Share it with the Congregation, and use it in ministry.

Response:

Discuss how the truths learned in the session could be be put into practice in their lives. Role play a situation in which that might happen. Find a way the truths could be incorporated in a ministry project by the group.

Conclusion:

Make sure that during the session you have personally recognized each child. Make sure you say "Good-bye," and encourage all members as they leave. Make an appointment to meet informally with at least one child during the week.

After the group has left, compile in a notebook things that you need to remember as a result of the session. For example, this might include approaching events, information about class members and their families, any sensitive points that need pastoral care, or items for you to be praying about between now and the next meeting.

Three Special Areas Of Sensitivity

1. Leaders should always be sensitive to the moving of the Spirit in the life of a child. When he or she is ready to make a step towards God which is appropriate to his understanding, guidance and encouragement should be provided. A simple step of faith at age five might be amplified and confirmed at age thirteen.
2. Leaders should develop friendly relations with parents, so they can cooperate together in the Christian growth of the child. The leader supplements the role of the parents, never supplanting them.
3. Leaders should be aware of a child who may be hurting or abused through a violent situation in the home. They should talk to the Shepherd about ways the child can be helped. Such situations should never be handled alone.

A Final Word

We are all learning as we seek to serve children. You may make some discoveries which would benefit others, so try to share your insights with others who are ministering in children's cell groups. You may be able to help one Shepherd, a group, or a whole church. Whatever you learn is God's gift to you. Share it with others!

21 EQUIPPING CHILDREN'S CELL LEADERS

(Note: this material was contributed by Dr. Lorna Jenkins of Auckland, New Zealand, adapted to suit the American scene.)

Servant Leader's Equipping Sessions

It is suggested that this equipping course be given to small groups of no more than eight to ten, allowing maximum interaction between participants. The following outline is designed for a weekend "Getaway" which would begin on a Saturday morning and extend through Sunday, with one session scheduled for the second day. It could also be done on two consecutive Saturdays. The sessions can also be adapted for other time frames.

Have on hand: a hymn book, blank paper, pencils, a large newsprint flip chart on an easel in one corner.

Setting: a living room or den, with refreshments available nearby.

Session 1: 9:30 A.M.

As trainees gather around the refreshment table, have two or three "Initiators" bring up the topic of "Family." Let them ask questions like, "How's your family?" "How many do you have in your family?" "What region did your family come from?" "How does your family get along together?"

When all have arrived, sit in a circle in the living room or den. Be sure all persons can have good eye contact with the rest of the group.

Opening: Warmup

Ask several people to suggest a hymn which was often sung in their family. Get one assistant to write up one verse of each hymn on the pages of the flip chart. (Have these verses ready to sing later in the session.)

Ask the group to recall occasions when their family...

*   Sang hymns together
*   Read or told Bible stories
*   Played games together
*   Talked to each other about the events of the day
*   Prayed together

If someone in the group did not experience any of these things as a child, ask: "What *were* the warm moments you remember your family shared together?"

Ask the group, "What do you feel you learned from those occasions? What kinds of things impacted you?" As they share, create a list on the flip chart of their comments. Briefly review it.

Ask, "What kind of learning takes place in the home?" Encourage people to give examples.

Pass around blank sheets of paper. Ask each person to draw stick figures representing the members of the family in which they grew up, including themselves.

They may include grandparents or other significant relatives if they wish to do so. If some of the family members were particularly significant in the life of the person, ask them to draw a line from that person to themselves. Write alongside the line the values they received from that person. Let each person share their drawing with the others.

Count fathers, mothers, etc., who were listed as the most significant people in their lives. Let the group evaluate these results.

Ask the group, "How many of you can remember a significant Sunday School teacher who was also a model to you during growing up years?" Evaluate the response with the group.

Ask, "What were the qualities that made that teacher a significant model?" Discuss these, using the flip chart to list them if necessary.

Ask the group to write down the qualities they would like to see in a child who has been reared in a Cell Group Church and is about to enter adulthood. List these in a column on the left half of a flip chart page.

In a right hand column, mark those qualities which can be best developed in a classroom, and which can best be created in a family atmosphere. Point out that all of the goals mentioned can be achieved best in a Children's Cell Group.

Break Time: 10:45 A.M.

Session 2: 11:00 A.M.

Have a short Bible study (20 minutes) related to Jesus and His small group, using John 13:1-20. Note the setting: a small group.

Points to emerge:
1. Jesus taught by action: v.1-5.
2. Jesus taught by answering their questions: v. 6-11.
3. Jesus taught by explanation: v. 12-15.
4. Teaching must result in action: v. 16-17.
5. Jesus knew the members of his group: v. 18.
6. Jesus was preparing them and interpreting for them a coming life experience: v. 19-20.

Discuss:
What was the style of leadership Jesus demonstrated?

Could Jesus have taught these lessons just as well in a classroom setting?

Introduce the FORMAL INSTRUCTION METHOD compared with the FAMILY GROUP MODEL. Ask the group to interpret the chart, filling in the misunderstandings or omissions. Ask the whole group to discover and explain the differences between a small class and a cell group.

Role plays:
Call on a prepared person to teach his group the story of the rich young ruler. (Mark 10:17-22)
(10 mins., as a class demonstration)
Call on a prepared person to lead the group in a discussion of what the rich young ruler might look like today. Include the question, "What was his real problem?"

(10 mins., as a class demonstration)

Ask the whole group if they could sense any differences of approach in the two methods used. What were the differences? Which method did they think children would better be able to learn from? Did anyone feel that there was some response they wanted to make, prompted by either of the presentations?

Encourage them to discover the differences between a teacher and a cell group leader. Add further material on the idea of the kinship of the leader and on the adult/friend.

Meal Time: Noon

Key Questions For Discussion: "Can a Shepherd Group meeting be like a family meeting? How could you encourage that in your group?" At the close of the meal, sing some of the hymns which have been placed on the flip chart.

Session 3: 1:30 P.M.

Divide into pairs. Take a short walk, sharing together some incident in your childhood when you misunderstood something which happened, or something painful that was said to you. How did you eventually find out the truth? How long did it take? Did you ever misunderstand what was going on in church?

Return at a designated time; sing some more hymns which have been written on the flip chart.

Spend time in prayer, praying for wisdom to know how to deal with the misunderstandings of children in the groups.

Discussion Question:
"Why do youngsters in Children's Cell Groups need to also participate in the Shepherd Groups?"

Possible Answers:
- "To see Christian adults, other than parents, up close;"
- "To develop strong friendships with other Christian children;"
- "To reinforce the values that are being taught in the home;"
- "To have a place where questions can be asked, life experiences can be interpreted, and misunderstandings can be resolved;"

- "To gain the support of the leader and the other children in the conflicts and frustrations of school life;"
- "To receive help and pastoral care with problems;"
- "To discover how the Bible speaks to us about these areas of conflict, confusion or hurt."
- "To celebrate together in thanksgiving for God's world, and in appreciation for the fun and joys of childhood."
- "To take delight in each other's skills, and to encourage each other to use them in ministry."
- "To learn and practice Christian skills such as prayer, Bible discovery, interpersonal relationships, and service."
- "To have a peer group in which a child is safe and accepted, where he feels appreciated and has an identity."
- "To help the many children who are excluded from secular peer groups, or have to achieve a certain status to belong to them."
- "To allow the Shepherd to sense signals of serious distress in the life of a child, and to follow up on an individual basis in consultation with the parents and/or the Zone Servant and Zone Pastor."

Discussion Questions:
- Can these needs be met within a Christian home?
- Which needs sometimes get overlooked?
- Could the Shepherd group be a support to children who do not have Christian homes?
- Could the home and the Shepherd group work together to help the child in these areas?
- Spend a brief time in prayer for Christian homes and Shepherd group life.

Break Time: About 3:30 P.M.

Session Four: 4:00 P.M.

In Full session:

Introduce the idea of Bible covenants. Talk about covenants we already practice, and covenants children practice.

How would covenants seem natural to children?

In small groups:

Ask each small group to compile a list of things that might be included in a Children's Cell Group covenant. Which of those things would the children be likely to suggest themselves? Ask the group how they would raise matters which the children did not think of.

Ask the groups to pass their covenants from group to group reading them and comparing them. Hand them in at the end.

General Discussion:

What should be included in a Children's Cell Group meeting?

Ask the whole group...
* ...to contribute ideas of what ought to be part of an average Children's Cell Group meeting. Collect the ideas, group them, and add any that have been left out.
* ...what they think the setting for such a group ought to look like.
* ...to suggest a way to uncover needs in the lives of the children in a group. What Bible passages might be appropriate to draw out those needs? Ask , "What kind of responses would you like to see as a result of the children's group experiences?"

Evening Meal: 6:00 P.M.

Ask for one group to prepare the eating area, and another group to prepare the food. All will share in cleaning up after the meal has been eaten.

If possible, have the groups eat at separate tables. Remind them that they have a covenant to create during the evening meal. They can choose from the prepared covenants, making revisions as they desire, and call on you for advice as needed.

Select a trainee to work with you in preparing a Children's Cell Group experience for the evening session.

Session Five: 7:30 P.M.

Preparation: select eight children of mixed ages, between 5 and 13 years of age. These may be the children of those being trained, or selected from Shepherd Groups nearby the home where you are meeting.

The whole group reconvenes to witness the Children's Cell Group event.

Setting:
All the adults sit around the edge of the room, a little distance from a circle of children. The children sit on the floor, perhaps on cushions. You are included in their circle.

Sharing:
- The children learn each other's names, and find out some special things about each other (5 minutes).
- You tell them some things about yourself (2 minutes).
- Have refreshments set out on a low table—perhaps on individual plates. Ask some children to serve it to the others.
- Discuss a topic relevant to their lifestyles.

Suggestions:
Friends who have let you down...
How and when do we pray? Does it work?
Talk about their experiences, and your own as well.

Praise:
Using a guitar or autoharp or similar instrument (even a ukulele), sing some songs which are suggested by the sharing. Ask, "What would be a good song to sing in that situation?" (Use an Overhead Projector if possible. Get one of the children to operate it.) Lead from one song to the next with sentences of praise. The children may wish to look up assigned psalms and explain how they fit the theme. Be sure to include some action!

Storytelling:
Move into the Bible material naturally *(10 minutes)*. Devise questions which will lead naturally towards the desired response to the lesson—not questions the children know there are pre-set answers. The questions should encourage discovery both of facts

and feelings. Don't tell them the answers, or even where to look for them. If they are having problems finding the answers, put them in pairs to search the Bible passage or to discuss the question. Let them report back. Write up conclusions as you go along. Refer back to the questions brought up by the children during the sharing time. Be sure all their questions are included.

Here are some examples:

First Example:

Jesus had two special friends who let Him down. Who were they? *(Tell the story, or draw out the story from them if they know it.)*

Let the children live through the story!

Ask, "Was Jesus ever friendly to Peter and Judas again?" (Peter: yes; Judas: no.) Peter was sorry for what he did, and he could be forgiven. Judas did not think he could be forgiven, and so he died.

Ask, "If we have friends who do something cruel to us, can we forgive them?" "What has to happen so you can be friends with them again?"

Second Example:

Ask, "Can you think of a time when the disciples were praying very hard for something and God answered?" Turn to the story of Peter's release from prison. *(Once again: tell the story, or draw out the story from them if they know it.)* Ask, "Was it an easy prayer for God to answer?" "Did the disciples believe that God could do it?" "Who found out first that God had answered their prayer?" "Did God *always* get Christians out of prison?" "Why did God answer prayer sometimes, and not other times?" "Have you ever had that happen to you?"

Response:

Talk about how the idea of the session could be be put into practice in their lives (5 minutes). Role play a situation in which that might happen. Or, plan a way in which this idea could become a ministry project towards others in the Cell Group Church, or outside it.

Give each child a small notebook and ask them to start a

prayer diary in it. Explain they can bring the diary to each Cell Group meeting, and there will be a weekly review of their prayers. Indicate they can discuss with you why some of their prayers were answered and others were not answered.

Ask the children to prepare a prayer they can share to bless the adults who have been observing their time with you.

Join hands; pray for one another.

Conclusion:

The session should not last longer than 60 to 75 minutes. Make sure during the session you have personally recognized each child. Make sure you say "Good-bye" and encourage each one as they leave. Make an appointment to meet informally with at least one of them during the week. Let the children leave, encouraging them to say goodbye to each one of the adult trainees who have been watching.

Session Six: 9:00 P.M.

After the children have left, compile in a notebook things that the trainees need to remember about them as a result of the session. This may include approaching events like someone's birthday, information about the children and their families, sensitive points that need pastoral care from the Shepherd, items for you to pray about during the week.

Lead the group in an evaluation of the Children's Cell Group experience; discuss potential problems in the lives of the youngsters. Seek a problem-solving group approach to them.

In small groups:

Ask each group to work out how much preparation would be required to plan for each week's Children's Cell Group. Ask them to make a list of the things which need to be done, reporting back so a master list can be compiled.

Session Seven: Sunday, At An Appropriate Hour

Discuss the proper relationships between individual families and their cell group life.

Conduct a role play of a "home visit" to be made by a Children's Cell Group leader to the parents of a participating child.

Teaching Session:
1. *Blending Children Into The Cell Church*
   Encourage participation. Frequently ask each trainee what he/she is thinking.)
   Material to be presented may include:
   - The facilitator of the Children's Cell Group could be a threat to the family. There is a need to spend time with the parents, explaining the nature of a Children's Cell Group and what you are seeking to do with the children. Discover their dreams and standards for their children. Try to support them in their goals; be ready to help where you can.
   - Take time to create a friendship with the parents; get involved with the whole family. For example, visit a family member's birthday party—even prepare some games, or bring some food. Or, give a harried mother a night out with her husband by baby sitting for them. Invite the whole family of a child to your home for a meal, or plan a joint outing. Be prepared to assist in some family project, such as moving to a new apartment or laying a concrete drive - or, sharing sewing skills, etc.
   - Be ready to talk to the parents about what their child has shared about personal concerns or perplexities being faced (without unnecessarily breaking the child's confidence). Pray with them about these needs. Does the Cell Group Church have some equipping programs which are available in the area of parenting skills?
   - Are the parents a part of a Shepherd Group? If not, introduce the family to cell group members in the neighborhood, and invite them to a cell group social event, like a barbeque. Suggest that the parents might also like to belong to a Share Group or a Shepherd Group, as visitors at first and later as participants. If they have a special need, alert other Christians in a nearby cell. Let them meet the Zone Pastor informally, preferably in his casual clothes.
   - The children are part of the church community.
   - The Children's Cell Group should not become an entity in itself. It needs to network with other age groups, with the Shepherd Groups, and with the Congregations.

In small groups:

Give each group some sealed instructions. When they run out of ideas they can break the seal and find some further ideas to add to their collection. Here are some suggestions:

- Have a "hot spot" in the Children's Cell Group. Invite members of the Shepherd Groups, all ages, to come to visit the Children's Cell Group one at a time. Allow the children to ask them questions.
- Invite the Zone Pastor to be a member of the Children's Cell Group at least annually, to participate and answer questions—not to give a short word and then leave.
- When there is a special church event, give the Children's Cell Group a chance to find out what is happening, to witness it, and to ask questions.
- Try to ensure that Children's Cell Group members are able to attend the Congregation and Celebration meetings for at least part of the time—preferably during the praise times, sessions which include prayer, testimonies, the Lord's Supper or baptism, and special events.
- Give the children opportunity to minister in the worship of the Shepherd Group or the Congregation meetings, through offering prayer, singing music, displaying their activities, making special gestures such as giving flowers to the mothers, taking up the offering, or presenting the Bible reading through drama.
- Hold a Children's Rally of all the Children's Cell Groups. Let the children talk briefly to the Senior Pastor about the concerns of their week (Use a microphone). Have a "CHILD OF THE WEEK" when the Congregation meets, so the adults can learn the names of the youngsters.
- Have special times when the past is remembered, showing the children how God has led the church and its members through the years and the mighty acts he has done. Make sure that if there is a miracle or answer to prayer in the church family, the children hear about it and meet the persons involved.
- Send an evaluator to each Children's Cell Group. Evaluate

their conclusions; make a report to the Children's Leadership Team.

- Give each group a situation in which children and adults might get to know each other: e.g., within the Shepherd Group, in Congregational Meetings, or during Celebrations.
- Ask each group to recommend some special events the children would enjoy. Ask them to work out ways in which children could have meaningful relationships with the rest of the church.

2. Areas of complexity

- The Zone Pastors need to know about the families you are dealing with, and how the church can serve those families. Avoid the temptation to put pressure on parents to come to a Share Group or a Shepherd Group immediately. If you push them, they may even come one time, but the chances are they won't come back. Parents need to feel comfortable with a group, affirmed that they are among friends, and that the Shepherd is a real person.
- If you discover a child who is in an abusive or conflict situation and is in need of care and counselling, don't try to handle it alone—beyond showing your love and deep concern. Try to find people who can join you in offering the child care and protection, and assistance to the parent(s) involved.
- In building a trust relationship with a child, they need to have complete confidence in you. This means that not everything they tell you is intended to be reported back to their parents, or to anyone else. If they had a fight with another child or stepped out of line at school, they may not want their parents to know about it. What you divulge to the parents depends a bit on your judgment of how they are likely to handle it. On the other hand, sometimes you may hear things which parents need to know, or which parents need to interpret for you. In that case, you should arrange to see the parents— preferably with the child's knowledge. If you think the parents cannot handle the information you have, seek outside help. Never report "cute sayings" if you think they will become a cause for adult laughter.

Break Time: 15 Minutes

Session 8: Sunday, At An Appropriate Hour

Ask each group to withdraw to a quiet place and to write down the names of the children they are personally involved with, both their own children and others as well.

With those children in mind, compile together a list of the things children need and expect from their parents and leaders. When each person has prepared a list, ask each trainee to check the areas where they know they may have problems meeting those needs.

Ask each person to silently ask God what they *could* do, and what they *intend* to do, to better serve these children.

One member of the group may now be asked to read aloud Matthew 18:1-6 and 10-14. Ask each member of the group to formulate an "Act of Commitment," in which they indicate, with God's help, how they will serve the youngsters in their Children's Cell Group as their spiritual calling.

Ask every trainee who is willing to do so, to read their commitment aloud to the group. Spend time praying for each other, that all will keep that commitment. Pledge to phone one another a month from now, to review the life which has backed up this commitment.

The groups should disperse quietly. The training leader should be available to answer questions and to give counsel if necessary.

TIPS FROM DR. LORNA JENKINS FOR SERVANTS OF CHILDREN'S CELL GROUPS

The Children's Cell Group should be a group to belong to, because children love to belong and feel they're needed and wanted.

IT SHOULD BE A GROUP...
- For talking and sharing.
- For acceptance, but not for competition.
- For trust in adults.
- For asking questions.
- For sharing troubles.
- For mutual support and prayer.
- For ministering together.

FLEXIBILITY
Groups can meet any place, any time. Thus includes after school, Saturday mornings, Sunday afternoons, etc.

PERSONAL RELATIONSHIPS
The Servant Leaders need to be trusted friends...more like a caring relative than a "teacher."
Be alert for "silent" problems. Know the parents: be on their team.

PASTORAL CARE
Provides an "early warning system" for hurting ones.

DISCIPLESHIP IN ACTION
Children learn to minister to other children.

Mixed ages give children the opportunity to care for younger children.

For the Servant Leader, quality time can be spent one to one, outside the group.
Teens are good disciplers!

Supporting the child's parents may make a great difference in the home environment.
Keep good records on all the children.

GROUP INTERACTION
Skills in group life are developed...something the child doesn't get in school.

SAFE ENVIRONMENT
For the rest of his/her life, the child will remember this first taste of true community...even when it doesn't exist at home! In years to come, you will be a trusted friend to share in solving adolescent problems.

FIGHTING BOREDOM

SINGING

"Why don't they sing?"
- *Boys hate singing. It isn't "cool."*
- *Many songs are too old, or too juvenile.*
- *There's inadequate accompaniment or direction given.*

"How can we improve things?"
- *Better up-beat music.*
- *Use tapes for background and for teaching.*
- *Use instruments, ones they can play.*
- *Use movement, but not "actions."*

PRAYER

- *Prayer is only interesting if you are doing it.*
- *Construct prayers that the group can share aloud.*
- *Collect prayer items from the children themselves.*
- *Ask, "What are the most boring prayers you've heard?" ...Avoid those methods of praying with the group.*
- *Ask, "What do you think God would like to hear about?"*
- *Keep a group Prayer Diary. Record answers to prayer.*
- *Encourage brief, spontaneous prayers in ordinary words.*
- *Write letters to God as prayers.*

STORIES

"Why won't they listen?"
- *They've heard them before.*
- *They seem unreal—like fiction.*
- *They have morals tacked on the end.*
- *They are heavy reading, or use heavy language.*
- *There is no relevance to their daily living.*

"How can we improve things?"
- *Use skilled storytellers; train yourself to be one!*
- *Open up the story to discussion instead of narration.*

STORIES, continued

Use questions like these:
- *"What did you think about that story?"*
- *"Do you think that really happened? When? Where?"*
- *"Can you picture this in your mind? Can you act it out?"*
- *"How would you have felt if you had been there?"*
- *"Have you ever had an experience like this?"*
- *"Why did God put this story in the Bible?"*
- *"If you could have given _____ some advice, what would you have said to him/her?"*

ACTIVITIES

- *Keep them occupied.*
- *Fill in answers to questions.*
- *Coloring or drawing pictures of events from a story you told.*
- *Art–murals, clay sculptures, etc.*
- *Nature–walks, collections.*
- *Discovery–finding things; developing scrapbooks.*
- *Videotaping a Bible story: some acting, some producing.*
- *Music–composing songs, developing a group.*
- *Ministry–caring for special people with special needs.*

THE UNWELCOMED CHILD

Sarah: "May I come to your church today
To see you worship, sing and pray?"

Mrs. J.:   "You wouldn't find it any fun.
When you are older you may come."

Sarah: "But I would like to come and see
And worship with the family."

Mrs. J.:   "You wouldn't like our songs at all,
The children's church is down the hall."

Sarah: "But I love Jesus, this is true!
Can't I be a disciple too?"

Mrs. J.:   "Just wait, the time will come to pass
For you to join Disciple's Class."

Sarah: "May I tell you why I'm crying?
Did you know my Grandpa's dying?"

Mrs. J.:   "When you grow old enough, you'll know
That there's a time we all must go."

Sarah: "Can you tell, I'm asking you,
Are all the Bible stories true?"

Mrs. J.:   "Please put aside your questions, do.
If I believe it, why can't you?"

Sarah: "My friends at school say I'm a freak
Because I go to church each week."

Mrs. J.:   "You take no notice to what they say.
You're growing up the Christian way."

Sarah: "Can I come in? Do I belong?
Can't I do something brave or strong?"

Mrs. J.:   "Be patient! You're the church tomorrow–
When you have learned our ways to follow."

As time went by, the child grew bolder
Growing taller, growing older
Looking for love and care and nurture...
Some day, later, in the future.
Someone in the church will say,
"Come! You may join the church today."
But–alas–the child has gone away.
     • Dr. Lorna Jenkins

*"Whoever welcomes in my name,
One such child as this welcomes Me."*
     • Matthew 18:5

22 CELL GROUPS FOR TEENAGERS

The Way It All Began

When West Memorial was launched, I had senior high and junior high sons living in my home. The spiritual growth they experienced in our new lifestyle was a great blessing to us. They had been attending the First Baptist Church of Dallas for five years, so you can imagine the culture shock they experienced when we brought them to Houston—but it didn't last long!

Ralph, my oldest son, began to penetrate the high school kids. He and I would go down to "Pimple Park" (nickname given by teens, of course) on Friday and Saturday nights to contact the kids on drugs. Mom was never surprised when we brought home a car full of stoned kids to sleep on the living room floor. Another hangout was an all night doughnut shop in a shopping mall. It didn't take long at all before we had a large group of teens who needed the Lord and needed groups.

God sent along a couple who committed themselves to work with these teen cell groups. They opened their home for them, offering among other things help with their homework. Their home would be packed with kids who studied from 7 to 9 p.m. The last part of the evening was a jamboree!

Soon, the teen cells grew to a point that their house alone would not accommodate them all for these gatherings. The teens scrounged samples of rugs from nearby stores and sewed them together to carpet their two-car garage. For many months, this was the focal point of the ministry and fellowship activities.

We later found an old, abandoned house that was to be torn down in a year or two. We offered to take care of it rent free, and the owners jumped at the offer. We transformed it into a "hangout" for teenagers. Two of our single men moved into the second level of it and kept the ministry going from that location into the wee hours of the night. The stories of power encounters with teens who were set free from drugs and problems there would have made a great film.

Ralph, my son, began to form cell groups in another part of the city where a pastor of a P.B.D. church wanted to touch immigrants from Mexico. There he met a lad on drugs and led him to Christ. His new friend spent a lot of time in our home, learning to play the guitar from Ralph. The small groups in that district of the town grew and grew.

That lad had a real burden for Mexico, so one day we took up an offering to give him food money and prayed him off to hitchhike to Monterrey with his guitar. For many months we heard nothing from him. Then he called Ralph to report that he had reached hundreds of teens who were on drugs. They were travelling from town to town, witnessing on the streets to young people on drugs. A "cell group movement" had been formed by the Holy Spirit, and it was harvesting scores of youngsters.

Ralph and I flew to Monterrey, then drove in an old van, to a "retreat center" where all the groups were gathering for me to teach the Bible to them. Several hundred came, all converted off the streets and formed into cells from many parts of Mexico. I shall never forget the challenge of being the first Bible teacher most of them had ever heard. Since they had all been truly delivered by the power of God from drugs, they needed no teaching on what God could do in their lives. They could have taught *me* much!

Then Came Jimmy Dorrell

Upon our return from Singapore, I searched for a man who could understand cell church life to work with the youth. I found a bearded lad who had graduated from seminary and who wanted nothing to do with P.B.D. structures. He was just perfect for the job. When he began, there were eight kids in the back row of the church on Sunday nights, including my last son who was now a teen ager. (You remember the church fell apart in our absence.) Within 18 months, Jim had three on his staff and had 600 teen-agers on his mailing list, all in groups!

Cell Groups Were Led Only By Teens

God had given Jim a real vision for reaching high school kids. His philosophy was one I heartily agreed to endorse: *we would treat every teenager as a minister, and equip them for that work.* He would develop adult workers who would never, ever conduct a cell; they were to *equip and supervise* the teens as *they* conducted the cells. In house after house, week after week, kids would gather for cell groups in living rooms without a single adult present. Praying in the kitchen, the adult workers were nearby if they were needed, often witnessing to the unsaved parents of the homes they were meeting in. Every teen who *could* was encouraged to take a turn sponsoring the cell in his or her own home.

I smiled as I saw my high school sophomore struggling to prepare for his Sunday night cell group. I was under *strict* orders from Jim to give him no help as he led his cell meetings. My, how he grew!

We had a 24-hour a day prayer room in Touch Center, and I regularly spent time there with some of my men from 6:30 to 7;30 a.m. We were soon joined by a dozen or more teens, who had prayer burdens for unsaved parents and friends. Then the thirst for prayer become so intense that Jim opened up the chapel every morning before school began for them to meet and pray.

When I would give an invitation at the end of my messages, usually groups of three or four would come together to present to the church another member of their cell who had accepted Christ. God was at work in a most powerful way. Pregnant girls chose not to get an abortion. Kids who were thieves were set free from their evil habits. Teen cells were high drama!

"Tickets" were mimeographed in the church office each week and given to the members of each cell group to distribute in school. The ticket announced the topic for the next meeting; on the back was a little map showing how to get to the house where they would gather. Each cell group would pass these out to friends and strangers during the week. Those who arrived with a beer can in their hand to attend the meeting were lovingly informed that beer, drugs, and cigarettes were off limits during meeting times.

Swimming pools were sometimes used for baptizing converts. I was quite liberal in my conviction that if Philip, an "unordained layman," could baptize an Ethiopian eunuch without a formal vote of the church approving it, we were quite scriptural in letting converts decide if they wanted one of the pastors to do the baptizing, or whether it would be more meaningful for the ones who led them to Christ to do it. We saw wonderful things take place in the lives of those who shared that beautiful moment with each other.

Jim started the first group, and called it "Alpha." In a few months, the groups had grown so fast that he started in on the Hebrew alphabet with Junior High groups. It made me smile to hear a 13-year-old talking about belonging to the "Theta Group."

After the Cells, A Gathering!

It was learned that the groups should meet simultaneously in the different homes being used. After the cell meetings, all held at 6 p.m. on Sunday nights, there was something special for them to attend together. One hot night in July, a truck that made snow for packing vegetables on the way to market deposited a ton of white stuff on the lawn in front of Touch Center. Hundreds of kids showed up for the first time for the snowball fight!

On another occasion, the cell members spent Saturday afternoon filling balloons with water. Sunday night, they soaked each other in a big "battle." The Godfather's Pizza Restaurant was requisitioned for another evening, as was a roller skating rink, a health club, and quite frequently our gymnasium.

"Getaways" Were Important

West Memorial had the use of Touch Ranch for retreats, and the teen cell groups took maximum advantage of it, along with many other locations the staff uncovered which were perfect for youth activities. We bought two vans for them to use. "Getaways" were important to the ministry. Teenagers who are pulled out of their normal environment are able to rethink their values in a new way. Each retreat "targeted" a certain segment of teens. In some, no Christian could go unless he or she brought an unbeliever as a guest. In others, only cell leaders were invited. The retreats were all focused on special groups: new converts, girls with problems in their homes, etc. This intermingling of the members of cells for special emphases was important to their development.

Wednesday Nights Was For Bible Study

Jim and his lovely wife, Janet, along with all the staffers and volunteer workers, would gather the teens on Wednesday nights for biblical teaching and discussion. Occasionally our parents who were church members were horrified at the frank discussions carried on in these Bible studies; it reflected how out of touch they were with today's teen world.

After a while, so many teens showed up that other adult functions could not be held in Touch Center. They literally took over the place!

Impact On The High Schools

Jim became a legend in the three or four high schools we drew students from for the cell groups. He and the other staffers were highly respected by the administration and faculties, for they saw the results in changed lives in the classrooms. We were all delighted when he was voted by two graduating classes in a row to bring the baccalaureate messages at Stratford High School.

Suggestions For You:

1. Expect the best from teens who are Christians.
2. Expect them to be accountable for their ministry.
3. Expect Christ to fill and use them; their age is no handicap.
4. Model a totally committed lifestyle for them. Their parents and their society may only provide negative models.
5. Use high school Seniors to shepherd junior high groups. They love to relate to one of the "big guys."
6. Multiply all the groups simultaneously. They need the feeling of "togetherness" this provides.

Some Topics Used Effectively In Teen Share Groups

From the Touch Basic Training Facilitator's Guide, here are some tried-and-true topics to help you get started:

Relationships
The Family
Drugs
Self-image
Sex
Sports
Teacher/Student Relations
Temptations
Parent Conflicts
Love
How To Have Peace
Being Independent
Dating
Brothers And Sisters
The Future
School
World Problems
Going To War
Does God Care About Us?
Are Miracles True?
Is There Life After Death?
How Important Is Church?
Betting: Right Or Wrong?
Why Am I Here?
What's Wrong With Porn?
Are All Movies OK to see?
How To Ask For A Date
How To Refuse A Date
Getting Over Grudges
How Important Are Clothes?
What About Cheating?
Borrowing
What To Tell Your Parents
Breaking Up

Peer Pressure
Divorce
Loneliness
Depression
Alcohol
Grades
Putdowns: How To Bounce Back
Music
Emptiness
Suicide
Do you need Joy?
Respect
Family Problems
College
Financial Needs
Friendship
Loving Others, No Matter What!
How To Know Truth From Error
Are All World Religions True?
Does Praying Do Any Good?
Was Jesus Really God?
Why People Want Power
Should Pot Be Legalized?
Are All Of Us Created Equal?
Is Truth Absolute Or Relative?
Speeding: Right, Wrong, Or
    Neutral?
How To Leave A Party That Gets
    Out Of Hand
Are White Lies Wrong?
Best Friends
What Makes Me Significant?
Going Steady
What About Rock Festivals?

23 EXPANDING CELLS INTO THE CITY

Before launching or expanding a ministry, nothing is as crucial as the creation of an Urban Strategy. It is as important to the cell group church planter as is a business plan to the launchers of a new venture. In urban settings, a strategy is absolutely necessary if an entire metroplex is to be evangelized. While traditional church leaders tend to think in terms of parishes or "church fields," a cell group strategist seeks to develop a pattern that will be effective in reaching all the people groups present.

For several years, I have taught M.Div. and D.Min. students from Columbia Biblical Seminary and School of World Missions classes which use World Class Cities as a laboratory. These students travel the world with me, surveying church life in major cities. In each place, they are exposed to rapidly exploding cell group congregations. They focus on one major city for thirty days, learning the "tools of the trade" used by cell group strategists.

In 1962, when Dr. Leonard Irwin of the Home Mission Board, Southern Baptist Convention, introduced these tools to me, I felt something like Cinderella when she stepped through the looking-glass! After planting over a dozen churches without knowing what I was doing, a new way of praying and strategizing was opened to me through them. Those were the days when home computers were not in existence; we would rent a huge office machine at $50 a day to do computations which now can be done ten times as fast with a little laptop!

Without any exception, I have found it possible to collect the necessary data to develop an urban strategy in every part of the world I have visited—even when local missionaries said it did not exist in their third world nation. Thus, reports have been created for Nairobi, Bangkok, Singapore, Jakarta, Brussels, Auckland, Brisbane, and London without any problem.[1] In the United States, not only is data readily available, but special reports can be secured for a nominal sum which will give one, five, and ten mile detailed population reports from the intersections of any specific streets or highways.[2]

Developing an Urban Strategy includes the following steps:

1. Create A Prayer Base For Your Activity

Nothing is more fraught with danger than seeking to do the work of the Master without "Listening Room" time. Taking daily findings to the prayer closet provides spiritual insights not provided by the crunching of numbers. It is recommended that the strategy team spend daily periods in prayer. There will be moments in the study when there is simply nothing to do but weep and pray over the lostness of the neighborhoods being studied.

Without question, spiritual eyes will discern "strongholds" of Satan within a city as the study develops. When one evaluates districts of sin and evil in a city, it is necessary to remember that the battle we fight is not against flesh and blood, but against principalities and powers in the air. Let those who are spiritually blind to eternal warfare stay away from developing urban strategy!

2. Secure Data

The first step will be to collect all available census data, sociological studies, and previous reports which have been done about the city, suburbia, and the exurbia surrounding it. Sources include United Nations studies, national census reports, regional reports (including "Standard Metropolitan Statistical Area" data), city and county studies, and research materials completed through grants by local universities. Visits should be made to agencies developing highway systems for the area, and any Planning Commissions sponsored by national, state, regional, county, or city governments. Much information can be gleaned by interviewing utility companies in the region. Their forecasts of where telephones, electricity, and gas will be needed can be valuable tools for studying both suburbia and exurbia. Urban Renewal Commissions make recommendations about decaying inner city areas, and have much data available. Even the slums of third world cities have been carefully mapped, with lifestyles of inhabitants described. (In Bangkok, a huge multicolored set of maps has been published showing the location of hundreds and hundreds of slums.)

Basic questions to be answered about the city include:

1. How many children live here?
2. How many single-parent families are present?
3. How many retired and elderly, and where are they housed?
4. Where are the poor?
5. Where are the rich?
6. What ethnic groups are there, and where?
7. What are the educational levels and occupations?
8. What will the population be in five years? Ten years?
9. What urban redevelopment will take place?

One must enjoy being a Sherlock Holmes during this investigative step, making friends with officials at each office visited and asking endless questions. Often key documents will be "passed on," not usually given to the public, once the respect of the official you are interviewing has been gained. In Singapore, I created the "Baptist Centre for Urban Studies" (that was just me!), had calling cards printed, and left them behind with each government official. I was soon being invited to all sorts of functions held by sociologists, demographers, and urban planners. Most of the best "leads" came by asking, "Who has additional information that might be of value to the study?" Offering to share the results of your own research when completed is greatly appreciated.

Include in this procedure visits to all religious headquarters in the region. Many denominational leaders have done studies which can be of great help. In doing an urban strategy for Brussels, interviews with the head of the state protestant church and a key Catholic cardinal provided significant data which influenced preparation of the strategy.

Include a study of cults, and why they have succeeded in penetrating the society. In Singapore, we learned much from a study of how the Japanese *Sokka Gakkai* cult had exploded in size in just a few short years. The study of how the Mormons had deeply penetrated the Maoris in Auckland, New Zealand gave insights into how that cult had tapped into their needs to get a foothold among them.

Secure listings of all known churches, synagogues, temples, shrines, etc., from all available sources. In some areas this is a simple matter: the research has already been done. In other cities, it will be the first time anyone has bothered to consider the matter. Your research will help you discover where ethnics and migrants have settled in the city: they are found by their faith and their food!

3. Create A Strategy Map

From a government or private mapping source, purchase the largest, most detailed map available of the region. For Singapore, I purchased segments of a map from a government office and had them mounted on a cloth base. The map was eight feet high and thirteen feet wide, and showed every street and track on the island. In Brisbane, we secured multicolored maps in sections about three feet by four feet in size, and developed each one separately, so they could be transported easily from place to place.

4. Separate The City By Neighborhoods

This has often been done by urban planners, but in many areas you may be the first person to delineate the actual boundaries of neighborhoods. Much help can be gained in doing this by scrutinizing the "Enumeration Districts" of the "Census Tracts." While the "C.T.'s" are shown on the census reports purchased from the Bureau of the Census, the "E.D.'s" are available only upon request. Expect to pay a special charge for this material.

The "E.D." shows the area assigned for one person to survey when a census is taken. It will be a "bite sized" area which can be covered on foot, not crossing any major highways or rivers to complete the task. This material is helpful in giving block-by-block reports of the number of residents, their incomes, education, religious preferences (in many countries), and even the number of toilets in their residences!

The boundaries of the city's neighborhoods should be carefully marked on the map, or maps, of the region. Use 1/16" bendable red ChartTape for this purpose, carefully pressing it over the streets which mark the edges of each area. As you do so, put a 1/4" round sticker in each neighborhood, with a number written on it. Create a list of these numbers, designating it with the commonly used name for that territory: e.g., "Woodlands, Section 1."

Also use round stickers to mark the exact location of all existing religious structures. In Philadelphia, doing so quickly revealed ethnic groups from Italy, Russia, Greece, etc., and where they had clustered. In Singapore, Indian, Buddhist, and Sikh temples attract people who mingle together in hawker stalls which prepare their ethnic foods; many live in housing estates miles away.

5. Make Population Pyramids

Let's look at two population pyramids which help us decide what strategy to plant cells we should use in each area:

In this first pyramid, we see a slum area of Brisbane (Fortitude

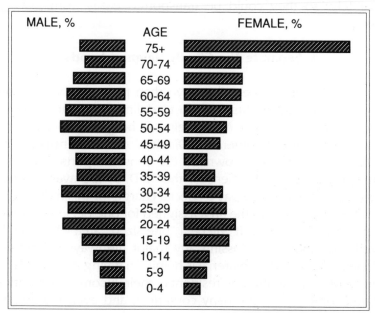

Valley). It includes prostitutes, night clubs, Chinatown, and a business district. Note the absence of children of either sex. A significant falloff of women in the 40-44 age group reflects the presence of the younger women of ill repute. Note also the large number of elderly people who are trapped here by their poverty. Here's a mystery: why should so many women above the age of 75 live in a place like this? In our research, we discovered that the Catholics had established a retirement home for nuns in this neighborhood generations ago, when Brisbane was young and the district was on the edge of town. The retirement center remains today, an imposing stone fortress in the midst of a hell-hole called Fortitude Valley.

In the next example, we see a typical pyramid of a community settled by young couples with lots and lots of little children in the family (Ferny Grove, Brisbane). This would be a prime area for the planting of new work among young couples.[3] Note the massive clustering of preschoolers, their parents reflected in the 25-39 bars of the chart.

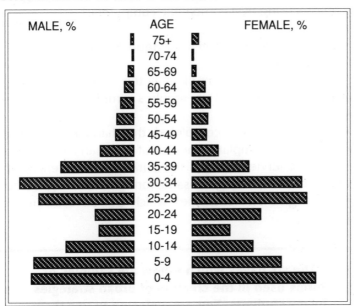

NOTE: *a population pyramid is created by obtaining the percentages of each male or female age group in a census tract. These samples were created in Microsoft multiplan, using a Macintosh Plus computer.*

6. Create Templates For Your Report

Once the material has been collected, a special Survey Form can be created to collect the data for each neighborhood. A sample of this form is provided on the next two pages.

It is also possible for you to create a Template for your actual report (see samples on the two pages which follow the Survey Form). I usually prepare a double-page spread for each neighborhood, showing the following information: population pyramid, small map showing boundaries of the neighborhood, housing information, inmigration patterns, marital status of population, incomes, employment, religious preferences, brief description of the community, neighborhood category (see part 7), and recommended strategy for planting appropriate cell groups.

I am an avid fan of the Macintosh computer for this task, using *Ready Set Go!*, *Cricket Graph*, and *Excel* or *Wingz* for the project. Dr. David Finnell at Columbia Biblical Seminary and Graduate School of Missions is developing a special program to make reports using IBM compatible computers.[4]

7. Develop Neighborhood Analyses

Using the Survey Form, fill in all the data for each category of each neighborhood. This requires simple compilations of statistics.

Once this has been completed, the charts are prepared for insertion into the Template. The use of pie charts and bar charts give graphic overviews of the similarities and differences of the neighborhoods. Repeating the same format for all neighborhoods provides insights into strategies which can be used in similar settings.

The six pages which follow are samples of forms used in the creation of urban strategies by my students. You are welcome to use them as they are, or to create forms adapted from them.

WORKSHEET FOR: _____

POP. PYR. LOCATED ON DISK _____

NAME OF LARGER AREA (BOROUGH, CITY, U.A., ETC.) _____

TOTAL POPULATION OF LARGER AREA (MALE + FEMALE=TOTAL) _____

POPULATION PYRAMID OF LARGER AREA IS LOCATED ON DISK _____

RESIDENT POPULATION (TABLE 2)

MALE + FEMALE = TOTAL _____

TOTAL HOUSEHOLDS (TABLE 14) _____

THE FOLLOWING INFORMATION IS IN TABLE 5:
NEVER MARRIED,
   OVER 15 YEARS: _____

MARRIED _____

REMARRIED _____

SEPARATED _____

WIDOWED _____

DIVORCED _____

DE FACTO RELATIONSHIP _____

WITHIN THE TOTAL POPULATION ARE...

N. Z. MAORI (TABLE 4) _____

POLYNESIAN (TABLE 4) _____

NOT WORKING (TABLE 6;
   ADD MALE+FEMALE) _____

BORN OUTSIDE N.Z.
(USE TABLE 3) _____

ADD M+F FOR **TOTAL:** _____

ADD M+F FOR **N Z :** _____

SUBTRACT: **USE THIS TOTAL:** _____

AMONG THE OVERSEAS BORN ARE...
(NOTE: SELECT THE 4 CATEGORIES WITH HIGHEST
TOTALS. THIS WILL VARY WITH EACH AREA. USE TABLE 3)
AREA (USE CAPS ONLY!) TOTAL
  (ADD MALE+FEMALE)

_____ _____

_____ _____

TYPES OF DWELLINGS (TABLE 15)

For the next two figures, use
Aggregate Number of Occupants:

Living in Private Dwellings _____

In Non-Private Dwellings _____

Separate Houses _____

2 Houses/Flats, joined _____

3 or + joined together _____

Joined to business/shop _____

Bach, Crib, Hut _____

Temporary private dwelling _____

INCOME (TABLE 11)

In all cases, add M+F to get one total.
Then, add together columns to produce six
totals.
E. G.: Add 5 columns to get $1-10,000, etc.

NIL OR LOSS: _____

$1 - $10,000: _____

$10,000 - $15,000: _____

$15,000 -$ 25,000: _____

$25,000 - $50,000: _____

Over $50,000: _____

OCCUPATIONS (TABLE 8. ADD M+F=TOTAL)

Professional, technical _____

Administrative, Managerial _____

Clerical _____

Sales Workers _____

Service Workers _____

Agricultural, etc. _____ Laborers,
   etc.

FAMILY TYPES (TABLE 14)

1 Family Only _____

1 Family + Others _____

2 Families _____

Non-Family Households _____

One Person Households _____

WORKSHEET FOR: _____

WRITE A 75 WORD DESCRIPTION OF THIS AREA. INCLUDE FACTORS WHICH WILL IMPACT THE CREATION OF AN URBAN STRATEGY (Institutions present, geographical distinctives, hospitals, schools, factories, railways, comment about the pop. pyramid, your own observations from visiting the area, etc.) Type into proper area on book page when polished.

_____

_____

_____

_____

_____

_____

_____

_____

RELIGIOUS STRUCTURES FOUND IN THIS AREA

List the name in caps. Put the exact address of the church on the next line. Type into book page.

_____

_____

_____

_____

_____

_____

_____

_____

_____

_____

_____

RELIGIOUS PREFERENCES IN THIS AREA

(USE UNPUBLISHED TABLE 25)
ADD M + F = TOTAL

ANGLICAN _____

PRESBYTERIAN _____

ROMAN CATHOLIC _____

METHODIST _____

CHRISTIAN N. O. D. _____

BAPTIST _____

MORMON _____

RATANA _____

BRETHREN _____

SALVATION ARMY _____

PROTESTANT N. O. D. _____

JEHOVAH'S WITNESSES _____

ASSEMBLIES OF GOD _____

AGNOSTIC, ATHIEST _____

OTHER _____

ADD TOGETHER:

NO RELIGION _____

OBJECT _____

NOT SPECIFIED _____

TOTAL OF ABOVE _____

WORKSHEET FOR: _____

SURVEY DATA

As you work with 43 people in your area, list and tabulate the total results here:

Leisure Interests	Ch.Pref.	Attend.	Looking	Bible	Problems	Solutions	Group?	Seeker?

THIS SUMMARY PAGE IS USED WITH THE SURVEY FORM ON PAGE 354

TOTALS								

WORKSHEET FOR: _____

WHAT COULD BE DONE?

Pray much about what you write here! This will be completed only after you have done all your field surveys and completed all other statistical analyses. Interviews with Pastors, residents, etc., will give you insights. Discuss your conclusions with your Team when you are in need of additional insights. Recognize that your suggestions may well influence the conversion of many people in the area. (Max. 400 words). Type into proper area on book page when polished.

_____

_____

_____

_____

_____

_____

_____

_____

_____

_____

_____

_____

_____

_____

_____

_____

_____

_____

_____

_____

_____

_____

_____

_____

PAKURANGA CENTRAL

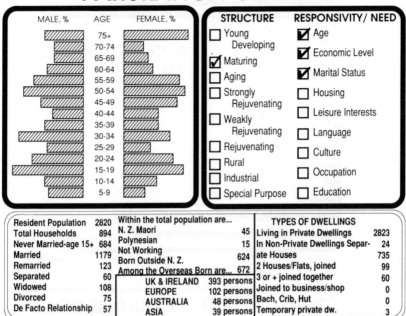

MALE, %	AGE	FEMALE, %
	75+	
	70-74	
	65-69	
	60-64	
	55-59	
	50-54	
	45-49	
	40-44	
	35-39	
	30-34	
	25-29	
	20-24	
	15-19	
	10-14	
	5-9	

STRUCTURE

- ☐ Young Developing
- ☑ Maturing
- ☐ Aging
- ☐ Strongly Rejuvenating
- ☐ Weakly Rejuvenating
- ☐ Rejuvenating
- ☐ Rural
- ☐ Industrial
- ☐ Special Purpose

RESPONSIVITY/ NEED

- ☑ Age
- ☑ Economic Level
- ☑ Marital Status
- ☐ Housing
- ☐ Leisure Interests
- ☐ Language
- ☐ Culture
- ☐ Occupation
- ☐ Education

		Within the total population are...		TYPES OF DWELLINGS	
Resident Population	2820	N. Z. Maori	45	Living in Private Dwellings	2823
Total Households	894	Polynesian	15	In Non-Private Dwellings Separ-	24
Never Married-age 15+	684	Not Working		ate Houses	735
Married	1179	Born Outside N. Z.	624	2 Houses/Flats, joined	99
Remarried	123	Among the Overseas Born are...	672	3 or + joined together	60
Separated	60	UK & IRELAND	393 persons	Joined to business/shop	0
Widowed	108	EUROPE	102 persons	Bach, Crib, Hut	0
Divorced	75	AUSTRALIA	48 persons	Temporary private dw.	3
De Facto Relationship	57	ASIA	39 persons		

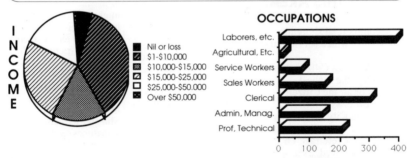

INCOME

- ■ Nil or loss
- ▨ $1-$10,000
- ▩ $10,000-$15,000
- ▧ $15,000-$25,000
- ☐ $25,000-$50,000
- ▨ Over $50,000

OCCUPATIONS

Laborers, etc.
Agricultural, Etc.
Service Workers
Sales Workers
Clerical
Admin, Manag.
Prof, Technical

0   100   200   300   400

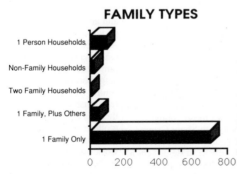

FAMILY TYPES

1 Person Households
Non-Family Households
Two Family Households
1 Family, Plus Others
1 Family Only

0   200   400   600   800

Generally, Pakuranga Central is made up of high cost housing estates 10 to 20 years old. There is a high turnover of residents in the middle cost housing bracket as jobs transfer people in & out of Auckland. Families may stay two to three years, then move on. There is a large young population under 24 years old which makes up about 30% of the population. Income is similar to that of greater Auckland, except for a slightly larger distribution of $25,00-50,000 incomes. It is also evident from the occupation chart that the labourers' & clerical categories are relatively higher.

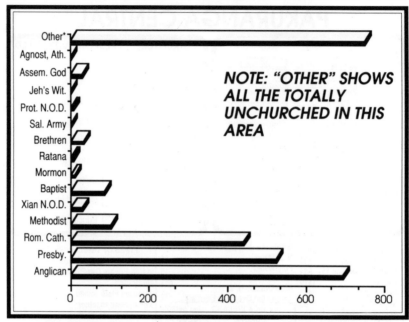

NOTE: "OTHER" SHOWS ALL THE TOTALLY UNCHURCHED IN THIS AREA

(Chart categories, top to bottom: Other*, Agnost, Ath., Assem. God, Jeh's Wit., Prot. N.O.D., Sal. Army, Brethren, Ratana, Mormon, Baptist, Xian N.O.D., Methodist, Rom. Cath., Presby., Anglican; scale 0 to 800)

REFLECTIONS ABOUT THIS AREA:

•It is valuable to note there is a large commercial shopping centre here, which services the region.

•The Pakuranga Citizen Advice Bureau had the highest referrals of all the Citizen Advice Bureaus in Manukau City for the year ending May 1986. They had a total of 4,477 referrals. Of the calls they received, 29% were enquiries related to personal, family, health or welfare issues. The Bureau also reported, "the abuse of alcohol amongst women is causing concern...Relationships between parents and children is another significant area of stress... remarriage to new partners is common."

•It is significant to the development of any strategy for this area to keep in mind that the fifteen to nineteen age group is the largest age category in this community.

WHAT COULD BE DONE?

Ministries designed to touch whole families, using a household evangelism approach, are applicable here. Various leisure and social activities, such as neighbourhood get-togethers and sports events could be initiated by resident Christians. Unemployment has been a problem in this area. Ministry could include: assistance for job seekers, family counseling, etc. The percentage of teenagers is high in this community. Special interest activities, such as teaching guitar lessons, driving instruction, grooming classes and sports teams, could be used to gather these young people into Share Groups. For young adults (20-34), evangelism strategies could include the development of Share Groups around common interests. These might best be offered in a home, where young adults will feel relaxed and make friends with their peers.

Young couples frequently need relief in the midst of the stress of living with infants. Ministry to them can sometimes avert the danger of child abuse. They also need someone to give them reassurance and advice when things go wrong.

Another means to reaching these young families is through the neighborhood play centre. Strong relationships can develop there as Christian mothers meet other mothers once or twice a week on neutral ground as they supervise their children's activities together.

8. Cluster Neighborhoods Into Categories

After creating all the data for the neighborhoods, they can then be broken down into these categories:

A. The Young Developing Suburb

These suburbs are still in the process of subdivision and construction. Their populations are, therefore, increasing rapidly as a result of in-migration and the establishment of families by young parents who are the principal buyers of the new houses. The population up to and including age 9 comprises as much as 27%, and always more than 15%, of the total. The age groups 60 years and over usually comprise less than 5% of the total except in those young suburbs containing a large senior citizens home. The social infrastructure needs of this type of suburb include kindergartens, child care facilities, primary schools, and playgrounds.

These areas should be targeted by churches, for they contain some of the most responsive segments of the city.

B. The Maturing Suburb

This type of suburb has been in the process of development for at least 20 years. The population total tends to be fairly stable although the composition of the population is undergoing change with a marked out-migration of young persons in the 15-24 age groups as families mature and grown children leave the parental home. Such outmigration is partially balanced by new births (but at a much lower rate than in the young developing suburbs) and, in some suburbs, a small net inmigration as the last remaining vacant lots are filled.

The population structure is characterized by a concentration of older families. The age groups 10-24 and 45-59 are usually predominant.

The social infrastructural needs of this type of suburb include a heavy demand for secondary schools, playing fields and recreational opportunities for older children and younger adults.

An aggressive ministry to young people, utilizing "Share Groups" led by themselves, can become a significant means of

SEEING THE CITY

Note: The "Rings" as described in this model are quite artificial. Terrain and historical events contribute to the actual
locations of these areas.

Third world slums in cities always require: water source,
government toleration, access to means of making an
income. Slums are found along rivers, railroad track right-
of-ways, public land, swamps, etc. Cells planted among them
grow rapidly!

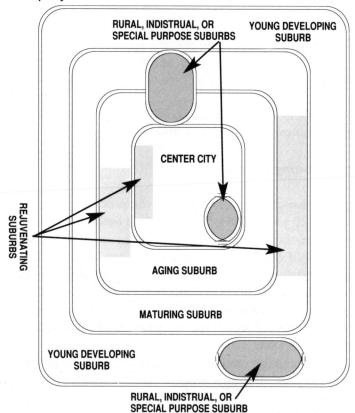

RURAL, INDISTRUAL, OR
SPECIAL PURPOSE SUBURBS

YOUNG DEVELOPING
SUBURB

CENTER CITY

REJUVENATING
SUBURBS

AGING SUBURB

MATURING SUBURB

YOUNG DEVELOPING
SUBURB

RURAL, INDISTRUAL, OR
SPECIAL PURPOSE SUBURB

Find similar responsive segments in areas of the city that
may be geographically separated. Use the same strategy in
each area. Launch with the *easiest* group to reach!

penetrating these areas. As adolescents and young adults seek to establish their own identity, they often search for a new set of values which contrast with those of their parents. If their peer group includes committed Christians, they will often choose to follow Christ. At this age, peers have more impact than older persons who may seek to work with them.

In turn, when the young people in a family come to know Christ, they create a natural bridge to share their faith with other family members.

C. The Aging Suburb

This type of suburb typically consists of predominantly single family homes more than 40 years old. The population totals of all the suburbs in this category are declining, some by more than 5% per annum, because of grown children leaving the family home, and natural mortality or movement to retirement homes out of the suburb by persons in the older age groups who form a major proportion of these communities.

In these suburbs, persons over 60 years of age always comprise more than 12% of the total and in some cases as much as 26%. There is a marked lack of young children, the 0-9 age groups usually forming less than 12%, and always less than 14% of the total.

An important result of the population structure of this type of suburb is a low household size; many houses are occupied by widows or widowers living alone or by elderly couples whose children have grown up and left home.

The social infrastructure needs of these communities centre around the provision of services to the elderly such as meals on wheels, home nursing care and social clubs. These suburbs often contain underutilized school facilities.

The gospel has particular relevance to these persons when shared in the context of relational small groups. Quite often they are neglected by their younger family members, who are intent on pursuing their own agendas. They want people who will care about them, listen to them, and encourage them. The leisure time of the elderly makes it easier to reach them during the daytime. The effective church in these areas will offer the type of social and recreational life which is appropriate to senior citizens.

D. The Rejuvenating Suburb

This type of suburb is defined as one other than a young developing suburb in which the population of at least one young adult age group showed a net increase between censuses. A further distinction may be made between strongly rejuvenating suburbs, in which a decline in population has been reversed and the total population is now increasing, and weakly rejuvenating suburbs in which the population decline has been slowed but not reversed.

Rejuvenating suburbs include most of the old inner suburbs where the housing stock has been through more than one cycle of ownership. Their age structure is similar to that of the aging suburbs, showing a heavy concentration in the older age groups and very few children. One marked difference, however, is a concentration of people in the 20-29 age groups which usually comprise more than 20% of the total.

Household size in rejuvenating suburbs is small. As in the aging suburbs there are many elderly people living alone while the young in-migrants are most often single persons or childless couples occupying rental accommodations in old houses or in multiple dwellings.

The social infrastructure of this type of suburb will be those of the aging suburb supplemented with the lifestyle requirements of the unattached adult: dining and dancing venues, sports centers, clubs, theaters and other facilities for social intercourse.

Reaching this area must be done by two branches of Christ's body: one which focuses on the young adult, and another which concentrates on the aging persons. Many creative approaches can be used in these outreach strategies, including musical and drama groups, forum discussions, sports contests, etc.

E. The Rural, Industrial Or Special Purpose Suburb

These areas are rural or semirural in character. They have a small population whose structure often cannot be characterized into any of the foregoing types.

To these suburbs may be added those which are of a primarily industrial nature with virtually no resident population, and those in which dominant residential institutions distort the pattern of the population structure. These would include such things as a prison farm or migrant hostel, a retirement village, nurse or student hostels, or military camps. They may also include seaside communities which contain many "second homes," often used seasonally or on week ends.

9. Take Surveys Of Population Awarenesses

Once the neighborhoods have been systematically examined, there is a critical step which must follow: the interviewing of population categories to determine responsive segments. Local, cultural factors may influence this significantly in some areas. For example, those working in Belgium a few years ago discovered that young couples with their first baby and who spoke Dutch were unusually open to discussing salvation by grace through faith in Jesus Christ. French-speaking couples in the same condition were not as responsive.

On the other hand, some responsive segments exist in many differing cultures among the same groups. Youth and young marrieds are usually more responsive than middle and older aged persons. Better educated people may often be less steeped in the pressures of family religions than the poor. Conversely, in some cultures the elite are resistant, and the poor are more responsive.

These matters must be discovered by surveys taken within the population. There are at least two ways to do this:

1. Discover which population segments are turning to Christ in existing churches and parachurch groups.
2. Discover which population segments are most vulnerable to the evangelism of the cults, and what causes them to respond.
3. Interview people in different neighborhoods of the city. If it is discovered there is responsiveness in a certain segment of people, then use the previous research to locate where pockets of such people are located.

On the next page, a simple survey form is reproduced which has been widely used to gain insights into the needs and attitudes of people in different areas of cities.

District	Address		Apt.	

NU HH	How long do you plan on living at this ad?	Like it here?

ANYONE IN HOUSEHOLD BETWEEN AGES OF...

	M	F	LEISURE INTERESTS
0-5			
6-12			
13-17			
17-23			
35+			
Retired			

CHURCH PREFERENCE: _____

(Circle:) ALL   HUSB   WIFE   CHILDREN   OTHER

COMMENTS:

Have you considered looking for a new church in this area?
Would it have to be the same denomination you are used to?
When is the best time for you to worship? (Circle:)   AM   PM
Would you say you know the Bible...(Circle:)

Very Well   A Little Bit   Not well at all

What personal problems do people in this area face today?
What solutions do you see to these problems?

Would you be interested in a group which meets in the homes of its members and where folks can develop warm friendships?
Do you have an interest in knowing more about becoming a follower of Jesus Christ?

Family Name	Language Spoken

Surveyors:	Date ___/___/___

10. Create Your Strategy Document

As shown in the sample pages in this article, this strategy report should include a population pyramid, basic information about the geography of the neighborhood, income, marital status, inmigration patterns, racial/ethnic mixes, types of employment, religious preferences, etc. Neighborhoods can be listed in several ways: by zones, census tracts, or alphabetically.

The entire presentation should be preceded by an overview of the city itself, providing the same data given for neighborhoods for the entire region. In addition, this introductory section should give population forecasts and other general information gleaned from the surveys taken and documents studied.

It is now possible to publish the results in whatever form seems most suitable. A document published jointly by Columbia Biblical Seminary/Touch International Ministries on Auckland, New Zealand is an example of a comprehensive report. Over 450 pages in length, it covers every single neighborhood of the city, and includes an overview of the metropolis with population projections into the next century. It is useful to all churches and parachurch groups, and may be sold at a cost designed to recapture the cost of production.

11. Select Key Areas For Penetration

With the strategy report available, it will now be possible to reach neighborhoods with similar characteristics. For example, young couples with young children may be scattered throughout the metroplex, but would be reached by a common strategy. Another area may reveal a large number of middle aged couples with teens; this would be of special interest to those seeking to reach youth. Through this selection, cell group churches seeking to penetrate an entire city will be able to plant cells appropriate to each area, targeting people with similar needs and interests.

In addition, much can be learned about specific population groups. Cells seeking to build around university students will be able to accurately pinpoint locations where they live.

When it is possible to include religious preferences in the strategy report, a further narrowing of the strategy can take place.

Some nations regularly include information about religious preferences in their nationwide census (Australia and New Zealand, for example). In other areas, this must be developed by examination of membership figures from various denominations and religious structures.

When certain religious groups are open to the Gospel, they can be targeted through studying the report, and a strategy developed to reach them. For example, if there is a responsive segment of immigrants within a city, they will be located for evangelism activity. The strategy might include radio broadcasting in their language, as well as reaching them personally by direct mail and house-to-house visitation in the districts where they have clustered.

12. Use A Checkerboard Planting Pattern

The ICHTHUS Fellowship in Southeast London has a full time staff worker who shapes their strategy for penetrating the city. With over one hundred cells in operation, their strategy includes creating a task force using several cell groups to penetrate an unreached territory between them.

For example, the Woolwich project mentioned in an earlier chapter was sponsored by cells from either side of the area. Such "checkerboard" planting of cells can provide a powerful tool in evangelizing unreached areas.

Many years ago, I used this strategy to develop the ministry of "The People Who Care" in Houston, Texas. When we first began, the gap in our "checkerboard" was so large we would drive fifteen minutes or more between our homes for our cell meetings. Within a year, Ruth and I were walking on foot to our cell group gathering.

The Full Gospel Central Church in Seoul has done the same thing through the years with their "Districts." When I first began to study them, they had only fourteen districts covering the entire city. As their cells grew, they gradually reduced the size of each district and added new ones. There are currently several dozen—and they continue to plan for further ones as they move past the 600,000 membership figure. It is important to have a vision that reaches far beyond the primitive beginning stages. An urban strategy will be constantly reviewed and updated.

13. Create The Actual Strategy

Questions for the church planter team to answer may include the following:

1. Who are the responsive segments we have discovered? Do they have anything in common? If so, what are these things?
2. Should we seek to penetrate several groups as a test of receptivity before focusing on only one?
3. Which group, or groups, within the community should first be reached? How will this strategy lend itself to the expansion of the ministry into other segments of the community? Prepare both short and long range plans.
4. As we view the metropolis, where do these segments live or gather?
5. How should we seek to communicate with them? Should we use direct mail, word of mouth only, house-to-house surveys, etc.?
6. What will be our reason for contacting them? Should we offer special small groups which focus on their problems or interests? (Examples: a "Target Group" for expectant mothers, or a group for lonely people?)
7. Where will we meet with them? Can we use their own homes? If not, what facilities in the areas where they live might be available for us to use? Can we use our own homes for this purpose?
8. How many groups can we launch in the first six months, given our manpower and their available time?

In most cases, the original strategy is only theoretical. As the ministry is launched, the church planting team will require many adjustments to their preliminary plans. Above everything else, the initial penetration of the unreached in the community should be given much higher priority than the establishment of a worship service on Sunday mornings. The many hours spent in preparing and executing this service may be better invested in ministry to the target group.

THE EQUIPPING TRACK FOR A CELL GROUP CHURCH

INCOMING MEMBER	**SPIRITUAL FORMATION WEEKEND** *Spiritual Gifts Inventory* *Journey Guide Interview*
"LITTLE CHILDREN"	*The Arrival Kit For* *New Christians* *Cover The Bible*
"YOUNG MEN"	**SPIRITUAL WARFARE WEEKEND** *Knocking On Doors, Opening* *Hearts*
"FATHERS"	**MINISTRY OUTREACH WEEKEND** *Touch Ministries Seminar* *Touch Basic Training* *The Way Home New Testament*
SHEPHERD INTERN	**SHEPHERD INTERN FORMATION WEEKEND** *Shepherd's Guidebook*
SHEPHERD	Regular equipping sessions with Zone Shepherd
ZONE SHEPHERD	**ZONE SHEPHERD FORMATION WEEKEND** Regular equipping sessions with Zone Pastor
ZONE PASTOR INTERN	ONE YEAR OF TRAINING IN ZONE PASTOR'S SCHOOL

24 EQUIPPING *ALL* THE MINISTERS!

"Equipping all the saints for the work of ministry" is a nice sounding phrase, but it can be a real nightmare to implement it in a modern society. Time pressure upon urban Christians exceeds anything experienced by first century believers. With many people having to work eleven or twelve hour days, how can they be expected to be active in their Shepherd group, spend time with unbelievers, and simultaneously devote evenings to attending discipleship classes?

When Singapore's Lawrence Khong asked me to attack the problem at Faith Community Baptist Church, we came up with the equipping pattern outlined in this chapter. Our goal is to have a comprehensive plan that begins when an unbeliever receives Christ, and is completed when a full time Zone Pastor has been trained. It will begin to be implemented in 1991, and should be fully installed by the end of 1992. I share it here with the desire that others may profit from our experiment, sharing their experience in return.

A Taxonomy Is Required

Taxonomy comes from two Greek words: *taxis,* "order," and *nomia,* "distribute." A *taxonomy* expert would say, "If you are going to talk about C and D, it's necessary to first introduce A, and then B. Otherwise, the learner will not know what you are talking about."

Sounds logical, doesn't it? Would it surprise you to know that to my knowledge all Sunday School curriculums now in use have been developed *without regard for a taxonomy?*

In 1970, our newly formed Shepherd group church became aware of this surprising matter through discussions with W. O. Howse at the Baptist Sunday School Board in Nashville. We contacted every denominational and interdenominational publisher of Sunday School literature. We asked, "If we train people using your literature, we want to know they have been given "A" before you introduce them to "B." We want a curriculum that will take a child and put him on a journey that will faithfully show him how to further develop as a minister as he graduates from department to department, until he is an adult Christian. Does your literature do that?" *None qualified.* Most publishers had never even thought seriously about the matter. Thus, the only "training" in the P.B.D. Sunday School is a helterskelter combination of materials. The local church makes it worse by buying a little literature from here, a little from there. Few Christian workers have worried about the lack of *taxonomy* in what's being used in their training structures.

Imagine a child being introduced to the death of Jesus on the cross without first knowing *how* He is God, and without understanding the meaning of the word "sin." Imagine a person seeking to know the *will* of God who has never been taught how to *hear God speak.* Imagine a believer seeking to build up a fellow Christian with little or no knowledge of spiritual gifts. *It's not hard to imagine: it's taking place all around us, all the time.*

What Should Be The First Things A New Christian Grasps?

That question bothered me for years. The tepid-water "New Member's Orientation Class" of the P.B.D. church was solidly based on *institutional* needs, not the needs of the convert. I spent many years trying to understand what was needed, and finally wrote the *Survival Kit For New Christians.* It has sold over two million copies in English and is probably in 50 foreign languages. It meets a need!

However, it *doesn't* meet the need of the Shepherd group church, and for that reason I will be creating *The Arrival Kit For New Christians* exclusively for use in Shepherd group churches. Several issues must be addressed in this new publication for the new believer to be properly oriented to living as a believer. Of course, many of the areas covered in the original book will remain, but the whole area of corporate life in Christ must be developed:

1. You have received two spiritual baptisms at the moment of your conversion: baptism into Christ, and baptism into the body of Christ (Romans 6:3, 1 Corinthians 12:13, Galatians 3:27).
2. Your value system as of now has been totally shaped without the mind of Christ influencing it. Most of your values must be be radically changed, or at least revised, as you enter your new life.
3. The Bible is the source for the restructuring of your values. Within this first year of your Christian life, you will be helped to review its contents from cover to cover, using Cover The Bible, which not only gives you a "bird's eye view" of all 66 books, but also focuses on evaluating your value system.
4. Your life in the Body of Christ is most precious. That Body is composed of cells we call Shepherd groups. Your maturity into Christian life is dependent upon your participation in one. You can't grow in a vacuum. Christ comes to you through your brothers and sisters in His family.
5. The understanding of how Christ flows through others to you, and how He flows through you to others, involves your use of spiritual gifts. You need to understand them and how they are used to edify others.

The following equipping structure has been developed with a taxonomy in mind. It begins with the moment of conversion. It assumes true growth can only happen by living in a "Basic Christian Community." Thus, it anticipates the Christian's total commitment to a Shepherd group. It seeks to strengthen the Shepherd groups by not competing with them through unnecessary time commitments.

Believers need to be equipped in two areas: Bible knowledge and ministry skills, leading them into ministry through Shepherd group life. Materials have been, and are being developed, with a *taxonomy* in mind.

No Classrooms Required

A Shepherd group church must equip believers as a part of Shepherd group life. With few exceptions, the equipping ministry of a Shepherd group church should not utilize classrooms. Classroom training neither tests nor screens people to determine how lectures have changed personal value systems. Classroom examinations only discover how well the subject material has been remembered. Below the level of Zone Pastor Intern, the traditional pattern of lectures should be replaced with "Equipper-Intern" relationships.

How Do People Learn?

We must take into full account the way people learn! We must stop assuming that the best way to equip people is to sit them down in rows and teach them. This destructive thesis has used up thousands of hours of time without producing effective ministers.

We must change the word "teaching" to "apprenticing." There are very few things we actually do unless we work with someone who both *informs* and *demonstrates* for us. We must begin with the premise that every true Christian is both in the *process* of being equipped, while simultaneously equipping someone else. This must begin with the first person entering a Shepherd group, and must continue right up through the Zone Pastors to the Senior Pastors! We must constantly be functioning on the philosophy that true equipping requires *both* activities to be taking place *simultaneously.*

Shepherd Group Schedule

Prior to the launching of the actual Shepherd Group, a 40 minute period will be set aside for equipping. The total time required for the two periods will be approximately two hours. A typical schedule will look like this:

Equipping	**Equipping Time 1 (20 minutes)**
	Equipping Time 2 (20 minutes)
Edification	**Shepherd Group (80 minutes)**

A. Part One: Equipping Ministries

**EACH ONE TEACHES ONE,
AFTER BEING TAUGHT BY ONE**

Premise: each person in a Shepherd group is equipping someone, and is being equipped by someone else.

1. First 20 minutes: Equipping Time 1

   Examples:
   - Each of the "Little Children" meets with a "Young Man" sponsor to discuss the SURVIVAL KIT.
   - The "Fathers" meet with the Shepherd and Intern to discuss their Share group ministry.

2. Second 20 minutes: Equipping Time 2

   Examples:
   - Each of the "Young Men" meet with a "Father" sponsor to discuss KNOCKING ON DOORS, OPENING HEARTS.
   - The "Little Children" meet with the Shepherd and Intern to discuss their COVER THE BIBLE studies.

B. Part Two: Edification Ministries

Premise: each person in a Shepherd group must learn to become an "edifier," actually using spiritual gifts in building up the body.

Schedule:

- 10 minutes: Ice Breaker
- 20 minutes: Worship
- 40 minutes: Edification
- 10 minutes: Share The Vision

Levels To Be Included In The Equipping Ministry

1. For the Incoming Member

Spiritual Formation Weekend

This event fills a Friday night through a Saturday night, beginning and ending with a meal. It may be held in a home, a retreat center, or any pleasant surrounding. The church should provide these weekends as frequently as needed. Where there is a constant harvest, it should be conducted monthly. In churches with Zone Pastors, they may be assigned to conduct them.

The following book is designed to be used in this weekend:

- **The *Spiritual Gifts Inventory* booklet**
  This booklet is designed to provide a presentation about spiritual gifts in the first half, and an inventory to be completed in the final pages. After the presentation about the importance and place of spiritual gifts, each person prayerfully examines the awareness of times when gifts have been manifested in life situations. Obviously, gifts are discovered in ministry, rather than in an inventory. Nevertheless, there must be a starting point for the "ungifted," a place where they are given some basic instruction about the gifts. The inventory in this booklet took over two years of testing to develop. Dramatically, after six months in a Shepherd group where edification has taken place, the inventory will reflect a different pattern of spiritual gifts. (For more information, see the later chapter *Touch Tools To Use.*)

There should be a loving, relaxed spirit in all that takes place during the weekend. The spirit of the pastor and other leadership team members should be considered to be as important as the content. There should be informal times for fellowship as well as training sessions. Each person should be made to feel they have entered a new world, the Kingdom of Christ, and that it is a place where one need not fear being manipulated.

A personalized notebook has been prepared by Faith Community Baptist Church for those attending this event. It's a good idea! It should be an item prepared "in house," rather than a book published professionally.

Experience has shown those entering the life of a cell church usually form special bonds during this weekend, even though they will not be in the same Shepherd groups when it is over. Every attempt should be made to make this take place.

The incoming believer must be shown how the vision of the church includes him or her. Only if there is a "handle" to get involved will people become more than observers of the vision. They must share as implementers!

Among other important topics the Leadership team should consider including in the weekend are:

- The "Vision" of the church.
- The Shepherd group as Community.
- The place of edification through your personal use of spiritual gifts in the Shepherd group.
- A practical demonstration of what it means to be an edifier of others through the use of spiritual gifts.
- A basic practice session in how to get into using your spiritual gifts to edify.

The final event is a "banquet," no matter how plain the food. All the Zone Pastors who have potential group members should participate, sitting at a table with these people. Shepherds may also be invited to give their testimonies of how they came to serve in their pastoral role, encouraging the new folks to seek God's best for their own ministries.

Special needs may be dealt with at this time, tailored to the particular problems present in the lives of those attending. These may include:

1. The wife or husband who has an unsaved spouse.
2. Persons who have a family situation which makes it impossible for their home to be available for Shepherd groups.
3. Family members who strongly oppose this commitment.
4. An explanation about the meaning of baptism and why it is necessary.
5. An explanation about the meaning of the Lord's supper, and how and where it is observed.
6. The use of Sponsors for those on their journeys.

7. The stewardship of life—both of our bodies and our assets.
8. The way the cell church receives offerings (in the Shepherd group meeting and/or in the Celebrations or Congregational meetings).

Much thought should be given to the pattern for this important weekend, tailoring it to the locality, the size of the church, and the special needs in the lives of the people.

The "Journey Guide" Interview

A spiritual journey must be outlined for incoming members using the *Journey Guide* by the Shepherd as soon as possible. This should be done in the person's home immediately after the weekend. (See complete explanation in the *Shepherd's Guidebook.*) Depending on what is needed, incoming members may be assigned to begin with any combination of the journey stages presented in the later chapter *Touch Tools To Use.*

2. For "Little Children:"

New converts should be located immediately in a Shepherd group, if they have not already made contact with one. (Faith Community Baptist Church requires Shepherd group attendance for four weeks before actual membership can commence.)

The "Little Children" will, of course, participate in the Spiritual Formation Weekend. They will be visited by the Shepherd and the Shepherd Intern, and the Journey Guide will be prepared for their first year in church life.

The object is to give a *thorough grounding* to every new believer within one year's time. At the end of one year, this will include a comprehensive survey of the Bible, and experience in reaching both Type "A" and Type "B" unbelievers, as well as the ability to use spiritual gifts in ministry. The following materials are designed to accomplish these objectives:

1. The 11-week *Arrival Kit.*

This is a self-study programmed learning tool requiring 5 days a week for personal study. It takes no more than 15 minutes to complete the daily material. Each week of self-study is then discussed in the Equipping Time with the person's Sponsor (Refer to diagram on page 242).

2. The 52-week *Cover The Bible* course.

This is a self-study requiring 5 days a week of personal study, using 5-minute-per-day cassette taped messages. At six week intervals, the Leadership team should provide a special question/answer evening for all who are taking the one year course. It will be a general session for anyone to attend. The person or persons leading it should be well versed in the Bible, "apt to teach," and able to apply Bible truth to personal values from a Kingdom perspective.

Note: "Little Children" will invest about 20 minutes a day in self-study.

3. For "Young Men:"

Spiritual Warfare Weekend

This is a continuation of the *Spiritual Formation Weekend.* It provides a basic orientation for new believers who are moving from the "Little Children" stage to the "Young Men" stage. For the most part, these will be Christians who are only three or four months old in the Lord. The teaching on spiritual warfare should be very basic, providing them more with a defense mechanism than instruction about how to take the offensive in this matter.

For those who feel a new Christian should not be so quickly exposed to instruction in this area, may I remind them that one is not a "Young Man" until he or she has learned how to "master the evil one." If there is no instruction, *how will that mastery happen?*

Every new convert, within three months, has come face to face with the enemy many times. It's no surprise that Satan is moving about like a roaring lion, seeking to devour new believers. The great need is to answer the question, "How do I overcome his attacks?"

In all cases, they should be instructed to serve under a more experienced Christian in understanding spiritual conflict. Once again, the apprenticeship pattern within the Shepherd group family is required.

The contents of the Spiritual Warfare Weekend should include:

- Further teaching on how to exercis their spiritual gifts for edification within the Shepherd group.
- The place of prayer in warfare.
- How to recognize demonic activity.
- How to pray for a person who is oppressed.
- Instructions on how to minister with a more mature Christian before, during, and after a person has been set free;
- Healing: basic Biblical teaching on the subject, and how to pray for healing.

Along with this training, the "Young Man" is guided into the penetration of the darkness Satan has implanted in the minds of unbelievers. At this stage, the believer is to be equipped to bring Type "A" unbelievers to faith in Christ. Under the mantle of the Sponsor, the journey involves visitation to them and sharing the message of salvation. The following book is designed to accomplish this objective:

- **The 11-week *Knocking On Doors, Opening Hearts.***
  Names of visitors to worship services/special events will be channeled to the appropriate Shepherd groups to be visited and enlisted as a Shepherd group or Share group participant. (Most will be candidates for the Shepherd group.)
  1. The "Young Men" will be introduced to a visitation ministry for a period of 11 weeks.
  2. They will be guided by a more experienced member of the Shepherd group during this 11 week training.
  3. They will be assisted to lead another person to accept the Lord and become active in their Shepherd group.
  4. This will require the study of one chapter in the book *Knocking On Doors, Opening Hearts* each week for 11 weeks, with review by the Sponsor during the Equipping Time.
  5. Most important of all, the person being equipped does not "finish a course." The criteria for completion is to actually bring another person to accept Christ as Lord. While in the P.B.D. circles this is a rare person, it *must* be

the standard for the authentic Christian. When the words "layman" and "laity" and "lay pastor" are eliminated from one's vocabulary, the gap between "clergy" and "laity" disappears forever—we are *all* ministers, and that means *all* can be involved in reaping.

4. For "Fathers:"

Ministry Outreach Weekend

1. The focus of this workshop-type weekend will be to form teams of three from Shepherd groups and release them to minister to six Type "B" unbelievers during a period of ten weeks.
2. This weekend will be limited to those who have:
   - Completed *Knocking On Doors, Opening Hearts.*
   - Made at least 11 visits in a period of 11 weeks.
   - Personally experienced leading one person to Christ.

   Note: there isn't any sense in equipping Christians to reach out to Type "B" unbelievers if they can't win a person to Christ. This is a mandatory prerequisite!

3. The five hour **Touch Ministries Seminar** is presented during this weekend. Video segments, overhead projector transparencies, and student workbooks are used for each person present, and teams are formed at the close of the sessions.

   The following materials are designed to accomplish the objective of forming Share groups:

- **The 20 week *Touch Basic Training* course.**
   1. This weekly equipping immediately follows the *Ministry Outreach Weekend.*
   2. It is provided for teams, not individuals, and is to take place during EQUIPPING TIME 1 in the Shepherd group gatherings.
   3. Shepherds must be trained to conduct these 20-minutes-per-week sessions. All Shepherds should have already been through the training themselves when previously

serving on a Share group team, making this easier than it might seem.

4. When a videotape player is available, the Shepherd can make use of the six hours of video segments produced for use in the training.

5. The *Facilitator's Guidebook* provides complete guidance for the use of the Touch Basic Training materials, and includes overhead transparencies which can also be used as flash cards in a living room setting.

5. For Shepherd Interns

The Shepherd Intern is to undergo six months of training, following which he or she becomes responsible for a Shepherd group and begins to supervise the equipping of another Shepherd Intern.

Shepherd Intern Formation Weekend

1. This should be a full Saturday session, orienting the Shepherd Intern to what is expected of him/her. It could be held in a hotel with the church picking up the cost of the meal, beginning at 8:30 a.m. and finishing at 4:30 p.m.

2. The structure of the sessions should be as follows:

    a. A beginning word from the Senior Pastor about the importance of their task, and a sharing of his heart concerning the vision for the Shepherd Groups.

    b. He adds a word of thanks for their faithfulness as a "Little Child," a "Young Man," and a "Father" in their Shepherd group experience. He should tell them he is looking forward to laying hands on them at the end of the day as they are set apart for their ministry.

    c. A testimony from a Shepherd about the joy of the work, and the way his/her life had to change in order to be an effective Shepherd.

    d. A season of fellowship with the Senior Pastor and the Zone Pastors. This might include recreation or hiking, etc. A real effort should be made to make each person feel that he/she is a part of a leadership team that cares deeply about them, and that they are fully accepted on that team.

e. An IPAT or Taylor-Johnson Temperament Analysis test or similar instrument is given early in the day so it can be processed for a later session.

f. A review of the six months period they will be in training, week by week. There should be no "hidden obligations" as they enter their ministry.

g. A review of the job description of a Shepherd Intern.

h. An outline of the time investment required to be effective in their ministry.

i. A discussion of their lifestyle, and a preparation of a "Time Chart" revealing how they *now* invest their time.

j. A small group activity with a Zone Pastor leading each group, discussing the adjustments required to their time investment, and helping each person come to terms with the matter of "Living Christianly" instead of "Living, Cultural Style."

k. A review of the **Shepherd's Guidebook,** outlining the importance of each chapter. At this time, a schedule should be given for the completion of their study of the book.

l. Evaluation of their temperament analysis test and a discussion of the findings in small groups.

m. An intense period of prayer.

n. A signing of a Preliminary Covenant, in which they commit themselves to the ministry of being a Shepherd.

o. Pastors lay hands on all who sign the Covenant.

p. Preparation is then provided so they know how to conduct themselves at the next Celebration, where they will all be presented. Specific ones (two is enough) are asked to prepare brief two minute testimonies to share with the audience their feelings about the step they are taking.

Shepherd Intern Training Period

1. The Shepherd Intern studies a chapter a week in the *Shepherd's Guidebook.* He or she meets with the Shepherd to review the chapter and discuss the "fleshing out" of the principles in the Shepherd group meeting.

2. The Intern is regularly assigned tasks within the Shepherd group by the Shepherd. Within 4-1/2 months, the Intern

begins to give full direction to the cell as the Shepherd observes. The pattern to be followed by the Shepherd, as a chart in the later chapter *How To Form A Leadership Cell* illustrates, is:

Stage 1:
   High directive, low facilitative—"Watch me!" (7 weeks)
Stage 2:
   High directive, high facilitative—"Here's how; now you try it!" (7 weeks)
Stage 3:
   Low directive, high facilitative—"Do it; I'll sit back and watch." (7 weeks)
Stage 4:
   Low directive, low facilitative—"You're doing very well. Keep it up!"

3. All the activities of the Shepherd should be shared by the Shepherd Intern, who is literally a "shadow" during the entire six months of internship.
4. At the time an Intern is finally set apart as a Shepherd, there should be a public "ordination" service in the Celebration, with the laying on of hands by the Zone Servants and the Zone Pastors. A *Covenant of Ministry* should now be publicly signed by the Intern as the congregation watches.

6. For Shepherds

The primary responsibility is to pastor the members of a Shepherd group. A Shepherd needs some form of identification. At the time of "ordination" mentioned above, he/she could be given a lovely pin or badge to wear, or whatever is appropriate in the culture. The identification should mark the person as a Shepherd in all places, not just around other members of the cell church. Thus, a locket or a pin can be used. *(We have produced lockets and pins with the Touch logo on them for those who don't have budget money to produce specialty items.)*

The TOUCH Logo

The Shepherd meets on a regular basis with the Zone Shepherd. The agendas for these meetings are to be set at least one week in advance, and should be based on specific needs or problems of the five Shepherds who meet together.

The Shepherd spends special time with the Zone Shepherd and the Zone Pastor on a fortnightly basis. This appointment is to provide time for the Shepherd to learn from these men how to handle certain ministry areas, and for them to observe him at the same time. Those to be visited or ministered to on these occasions are chosen by the Shepherd, and may involve healings, deliverances, visits to lost family members of cell members, etc.

After numerous trips to Korea to study Yonggi Cho's Shepherd group model, I *finally* discovered this "three tier" pattern is used by him. (Digging out the mechanics of how his church is run is not easy, and is regretfully not included in his annual conference!) A precious missionary lady who has been with him from the beginning explained this "three-tier" pattern of discipling to me. Later, I discovered the same identical process was being used by the 50,000 member Kwang Lim Methodist Church, pastored by Dr. Sun Do Kim, and the Yong Nak Presbyterian Church. It fits Paul's admonition in 2 Timothy 2:2!

7. For Zone Shepherds

A Zone Shepherd shall have satisfactorily completed his six months of training as a Shepherd Intern, and have served for two full cycles as a Shepherd. This minimum experience is necessary for effective ministry as he becomes the pastor to Shepherds. He will be assigned three or four Shepherds, never more, and will assist them in every possible way. This will include meeting together with them to discuss problems they are all facing, rotating between their group meetings, and providing private counseling for them. This is in addition to the "Three Tier" visits mentioned above.

Zone Shepherd Formation Weekend

At church expense, this event will cover a period of Friday night, all day Saturday, and all day Sunday. It should be held in a lovely setting—a hotel or a resort spot. It's a major event in the life of the person and of the church. Wives or husbands are most assuredly included!

Some areas to be covered in the weekend are:

1. How to minister to the Shepherds under your care.
2. The relationship between you and the Zone Pastor.
3. Visitation of the Shepherd Groups on a rotating basis.
4. Reports: their importance, their use.
5. Visiting Shepherd group people with the Shepherd and the Zone Pastor on a cyclical basis.
6. Handling Shepherd group problems effectively.
7. Advanced Spiritual Warfare.
8. Advanced Spiritual Gifts; their use in your new ministry.
9. Basic principles of counseling.
10. Prayer warfare and prayer intercession.

Zone Shepherd Conferences

These are suggestions gleaned from my own personal experience and from observation of Shepherd groups visited:

1. Systematic conferences conducted by the Zone Pastors are to be conducted on a monthly basis.
2. These conferences must be extremely worthwhile for the Zone Shepherds! If they are not conducted with practical assistance offered each time they meet, the Zone Shepherds will begin to skip them. Too many Zone Pastors observed simply give some inspiration and their thoughts on a scripture passage. *They must leave the preaching to the Senior Pastor!* Worthy preparation must be put into each of these sessions.
3. Another important point to remember: going around the circle and having reports from all Zone Shepherds becomes boring after a few sessions. The Zone Pastor must do his homework and have personal conferences first. Then, in the Conference, he should provide to all a copy of the attendance, discuss a list of problem areas in the groups supervised by the Zone Servants, and provide carefully researched solutions.
4. The Zone Pastor should then follow up and see if the prob-

lems were corrected by his counsel. This should be done by visiting problem groups with Zone Shepherds.

8. For Zone Pastor Interns

For one year, the Zone Pastor Interns will meet with teaching members of the Ministry Team for training in their ministry. There shall be a regular regimen for this period of equipping, and this regimen will take precedence over all other matters. Ordination as a Zone Pastor shall require the completion of all requirements. There shall be nine hours of class time and fifteen hours of study time per week. In addition, each Intern will be given 24 hours of specific weekly assignments by the Zone Pastor, with evaluation of the Intern's effectiveness submitted by the Zone Pastor on a biweekly basis to those responsible for his/her training.

A marvelous example of this training is the *Network* offered by ICHTHUS Fellowship in London. Dion Robert's classes now number over 100 Zone Pastor Interns; he's ordaining over 50 men at one time! Below is the pattern I am participating in at the Faith Community Baptist Church in Singapore:

Suggested Schedule:

Wednesday, Thursday, And Friday: 8 a.m. to 10:50 a.m.:

8:00-8:50: First Class Session
9:00-9:50: Second Class Session
10:00-10:50: Third Class Session

Faculty members should include leadership team pastors, specifically selected Zone Pastors, and visiting teachers. Extension courses are readily available for use in this training. For a catalog, write to: Columbia School of Biblical Education, Post Office Box 3122, Columbia, South Carolina 29230-3122.

Tentative Subjects To Be Offered:

1. Christian Life 1 (Lecture)
2. Christian Life 2 (Groups)

3. Inductive Bible Study
4. Old Testament Survey
5. New Testament Survey
6. Christian Theology: An Overview
7. Galatians and Romans
8. Hermeneutics
9. A Theology of Christian Community
10. Prayer; Listening To The Voice of God
11. Animism and Your Ministry
12. A History of the "Radical" Christian Church
13. Your Personal Value System
14. Power Healing, Warfare, Evangelism
15. Principles Of Spirit-filled Teaching
16. Preaching (Optional; evaluation of gifts required.)
17. Leading Worship
18. Practical Pastoral Ministries:
    - Dedication of Babies
    - Conducting Baptisms
    - Conducting the Lord's Supper
    - Premarital Counseling
    - Conducting Weddings
    - Conducting Funerals
    - Principles of Leadership & Management
    - Serving under authority
    - Servanting those under your authority
    - Planning
    - Scheduling
    - Record Keeping and Analysis
    - Cell Group Planting
    - How to plant a Cell Group in virgin territory
    - How to equip leadership within a new Cell Group
    - Zone Servant Supervision
    - Zone Development Strategies

Additional Subjects To Be Offered To Missionary Interns:

This requires an additional four months of study. The goal of Faith Community Baptist Church is to send 100 of our members to mission fields by the year 2000 to plant cell churches. We have a very strong budget and already are supporting many workers, including Africa, Hong Kong, and Indonesia.

The missionary vision of a Shepherd group church is phenomenal! Yonggi Cho has Koreans all over the globe. ICTHUS Fellowship, as mentioned earlier, has targeted areas out of Cyprus. The type of missionary sent out from a cell church is experienced in his or her work and is exceptional in developing new work using a pattern which has been well learned. The courses added for them include:

- Practical Missionary Living
- Introduction to Missions
- Cultural Anthropology
- A Philosophy of Church Planting on the Mission Field

Practical Application Requirements

Before an Intern may graduate, there must be proven skills in these areas:

1. At least four people who have been personally led to a saving knowledge of Jesus Christ, and who have become a part of a Shepherd group.
2. At least two new Shepherd groups that have been formed by the Intern.
3. The first of these Shepherd groups is to be started with the close supervision and assistance of the appropriate Zone Pastor.
4. The second new Shepherd group must be started "from scratch" in an area where the church did not previously have a Shepherd group.
   - This Shepherd group is to be started by the Intern using his/her own strategy, gleaned from the training.
   - This project is to be closely supervised by the appropriate Zone Servant, but there is to be no assistance given other than proper cautions if the Intern plans strategies deemed unwise.
   - For the Missionary Intern, this second project may, at the discretion of the church, be carried out in an overseas setting, under another missionary cell church planter.
3. It is to be understood that until these goals have been met, the Intern will not be eligible for graduation or for employment as a Zone Pastor or a Missionary.

25 ORGANIZING FOR THE HARVEST

History of the *Eglise Protestante Baptiste Œuvres et Mission*

The *Eglise Protestante Baptiste Œuvres et Mission* in Abidjan is a classic example of a cell group church that has adapted to its surroundings. For you to understand the way Dion Robert has organized for the harvest, it's necessary to share the history of his ministry.

The son of a witch doctor in the village of Douleu, Dion made his way to Abidjan at age 21. There he joined the police force, and was so talented he shot up through the ranks to become a detective. At this point, he was sent to Senegal for a six month training course. While there, he was led to Christ by a missionary, and absorbed all the American could teach him in his free hours. Upon returning to the Ivory Coast, he set himself on a three to four hour sleep schedule so he could study the Bible undisturbed. With a mind like a sponge, he absorbed the scripture until he was filled with its message.

In 1975, he went to see a missionary and asked him if there was a place he could preach out what was burning in his bones. He was driven to the armpit of the city, a slum called Yopougon, and shown two small buildings with an "auditorium" added in the space between them. Dion moved into a couple of rooms with his wife, Helen, and two children. They were the only members at the start.

Two years later, the church had grown to 25 members. On May 1, 1976, during an all night prayer meeting, the little band of slum dwellers were deeply moved by the filling of the Holy Spirit, and received a vision for the evangelization of the entire

Ivory Coast nation. A year later, the church had doubled. Satan sought to destroy the church, and half of the 50 or so members left over Dion's biblical stand on the divorce issue.

In 1979, the missionaries who had sponsored the work wrote a letter giving the church autonomy. One year later, the little band planted a second church. In mid-1981, the group had grown to about 350 members, and realized they must build a better building for their meeting place. Dion still lived with his family in some side rooms off the small auditorium that would seat 100 Westerners, now packed tight by the 350 who squeezed in "African style." It was in this year the slum dwellers decided to build a larger structure. They had extremely limited funds, since 80% of the people in the city are unemployed. Bag by bag, they bought and poured cement on a site a few miles away they purchased from the missionaries. Little did they know that this project would not be fully completed until 1990, and not entered for use until Easter of 1989!

Once again Satan sought to split the little congregation, this time in 1982. This time it was over Pentecostalism which sought to infiltrate the structure. The Pentecostals withdrew.

Three more years of slow growth took place as Dion struggled to break from the P.B.D. model to the cell group church model. Dion took the limited information he gleaned from the scripture and his reading to his nightly sojourns before the Lord, and divided his membership into cells. Following the culture, these were composed of separate cells for men and women.

Growth Began After Structures Were Fully Developed

Their next step was to organize the church structure into "Departments" (see chart) which provided a *root system* to penetrate the community and win the lost to Christ. Responsibility was prayerfully delegated to Godly men and women. The graph of his growth does not explode until after he had taken this step to provide the superstructure for rapid growth.

Within a year, the church had gone to four worship services, and then exploded to seven—all preached by a man who was now sleeping on the floor of his own office because of the limited space available for the church's needs and the need for additional offices for the other pastors.

Eglise Protestante Baptiste Œuvres et Mission
Organizational Chart

MINISTRIES TO THE CELLS

Deacon Department

Religions, Sects & Traditions Department

Family Life Department

Teaching & Personnel Department

ADMINISTRATION OF THE CHURCH

Missionary Department

Music Department

Administration Department

Correspondence & Archives Department

Publications Department

Audio-Visual Department

Press Department

Gatekeeper Department

Public Relations Department

Social Services Department

Secretarial Department

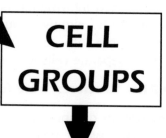

CELL GROUPS

MINISTRIES FOR CELL GROUP PENETRATION

Hospital Department	Evangelism Department	Youth Department
Prison Department	Demonology Department	Women's Department

By 1987, there were 5,214 members and 232 cells. It was at this time Ras and Beverly Robinson visited the church, with the cloud of Bev's growing brain tumor threatening their future. The Lord flowed His healing gifts into her while they were there; they returned to Fort Worth to discover she had been totally healed. This was one of many precious acts of God's power then being regularly experienced by the cell groups.

In 1990, the date of my writing, there are 1,500 cells in the nation. Robert says these are the only ones they have reports from; he estimates there are another 500 or more who do not turn in reports. Their ministry has literally covered all of the major cities of the nation, including 45 in Bouaké, the second largest city, which also has an additional 8 "Zone Churches" who do not now turn in figures to the central office. He estimates there are now over 2,000 members of *all* the Bouaké cells.

A Movement Doesn't Stay Put!

The church has extended into several nations around them. Four of their pastors have established extensions of the work in Guinea, two are in Burkina Faso. In 1989 they sent two of their couples, trained in their school, to plant a church in Paris, France among African Francophone people. It now has 250 in cells.

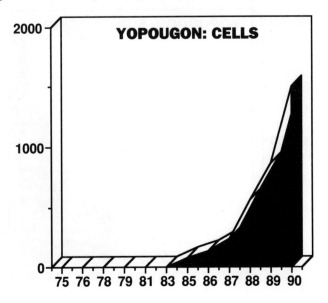

So committed is the church to its original vision of being a *movement,* not just a local church, that it changed its name in 1987 to "Protestant Baptist Church, *Works and Mission.*" Its training school has produced scores and scores of pastors for the ever expanding work. On Easter Monday, 1990, 57 more men were ordained to participate in the pastoral ministries. There are 198 full time pastors on the payroll as this is written.

Through much needed and prayed-for assistance from America and Singapore, the "Temple" and two multi-story buildings have now been completed. A 6,000 seat auditorium, offices, classrooms for their training school, and dormitories now assist them in their growth. Amazingly, the 20,000 people in the cells are reaching out and harvesting so rapidly that the typical time before multiplication of cells is only ten weeks!

Like many of the men I have surveyed around the world, Dion Robert had no model to follow except the scripture. The passage that helped him understand how the cells were to be managed was in Exodus 18, where Jethro gave Moses the pattern for guiding Israel. He says, "I got serious about the structure for the cells." On June 10, 1984, he instituted the structure which has caused the significant growth.

Robert's graph of growth reflects a pattern that is seen in other cell group churches I have studied around the world: a

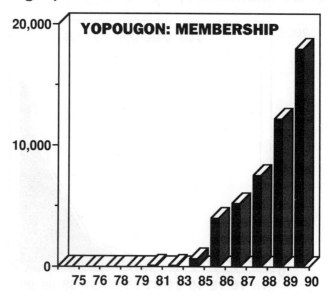

period of seven to ten years was required before the significant growth began. When asked about this, Pastor Dion said, "Leading people to go to the cross and die is not easy. Until they do, there will be no growth. The cells are not the secret; it is in the crucified lives of Christians who have finally come to the end of themselves and are totally dedicated to doing the work of their Lord."

Growth Results From Dedicated Christians

The growth is the result of *dedicated Christians,* whose lives are not fragmented and divided between many interests and ambitions. A serious ministry begins at the cross! Leaders must be men and women who are deeply committed to what the church is going to do and to become. He comments, "We have lost many people along the way when we brought them to obedience to the Lordship of Christ. If seed doesn't die, it bears no fruit. We lead people to die! We demand of all our cell leaders a maximum number of hours per week devoted to their ministry. It's hard work to serve a cell. If they are not dead to themselves, they will not give time to the Lord."

I was deeply moved by the personal modelling done by this pastor. With 20,000 members, he doesn't even own a car. He says, "If I drive a car, then all the people want one, too. I put everything aside that might give the people the impression I am not giving my all. I put all aside in order that the church may keep growing and winning the lost."

Dion has also pointed out that the development of a cell is like driving a car: you can't take your eyes off what is happening for a moment. Cell workers must be constantly supervised. "If you don't work at training every single week, you won't maintain a cell group vision. People will fall into a routine of just attending their meeting, and they will lose their zeal."

An Exposition Of The "Departments"

Dr. Charles Deevers, dental missionary attached to the church, has graciously provided us with this outline of the Departments. This study took several weeks for him to prepare, for those involved in the work had never written an explanation of what for them is a way of life.

1. DIRECTION OF THE CELL GROUPS

House Church Department

BOKA Boka Faustin, Director

The House Church Department is in charge of establishing and maintaining all local house churches [cell groups].

Disciples [in this book, called "Zone Interns"] are cell group members that are in training to become *Cell Group Pastors* [in this book, called "Shepherds"] when the cell multiplies itself.

The cell groups are divided into six Sections. Each Section has a full time Section Head. The sections are:

Section 1: Men
Section 2: Women
Section 3: SESAM (Cell groups for professional people.)
Section 4: Children
Section 5: SEMUS (Cell groups for students in high school and the university.)
Section 6: SECT. INT. (Cell groups in the interior of the country)

All of the 6 sections are divided into Zones. The Zones are divided into Sectors and the Sectors into Cells.

Each Saturday afternoon at 3:30, all house church pastors in Abidjan come together for a meeting. Over 1,500 pastors and workers attend these meetings. The local cell groups take up offerings that pay the transportation of their pastor. All offerings are brought in on Saturdays, and the pastors are then given back their transportation money. This is a self-supporting ministry and no church budget funds are used.

The Saturday program consists of the pastor teaching a 15 minute Bible study that will be shared with the cell groups at their next meeting.

Subjects are selected as needs arise within the cells. As each cell group turns in its weekly report, it includes spiritual problems faced by the members. These may be personal, family, job-related, etc. Topics for the pastor's sermons and for cell group discussion are selected as a result of what the groups have reported.

This period is followed by a 1 hour Bible study for the edification of the cell pastor [Shepherd], followed by 30 minutes of questions from the workers to the pastor.

2. ADMINISTRATION OF THE CHURCH

Missionary Department

Pastor OKOUBO Gadou Desire
Pastor KIMOU CLAUDILE

Coordination
This section coordinates all the activities of the department.

Ivory Coast Missions
This section is responsible for all of the 52 congregations of cells in the Ivory Coast. 17 of these congregations are in the Abidjan area. The latest figures show that the total adult membership of the church is 18,488. The Yopougon mother church has 6,000 members and the 51 other churches have 12,488 members.

When it is decided that because of location or growth a cell group should become a point to be developed into a congregation, the Zone Pastor requests that a pastor be sent from Abidjan to launch the new work. A new zone is created, and church planting begins using members of the existing cell as the foundation for expansion.

There are 23 *cellules* [cells] that they have selected to become Zones that are waiting for pastors. After the next graduation from the missionary school in December, 1990, many of these *cellules* will be assigned pastors. Their status will be upgraded to that of a zone, and each one will spawn new cell groups.

Each three months the Missionary Department has meetings for the Zone Pastors. The purpose of these meetings is to transmit decisions made at the Abidjan headquarters and to encourage the local churches.

The first zone outside Abidjan was started in 1975, and the second was launched in 1982. Since 1982, 50 zones have been started and 23 are waiting to be formed, lacking only a full time pastor.

In addition to the 52 zones there are 56 villages that have cell group churches. The extension into the rest of the nation is a high priority for the church.

Foreign Missions

In 1988 a church was started in Paris, France and the church sent its first foreign missionary. A second couple has now been sent to work with the growing church there.

Other churches are now planted in Guinea and Burkina Faso. Mali, Ghana, and Togo are soon to be entered, using future graduates of the Bible school.

Music Department

BEN, Director
N'GUESSAN KOUAME Lambert, Choir director

At present there are 82 choir members, 62 women and 20 men. They meet in classes on Monday, Tuesday, and Saturday, for Bible studies, music lessons, and choir practice. They sing each Sunday, and at all special events of the church.

M. Lambert said that since musicians are often prideful, racists, and nervous, their Bible studies are directed towards these areas.

Administration Department

GRAN Pierre, Director

92 people work in the Administration Department. There are 8 in Abidjan and 2 at each of the 42 churches in the interior of the country. The Department of Administration is divided into three sections:
1. Accounting
   a. The accounting of all funds, tithes, gifts, offerings. church budget, building, various enterprises such as the soap factory, bookstore, ELECTROMIS, etc.
   b. The payment of all bills.
   c. The paying of support to all missionary personnel.
2. Supervising the accounting procedures of each of the 42 churches.

The total church budget for 1989 (not including construction) is $175,000.00. The 122 missionaries of the church are given their support money three times a week as money is available. Since there are not sufficient funds to pay them one time per month, they are paid after each service from the tithes and undesignated offerings. This takes hours of time; sometimes the administration staff stays at the church until 2 a.m. When there is not enough money to pay everyone, the pastors and missionaries return after the next service to receive their stipends. They are living at the edge of faith, learning what it means to pray *"Give us this day our daily bread."* Salaries paid are not enough to provide more than food, so each staff member *really* lives by faith. There is no church with *so many* workers devoted to the vision!

Correspondence and Archives Department

Workers in this Department file away and look up all correspondence, and carefully archive the week-by-week activities by filing bulletins, brochures, etc. In the future, this archive will be of great assistance to those doing a historical study of the work.

Publications Department

Bookstore
During the first six months of 1989 the bookstore sold:

Bibles	1,270
New Testaments	624
Individual books of the Bible	1,283
Tracts	8,368
Books (mostly from VIDA in Miami)	3,101
Bible covers	254
Concordances	3
Cassettes	254

From these sales there was a profit of $2,354.71 of which $1,218.03 was transferred to the church construction account and $1,136.68 stayed in the Mass Media account. They also had enough profit to pay their workers $1,109.28 in benefits, rent bookstore space in Bouaké and Gagnoa, and start ELECTROMIS.

Print Shop

At present the print shop has only one offset press and its activities are limited to:

1. Printing weekly church Bible study outlines for the Wednesday services.
2. Printing church emblems on T-shirts. These shirts are resold to the members for $4.37.

Audio Visual Department

FLAN Koré Thomas (Director of personnel)
YAO N'Guettia (liaison to Department of Administration)
OHOUO Roger (Accounting and director of Bookstores)

Responsibilities:

1. Maintenance of all church audio and video equipment.
2. Recording of all services on cassette.
   · For historical record
   · For resale

Audio Ministries:

The second and the fourth of seven services are recorded, and the cassettes are edited. This takes about eight hours per cassette. As orders come in from the bookstore, the master cassettes are taken to a duplicating service in Abidjan. The cassettes are then sold through the bookstore.

Video Ministries:

This Department will be further developed in the future as the church occupies its new facilities. A full sized studio and control room for videotaping has been built into the ground floor of the five story building. For the moment, this Department consists of one photographer who photographs all important events of the church. Some photographs are sold.

ELECTROMIS (A word combining *Electronics* and *Œuvres et Mission*)

The church has rented a storefront three blocks from the new church building for an audio and video repair shop.

1. There they repair all church equipment (audio and video, including amplifiers, tape recorders, etc.)

2. They repair equipment that customers bring to them. From this there is a profit used to pay rent and employees' salaries.
3. They also sell parts, such as belts and motors to repair equipment.

Press Department

This department is in charge of all press releases and coordinating all newspaper, radio and television coverage of all major events of the church.

Gatekeeper Department

N'GUESSAN N'Da N'guessan Raphaiel, Director

It is difficult to translate even the name of this Department into English. One is tempted to call them "Ushers," but their activities go much further than ushering. Using 1 Chronicles 9:17 for their ministry verse, they call themselves "Gatekeepers."

There are 350 Gatekeepers in the church, divided into seven specialty sections:

Section 1. Administration
> (Direct, coordinate and compile data)

Section 2. Youth
> (Recruit and teach youth to be gatekeepers)

Section 3. Reception
> (In Abidjan this consists of 12 people who receive visitors and members that have come to the church for private appointments with the pastor or one of the church staff. If the visitor has no appointment, they refer them to the appropriate section for counseling.)

Section 4. Gatekeepers
> (Insure security and order in all services of the church, including conferences, baptisms, all night prayer meetings, etc. Provide for parking and surveillance of cars during meetings. Keep an accurate count of people attending meetings and report to Division Directors.)

Section 5. Interior And Exterior
(Recruit and train personnel in churches in the
interior of the country and exterior, including Paris,
to become Gatekeepers.

Section 6. Women's Training
(Recruit and train women as gatekeepers for
women's work and for women's meetings.)

Section 7. Church Property Maintenance
(Maintain all church property. This includes cleaning and maintaining buildings and all items in
those buildings, as well as inventory of church
property.)

The personnel meet each Saturday for training. They study
the role of the Gatekeeper in the Bible. They have their own prayer
meetings, fasts, and all night vigils.

Ten of the gatekeepers spend all night Saturday night at the
church so that they can be sure that the church is ready to receive
its first members on Sunday morning. Before entering their new
space, some people came as early as 4:30 a.m. to be sure and get
a seat for the 6 a.m. service. When people came for each of the
seven services, they were given a number. This insured an orderly
entrance before the service started. Those not able to attend one
service were asked to wait for the next one. The bodyguard of the
President often worshipped at the 6 a.m. service.

When visitors come to one of the services, they are first
introduced to a member of the evangelism department. As they
get to know the evangelist, information is gained about their
spiritual needs. They are then counseled accordingly. Follow-up
appointments are made at this time.

Based on the reports for the month of July, 1989, there were
the following number of visitors in the Abidjan churches:

Yopougon Central Church: 420 visitors
Other Abidjan Congregations: 435 visitors

Public Relations Department

In a cell group church without a myriad of P.B.D. structures,
the people of God can utilize both their *gifts* and their *talents*.

Within this church are many talented people who can use their skills in the area of public relations. Advertising, press conferences, radio broadcasts, etc., are ways the church reaches out and shares its life with untouched people. Volunteer workers with abilities in this area serve under a full time worker on the church staff.

Social Services Department

Director DJAGBO Mahi Julien

As pastor Dion saw the great need of his flock, he realized he could not be God's man among them if he did not do something to develop employment. With eighty per cent of his congregation unemployed, as many as 15 relatives live off the income of one person who is salaried. One of his first ventures was to develop a mobile sandwich business. With a small amount of investment, members were able to make sandwiches and sell them to factory workers at lunchtime.

As the potential was seen, the organization of this Department took place. The Social Services Department organizes social services in order to:

1. Benefit the general population.
2. Give work to church members.
3. Increase church income.
4. Encourage church members to give to worthy causes.

The three classes of social services are:

1. *Non-lucrative,* such as a halfway house, orphanage, etc.
2. *Semi-lucrative,* such as working in the dental clinic.
3. *Lucrative,* such as ELECTROMIS, a chicken farm they have developed, and the manufacture of GRACE soap in a factory they have developed.

Secretarial Department

Six Secretaries are in this department. They are divided into 6 "Missions:"

Mission 1
Secretaries for General Ministry, Evangelism, Youth, Hospital, Demonology, Prisons, Women, Music, Public Relations, House Churches.

Mission 2
Secretary for: Missionary school, Missionary Department, Religions, Sects & Traditions.

Mission 3
Secretary for: Administration, Deacons, Family Relations, Social Services, Gatekeepers

Mission 4
Secretary for: Mass Media, Audio-Visual, Print Shop, Press.

Mission 5
(Tasks not described in Dr. Deever's report)

Mission 6
Communications and Telephone Secretary

3. MINISTRIES TO THE CELLS

Deacon Department

ANDRÉ Baye, Director

Deacons are attached to each Congregation in each Zone, and serve the needs of the cells which compose it. They serve the Congregations and the church in general in the following ways:

1. Matters of Discipline.
   At such time as a member is not willing to turn away from sinful deeds, the Deacons seek to minister until it is obvious the person is rebellious. As Pastor Dion says, "The Body of Christ is made up of those who are tired of their sin. If a Christian is *not* tired of sin, he has no place in the Body until he has *become* tired of it." It is the task of the Deacons to look after the separation of such a person and to minister further until the person is prepared to make a full break with sinning.

2. Weddings.
   All counseling in preparation for marriage is in the hands of the Deacons. In some cases, the young man will first consult with a Deacon about his interest in a young lady and the

Deacon becomes a go-between. In addition, all preparations for the wedding are cared for by this Department. The pastor will perform the ceremony, but the Deacons minister to the couple.

3. Funerals.

All visitation of the family and assistance required for the funeral service is conducted by the Deacons. In many cases in this culture, people die without family or funds for burial. In such cases, the Deacons will order the casket, arrange for a burial plot, and care for all other matters related to the burial. The pastor performs the actual funeral services.

4. Benevolence.

Funds for benevolence are channeled through the Deacons. They are alert to special needs and respond with food, clothes, or whatever is appropriate.

Religions, Sects and Traditions Department

BOYER TEHE Justin, Director

When the evangelists discover a person has problems in accepting Jesus, or cannot grow spiritually because of his former ties with a religion, a sect, or a tradition, this person is referred to this Department for counseling.

The main problem faced is that the person believes that it is the religion, sect, or rite that saves. He is led to experience Jesus as his personal Savior.

This Department does extensive study and research into the myriad cults, sects, religions, and animistic practices which infest this part of the world.

Family Life Department

AMESSAN AHOZIMANE Delphine, Director

This Department has three Sections:
1. Counseling Section
   a. Give family counseling to christian couples and Christians who are already married to non-Christians.
   b. Pre-marital counseling.

  c. Birth control counseling (They recommend the rhythm method instead of medicines or chemicals.)
2. Home Organization Section
  a. Organizes meetings for couples to discuss home organization.
  b. Topics: What Is Purpose Of The Home? Why Did God Create It? The Home As The Headquarters Of God. The Home As The Mission Field. The First Church: A Home Meeting. The Home With Two Disciples: A Man And A Woman.
  a. Physical section
    Role of man: Should help woman in housework, etc.
    Role of woman: The woman is not a slave of man, but a help mate. There must be friendly relations. The women are taught how to cook and clean; home organization is taught.
  c. Spiritual section
    Role of man: the symbol of Christ, the bridegroom.
    Role of woman: the symbol of the Church, the bride.
3. Counselor Training Section
  a. Train church members to be home and family counselors. Teach them how to deal with couples. The counselor is a listener—not to take sides—but, in the end, to explain to the couple what the Bible says about the subject at hand.
  b. Problems often encountered:
    • The wife does not know how to be hospitable to visitors.
    • The man wants to have sex every day.

All Congregations have at least one counselor. Some have more, depending on their size.

Family life in this African city is in desperate need of guidance. The traditions of animism are difficult to break for the new believer without some guidance. This Department fills a great void in the lives of couples coming to know Christ as Lord.

Teaching And Personnel Department

AYE Ernest, Director
DJIKE Gastien, Associate Director

The two functions of this Department are the training and placement of personnel. As of mid 1989, they had placed 122 full time workers and 77 students after graduation from the Missionary Training School.

The Church's Missionary Training Center

77 students were enrolled in 1989 at the Missionary Training Center in Andokoua, one mile east of the Yopougon Baptist Church. Pastor AYÉ Touali Ernest, Chairman of the Department of Personnel And Their Formation, is Director of the Center. Pastor DJIKE Gastien is the Associate Director.

The curriculum covers subjects such as music appreciation, preaching, and children's ministry. It is a broad based program consisting of 33 weeks of instruction. Students start classes at 7:30 each morning and classes last until 6 or 6:30 in the evening.

Each student is being watched over, or discipled, by one of the older, more experienced church staff members. Each week the student spends time with the staff person learning more of the practical side of his ministry. For example, a student aspiring to become a pastor spends time with one of the staff pastors. Another, aspiring to be a church administrator, spends time with one of the church administrators. All are assigned to the different Congregations in the Abidjan area.

To be accepted at the school, the student has to be at least 25 years old (Numbers 8:24), write a formal request, write his testimony, and fill out a questionnaire consisting of 29 questions. He must have the recommendation of his pastor and be approved by the Director and the Central Committee of the church.

The teaching staff is composed of 17 professors, most of whom are Department heads of the various Departments at the church. Each Department head teaches four hours a week for the 33 weeks, for a total of 132 hours.

The student body is divided into two classes. *Class A* is composed of students who have the equivalent of a high school diploma or higher. *Class B* is composed of students who have not finished the equivalent of high school. Class A students will go on to be urban church leaders, and Class B students will become rural church leaders.

The two classes are taught the same subjects, but more time

is spent in illustrations with the Class B group. For example, Pastor AYÉ was teaching about the books of the Bible. For Class A, he taught them that the Bible was composed of 66 books. For those in the Class B section, he not only taught them that the Bible was *composed* of 66 books, but he brought 66 books into the class-room—each with the name of a book of the Bible written on it.

There are no tuition fees for the students. Often their local Congregation will provide them with transportation money, but they do not receive scholarships.

At the beginning of the 1989 school year, the school had no place to meet. A shoe factory was found in the quarter of Ando-koua, not far from the church building, and it was decided that it would make an excellent school, plus an excellent meeting place on Sunday for a new Congregation. However, the rent was US$800.00 per month. Faced with this challenge, the student body and the local Congregation members (in Andokoua) gave enough money for the rent to be paid through October.

The school is now housed in the new facility. They have about 100 students at present, with an additional 30 students, now pastors, that will take Audio-Visual courses. This will include videotaping and critiques of their sermons, as well as studying the sermons of great preachers.

4. MINISTRIES FOR CELL GROUP PENETRATION

Evangelism Department

> KPESSOU Abel, Director
> CAMARA Issouf, Assoc. Director

This Department is divided into nine zones which corre-spond to the nine Abidjan zones of the central church. There is a full time Director Of Evangelism for each zone. Each zone is divided into sectors, and each sector has a director. The Sector Directors are not full time church workers. [Note: they use the French term *secteur* for what this book calls "Zone Shepherds."]

Training for Evangelists
The evangelists are trained in three ways:

1. Each Saturday at 3:00 p.m., all of the Abidjan evangelists meet for a teaching session.
2. Six of the students at the Missionary Training School are training to be full time evangelists with the church.
3. After graduation from the missionary school, they are given an internship where they become an acting evangelist for an area. They are given goals and are followed up to see if they need more training before they are assigned to the field.

The goal of this Department is soul winning, and the promotion of soul winning, by the cell groups. They believe that the more the church evangelizes, the more the church will experience revival. Their stated goals are:

1. To lead every church member to become a soul winner.
2. To welcome new members into the fellowship and disciple them until they become members of a local cell group.
3. Organize campaigns of evangelism. These include open air crusades, etc., in different areas of the city.

The July-August, 1989, report reveals that 1,479 visits were made by appointment with one of the evangelists. 400 of them became members of a cell group. There are detailed reports on why only 27% of these visitors became cell group members. Two of the reasons given are: that visitors to the public services found standing in line to get into a meeting too difficult; they joined other churches after accepting Jesus; visitors became regular attenders of the large meetings, but have not yet joined a home cell group.

[Note: it is to be remembered that this Department, like all the others, is staffed by volunteer cell group members. The ratio of salaried to volunteer workers is extremely small—in the neighborhood of 1.5%.]

Youth Department
DAINGUI Adja Julien, Director

There are four sections in the Youth Department:

1. Teaching Section
a. Teaching and training of youth workers:

Missionaries (graduates of missionary school)

Assistants (part-time workers)

Course includes 6 months of training and then working as an associate for 3 months with an experienced assistant.

b. Teaching and training the youth. These are the divisions:
1. 4-5 year olds
2. 6-8 year olds
3. 9-12 year olds
4. 13-17 year olds

2. Follow-up Section
Division 1: Student follow-up (4-18 year olds)

Division 2: Young women's follow-up

Division 3: Delinquents follow-up

Division 4: Contact youth's parents and follow-up

Division 5: Contact youth's friends and follow-up

3. Field Relations Section
Interior of the Ivory Coast

Headquarters (Abidjan)

Exterior of the Ivory Coast

There are 4 Zones in Abidjan. Each zone is divided into Fields. (A Field will correspond to a congregation area.)

4. Coordination With Other Departments Section
This Section relates to the other Departments of the church, assigning youth to work with adults in other Departments to be trained. *The Youth Department is a carbon copy of the church.* In the Youth Department, young people will be the Administrators, Missionaries, Evangelists, Demonologists, etc.

At present, they have two youth church services. On Thursday, youth prayer cells meet.

In the Youth Department they have:
- 6,000 youth enrolled
- 6 full time missionaries
- 156 assistants (adults) in the nation outside Abidjan who

work with children.
- 683 workers (youth themselves who are engaged in the work)

The youth are an active part of the church. In May, the youth contributed $350.00 to the construction. They paid for their own retreat in the Banco forest, $4,062.50, and gave $1,875.00 toward the annual Easter Retreat held in Bouaké this year.

Note: In the Ivory Coast 90% of the youth attend public or private schools. 80% of youth reach the ninth grade before dropping out of school, and only 20% of the youth enter the twelfth grade.

Women's Department

Pastor WAKOUBO Kouohon Josephine, Director
Pastor ONIN Clementine, Associate Director

In the women's Department there are three sections:

1. Follow-up and training
2. Interior of Ivory Coast
3. Exterior of Ivory Coast

Each of the 9 church zones has a Director, and each of the 52 Congregations has a local Director. The Zone Directors are single women missionaries working full time with the church. The local Congregation Directors are women, often married, and do not work full time in the ministry.

After each of the Pastor Training Seminars, held four times a year, they have special Women's Work Meetings that last three days. They cover such subjects as "The Missionary And Her Calling," etc.

Each Sunday afternoon the Department sponsors a course for Pastor's wives. This provides fellowship between them, as well as inspiration for working with their husbands.

As new women come into the church, they are asked to fill out a Questionnaire. From this form, the women's workers provide in-depth counseling that can last for months. This insures that the women coming into the church are delivered from past evil experiences, and are given a solid Christian foundation.

Demonology Department

> GUE Jacques, Director
> KONOU Christine, Assoc. Director

[A note to my Western readers: if your worldview does not permit you to accept the reality of demon possession, you really should take a trip to visit this church. The manifestations are so clearly *not* the work of manipulation that one is forced to accept both the presence and the power of evil spirits which have inhabited the lives of unprotected unbelievers! As I observed 500 cell group members who had been developed into 100 teams of five, I was amazed at the ability God had given them to minister to people who rolled back their eyeballs until only the whites could be seen, kicking and screaming all the while. When the release came, the love shown to these victims was pure Calvary love. I asked Dion Robert, "How many of those 500 workers have, themselves, been possessed in the past?" He replied, "About 90% of them."]

The Department of Demonology is divided into seven sections:

Men's section
(Specializes in demonic problems of men.)
Women's section
(Specializes in demonic problems of women.)
Youth Section
(Specializes in demonic problems of youth.)
Intercession Section
(Intercedes and calls the church to intercession for special problems.)
Counseling Section
(Specializes in follow-up counseling to insure that all strong-holds are broken and that the individual understands what must be done to stay delivered).

In the Counseling Section there are 5 divisions:

1. Witchcraft.
2. Spell Casting.
3. Depression.
4. Bonds.
5. Physical illness caused by mental conditions.

The ministry is divided into five *Divisions.*
(Abidjan is a Division.)
The Divisions are divided into *Forces.* (Abidjan has 5 Forces.)
The Forces are divided into *Troops.* (Abidjan has 18 Troops.)
The Troops are divided into *Teams.* (Abidjan has 50 Teams.)
Each Team is composed of 8 *Sentinels.* There are over 400
Sentinels (workers) in Abidjan.

Each Team has three *Guards* (meetings) per week. During
these meetings, they study the Bible together, pray, and focus on
prayers of intercession.

On Saturday at 2:00 p.m., the Division, Force, Troop and
Team Leaders have a training meeting. At 3:00 p.m., there is a
general meeting for the Leaders and the Sentinels. They study
such subjects as how to counsel a possessed person, how to talk
to him to find out his problem, how to pray for him, the world of
spirits, and how to exorcise demons.

Hospital Department

BLAHOA Pépé Ignace, Director
FLEHI Frederic, Associate Director

The Hospital Department is recognized by the government
and the Minister of Health. The Department consists of 39
workers. These workers attend a training course each Saturday at
the church led by Pastor BLAHOA. Subjects include bedside
manner, how to win the sick to the Lord, how to counsel the sick
and grieving patients and their families, and how to pray for
release from demons in the hospital setting.

Hospital visitation is conducted at the Cocody and Treichville
hospitals in Abidjan under three divisions or specialities: Men's
Visitation, Women's Visitation, and Children's Visitation.

Sunday afternoons are for evangelization or first contact. A
detailed, Bible-referenced questionnaire is filled out for each
patient.

Follow-up visitation is on Tuesdays and Thursdays for the patients that are in the hospital, and on Wednesdays and Fridays for those patients that have been dismissed from the hospital. They are followed up after they have been dismissed from the hospital by the Hospital Department until they become active in a cell. They then fall under the responsibility of the House Church Department.

Individual appointments are made with family members to come to the church and meet with Department members during the mornings.

Great effort is taken to put the patient at ease and to discover what his spiritual position is, including what roots of sin may have led to his present condition. These are then dealt with in an organized manner.

Prison Department

KEIPO Govret, Director
KOUOTO Dagbalé Hélène, Women's Section

Four divisions exist within this Department:

Men's Division
Women's Division
Minor's Division
Re-education Division

The prison work started in 1986 with visits to the Yopougon Prison. It has a prison population of about 4,500 inmates. Weekly visits are made to the men's section, the women's section, and the minor's section. Work is centered around evangelism and discipling, but also includes providing clothing and medicines for prisoners when available. In addition, the Congregations are encouraged to support the prison work through their prayers, their personal visits to prisoners, and their offerings.

Dr. Charles Deevers, missionary dentist, visits the prison on Monday and Wednesday and treats about 30 dental patients per week.

How Can So Many Ministries Function?

Several things make this model of cell group church life unique. The first is the *total devotion* of the members to the vision of reaching the Francophone world for Christ. The vision of Dion Robert is now the vision of 20,000 Christians, all dedicated to be a part of the army to make it happen.

A second factor is the *significant amount of time* available to these people. As already mentioned, with an 80% rate of unemployment, many of the members are actually "full time" workers without pay.

Another reason is the manner in which this structure provides a *ministry for everyone,* always relevant to needs in lives. The more you study the structure, the more you realize that this is about the purest *people based* church life one can ever see! A visit with this dear congregation affirms that.

Still another reason is the joint relationship between the *cells,* where true community is found and edification takes place, and *ministry,* where people are involved at different levels of ability to reach out. Those who may begin as Gatekeepers mature through the training and the interviewing of visitors, and are soon found developing evangelism skills and ministering to the lost in a brand new way.

Most important of all, *there is no competition with cell group life.* As Pastor Dion said to me, "Everything we do is to make the cell the heart and soul of our church life." From this chapter, it is obvious that more people are equipped, and more are reached, than other styles of church life can accomplish.

While the model we have seen is pure African, there are many ways it can be adapted or adjusted to other cultures. Read it over several times as your cell group church develops, and plan in advance for growth. Robert didn't need all these Departments when he had 650 members—but he couldn't survive without them at this point in the church's life!

26 TRANSITIONING A P.B.D. CHURCH

After all the comments I have made about P.B.D. church life, I want to come to the end of this book and emphasize that while a church structure based on programs is unbiblical, inefficient and impotent in today's society, the Godly people on the staffs and in the pews of those churches have produced *every reader of this book, including the author!* On a scale of one to ten, you may rate the P.B.D. church structure as you will, but give the saints a great big "10."

Tribute must be paid to all those Godly believers who love their Lord more than they love the next breath that fills their lungs. The world *may* be harvested more rapidly, and people *may* be edified in greater numbers by the cell church movement, but the saints of God have not been asleep. The dedicated men and women within the P.B.D. churches have poured their lives and their funds into doing the work of the Lord in the best way they knew to do it. It's overwhelming when you travel the world among God's people and see the suffering, the steadfastness, and the devotion of their ministries. It's a tribute to them that they have accomplished so much using such inefficient structures.

At the same time, it's pretty obvious that the second Reformation has begun. Not only is the dry rot within church life now obvious to both saint and sinner, but recent events have soured the unbelieving public more than ever against institutional religion.

My heart goes out to all the wonderful people of God who now feel trapped inside church structures, and who don't see any way out. It also goes out to the tens of thousands who have *left the church,* who still believe in the Lord, and who wander like sheep without a shepherd to lead them.

We regularly take calls from pastors or church members who are saying, "Where do we go from here?" For those within the P.B.D. structure and who want to bring about change, I want to share what I have learned over these past 25 years as I have watched men attempt it. Perhaps some of the suggestions which follow will be helpful to those who wish to birth a cell group church by "renewing" a traditional one.

Go To The *"Listening Room!"*

Before someone deeply rooted in P.B.D. life should attempt to bring change into an existing structure, there should be a very clear calling from the Lord about the matter. It's not something a person does because he is frustrated with the system, or because he is angry with a certain group. Negative reasons for causing change won't have the mind of Christ, and the work so established will not have his blessings.

The person seeking to bring a traditional church through a transition to become a cell group church must devote at least five to seven years to the task. He will have to unlearn much of what he thinks church life is, and step into a new world where all things are new. That's not easy to do!

On the wall of my office I have a print signed by Fred Machetanz, the famous Alaskan artist. It's a picture of an eskimo with a dogsled who had gone onto new ice to hunt seals. The weight of the dogs, the sled, and his own body has caused the ice to crack away from the mainland. He is standing on the floe, his lead dog sitting pensively by his side, watching the water gap widen between them and security. The painting is titled, "What Every Hunter Fears Most."

I can tell you from my own journey that when you decide to leave structures behind, there is a price to pay. Every man since Martin Luther who has done so by choice or by circumstances can attest to the reality of this. Unless one has been to the *Listening Room* and has a clear word from the Lord, he will be unable to say as Luther did, "Here I stand. I can do no other. God help me!" One must know that his constant Companion has called him forth, and that he has little say in the matter of what comes next. Only then will the anointing remain when rejection comes from old friends.

Ask The Hard Questions

As I reflect over the dozens of times I have been involved in the attempts of pastors to bring change to the church, the first thing I would suggest is that this hard question be asked: *"Is it really possible for this particular group of people to change? Should I attempt this?*

There are thousands of churches who should simply be left alone. They are unable to change, and the attempt is a futile one. People gain their personal significance from their positions and power bases in church life as readily as they do in business life. To change the system is to threaten their worth and self-esteem, often developed at a great price of time invested by them during years of devotion and sacrifice to a church program. Unless a spiritual explosion occurs in their lives, *they won't change.*

There are truly devoted pastors who cling to the security blanket of the salary provided by a congregation. Should he risk all for a new concept of church life? That's a question for the *Listening Room!* He will invest years trying to bring change into that church. At the end, he may be no farther along than when he started—and stands a good chance of being sacked for his effort!

Sometimes it's better to just start over. Sometimes it's easier to take a "remnant," as Jehovah said He would do within Israel, and start fresh. It's a painful thing to draw out people who want to go on with God and leave the rest behind, but that's what God had to do with Israel in the desert. It is a viable option, and we are going to see more and more of this as we approach the end of the century.

It's always something to be prayed over until the Lord provides the answer: *should the committed live in frustration because of the traditionalists who hinder the ministry, or should the uncommitted face a new future apart from them?*

In the early days of West Memorial Baptist Church, that's the situation I faced. My problem was the agony of *loving everyone in the flock,* and not wanting to hurt either the innovators who were excited about our new lifestyle or the tradition-bound folks who began to fight it tooth and toenail. My resignation caused the two sides to clash, and the result was the dissemination of the traditionalists into P.B.D. churches nearby. It was only then that we could make our changes in harmony and peace.

I understand how those feel who have close ties of love in a P.B.D. church family, and who are also torn by the idea of staying in the miserable structure. Such life-changing decisions are made slowly, with much grief, and must be done with love and not bitterness, in the *Listening Room.*

Have I properly conveyed to you my feelings about all this? If not, let me say again as clearly as I know how—I have the deepest love and affection for the *saints* everywhere! *It's their entrapment in the traditional church I have sought to criticize.*

If you are a church staff member or a church member, I would like to frankly say to you that you should not attempt to bring change to your church. Authority and responsibility are two categories which must exactly overlap. If the pastor is not going to endorse what you are doing, you will be a thorn in the church as long as you are there. Since you don't plan to be a part of the traditional direction of the pastor, it would be much better for you to move on. *You can't change a church without the spiritual oversight of it which God has assigned to its pastor. You are out of order when you attempt to do so!*

The rest of this chapter is specifically provided for a pastor of a traditional church who is trying to make up his mind about staying with the old or launching into the new. Please consider all the factors presented in this chapter.

Change And The Church

How many times have you tried to introduce a new concept, only to be met by a brick wall—or given only token support by a few? Or, perhaps your suggestion was enthusiastically received, only to fizzle in six months or so. The main cause of these responses was a failure to properly initiate change.

No society in history has faced rapid, shattering change as has ours. We now expect change. We assume that tomorrow will somehow be better than yesterday, that new technology will bring "better" things. We expect our children to be smarter than we are. At the same time, there's a feeling that things have gotten out of hand.

Alvin Toffler called this feeling "future shock." Most of us by now are sure that we have had enough of it. Note the middle class American quest for oak furniture which was sold from Sears catalogues 60 years ago! The church has become, for most persons, the last bastion of yesterday. The church is the one institution which can preserve "the good old days," when nothing else has stayed the same. More and more Christians, when thinking about their local churches, resist change there—even though they would not think of driving a 25 year old car.

There's a good reason for this: *all change is perceived as loss.* Even when the change is an apparently happy occasion—like marriage, or moving to a new job—there remains the lingering feeling we have left something behind, something we'll never recapture.

Christian leaders should be change agents. We are in the business of leading people to higher ground, new ministries to the lost. We have been told that change needs to be carefully "managed." But too often as we seek to do this, we fail to take into account the anguish for which we are responsible.

We need to change. We need to move to higher ground. We need to mature in Christ. We need to right the wrongs that are out in the world, to change them for the better. But, in the midst of our quest, however noble it may be, we need a deep appreciation of not just how to accomplish the goal, but how to bring about change in a manner that will produce a minimum of distress.

Change only takes place in people when they are discontent. If we are satisfied with the status quo, why should we change? Skillful union organizers and other mobilizers of public opinion have traded on negative discontent. If one can find enough people who dislike the same thing, then one has a group with a common goal, namely to get rid of that which they dislike. The role of the change agent is then to provide a solution to the common felt need.

But there are also those who are in the business of creating what might be called "positive discontent." When a pastor calls people to maturity in Christ, he is creating in them a holy discontent—a discontent with the way they are, and a desire to become more than they are.

Resistance to change takes place in the same way. If people are presented with new situations which threaten their "comfort zones," their discontent will be aimed at removing the cause of potential changes. The amount of resistance to change will be proportional to the threat of losing vested interests in the system.

It's important to understand that resistance may not be against the *change agent,* or even against *the change being proposed.* Both may be intellectually perceived as excellent, but however good the program is, if it's going to result in changing the way things have always been, it's normal for it to be resisted. Church committees or departments can present programs which are beautifully conceived, and would produce excellent results for large numbers of people, but are often shattered by those who simply do not want change—*any kind of change.*

Your task as a facilitator, then, is to introduce change in a manner that will *encourage* people, not *discourage* them. our culture focuses on individuality, not community. It is not the same in other cultures. Few other societies in the entire world pay as much attention to exalting the individual as does the British/ American culture. This emphasis on rugged individualism can blind us to a basic fact about how change takes place.

How Change Takes Place In A Church

For a number of years, sociologists have described the change process within groups of individuals as "the diffusion of innovations." That is, a new idea seeps slowly through the soil of the total group, moving from one level of persons in the group to the next level. They have recognized that when an innovator poses a new idea, or does something differently, there will be some who will see the personal advantages to them very early. Those who do so are called *Innovators.* The concept will next be accepted by the *Early Adopters,* followed by the *Early Majority,* the *Late Majority,* and perhaps never by the *Laggard.*

The important fact here is that, in all cases, each one of these groups of individuals accepts change because they observe its benefits in the lives of others first. They then see how it will be of benefit to their own lives. These important facts give us insight into how to plan for change in a "volunteer organization" like a church. People adopt a new idea by *diffusion* within the group, not by some formal vote that everyone is now prepared to simultaneously adopt the new proposal. It must be stressed that if people don't see benefits for their own situation, there will be absolutely no reason for them to adopt.

In Your Church, There Are Five Distinct Types Of People

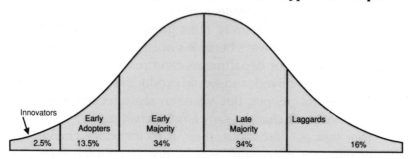

Note the five types of people in the graph above. Pay special attention to the fact that there are fewer people in the groups at the edges of the bell curve than in the center of it. Rogers and Shoemaker, in *Communication Of Innovations,* describe them:[1]

Innovators

In your church, you have a group of 2.5% who are eager and ready to try out new ideas. Their lifestyle is characterized by a wide spread of friends, many living long distances away. These "risk takers" are usually more affluent than the rest of the group, since they may have to absorb losses resulting from innovating. These people are venturesome, creative, and ready to try a new idea if it makes sense to them.

Can You Write The Names Of Such Persons Here?

_____

_____

_____

_____

Early Adopters

13.5% of your congregation fall into this category. They are usually the *opinion setters* in the church—certainly more than the Innovators are. Potential adopters in the next category, the Early Majority, will be friends of, and influenced by, these Early Adopters. They will be the "public relations" members, influencing those in the membership who ask them, "What do you think about this new cell group concept?"

Can You Write The Names Of Such Persons Here?

_____

_____

_____

_____

Early Majority

These are the "deliberate" people, about 34% of the total, who wait until they are sure the idea has a pretty good possibility of succeeding. They interact frequently with the Early Adopters. However, they probably subscribe to the idea, "Be not the last to lay the old aside, nor the first by which the new is tried." They seldom lead out, but will be the first to adopt after the Innovators and Early Adopters have working models of Share groups established.

Can You Write The Names Of Such Persons Here?

_____

_____

_____

_____

Late Majority

These represent a significant 34% of the church, and can best be described as the "skeptics." This group will not adopt a new concept until most of the others in the church have done so. The weight of "institutional endorsement" must be present before they will agree to share in what is going on. Indeed, they may appeal to the denominational hierarchy to step in and stop a new "unapproved by headquarters" proposal. It takes the pressure of the peer group to motivate them to adopt, even after they see how they will benefit from the change. However, once they have accepted the new idea, it will be hard to ever eliminate it.

Can You Write The Names Of Such Persons Here?

_____

_____

_____

_____

The Laggards

Traditional to the core, this 16% are the last to adopt. They possess almost no "world vision," and live in a tiny bubble of structured activity. They tend to seek out others who agree with their opinions about things, and are openly suspicious of all innovations and all innovators. They can slow things to a crawl if they are in positions of leadership. Sadly, over the years of a church's life, as Innovators and Early Adopters move away and leave official leadership positions empty, the Laggards are added to the governing boards until they are in control. When the "pillars" of the church contain a majority of Laggards, there's little or no hope of that church body being changed. This trend builds up over years, and it may require many funerals before this group loses control. Unseating incumbents is hard to do, whether it is in politics or in church life.

Do You Dare To Write Any Names Here?

_____

_____

_____

_____

How Long Does It Take The Change To Be Adopted By All?

According to Rogers and Shoemaker,[2] the length of time is as follows:

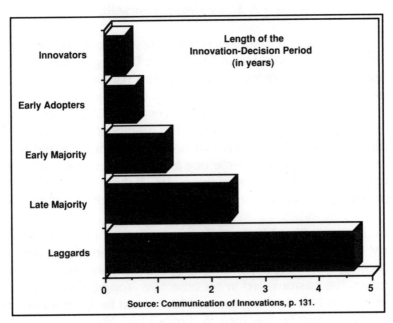

Length of the Innovation-Decision Period (in years)

Source: Communication of Innovations, p. 131.

Indicators Of Effectiveness Are Needed

How will the pilot project be judged? What indicators can be set up to measure the effectiveness of the ministry? What are the qualities we might expect to find? For example, if we are going to introduce a new form for the worship service in the local church, six months later there should be some indication that the new pattern is really bringing people closer to God. Or, if we are introducing a new policy on the use of offering envelopes, one year later there should be some increase in income as a result.

As you begin cell group life, how will you know, after one year, if your lifestyle evangelism ministry through the Share groups is effective? *Why one year?* While the Early Adopters may be very enthusiastic about the program shortly after it is begun, the majority of the staff or congregation will withhold judgment. They may even have negative feelings towards the ministry for a long period of time. How long is it going to take before all those who will eventually accept the innovation have adjusted to the presence of it? *About one year!*

Start A Share Group Yourself!

Remember the "monkey see, monkey do" principle! In some of the first churches that used Touch Basic Training to launch Share groups, it became obvious that the biggest handicap was that the pastor and his wife were not *personally* touching the lives of the lost, and that the only people they ever led to Christ were those within the church walls. What can the members be expected to birth if the shepherd and his wife are barren? There should be at least one growing group—*the one led by the Pastor and his wife.* That model is crucial to everything else. If there is one effective, working model led by the Pastor, in six months there will be two.

Pastors with multiple staffs sometimes tell me they are too busy to be involved with this, and they do not participate in launching a Share group. Every single time I have watched this happen, the pastor failed in his objective. Yonggi Cho has more pressure on him than any pastor I know, and he is adamant that the pastor *must* be involved in the cell life! No greater priority exists than for the pastor to restructure his own lifestyle. He must *personally* be vitally related to the population around him who would not be caught dead in their own coffin listening to him preach.

Some years ago, Jerry Falwell flew me in to talk with him and his key men about cell groups. As we began the session, he said,

"Ralph, I must close the session with you by 2 p.m. I must drive to the state prison to see a man who is serving a sentence for murder. The Lord has laid him on my heart, and I must talk to him about his soul." It's my conviction that the Lord has so widely used him because he has never lost his passion for *one person* who needs Christ!

Select Key Persons To Help You Launch Your Own Group

In your church, select three or four Innovators, perhaps two couples, who would be willing to begin this first group with you. In your living room, take them through the Touch Ministries Seminar. Next, take them through Touch Basic Training. Let them experience the process from the start. Grow from six or eight to fifteen through penetration of Type "B" unbelievers. Start these converts on their journey by forming a Shepherd group with them. Experience the cell church life for yourselves until you are caught up in the flow of its dynamic.

Preach Messages About The Theology Of Church Life

At the same time, preach series of messages on the topics related to Basic Christian Communities, *oikos, oikodomeo,* and *oikonomos* lifestyles. Remember that *theology breeds methodology.* Provide a solid biblical grounding for the membership from the pulpit as you are forming your Share group and later your Shepherd group. Use illustrations in your sermons taken from the group life you are experiencing. Use testimonies from converts.

Dig out messages that help the membership realize Kingdom life is much different than life in the kingdoms of this world. Carefully teach them the proper use of spiritual gifts, and that they are all to be exercising them. Share about strongholds in their lives and in the world about them. I preached a series on the word *segullah* (1 Peter 2:9), "a people for God's own possession," which was remembered for a decade by those who heard it.

Preach in these areas until the feedback from the members assures you that the truths have soaked into their hearts, and the desire to move into the deeper things of God is present. As the Early Adopters and the Early Majority begin to share their *Listening Room* experiences with you, move to the next step.

Introduce The Change First To A Group, Not The Church

Whenever possible, introduce the change within a part of the P.B.D. structure. Hopefully, that will be the Sunday School department of the church. Indicate to those selected for participation in this next stage that this is an experiment. They are really a "pilot" group. This not only raises the enthusiasm of those who are involved, but it also relieves the threat to the rest of the church.

Those chosen for this stage should usually be Early Adopters. The Early Majority, the Late Majority, and the Laggards will not be threatened by this, since their participation in church life does not change. The Early Adopters will *observe*, often coming to a point where they are not only ready to accept the new idea, but actually clamoring for it.

In the event that the Sunday School leadership is closed to the possibility of the experiment, look for a department of church life which is in existence, but not controlled by anyone. For example, if the Church Training Department is virtually dead, ask to use it for the pilot project. If no one cares about its programs, it's a sleeping program which can be resurrected to begin Share Groups.

Install Share Groups In Selected Sunday School Classes

Using the original couples you equipped in your own Share group, place them in Sunday school departments to form new groups and train team members in the way you trained them. The Touch Ministries Seminar and Touch Basic Training should be taught in homes by each couple to their new coworkers.

Converts from the original cell should be distributed into these new groups to receive the training. By this time, these new Christians will have been through the *Arrival Kit For New Christians* and *Knocking On Doors, Opening Hearts!*

With your General Superintendent, examine the class rolls of your Sunday school. Which classes have members who are potential candidates for developing Share groups? Discuss the possibility of installing your "pilot project" with the teachers of these classes. Indicate if the groups do well, there will later on be a suggestion that the entire class be restructured to hear the Bible study presented by the teacher, followed by small group application of the content.

You may hear the old excuses: "Groups are dangerous;" "This will lead to doctrinal problems;" "These people will never agree to this;" etc. Have your answers ready for every excuse.

Conduct A Church-wide Touch Ministries Seminar

Wait until your Sunday school groups are "up and running." About four months after they start, you should be ready to conduct the Touch Ministries Seminar for the entire church. Be sure you have all the "pillars" of the church present, even though they may not enter into the ministry at first, plus the all important uninvolved church members. Use the members of your own team to give testimonies, to work with you, to get the vision of what you are doing. Seek to enlist several new teams at this time.

Revise Entire Sunday School Departments

Using the original cells you planted in a department, convert the entire department into Share groups. The teacher will present the lesson in 20 minutes, with 40 minutes spent in application by the groups. These groups then conduct home meetings with Type "A" and "B" unbelievers, church visitors, etc. Thus, the entire department is now involved in reaching out to the lost. If there are Laggards who do not wish to participate, seek to transfer them into the more traditional classes.

Pastor Rod Masteller led the Putnam City Baptist Church in Oklahoma City into this pattern. He and his wife were among the first to see neighbors converted through their cell. Joe Perry has done an excellent job of blending the groups into their Sunday school departments. It works!

Consider The Loss Of Members Which Will Occur

Who will be influenced by the change? Some people are going to lose authority or responsibility if Share groups and then Shepherd groups are effective. Familiar patterns will eventually be disrupted. Perhaps times for groups will conflict with something already in existence, like choir practice or teacher's meetings.

Whenever possible, build into the change of plans a way of replacing all losses with a greater benefit. All change is experienced as a loss, but the reason people are willing to accept change is that they see the gain to be greater than what they are losing. For example, help your Sunday School leadership see these advantages:

1. The Sunday School could begin to explode with unbelievers and new converts.
2. Those now uninvolved and unenlisted will be the target for training.
3. A small group of committed class members will be like yeast in the midst of complacent class members.
4. The primary expenses of the ministry will be minimal.

Build In An Evaluation System

Be able to identify the Early Adopters, as well as the Late Adopters. The reason people adopt late is because they like stability. If you disrupt stability, they are going to be hurt in some way. If you can identify these hurts—which may not be anticipated ahead of time—you can often modify plans to offset the anguish people feel.

For example, suppose there are two members who become friends while serving on a committee. One of them drops out to participate in a Share group. The other one complains, "This new activity is hurting the church." This unhappy person could be encouraged to attend the new Share group with his old friend, providing an opportunity for the two to continue working together in the new ministry.

Look For Win/Win Situations

Too often, in trying to overcome the objections of other people, we view them as adversaries who have to be won over or even (if only subconsciously) "beaten." If we can remember that the people we are dealing with are brothers and sisters in Christ, members of the same Body of Christ we belong to, we can try to understand the impact our actions are going to have on them and seek to edify them. Our very spirits must communicate to them our desire that we want the best for them. Spending special moments with those who oppose what you are doing is important. Original members of your Share group must do the same.

Practical Suggestions

1. *Take Your Time*
   It is true that sometimes a leader can move an entire organization just by the strength of his or her conviction and force of personality. However, too often the result left is a feeling that people are working on the *leader's* goals, rather than their *own* goals. Don't try to accomplish too much in a short time. Keep your dreams big but your aim low. For example, you may seen a need to eliminate some present tasks to open personal time for being with unbelievers. If you boldly announce the elimination of things you have done in the past, without taking the time to let the people involved come to their own conclusions about the worthiness of the move, you will meet a great deal of opposition.

2. *Share Your Vision With The Congregation From The Pulpit.*
   For example, point to the low number of baptisms last year caused by the total activity of the P.B.D. structures. This could be a point on which to motivate a desire for change.

3. *Involve As Many People As Possible.*
   Ownership of the goal is gradually imparted, first among the Innovators and Early Adopters. Then, when the time is right and several Share groups are functioning properly, conduct the Touch Ministries Seminar for the entire congregation. The whole church must be familiarized with what is happening. You can then begin to initiate the change within entire Sunday school departments.

4. *Affirm Progress*
   Use charts on the wall of the church to show the weekly attendance at the Share Groups, the number of new persons attending, the number of unsaved reached. In addition, affirm people by handwritten notes, announcements in the bulletin—any way that seems appropriate.

Remember: The Focal Point Must Be Upon God's Power

As the transition takes place in the formation of the cell groups, the greater transition will be the development of *oikodomeo* within the lifestyles of the people. In your original group, you must be the first to discover how to receive and manifest Christ's power flowing through you as gifts are used. Forget about your role as a clergyman, and become a man who seeks Christ's direction for building up others through the "spirituals."

When your original cell experiences the power of God in their midst, healing of bodies and minds will take place, along with the discernment of strongholds and true and false spirits. Don't try to *push* this along: if He is not hindered, the Holy Spirit will make it happen. He has waited patiently for the opening in your church to show His mighty power!

Evaluate Teams Weekly

When the reports from Share group meetings come in, look them over carefully. They are indicators of what is happening. Do some attend one time, and not return? *Why?* Is there inadequate follow up in person and by telephone? Are new people not being brought in? *Why?* Are some bringing new people, and others no one at all? *Why?*

Provide Contacts Where People Run Dry

Do not let a trainee fail! Helping each person be successful is all-important. One success leads to another, and self-confidence must be developed. Remember that you are asking people to do something they have probably never done before. They need to replace fear with faith, developing a personal vision of what it would be like to reach their world for Christ.

Bring Converts To Share Their Testimonies With The Church

Share the victories first hand with the entire church! Letting members talk personally with new converts will enforce their awareness that God has already started to do His work in their midst.

Make The Shift To Cell Group Church Life

When at least 50% of your membership are committed to the cell group church life, there will be a dissatisfaction with the many conflicts with the programs that are still running. Drop your organizations, one by one. Move to a pattern where everyone equips someone, while being equipped.

Those who are still gaining their significance and holding down a power base through controlling a program should be given special attention. It would be easy for these folks to just get angry and fight what you are doing, or leave the church in a huff. However, their mixture of ego with power in the church reveals a serious flaw in their Christian life. How much better it would be for you to minister to them, perhaps through small groups designed to work with you on their needs, until they are brought to a spirit of true servanthood and ministry. In a cell group church, no one should be declared to be "off limits" to the power of God.

Restructure The Church Staff

I really enjoy hearing Dale Galloway tell about the way he finally called in his staff and reassigned them to serve as Zone Pastors! What a day that must have been—the final clod of dirt had been dropped on the old coffin. From that day one, that dear church has skyrocketed into a ministry that extends for miles and miles across the greater Portland area.

Here's A Chart To Show You What's Ahead!

On the facing page, this chart will help you see the stages you are going to go through. Notice there's a cycle that causes you to return to the top of the chart and dream all over again. The mark of a true leader is his ability to get the mind of God for the next phase of cell church life and implement it before momentum is lost. No man in the world has done this any more effectively than Dion Robert in Abidjan! It requires more time in the *Listening Room* than most pastors have experienced. To have the mind of God is a glorious thing when guiding a church.

PROBLEMS	STEP	RESISTANCE
Lack of knowledge Lack of creativity Lack of a model "Not invented here"	CONCEPTION	*LIMITED AWARENESS*
	Innovation ⬇	
No previous experience No expertise No guardrails	DEMONSTRATION	*SKEPTICISM*
	System Design ⬇	
Unawareness of requirements No previous experience No trained staff	DEVELOPMENT	*LIMITED SUPPLY OF STAFF AND FUNDS*
	Developed System ⬇	
Development of training Trainers needed Expansion of management Cost-effectiveness	INTEGRATION	*EXISTING WORK STRUCTURES*
	Growth ⬇	
Expanded awareness causes cycle to begin again Reorganization threatens "turfs"	TRANSFORMATION	*INERTIA INNER FEAR OF "LOSING CONTROL"*
Triggers general unrest in denomination and generally intimidates "status quo"	↺ *CYCLE BEGINS AGAIN*	

27 HOW TO PLANT A CELL CHURCH

Probably the most often asked question I receive in sharing with those who want to launch a cell group church is, "Where do we go from here?" This chapter, and the one that follows, are suggestions to assist you in your journey.

If Possible, Apprentice Yourself To A Cell Church

Of course, the best possible answer would be to say, "Go and apprentice yourself to someone who has done it!" That's what we are doing at Columbia Biblical Seminary and Graduate School of Missions for our church planter majors. In addition to the courses I teach there, we have also planted the Columbia Community Church. In it, students who choose to align them-selves with it for their campus stay have opportunity to experience cell church life.

I recently visited in Madrid with a fine young missionary, who is typical of what is taking place worldwide. His assignment is church planting. *He has never seen a church planted, and his seminary experience didn't provide a single course on the subject.*

A few years back, I was retained by a denomination to work with five church planter couples, all recent seminary grads, assigned to begin new work in Chicago. I was to make three trips in one year to "trouble shoot" for them. Their greatest trouble was that they didn't have the foggiest idea of what to do, where to begin, or how to break into the kaleidoscope of kingdoms of this world in that city. Sadly, all five of them dropped out of their work in defeat. One moved to a small town church, and four of them quit the ministry entirely to go into secular work.

Study the book of Acts: there is a definite pattern to how the church planter was equipped by Paul. The first step was to *experience a church being planted.* This was the case with every single one of the men Paul trained. Indeed, it was also the case with *Paul,* who was placed in the Antioch church planting venture by Barnabas—who came to help Antioch get going *after he had experienced the birth of the Jerusalem church!*

The second step was to *work with a church planter.* We see the extent of this as we examine the names of Paul's travelling companions. I can just imagine the story-swapping of apprentices who had seen churches planted in different places in Acts 20:4:

> *He was accompanied by Sopater son of Pyrrhus from Berea, Aristarchus and Secundus from Thessalonica, Gaius from Derbe, Timothy also, and Tychicus and Trophimus from the province of Asia.*

We have arrangements with Les Scarborough in Sydney, Faith Community Baptist Church in Singapore, New Hope Baptist Church in Portland, ICHTHUS Fellowship in London, and the *Eglise Protestante Baptiste Œuvres et Mission* in Abidjan for placement of students for one year as they complete their degree. In addition, they are required to go overseas with me for courses taught "on the fly" as they are exposed to numerous examples of cell churches. You can't graduate from Columbia with a degree in church planting until you have spent up to a year under a church planter!

Form A Leadership Cell

My companion in the formation of the Shepherd Community in Houston, Bill Beckham, has provided us with this model. He and Mary come to this cell church planting venture after 15 years of distinguished service in Thailand as church planters.

The Leadership Cell is a hybrid. It looks a lot like the Shepherd Cell, but also functions as the cell group church, not yet developed. All of the principle elements are able to function within it. It creates both Share groups and visitation teams for outreach. This sets up a framework where core leaders can receive on-the-job training in every aspect of Shepherd group life.

As you study the diagram on the following page, remember that diagrams on paper don't always work out the same way in real life. *That's no reason to be cynical of them!* Every good football team studies the coach's diagrams on a chalkboard. Their next step is to practice the diagram on the playing field until they are "picture perfect" in execution. Then, they face the opposition on the gridiron. Sometimes the play works exactly as in the diagram, and sometimes it doesn't. If it doesn't happen as anticipated, *they go back to the chalkboard!*

Begin The Leadership Cell With Six Or Eight People

Duplication of strengths in the Leadership Cell may be necessary, but the best pattern would be to blend strengths so a wider ministry may take place. This would seem to be the pattern set in Ephesians 4, where the equippers of the saints include an Apostle, a Pastor-Teacher, an Evangelist, and a Prophet.

If the team members are moving to a new city, they should do an urban strategy study before deciding where to live permanently. While this may require renting an apartment for the first few months, it's important that the selection of locations be made on the basis of the *ministry,* not the needs of the *family.* This may sound harsh, but those who begin by putting their own needs first seldom become effective servant leaders.

The financing of the Leadership cell members will take many avenues. Missionaries have support raised before they begin. In the case of the Beckhams coming to form the Shepherd Community in Houston, Mary will have to work for certain, and Bill may also temporarily have to find secular employment. The "upside" of that is the many *oikos* contacts that will be made—something a "full time" worker cannot do without special effort.

The first purpose of the cell is to *bond* the leadership team. There must be a clear vision of what must take place, and a deep commitment to do whatever is needed to make it happen. There must be no question about the *calling* of each person to the task.

As it begins, the goal of the team should be to activate all elements of a cell group church. All members should become familiar with the lifestyle of a Shepherd group, effectively performing all the tasks to be found within it. Thus, everyone

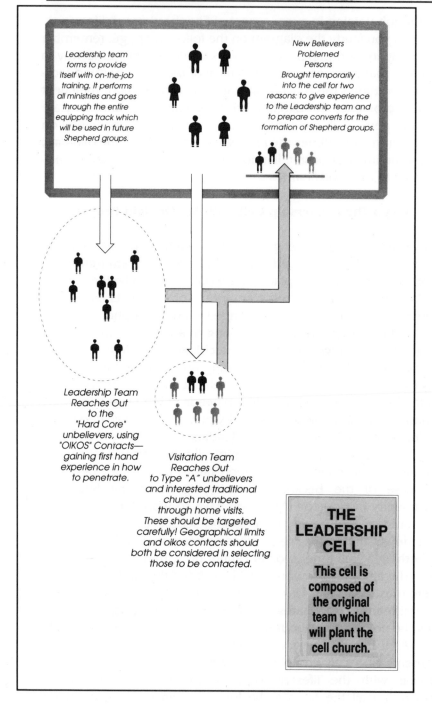

Leadership team forms to provide itself with on-the-job training. It performs all ministries and goes through the entire equipping track which will be used in future Shepherd groups.

New Believers Problemed Persons Brought temporarily into the cell for two reasons: to give experience to the Leadership team and to prepare converts for the formation of Shepherd groups.

Leadership Team Reaches Out to the "Hard Core" unbelievers, using "OIKOS" Conracts— gaining first hand experience in how to penetrate.

Visitation Team Reaches Out to Type "A" unbelievers and interested traditional church members through home visits. These should be targeted carefully! Geographical limits and oikos contacts should both be considered in selecting those to be contacted.

THE LEADERSHIP CELL

This cell is composed of the original team which will plant the cell church.

should go through the materials used in the equipping track. All should be able to effectively visit and should bring a Type "A" unbeliever to Christ. All should participate in the life of a Share group (see next chapter), and discover the dynamics which take place in that setting. All should serve as a Shepherd of the team for a period of time, evaluated by the rest of the group.

It really doesn't matter if this stage takes several months. There will be more growth in the future if the time is taken to bring the weakest member of the team "up to speed."

This, of course, must include the wives. Many a church planting venture has gone up in flames because the wife was treated as a "tag along," unable to effectively function. Excuses usually include the caring for the children, housework, etc. Our educational system commits a major blunder where wives of seminary students are concerned. The husband gets three years of education, while the wife remains dormant in her own development. I have witnessed many men weep as they have shared the burden of carrying on a public ministry while trying to carry their wives on their backs as a second burden.

The team should follow these guidelines for their initial times together:

1. Focus on God's vision for the work.
2. Develop an initial strategy.
3. Discover how to exercise gifts for edifying each other.
4. Be accountable to each other.
5. Target geographic neighborhoods.
6. Target special groups to be reached by Share groups.
7. Form the first generation of Share groups.
8. Form the first generation of Shepherd groups.
9. Identify, enlist, and train the first Shepherds.

Phase Two: Formation Of First Shepherd Groups

Once the team has set a pattern of outreach to the lost, the converts will trigger the second phase. It is now time for the first Shepherd group, or groups, to be formed. The Leadership cell should continue to meet alone—perhaps forever!—but the members now try their wings at forming new groups.

The Leadership cell members will, of course, serve as the

THE RIGHT ENVIRONMENTS FOR GROWTH

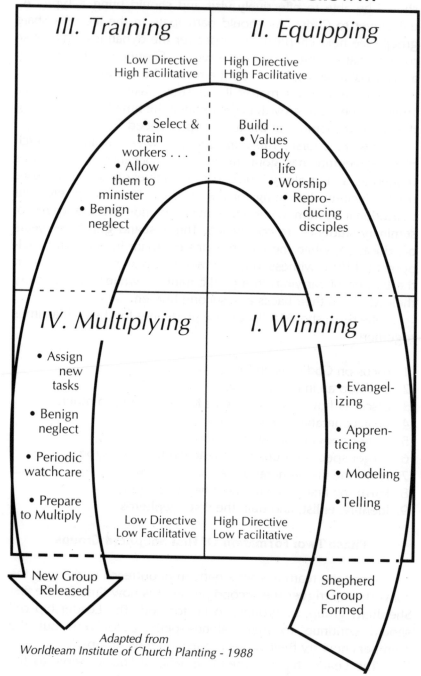

III. Training

Low Directive
High Facilitative

• Select & train workers . . .
• Allow them to minister
• Benign neglect

II. Equipping

High Directive
High Facilitative

Build ...
• Values
• Body life
• Worship
• Repro-ducing disciples

IV. Multiplying

• Assign new tasks

• Benign neglect

• Periodic watchcare

• Prepare to Multiply

Low Directive
Low Facilitative

I. Winning

• Evangel-izing

• Appren-ticing

• Modeling

•Telling

High Directive
Low Facilitative

New Group Released

Shepherd Group Formed

Adapted from
Worldteam Institute of Church Planting - 1988

Shepherd and the Intern of the first groups. Those who have accepted Christ will be moved through the equipping track. They will complete the *Arrival Kit,* move on to *Knocking On Doors, Opening Hearts,* and after winning someone to Christ will form Share groups as they train using *Touch Basic Training.* There will then be growth which will cause the second generation of Shepherd groups to be launched.

During the first stage, the Leadership team has been prayerfully evaluating each person. Initial Shepherd Interns must be identified, and invited to be equipped. Each one will then serve as an Intern during this second generation, under the watchful eye of a Leadership team member.

The functioning cell group church will not be launched until the third generation of Shepherd groups are formed. Consider now a potential time line for all this to take place:

FIRST PERIOD *(nine months?)*
   Leadership team begins to function.
SECOND PERIOD *(six to nine months?)*
   First generation of Shepherd groups formed with converts.
THIRD PERIOD *(six to nine months?)*
   Second generation of Shepherd groups formed; some converts invited to serve as Shepherd Interns.
FOURTH PERIOD *(six to nine months?)*
   Third generation of Shepherd groups formed; Shepherd Interns now move up to become Shepherds.

It is at this stage that the Leadership team must train themselves to serve in the role of the Zone Shepherd, assuming responsibility for the oversight of several Shepherd groups. They no longer function as Shepherds. They move between the groups assigned, advising the Shepherds and Interns. By constantly attending all the cells as an advisor, they grasp the areas which need to be strengthened. By constantly spending time with the Shepherds, visiting and praying with the sick, or counseling a marriage problem, the Shepherds are given their "on the job training" by having a companion in their ministry.

The Leadership team meetings are now devoted to sharing problems being encountered and strategizing for additional formation of cells in new areas of the society. They should stay at least one year ahead in their planning.

Note that nothing has been said about forming public Celebrations during these three generations. As we shall see in the next chapter, it's not a good idea to "go public" at the beginning. The creation of a "celestial funnel" should be avoided at all costs! Private gatherings in homes for worship are more appropriate at this time, along with "getaways"—weekends when all in the movement share a wonderful time of Bible teaching, fellowship, extended prayer, and play. These are infinitely more effective than public Celebrations, and bond the entire group in a special way.

One of the highlights of the early ministry at West Memorial in Houston was a weekend we all spent together in a hotel in Galveston. It was unforgettable! This led the Body to create a special retreat ministry near Bellville, Texas, at "Touch Ranch," a farm owned by the Paul Martins. The rug in the old living room there is permanently stained with the tears shed during prayer times.

Finally, Establish Zone Shepherds

Hand picking effective Shepherds to replace members of the Leadership cell members is the next stage. Since the only people qualified for this task are Shepherds, this usually requires his or her group to be distributed into other cells. While this may seem to be hard to do, if the entire movement has caught the vision of penetrating the city it is not traumatic. Friends go with friends when this reapportionment takes place, making the transition easier.

At this time, the Leadership cell members must focus their attention on thoroughly equipping the Zone Shepherds. They will be heavily involved in working with each Zone Shepherd, being a participant in all he or she does for at least six months.

The more time the Leadership cell invests in the launch, the stronger the cell church will be in the years ahead. It's much better to let the "rich young rulers" go sadly away in these formative stages, than accommodate their lack of commitment for the sake of numbers. And—by all means—send the traditional folks who don't want to change back where they came from!

Avoid The Temptation To Launch A Celebration

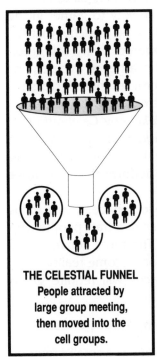

THE CELESTIAL FUNNEL
People attracted by
large group meeting,
then moved into the
cell groups.

Something in the blood of those coming from a P.B.D. background cries out for the formation of a Celebration, or a "Service of Worship," as the first step in church planting. Don't succumb to the thought! Imagine the countless hours which are required to hold a weekly public service. You must find the place to meet. Musicians are instantly needed. Song books, or at the least, song sheets, are required. Is there a sound system, or do you have to import one? What about a nursery for the children—and what will the young people do while the adults are meeting? Rented space means storing the furnishings required: does someone have a truck or a station wagon? How will we advertise it? Who will take the offering? Whew!

As I have journeyed over the globe among cell churches, I have discovered there are two different types of them. I call the first one the "Celestial Funnel" model. It's not a true cell group church, since it attracts people by a large production held on a weekly basis. It then seeks to hold the people who come by putting them in cell groups. My study of them reveals that only thirty to thirty-five per cent of the people who join this type of cell church ever participate in the actual cell groups. The reason is obvious: they didn't come for personal growth or ministry, but for *inspiration*.

That's not true in the pure cell group model. Among the pastors who have developed such a model are Yonggi Cho in Seoul, Les Scarborough in Sydney, and Dion Robert in Abidjan. It's also the reason Lawrence Khong in Singapore is seeking to make the change in his cell group church to building the growth through the groups rather than simply through his powerful preaching.

These remarks are not to disparage the place of the preacher and the Celebration in impacting unreached people. Every strong cell church has weekly services that bless all who attend. These gatherings are an important part of the "root system" needed to penetrate the community. The combination of an anointed leader with anointed cell groups is the maximum way to gather in the harvest. The point is not to be so dazzled by the preacher that the more important ministry of the cells is ignored. Every cell group pastor preaches with power, saying in his heart even as he equips his people, "I am doing this to equip them; let them increase— and let my importance to our growth decrease in proportion."

The recommendation is that you delay any Celebration for the cells until you have at least one hundred to participate. The assignments to develop the services can then be rotated among the cells, or certain cells can be asked to perform the same tasks in each service.

When you do finally create a public service, you'll focus them to build the life of the cells, rather than to attract people who may not be interested in cell group life. The more converts you gather in, the faster you will see your vision become reality.

Of course, in time the public services will require gifted musicians to be added to the Ministry Team.

Well, What Do You *Do* In The Beginning About Worship?

At the very start of the new work, meet as a small group on Sunday mornings to pray, to build up one another, and to train to effectively reach out through your Share group. After you have gleaned your first harvest, change this Sunday morning time to become the Shepherd group meeting. It will be a relaxed, precious time with all the families participating. Have an "Agape Meal" as the ladies feel like bringing covered dishes; begin it with the passing of the bread and ending it with the passing of the cup as the memory of Christ's death for His Bride.

Let those in the group bring messages God has given them from the scripture. If you wish, listen to a taped message and then discuss it. Or, read a chapter from an inspirational book or expository Bible study.

Without Fail, Multiply Each Group At Fifteen!

As the first Share group develops from three or four to twelve to fifteen, it's time to do two things: form your first two Shepherd groups and add a Share group to the new Shepherd group. From this time on, there should be about six to eight people in all Shepherd groups that are launched, and about three or four on each Share group team. The smaller the groups, the more involved they will be in ministering to each other. As you begin to form new groups, you or someone you designate will have to become a "Zone Servant" to minister to the special needs of these little cell churches. Remember—*the maximum load for a Zone Servant is five groups.*

The Church On Brady in Los Angeles has created a lovely video segment entitled "A Vision For Division," featuring "Sammy Cell." It's a part of the six hours of video segments in the Touch Basic Training materials. It's good to use this segment at the launching of each new cell. The time to inform people they must multiply at *fifteen* is not when they have *eighteen,* but when they have *eight!* The longer you wait, the more static you will get when it's time to make two groups out of one.

The reason for this is plain when you learn a simple mathematical formula:

$$(N \times N)\text{-}N = CL$$

Which, being interpreted, means: multiply the number of people present by the same number. Then subtract that number from the total. This gives you the number of communication lines in the group. Note how fast it increases: I talk to you, and you talk to me: there are *two* communication lines. A third person joins us: there are six lines now. With the fourth person, there are twelve, with ten there are ninety, and with fifteen there are two hundred and ten communication lines. In fact, after fifteen persons you can no longer expect to have small group dynamics. It's a "Large Group" then, and must be treated in that way. Intimate sharing and interactive discussion is not possible. Save large group activities for the Celebrations or, later on, for the Congregations and Celebrations.

Your *Second* Biggest Problem: Dealing With Frustrated P.B.D. People

(We'll get to the first biggest problem in a moment.) Avoid like the bubonic plague the temptation to grow by finding frustrated P.B.D. church members who want to join you, unless you

have an opportunity to evaluate their motives. Those who depart from P.B.D. life with a grudge seldom, if ever, have a passion for the lost. Take it from years of experience with them—they will drag their feet and slow you down in your mission of becoming the real family of God.

One dear pastor who is in his third year with a clump of folks who pulled out of a P.B.D. situation recently shared his frustrations over this matter. Out of eighty-nine people, seven families have dragged their feet from the first, reticent to abandon the "tried and true" ways of their pasts. They refused to participate in either Share or Shepherd groups, attending only the public worship times. They finally insisted on a youth program for their teens, a regular Sunday school for their tots, and regular Bible studies for themselves where they could "get fed." At the same time, in three years they had made no move whatsoever to share their faith or make friends with unbelievers. The rest of the cell group members finally asked them to *please leave, and join a church that pleased them.*

We went through great traumas over this when I pastored *The People Who Care* in Houston back in 1970. Half of our original group wanted to enter our new lifestyle, and the other half fought it at every turn. I hated to split a church, so I split myself wide open emotionally instead. I resigned after one year with no place to go and six mouths to feed. I was hurting so badly that I actually chose the concrete pillar on the freeway I was going to drive into at ninety miles an hour. I resigned the church with nowhere to go. My dear friend Jack Taylor invited me to come to San Antonio to work with him. Those were terrible months for me!

In His providence, He spared me from my dark night of the soul and also arranged for a precious lady, a psychiatrist in the group, to confront the Houston congregation with their conflict. The P.B.D. folks all moved *en masse* to a nearby church. The little band of 42 who remained called me to return to the work again, and I moved back to Houston.

From that moment on, and for all the years that followed, we were extremely cautious about people who visited us from local churches. I used to say to them, "What you see when you come to our Celebrations is not our church. You need to get involved in our cell groups for at least three months. If, at the end of that time, you are *still* interested in becoming part of our cell group life, we will provide a Spiritual Formation Seminar for you before you become a part of our lifestyle. Just remember that we don't plan to *change* who we are, and we are not looking for folks who want to *try* to change us." We didn't get large numbers from other congregations, and those who *did* join us were precious jewels. This also kept our focus on the growth which would come through targeting unchurched people.

Your *First* Biggest Problem: Helping Christians To Effectively Relate To The Unchurched

Expect it to be tough going when you form Share groups to reach the unchurched! The problem is not that these folks are difficult to reach: it's that the Christians you will work with have spent years ignoring the pagan world. *(Does that include you?)*

Restructuring personal values is a slow and painful task, but it's much easier when you're in a cell with a desire to reach out. The first steps in learning how to *oikodomeo* each other will come as you struggle together with your barren lifestyles.

Making contacts is not difficult, but it will require a new way of spending your time. Friends require the investment of hours spent together. When one is free from the P.B.D. rat race, there is time for this.

How many on your Leadership team have personally brought at least one other to Christ? Let them build up the ones who have never done so, by modelling and explaining how it is done as *Knocking On Doors, Opening Hearts* is studied.

Do one or two of the team have contacts ready to participate in a Share group? Let them show the way they developed such friendships to those who have no contacts. *It's "show and tell time," folks!* There's no way to learn how to do this except by watching and doing what you see demonstrated.

Early in the life of *The People Who Care,* I took men who had been deacons and church leaders into apprenticeship. They were wonderful guys who had been so busy in the church they had lost contact with unreached men. One at a time, I took them out with me to visit on Friday evenings. We went to taverns, to pool halls, to bars in local hotels, to all-night doughnut shops packed with kids on drugs. After I showed them how to make friends with people in our area in this way, they began to go out by pairs without me. We would meet on Friday nights at my house for prayer in the early evening, and they would return late that night to share and pray about the new contacts they had made. After they developed a "case load" of three or four men, they temporarily used those Friday nights to entertain the men (and often their spouses) in their homes.

Developing a lifestyle that focuses on reaching the unchurched will take some time. Expect this! Look again at the chart of Yonggi Cho's church growth in the first chapter, and realize it will take a while before you get your cell group church under way. In the beginning, you are sowing a lot of seed to be reaped in later months. Keep reminding yourself that once the ministry takes off, the growth is exponential!

Most important of all, remember that the first person you must train is—you! Until you have personally been able to accomplish what you want to train others to do, you will not be successful. Remember Dion Robert: with limited education, without a day of Bible college or seminary, he has developed the largest church in the history of his nation. The three things that made him successful was determination, determination, and determination.

Tan Tien Sur was my student in Singapore in 1977 when I taught these concepts. After I returned to America in that year, he tried and tried to make the cells work among taxi drivers and factory workers. To do so, he forced himself to learn Chinese dialects they spoke. Months went into years, and he couldn't get the right combination to touch this semiliterate, unreached segment of the population. When I returned ten years later, I discovered his exciting ministry called Care Corner had reached hundreds of these folks for Christ. He has cell groups which meet right in the factories. His dream is to create a "Seminary" to train leadership among these new believers. It will have to be a "school" without books, for few of them can read. Although he, too, has never had any formal Bible school or seminary training, his cell movement has won more unreached people for Christ than scores and scores of churches in Singapore have done in a generation! With scores and scores of cell groups, he has finally formed his own cell group church. The Chinese speaking congregations he *tried* to work with rejected these blue collar people!

Please—Move The Cell Meetings From House To House!

I have heard all the objections that can be used to doing this for many years: "People won't know where to come;" "It's too confusing;" "Why move around? There's security in having the same couple open their home every week for the meeting."

No, no, no! It's not true! I speak as one who has participated for many years in cell groups that moved every week, or at least every two weeks. In a Shepherd group with only a handful of members, keeping in touch with one another is a simple matter. The mentality of people who make these objections is premised on the fact that the cell meeting is just one more weekly event in a church schedule. If the cell is what it *ought* to be, it will be the focal point of life for each member. If someone is out of pocket for a few days, it's a simple matter to call the Shepherd and find out where the group is meeting. On the other hand, either the Shepherd or the Intern should call *every* contact, *every* week. Affirming who will be present at the cell should be known in advance.

When the cell meets at the same house all the time, several major setbacks occur. The first is the miserable task of the poor housewife to get her place cleaned up for company every Tuesday night. After a while, that gets old!

The second setback is that the group quickly establish that this is "Bill and Margie's group." Mutual ownership is destroyed. Accountability for the gatherings is watered down.

The third setback is that people never get to *really* know each other until they spend time in all the homes in the group. This is a very important matter! If you meet Ruth and me at "Bill and Margie's house," you'll never know that we have chosen to live simply, and that our Houston home is packed with furniture and pictures which reflect our deep love for all things Chinese.

Finally, the scripture *plainly says* that "they went from house to house." We never saw growth until we began to do that!

This chapter ends, then, with this recommendation:

How will you start your cell group church? With a vision so deeply rooted in your heart and soul by the Holy Spirit that it will not wane when the going is rough and you feel like quitting!

SELF-CHECK FOR YOUR OWN READINESS TO BEGIN

List five unchurched people you spend quality time with each week. They can be from your Primary or Secondary *oikos*.

1. _____

2. _____

3. _____

4. _____

5. _____

List those occasions when you have *personally* either brought a friend to accept Christ, or when you have *tried* to do so. It must have happened on a *one-to-one basis*, not just serving as a counsellor in an evangelistic meeting, etc.:

_____

_____

_____

_____

SELF-CHECK FOR STEPS TO TAKE AS YOU BEGIN

List the names of three or four other persons who are willing to participate in forming the Leadership cell with you:*

1. _____

2. _____

3. _____

4. _____

- Give each of them a copy of *A Guidebook for Cell Group Churches*. Assign them portions of it to read. Meet regularly to discuss the material. Work through all philosophical differences before proceeding.
- Spend *significant* periods of time together just praying and seeking the Lord's face about your project. *"Significant"* means three to four hour periods at least once or twice a week. Don't spend all your time talking; you did that as you discussed the book together. Learn to go into the *Listening Room* of prayer. Create prayer lists for each person to use in these times together. Share impressions the Lord gives you as you pray together. Take those impressions back to the Throne of God to discern whether they have been given by Him to you, or whether they are simply personal preferences. *Learn to be a Body related to the Head—to be living stones, built upon the Foundation!*
- List all unbelievers in your *oikoses* and include them in your prayer periods. Pray for openness and receptivity to your forthcoming invitations to join you in a Share group.
- Actively seek to build up *(oikodomeo)* one another by permitting Christ's presence to flow through you for each other.

*If you have a larger number of people, divide them into cells of no more than five. Underline names of possible servant leaders in each cell. Be sure each group includes at least one mature person with *oikos* contacts among the unchurched. Repeat the above suggestions with each group.

EQUIPPING RESOURCES AVAILABLE
FROM TOUCH OUTREACH MINISTRIES

ENTRY LEVEL	CHARACTERISTICS	COURSE OFFERED
NEW CHRISTIAN	Recent Convert	Arrival Kit for New Believers Cover the Bible
COLD CHRISTIAN	Not Grounded Never discipled Lapse of many years Past unconcern about personal growth and ministry	Life Basic Training Cover the Bible
LUKEWARM CHRISTIAN	Some previous discipleship; values are a mixture of secular and Christian; little heart for knowing God.	Life Basic Training "I Am Crucified" Cassette Tapes Cover the Bible
READY FOR SERVICE	Committed. Needs help in use of spiritual gifts in a specific ministry.	Cover the Bible Spiritual Gifts Inventory Spiritual Gifts tapes

PREPARATION FOR EFFECTIVE SERVICE

TEACHING GIFTS	Ready to learn the Bible in depth	Begin with Cover the Bible, offer advanced courses of your own choosing.
VISITING THE VISITORS (Type "A" Unbeliever)	Ready to serve on a visitation team	Knocking On Doors, Opening Hearts
REACHING TYPE "B" UNBELIEVERS	Ready to serve on a Share group team	Touch Ministries Seminar Touch Basic Training The Way Home New Testament
SHEPHERD INTERN	Preparing to lead a Shepherd group	Shepherd's Guidebook
WIDER MINISTRIES	Ready to become a Zone Shepherd or serve in another capacity	Personal time with Leadership or Ministry Team or other staff person

 # TOUCH TOOLS TO USE

During the last 14 years, we have been writing and testing materials for use in the cell church. Realizing there needed to be a complete "equipping track" for the church planter, the materials have been painstakingly developed. Inserted in the back of this book is an order blank for you to peruse. We would count it a great privilege to participate in your ministry as you use these materials in your cell groups.

Because so many have asked for a commentary on each of our products, this chapter will explain the items on the order form, following its outline.

Books About Cell Group Church Life

Where Do We Go From Here?
This is the book you hold in your hand. They may be ordered in bulk for study groups you form as you introduce the concept of the cell group church to others.

The Touch of the Spirit
Now out of print, we have copies left. It's one of my earliest books which talks about life in small groups. Contains many excellent illustrations of small group life.

The Seven Last Words of the Church
Now out of print, we secured the final supply of a book which tells the story of my own journey out of P.B.D. life into the cell group church. It's worth reading if you are about to do the same!

Equipping Tools For A Cell Group

Shepherd's Guidebook

    This equipping tool is crucial to the development of Shepherd Interns. It has already gone through three printings. I keep the amount published low, for I am constantly learning from the Shepherds I relate to, and plan to keep this in revision about every year or two. It's also published in Singapore for use in the Orient. After you have finished reading this book, it's the next thing you will want to digest as you consider developing a cell group church.

    These are the chapter titles in the *Shepherd's Guidebook :*

Part One: The Shepherd's Life
    Check List Of What Should Be In Place
    Description Of Congregations And Celebrations
    Welcome To The Life Of A Shepherd!
    The Shepherd As A Discipler
Part Two: The Shepherd's Tasks
    As You Go, Develop Apprentices
    Equipping The Flock For Ministry
    Using The Journey Guide And Map
    The Shepherd's Prayer Life
    "Kinning:" Creating Christian Kinfolks
    Reaching The Unreached
    Caring: A Work Of Tender Love
    Will The Little Children Suffer?
    Too Much Month At The End Of The Money
Part Three: The Shepherd Group Gatherings
    How Shepherd Groups Function
    Having Meaningful Gatherings
    Leading The Flock To Experience God
    Critical Moments In Group Life
    Get Acquainted Activities
Part Four: Twelve Shepherd Group Gatherings
    Shepherd Group Sessions
Part Five: The Journey Guide
Part Six: Useful Forms

Journey Guides

This little booklet has really been blessed by the Lord! As each new person enters a Shepherd group, the Shepherd visits the home for a personal interview. The *Journey Guide* is completed in advance of this visit. Through sharing together, a "Journey" of equipping courses is outlined to help this person grow spiritually and into greater ministry. The bonding which takes place as this is done is important.

The *Journey Guide* is a 12-page booklet, printed in color, and includes self-tests which help the user evaluate his or her spiritual condition.

Knocking On Doors, Opening Hearts

A paperback book, this guide to touching Type "A" people is to be used by the "Young Men" as they learn how to visit and bring others to confess Christ as Lord. There's a special *Equipper's Guide* section in the back of the book for use in the weekly sharing time between the apprentice and the equipper. It may be the first book ever written which approaches sharing Christ with a lost person in a relational way, rather than by utilizing "stranger evangelism" methods. The pattern for sharing Christ is deliberately developed with the expectation that the trainee will continue on as a "Father" to take Touch Basic Training, where the pattern is further expanded.

These are the chapter titles in *Knocking On Doors, Opening Hearts,* which has 144 pages:

Why Do We Visit?
Our Message—Part 1
Our Message—Part 2
Our Methods—Part 1
Our Methods—Part 2
How To Lead A Lost Person To Christ—Part 1
How To Lead A Lost Person To Christ—Part 2
Practicum, Part 1: Drawing The Net
Practicum, Part 2: Excuses
Practicum, Part 3: Questions
Equipper's Guide

Spiritual Gifts Inventory

This booklet is *excellent* for use in the Spiritual Formation Weekend. It provides basic information about spiritual gifts, followed by a carefully developed inventory for the person to use. Actually, gifts are uncovered *through use,* not inventories, but this is a pretty accurate way to help a person recall what gifts they have manifested in the past. It's also a great introduction to spiritual gifts for use with new believers (Paul speaks of them as the "ungifted ones"). It has been interesting for us to see that, after six months of involvement in Shepherd group life and ministry, the person who takes this inventory over again will see a marked difference. (It can be reused by the same person.) It has 36 pages.

Spiritual Gifts Inventory: Books and Tape

I was asked to prepare a cassette tape to be used in a small group setting, explaining the Inventory and commenting on spiritual gifts. This little set is also helpful for those who are going to administer the Inventory.

The Way Home New International New Testament

This lovely paperback New Testament has been published through cooperation with the fine folks at the International Bible Society. It contains the entire NIV New Testament, plus special "Successful Living" pages I have added to it. This was developed and tested with unbelievers, designed to be their first introduction to basic truths of the Christian message. It's heavily slanted toward touching the value system of the unbeliever. It is not meant to be handed to someone—rather, it is to be used in a one-to-one dialogue between a believer and an unbeliever. There are 11 sections to the study, which uses a programmed learning pattern.

Cover The Bible Materials

Cover The Bible Loose Leaf Notebooks

This is a one year Bible survey course for curious unbelievers and believers who have never gotten a "bird's-eye view" of the Bible. It's divided into 52 sections. This notebook version is best to use when you are teaching it to unbelievers. It makes it possible for you to give them one portion of the notes each week. Their interest is heightened as they know they must attend every week to receive all the notes.

Cover The Bible Paperback

This is a paperback version of the material, best to use with those in Shepherd groups who are going through the material on a weekly basis.

Cover The Bible Personal Tape Series

To assist the new Christian in a Shepherd group, this set of cassette tapes is a five-minute-per-day study of the materials with the author. The tapes provide 52 weeks of presentations. *(Available second quarter of 1991)*

56-Hour Cassette Lectures, In Briefcase

This set of cassettes tapes was produced in the studio of KHCB before a live audience. At the conclusion of 52 hours of lectures by Ralph Neighbour is his four hour dialogue with Bob Ross, expert in biblical backgrounds in the land of Israel. His tapes require the use of the excellent *Bible Map Manual.* Shepherds who will meet with students weekly during the equipping time will find these tapes provide excellent background.

56-Hour Cassette Lectures, four per month

To make the purchase of this rather expensive product available to more people, we offer them on a monthly installment basis without interest. The large brief case which houses all 56 tapes is sent with the first set of four tapes. Along with the final four tapes, we send the *Student Map Manual* free of charge. Your Visa or Mastercard will automatically be debited each month, with your authorization, for the 13 months tapes are sent out.

NIV Study Bibles, Hardback

This is the "official" Bible used with the *Cover The Bible* course. We have them available at below cost to you, and a further reduction when ordered in bulk along with the study guides.

Student Map Manual
> This amazing book of maps of the Holy Land is one of a kind. It shows the location of towns and road systems generation by generation. It retails for $39.95 in this hardback edition.

Free *Cover The Bible* Direct Mail Layout
> Through the years, I have discovered that one of the "root systems" a cell church can offer is the *Cover The Bible* course for totally unchurched people. Many are curious about what the Bible teaches, but don't want to get all tangled up with a P.B.D. church to find out. By direct mail, we have advertised a course which tells "All you wanted to know about the Bible, but were embarrassed to ask!" We have had a good response from this mailing. Many dozens have responded, including Muslims, Jews, and people who have *never* attended a church. We will gladly typeset the 2-page self-mailer for you to send to homes as you place a bulk order for the books. (We recommend using the loose leaf version for this ministry.)

Touch Ministries Seminar Materials

This five hour introductory seminar explains Share groups and the desperate need to reach Type "B" people, taking them from their complete lack of interest in spiritual things to a desire to know more about the Christian message. The typical believer doesn't understand *why* a relational approach must be made to these Type "B" people, and this seminar explains the impact made by 10-week Share group encounters.

It *must* precede the use of Touch Basic Training. It cannot be skipped over, because it is the foundation for all that is done in the longer course. It also helps everyone in the entire P.B.D. church to understand what the Share groups are all about.

Touch Ministries Seminar Facilitator's Kit
> You must have this Kit if you are going to facilitate a *Touch Ministries Seminar*. The cassette tapes walk you through the entire seminar. They are prepared for you to listen to at your desk as you get ready to present the materials. The videotape is used in the actual seminar, and includes several segments

to help you as you present the Share group concept. Printed instructions and transparency paper masters are also provided.

Touch Ministries Seminar Loose Leaf Workbooks

The loose leaf notebook, plus the pages used during the *Touch Ministries Seminar,* are needed for every person being trained. It includes a detailed explanation of what Share Groups are like, and recommendations for developing them. Please don't try to "cut corners" by ordering one copy for a couple; every person being equipped needs one for the personal and small group activities to be facilitated. After the seminar is over, the additional space in the notebook will be filled up with the *Touch Basic Training* pages.

Touch Basic Training Materials

Touch Basic Training Facilitator's Kit

This is *essential* for anyone planning to equip people using the *Touch Basic Training Student Kit. The Facilitator's Guide* took me 1-1/2 years to write, test, and rewrite. It explains every one of the 249 *experiences* provided in the Student Guide, provides written scripts for all six hours of videotape segments, and gives many other aids as you decide which materials you want to use. The kit includes 12 hours of instructions on audiotape for the Facilitator, covering both the Touch Ministries Seminar and Touch Basic Training. Provided are transparency paper masters, which can be used as "flash cards" if you are equipping one team in a home. You are encouraged to order one Kit, and duplicate it as you wish for use by Shepherds.

Touch Basic Training Student Kit

The materials provided for each student include a 300 page loose leaf insert to be put into the notebook received at the *Touch Ministries Seminar.* Also provided are logo materials, tracts for sowing, cultivating, and harvesting, and a plexiglass doorplate.

Life Basic Training Materials

A word about Life Basic Training

Many years ago, while trying to help P.B.D. churches insert cell groups into their church life, we realized one of the greatest heartaches facing a pastor were the "sit n' soak" members. Realizing their value systems were not Christian in many dimensions, we began to develop a small group approach for helping them face that fact. Through five generations of revisions, we finally put together a videotaped series and a workbook to achieve this objective. This 11-week small group series does not need a teacher or a leader. It's designed so one or more groups of five persons can watch the video, follow the small group guide for discussion, and then complete five days of self-study based on what they grasped in the group meeting.

The sessions start out without a great deal of challenge, laying a foundation from the Bible about ways we gain our significance. Mary and Martha are used as models of contrasting lifestyles: one gaining significance by her activity, the other by sitting at the feet of Jesus.

By the fifth or sixth sessions, each person begins to feel the challenge of changing values to "live Christianly." Moses is examined as a model of a man who went through two cycles before being brought to servanthood, and the participant is asked to make a personal evaluation in the daily growth sessions.

Experience with groups has indicated that before the series is over, some have broken through to a new awareness of Christian living—and others, like the rich young ruler, go away deciding the cost is too great. Anticipate some will drop out during the last half of the sessions. Usually the "reason" they give masks their true feelings: *they don't want to pay the price called for to live a servant life.*

However, those who finish the course have usually come to new terms with their value systems, and are ready to move out into a servant lifestyle. We have seen numbers of people make an authentic profession of faith during the last weeks of the course, admitting for the first time their previous "decision for Christ" was made without any idea it meant more than joining the church.

This series is developed so it can be used as an alternative for those who complete the *Touch Ministries Seminar* and who do not choose to enter *Touch Basic Training*. It has been successfully inserted as curriculum in Sunday school classes. Several pastors have made it a part of their New Member Orientation Class in a P.B.D. setting.

Several churches have used this for all incoming members, using it as a part of their orientation materials.

Life Basic Training Facilitator's Kit

This kit includes a brief Facilitator's Guide which includes the written text of all 11 video segments. The videotapes, along with 11 audiotapes of the voice track, are included. Thus, the material can be used with or without video being available, in a training class held in a P.B.D. church or in a home setting.

Life Basic Training Workbooks (paperback)

Each person in a group will need one of these workbooks. It includes a "readiness" activity to prepare each person for viewing the video, the discussion guide for the group, and then five days of self-reflection after each session. These five days of self study are truly important to the reshaping of values in the life of the "sit and soak" Christian—the target we had in mind when this was produced.

Touch Specialty Items

For groups choosing to use the *Touch* logo, these materials are available in quantity:

Logo Lapel Pins or Lady's Logo Pendant
Plexiglass Door Plates
3-Color Vinyl Stickers

Unique Tracts For Relational Evangelism Contacts

We have produced three types of tracts for use with unbelievers. The first type is for use with people who need to be "prodded" into thinking about their relationship to Christ. They are called "seed sowing" tracts, and are designed to be placed on the edge of a desk in an office, etc., to generate discussion. They do not explain the plan of salvation.

The second type is called a "cultivating" tract *(The Perfect Circle)*. It is prepared to be used prior to a person being open to discussing how to become a Christian. The Christian writes personal comments about what he or she lived for before accepting Christ, and hands it to the unbeliever for private perusal.

The third type is called a "harvesting" tract. It's used to train Share group ministers as they take *Touch Basic Training*. Once the pattern is understood, we recommend it *not* be used when bringing an unbeliever to Christ; instead, it should be hand drawn on a piece of paper as the sharing takes place.

21 *"Seed Sowing" Tracts, Assorted*
20 *"Master Plan" Tracts*
20 *"Perfect Circle" Tracts (English or Spanish)*

Important Books You Can't Easily Find Elsewhere

Gods of Power

Written by Dr. Philip Steyne, this recently released book is the most definitive and scholarly presentation of power encounters involving animistic practices that has ever been written. No matter *where* you live, no matter *what* culture surrounds you, this book will open your eyes to things you have never realized were going on around you.

Brisbane Urban Strategy Report
Auckland Urban Strategy Report

These two 8-1/2" x 11" books provide complete breakdowns of all neighborhoods in these two cities, and provide an urban strategy report both in macro and micro levels. Pages 347-348 in this book provide an example of the micro reports. Either or both of these reports will prove to be an invaluable model for those intending to develop an urban strategy. Many have been purchased by missionary executives who seek to develop an overall strategy for planting churches in World Class Cities.

Cassette Tapes On Key Subjects

The Cell Group Church Tapes
This five hour set of cassette tapes was recorded in the spring of 1990 in Columbia, South Carolina, at a seminar for chaplains and pastors held at Fort Jackson. It comes with paper transparency masters which were used in the presentation.

"I Am Crucified With Christ"
This little set of tapes, accompanied by an illustrated booklet, has blessed lives for over 15 years. It's a great series to give to a hungry Christian who doesn't understand the principles of the crucified life.

"Is It Fair? Why Are The Heathen Condemned?"
As soon as Share group teams begin to work with the totally unchurched, this question will be presented to them. Because it was asked so many times to our teams, this taped set was produced to help answer the query. They can either be used by Christians who need help, or loaned to an unbeliever to think through the entire issue.

Dion Robert On Cell Group Churches
Using Dr. Charles Deevers as his translator, Dion Robert made these four *Carpool* cassette tapes with Ralph Neighbour, who interviewed him about his cell group church. They are not only fascinating, but most informative and useful for the cell group worker.

The Arrival Kit For New Christians

When published, this will replace the use of the *Survival Kit for New Christians*. It is being written for the new believer who has been reached through a Share group and/or a Shepherd group. It clearly outlines the theology of the church, beginning with a description of a "Basic Christian Community." Those serving in P.B.D. structures will find this book may confuse converts who are not in the surroundings of a cell group church. Its use probably should be limited to the true cell church. Look at it and decide for yourself.

Survival Kit Series

Adult Survival Kit for New Christians, Plus Two Cassette Tapes
Many people asked me to prepare a "talk-through" of the material in the book. The great value of this set will be to the "Young Man" who is the sponsor for one of the "Little Children" in a Shepherd group. It gives insights into the weekly material which will be helpful as they have their weekly review of the material. This set provides one copy of the book and one set of the tapes by Ralph Neighbour. It is specifically designed for a person who is working through the book.

Survival Kit For New Christians, Adult Version, English
Survival Kit For New Christians, Youth Version, English
Survival Kit For New Christians, Children's Version, English
Survival Kit For New Christians, Leader's Guide, English
Sigueme, Spanish Version, For Adults
Sigueme, Leader's Guide
Suis-moi, French Version, For Adults
Kakudai Suru Jinsei, Japanese Version, For Adults
Chinese Survival Kit, Hong Kong Version For Adults
Living Your Christian Values , Adult Version, English
(Formerly *Survival Kit 2*)
Living Your Christian Values , Youth Version, English
(Formerly *Survival Kit 2*)

These can all be secured from us. We give generous discounts when they are purchased in volume.

Touch Basic Training Seminars

Touch Basic Training Facilitator's Seminar on cassette tape
This 14 hour set of tapes was recorded during a live seminar conducted by Ralph Neighbour near Fort Worth, Texas. It focuses on the *Touch Ministries Seminar* and *Touch Basic Training*. The notebooks provided in the live seminar accompany the tapes. Additional workbooks for *Touch Basic Training Facilitator's Seminar* are also available if a group wishes to share in the cost of the series and meet together for the sessions.

ENDNOTES

CHAPTER 1

1. John E. Cox, "Problems and prospects of shelter and human settlements to the year 2000 and beyond." *EKISTICS* 53, no. 320/321, (September/October-November/December 1986): 266.

2. Available from Population Reference Bureau, Inc., 777 14th St., N.W., Suite 800, Washington, D.C. 20005.

3. Information Division, Ministry of Communications and Information. *Singapore 1988* (Singapore: Government Press, 1988), 14.

4. Jonathan C. Ritchey, "A Survey of Muslim Work With Reference To An Urban Setting In The Cote D' Ivoire" [unpublished manuscript], 1989, Library, Columbia Biblical Seminary and Graduate School of Missions, Columbia, S.C., p. 4.

5. Research done by the Home Mission Board of the Southern Baptist Convention verifies these figures, first recognized by Lyle Schaller. The author has studied this phenomenon for the past ten years in nation after nation. It is a worldwide statistic.

6. Charles Arn, Donald McGavran, Win Arn, *Growth, a New Vision for the Sunday School* (Pasadena: Church Growth Press, 1980), 25-27.

7. See *Auckland, Resistant and Neglected* (Houston: Touch Outreach Ministries, [n. d.]), 9-18.

8. *Emerging Trends,* Princeton Relgion Research Center (Vol. 11, No. 9).

9. "Baptist pastor dismissals rise." *New York Times,* March 15, 1989.

10. Acts 2:42-46; I Corinthians 14:24-26.

11. Jean Vanier, *Community And Growth* (Homebush, NSW, Australia: St Paul Publications,1979), 18-21.

12. Personal interview with the pastor, Dion Robert, on *CARPOOL*, a daily radio broadcast conducted by the author.

13. The address of this church is: Yoido P. O. Box 7, Seoul 150-600, Korea.

14. Paul Cho, "Growth Remembered." *Church Growth* (June 1985): 4.

15. John W. and Karen L. Hurston, *Caught In The Web* (Seoul: Church Growth International, 1977), 11.

16. Reported by Dr. Cho in his address to the Tenth Church Growth International Conference, held July 25-31,1989, in the facilities of the Yoido Full Gospel Church.

17. Solhein, Datin, "Church Planting Since 1945," Paper presented to the Twenty-Seventh Hayama Men's Missionary Seminary, January 6-8, 1986, 9.

18. An excellent book not available in the United States is Church Growth International's *Home Cell System*. It is available from CGI, Yoido P. O. Box 7, Seoul 150, Korea. Address your query to Ruth Sholtis, Administrative Secretary.

19. Stated in an address made by him to the 1989 Church Growth International board meeting, Seoul, Korea, August 4, 1989.

20. Kenneth Dale, *Circle of Harmony, A Case Study In Popular Japanese Buddhism With Implications For Christian Mission* (South Pasadena: William Carey Library, 1975), x.

21. Lawrence Khong may be reached at this address: Faith Community Baptist Church, 50 Thompson Rd #02-05/06, SLF Complex, Singapore 1129.

22. Dr. Kriengsak Chareonwongsak may be reached at this address: Hope of Bangkok, G. P. O. Box 1390, Bangkok 10501, Thailand.

23. Dion Robert may be reached at this address: Yaye Dion Robert, Pasteur Principal, Eglise Protestante Baptiste Oeuvres et Mission Int. Ext., 03 B. P. 1032, Abidjan 03, Ivory Coast.

24. Roger Forster may be reached at this address: Dr. Roger Forster, ICHTHUS Fellowship, 107-113 Stanstead Road, Forest Hill, London SE23 1HH.

25. C. Peter Wagner, *Spiritual Power and Church Growth* (Altamonte Springs, Florida: Strang Communications Company, 1986), 126-127.

26. Charles H. Kraft, *Christianity with Power* (Ann Arbor, Michigan: Servant Publications, 1989), 8.

CHAPTER 3

1. Jean Vanier, *Community And Growth* (Homebush, NSW, Australia: St Paul Publications, 1979), 18-21.

CHAPTER 5

1. M. Scott Peck, *The Different Drum* (New York: Simon and Schuster, 1987), 59.

2. *OIKOS* is used by me to refer to the basic building block of community life. It is usually translated "household" in the New Testament. A later chapter will fully develop its importance to cell group life.

3. Servants Among The Poor may be contacted at: 691 E. Howard Street, Pasadena, CA 91104.

4. Bruce Bettleheim, *Home For The Heart* (New York: Random House, Knopf Publishing Co., 1973), 41.

5. Matthew 16:13-20.

6. Matthew 18:15-20.

7. Anyone who has tried to pastor a traditional church realizes the impossibility of following these instructions in a congregation made up solely of polite acquaintances! Discipline of members is either *never* done, or it is done with a blunt hatchet which leaves broken bones strewed everywhere.

8. Peck, 1987, p. 300.

9. Robert Banks, *Paul's Idea of Community* (Homebush West, NSW 2140, Australia, 1979), 96-101.

10. 1 Peter 4:12-13.

11. John 20:21-23.

12. Luke 3:16.

13. 2 Corinthians 3:18.

14. Colossians 1:27.

15. Acts 2:41-47.

CHAPTER 6

1. E. Mansell Pattison, *Pastor and Parish—A Systems Approach* (Philadelphia: Fortress Press, 1977), 19.

2. Acts 18:8; Romans 16:5, 10, 11; 1 Corinthians 1:11, 1:16, 16:15, 16:19; Philippians 4:22; Colossians 4:15; 2 Timothy 1:16, 4:19.

CHAPTER 7

1. Benjamin Tonna, *A Gospel for the Cities* (Maryknoll, New York: Orbis Books, 1982). See Chapter 2.

2. Charles H. Kraft, *Christianity with Power* (Ann Arbor, Michigan: Servant

Publications, 1989), 20.

3. See Philip Steyne, *Gods of Power* (Houston: Touch Publications, 1990).

4. Dominique Lapierre, *The City of Joy* (London: Arrow Books Limited, 1986), 214.

5. Robert McGee, *Search for Significance* (Houston: Rapha Publishing, 1985), 11.

6. Tonna, 1982, p. 38.

7. Matthew 13:33.

8. E. Mansell Pattison, *Pastor and Parish—A Systems Approach* (Philadelphia: Fortress Press, 1977), 19.

CHAPTER 8

1. *Encyclopedia Britannica*, 1967 ed., s.v. "Blood."

2. *Ibid*, s.v. "Circulation of Blood."

3. *Ibid*, s.v. "Arteries."

4. The *Spiritual Gifts Inventory* is further discussed in Part 3 of this book.

5. Romans 12:7, 1 Corinthians 16:15, Acts 9:36.

6. Romans 12:8, Acts 4:32-35, 1 Corinthians 16:2.

7. Romans 12:8.

8. 1 Corinthians 12:9, Romans 12:3, Hebrews 11:1.

9. 1 Corinthians 12:10, Hebrews 5:14, 1 John 2:14; 4:1-3.

10. Romans 12:8, Acts 13, John 17:18-19.

11. Romans 12:6, 1 Corinthians 12:10.

12. Romans 12:7, Matthew 28:18-20

13. Matthew 12:42; Acts 6:3; 7:10; 1 Corinthians 1:26; 2:6-12; 12:8; Colossians 1:24-27; 2:3; 3:16; 4:5; James 1:5; Revelation 5:12.

14. 1 Corinthians 12:8.

15. Romans 12:8; John 14:16.

16. 1 Corinthians 14.

17. 1 Corinthians 14.

18. 1 Corinthians 12:10.

19. 1 Corinthians 12:10.

20. 1 Corinthians 14:24-25.

21. D. A. Carson, *Showing the Spirit* (Grand Rapids: Baker Book House, 1987), 111-116.

22. *Ibid.*, p. 105; see 1 Corinthians 12:30 and 14:18.

23. *Ibid.*

24. *Ibid.*, p. 103-104.

25. 1 Corinthians 14:26.

CHAPTER 9

1. 1 Corinthians 14:23.

2. 1 Corinthians 14:12.

3. 1 Corinthians 14:26.

4. Charles H. Kraft, *Christianity With Power* (Ann Arbor, Michigan: Servant Publications, 1989), 8.

5. 1 Corinthians 10:24.

6. 1 Corinthians 12:4-6.

7. Romans 12:6.

8. Romans 12:4-6a.

9. 1 Corinthians 12:4-6.

10. 1 Corinthians 12:11.

11. 1 Peter 4:10.
12. 1 Corinthians 12:7-10.
13. 1 Corinthians 12:28.
14. 1 Corinthians 12:30.
15. 1Corinthians 14:1.
16. Hebrews 2:4.
17. Carson, 1987, p. 59.
18. *Ibid.,* p. 60.
19. Ephesians 4:15-16.
20. 1 Corinthians14:1.
21. 1 Peter 4:8.
22. Hebrews 10:24.
23. 1 Thessalonians 3:12.
24. 2 Thessalonians 1:3.
25. 1 Corinthians 16:14.
26. 1 Corinthians 14:12.

CHAPTER 10

1. 1 Corinthians 14:12, 26; Hebrews 10:24, 25.
2. Ephesians 4:30.
3. Romans 6:3 and Galatians 3:27;1 Corinthians 12:13.
4. 1 Corinthians 12:7.
5. 1 Corinthians 14:25.
6. Daniel 10:12-13.
7. Hebrews 5:13-14.
8. David Lowes Watson, *The Early Methodist Class Meeting* (Nashville: Discipleship Resources, P. O. Box 840, Nashville, TN 37202, Revised 1987),194.
9. *Ibid.,* p. 200.
10. 1 John 2:13-14.

CHAPTER 11

1. C. S. Lewis, *The Four Loves* (New York: Harcourt, Brace & World, Inc., 1960), 192.
2. D. A. Carson, *Showing The Spirit* (Grand Rapids: Baker Book House, 1987), 179.
3. This is not to say that all who publicly declare words of knowledge are frauds. I watched Sam Lai in Hong Kong hold a street meeting in the park on Temple Street. He walked up to a man in the crowd that ringed him as he preached, and spoke so plainly to him about sin in his life that the man trembled with fear. The rest of the crowd became so afraid he would do the same to them that they literally ran away.
4. 1 Corinthians 14:26-33.
5. Hebrews 10:24-27.
6. Elizabeth O'Conner, *Search For Silence* (Waco: Word Books,1972), 87.
7. *Ibid.,* p. 95.
8. Carson, 1987, p. 34.

CHAPTER 12

1. Psalm 127:3.
2. Psalm 139:15-16; Psalm 22:9-10; 71:6.
3. Exodus 22:29.

4. Deuteronomy 6:6-7; 11:19-21.

5. Deuteronomy 4:9-10.

6. Deuteronomy 6:20-21.

7. Joshua 7:11.

8. Exodus 32:31-32.

9. W. Robertson Smith, Lectures on the Religion of the Semites (new ed., rev.; London: A. and C. Black, 1894), p. 273. Quoted in H. Wheeler Robinson, Corporate Personality in Ancient Israel, p. 28.

10. Psalm 103:13; Hosea 11:1-3.

11. Deuteronomy 32:46-47.

12. Deuteronomy 16:16; cf. Luke 2:41-51.

13. Deuteronomy 6:20.

14. Joshua 4:6.

15. 2 Chronicles 24:2.

16. Deuteronomy 6:7; 11:18-21.

17. Psalm 78:5-8.

18. Jeremiah 31:29.

19. Exodus 20:5-6; Deuteronomy 5:9; Numbers 14 :17-18.

20. Deuteronomy 18:9.

21. Numbers 14:31.

22. Ezekiel 18:18-20.

23. Psalm 8:2; 148:12.

24. 1 Samuel 3:7.

25. 1 Samuel 2:26 (cf. Luke 2:52).

26. Judges 13:3-5; Luke 1:76.

27. Proverbs 1:8; 4:1-4; 6:20.

28. Proverbs 3:12

29. Luke 1:42.

30. Luke 2:39.

31. Luke 2:49.

32. Matthew 11:16-17; Luke 7:31.

33. Matthew 17:14-18; Mark 9:14-27; Luke 9:47-33.

34. Mark 5:41; Luke 8:54.

35. Matthew 19:13-15; Mark 10:13-16; Luke 18:15-16.

36. Matthew 21:14-16.

37. Matthew 7:9-11.

38. Matthew 11:25.

39. Matthew 18:5; Mark 9:36-37.

40. Matthew 18:6; Luke 17:2.

41. Matthew 18:10.

42. Matthew 18:14.

43. John 6:9.

44. Matthew 19:14.

45. Matthew 20:25-28.

46. Mark 9:36-37; Luke 9:46-47.

47. Luke 18:21-23

48. Acts 2:39.

49. Acts 16:33-34.

50. Acts 9:36-42.

51. 2 Timothy 1:5.

52. Ephesians 5:32-33.

53. Ephesians 6:4.

54. Ephesians 4:13.

CHAPTER 13
1. See *The Shepherd's Guidebook* and *Touch Basic Training*. Order form is in back of book.
2. Robert and Julia Banks, *The House Church* (Sutherland: Albatross Books, P. O. Box 320, Sutherland, NSW 2232, Australia.)

CHAPTER 14
1. Psalm 78:70-72.
2. 1 John 2:12-14.
3. Available in late 1991. In the meantime, use my *Survival Kit for New Christians,* available from Touch Ministries (see end of book).
4. 1 Thessalonians 1:5-7.
5. 2 Corinthians 10:4-5.

CHAPTER 16
1. See references in the *Touch Ministries Seminar* (order blank is in the back of this book).
2. If you are not a watcher of American TV, "Mash" is an old comedy program which told the story of doctors and nurses in a Korean battle zone. They treated casualties who came wounded, and were sent away "patched up."
3. Target Group booklets available from Touch Outreach Ministries are mentioned on the order blank. More are being created all the time. They include a Facilitator's Guide for the Share Group team, and a booklet to be used by each member in preparation for the group meeting.
4. I. Howard Marshall, *Commentary on Luke* (Grand Rapids: William B. Eerdmans Publishing Company, 1978), 419-420.

CHAPTER 19
1. Dwayne Huebner , "Practicing the Presence of God," *Religious Education,* Vol. 82, No 4 (Fall 1987), p. 573.
2. Don Dinkmeyer and Rudolph Dreikurs, *Encouraging Children to Learn* (New York: Hawthorn Books Inc., 1963), p. 104.
3. Virgil E. Foster, *Christian Education Where the Learning Is* (Englewood Cliffs, N.J.: Prentice Hall Inc.,1968), 67.
4. Susan Schaeffer Macauley, *For The Children's Sake* (Westchester, Illinois: Crossway Books, Good News Publishers, 1984), 76.
5. Vernie Schorr, *Building Relations with Children International Center for Learning* (Glendale, California: Regal Books, 1978), 16.
6. Macauley, 1984, p. 68.
7. Laura B. Lewis, "Sunday School Teachers and Teaching: Memories and Metaphors," *Religious Education* Vol. 83:3 (Summer 1988), 394.
8. *Ibid.*
9. Rudolf Dreikurs, *Children, The Challenge* (New York: Duell, Sloan and Pearce, 1964.).
10. Hans G. Furth, *The World of Grown-ups: Children's Conceptions of Society* (New York: Elsevier, 1980), 65.
11. John H. Westerhoff III, *Bringing up Children in the Christian Faith* (Minneapolis: Winston Press, 1980), 16.
12. Leontine Young, *Life Among the Giants* (New York: McGraw Hill Book Company, 1965.), 3.

13. Furth, 1980, p. 65.

14. Carrie Lou Goddard, *The Child and His Nurture* (Nashville: Abingdon Press, 1962), 159.

15. *Ibid.*, p. 176.

16. Foster, 1968, p. 68.

17. Conversation in Hastings, New Zealand on 30 September, 1989.

18. Virgil E. Foster, 1968.

19. Lawrence O. Richards, *A Theology of Christian Education* (Grand Rapids: Zondervan Publishing House, 1975.) 114.

20. I can confirm this research from over a thousand responses from teachers in training seminars I have conducted.

21. Laura B. Lewis, "Sunday School Teachers and Teaching: Memories and Metaphors," *Religious Education* Vol 83:3 (Summer 1988), 390.

22. *Ibid.,* 394.

23. *Ibid.,* 393.

24. *Ibid.,* 392.

25. Sofia Cavaletti, *The Religious Potential of the Child* (New York: Paulist Press, 1983), 49.

26. Dorothy Jean Furnish, *Exploring The Bible With Children* (Nashville: Abingdon Press,1975), 94-5.

27. Trevor Ross, *A Report on Children's Growth Groups Model..* Unpublished report for the Baptist Family of Churches in Queensland, 1986, p. 11.

28. Sara Little, *To Set One's Heart* (Atlanta: John Knox Press, 1983), 54. Sara Little quotes a group investigation in which a student asks, "If a person does not believe in Jesus Christ, does he always go to hell when he dies?" A school friend had died in a car accident the night before. He had always proclaimed himself to be an atheist at school and had challenged several members of the group about their beliefs. The teacher abandoned her lesson and set up a group enquiry to mobilize the young people to find out the answer. It took three weeks of study and discussion, but the group had talked the matter through and discovered what the Bible said.

29. *Ibid.,* 57.

30. Richards, 1975, p. 82.

31. L. Douglas DeNike and Norman Tiber, "Neurotic Behavior" *Foundations of Abnormal Psychology* (New York: Holt, Rinehart and Wilson, 1968), 355. Quoted in Richards, 1975, p. 83.

32. Lawrence Kohlberg, "Moral Development and Identification" *Child Psychology 62nd Yearbook of the National Society for the Study of Education* (Chicago: University of Chicago Press, 1963). 296. Quoted in Richards, 1975, p. 84.

33. Schorr, 1978, p. 4.

34. Kay Llovio, "Towards a Definition of Christian Education. A Comparison of Richards and Westerhoff," *Christian Education Journal* V:2 (Winter: 1985), 17.

35. Schorr, 1978, p. 9.

36. *Ibid.*

37. *Ibid.,* 26.

38. Ephesians 6:4.

39. Schorr, 1978, p. 5.

40. November 26, 1989, Northcote Baptist Church, New Zealand.

41. Judith Allen Shelly and Others, *The Spiritual Needs of Children: A Guide for Nurses, Parents and Teachers* (Downers Grove: Intervarsity Press, 1982), 30.

42. "Several churches mentioned the benefit of meeting in the leader's home

rather than on church premises. A homely atmosphere can in particular, help small group discussions [for children]. It is also a good link where churches have a house group structure for adults." Quoted from *"Suffer the Children"* Administry, December 1987, p.9, a comment in response to a local questionnaire.

43. Shelly, 1982, p. 45.

44. Zick Rubin, *Children's Friendships* (Cambridge, Mass.: Harvard University Press, 1980), 116.

45. Maria Montessori, *The Absorbent Mind* (New York: Holt, Rinehart and Winston, 1967), 228.

46. *Ibid.,* 227.

47. Rubin, 1980, p. 114.

48. Richards, 1975, p. 85.

49. L. R. Jenkins, *The Growing Child Scripture Union Video Script* (Queensland, Australia, 1987).

CHAPTER 23

1. The Brisbane and Auckland reports are available from Touch Outreach Ministries, Box 19888, Houston, TX 77079 for $25 each.

2. Contact Church Information & Development Services, 3001 Redhill Avenue, Suite 2-220, Costa Mesa, CA 92626.

3. See *Brisbane Report.*

4. Contact Dr. David Finnell, Post Office Box 3122, Columbia, SC 29230-3122.

CHAPTER 26

1. Everett M. Rogers with F. Floyd Shoemaker, *Communication of Innovations, A Cross-Cultural Approach,* second edition (New York: The Free Press, 1971) 182 ff.

2. *Ibid.,* p. 131.

INDEX

Abidjan, Ivory Coast	31
Africa, cell group church	31-32
Apprenticing	361
Apprenticing to a cell church	423
Arrival Kit for New Christians	215, 358, 366, 449
Auckland Urban Strategy	450
Australia, cell group church	33
Banks, Robert	59, 203
Baptisms, Southern Baptists	18
Basic Christian Community	194
Bettleheim, Bruno	101
Brisbane Urban Strategy	450
Carson, D. A.	157
Celebration	32, 196, 206-207
Celestial Funnel	431
Cell church, large church staff	265
Cell church, sample budget	266
Cell Group Church	11, 20-22
Cell group church tapes	448
Cell group church, urban model	135
Cell groups for teens	330-335
Cell, macro and micro descriptions	223-238
Cell, maximum size	220
Cell, multiply in six months	69, 217
Cells	197
Cells, must move from house to house	437
Census Tracts	339
Change and the church	407-409
Children, Shepherd groups for	309-312
Children, cell groups for,	267-274, 286-292
Children, equipping leaders	274-285, 295, 313-328
Children, festivals and ceremonies	307-309
Children, intergenerational settings	304-307
Children, mixed age groups	292-293
Children, place in early church	189-192
Children, place in Israel's community	181-185
Children, policy for cells	302-303
Cho, Paul Yonggi	53, 208, 264, 436
Christian Outreach Centre	33
Church of Praise	28
Church structures inadequate	14
Columbia Biblical Seminary and Graduate School of Missions	423, 424
Columbia Community Church	423
Communidades de Base	33
Community in the Body of Christ	108-111, 199-200
Community in the New Testament	100-102
Community in the Old Testament	99-100
Congregations	195, 204-206
Contemporary model	46
Cover The Bible	367, 443 ff.
Cyprus, launching pad	33
Deacon	44, 45, 46, 48,
Dion Robert On Cell Groups	451
Direct mail layout	446
Districts	356
Ecclesia	39, 40,
Edification in cell groups	161-164, 180, 239
Edification stage	225
Eglise Protestant Baptiste Œvres et Mission	31, 378-403, 424
Elder, bishop	45-48
England, cell group church	32
Enumeration Districts	339
Epworth Society covenant	165
Equipper	44
Equipping resources available	440
Equipping track for a cell group church	363
Facilitator's Guidebook	370
Faith Community Baptist Church	27-28, 261, 424
Fathers, spiritual	214, 369
Five types of people, bell curve explained	410-414
Forster, Roger	32
Fullness churches	39
Galloway, Dale	34, 209, 259, 421
Getaways	261
Gifts, and cell groups	151-156, 160-161
Gifts, and love	156-159
Gifts, and needs	164
Gifts, purpose of	145
Gifts, service	140
Gifts, sign	143
Gifts, spiritual	139
Gods of Power	450
Grace-gifts	40
Grupos de Amor	34, 209
Guiness, Os	239
Hong Kong, cell group church	30
Hope of Bangkok church	28, 29
House churches defined	203-4
House groups, impact of	43-44
I Am Crucified With Christ tapes	451
Ice Breaker stage	225
ICHTHUS Fellowship	32, 168-169, 356, 424
In Focus Churches	34
In visits and Out visits	252
Is It Fair? Why Are The Heathen Condemned?	451
Japan, cell group churches	25-27
Journey Guide	366, 443
Journey Guide Interview	366
Kang, Albert	28
Katartizo	41
Khong, Lawrence	27

Kingdoms of this world   122-135
Kinning   221-222
Knocking On Doors,
  Opening Hearts   216, 368,
                                435, 443
Koinonia   51
Kriengsak, Chareonwonsak   28
Leadership Cell   425-427
Life Basic Training   448
Life Basic Training Facilitator's Kit 449
Life Basic Training Workbooks   449
Listening Room   172-173,
                                405
Little Children   212, 366
Living stones   40
Logo lapel pins, pendants   449
Lordship evangelism controversy 53-54
Love feast, Lord's supper   45, 105-
                                106
Macau, cell group church   30
Mainland China, cell group church 29-30
Man of peace   250
Marshall, I. Howard   250
Megachurches   19, 38
Ministry Outreach Weekend   369-370
Ministry Team   196, 375
Missionary Interns   376-377
N x N=CL   433
Neighborhoods, categories of   349-353
Network   32
New Hope Community Church   34, 209,
                                259, 424
New Testament and
  today's church contrasted   58
New Testament model   45
NIV Study Bibles, hardback   445
O'Connor, Elizabeth   177, 178
Oikodomeo   40, 41,
                                121, 246,
Oikonomos   121, 246
Oikos   82, 114-
                                120, 246-
                                247
Oikos strategy   249-251
Oikos, primary and secondary   257
P.B.D. cell administrative models 70-77
P.B.D. churches   38, 47-58,
P.B.D. groups   59-70
P.B.D. Specialists   47-49, 56,
                                69
P.B.D., Program Base Design   47,
Pakuranga Central   347-348
Parish mentality   52
Pattison, E. Mansell   136
Peck, M. Scott   94
People Who Care   84, 85,
Population explosion   12-13,
Population Pyramids   340-341
Praise churches   38
Problems, Steps, Resistance chart 422
Program Base Design defined   39
Reddick, Lynn   34
Restoration churches   38
Restructuring church staff   421
Right environments for growth   428
Robert, Dion   31, 52-53,

                                54, 159,
                                167,
Rogers and Shoemaker   410
Rules of the Band Societies   166-167
Samaan, John   96
Scarborough, Les   33, 424
Senior Pastor   196
Seow, Eugene   223
Seven Last Words of
  the Church, The   441
Share group cells   194, 195,
                                203, 216,
                                254-261,
Share group cells, defined   254
Share groups, topics for teens 335
Share The Vision stage   225
Shepherd Group schedule   362
Shepherd group, three levels   212-214
Shepherd groups   194, 195,
                                198, 209-
                                210, 213,
                                427
Shepherd Intern (or, Servant Intern) 198, 217,
                                370,
Shepherd Intern
  Formation Weekend   370
Shepherd Intern Training Period 371-372
Shepherd's Guidebook   218, 222,
                                262, 442
Shepherds   210-212,
                                372-373
Singapore, cell group churches 27-28
South America, cell group churches 33-34
Spiritual Formation Weekend   364-366
Spiritual Gifts Inventory   364, 444
Spiritual Gifts Inventory,
  books and tape   444
Spiritual warfare   170
Spiritual Warfare Weekend   367-369
Sponsors, each one teach one   362
St. Marys Baptist Church   33
Steyne, Philip   450
Stranger Evangelism   50, 239-
                                242
Strongholds   220
Student Map Manual   446
Sunday school enrollment   17
Survival Kit for New Christians 360, 451-
                                452
Tan Tien Sur   436
Target Group Evangelism   86
Target groups   87, 247-
                                248, 258-
                                260
Taxonomy, defined   359
Taylor, Jack   57
Televangelists   19
Tender Loving Care groups   209
Texas Baptist Convention   79
Thailand, cell group churches   28-29
The Unwelcomed Child   329
Third Wave theology   35-36
Touch Basic Training   217, 246,
                                256, 369
Touch Basic Training Facilitator's Kit 447
Touch Basic Training seminars   452

Touch Basic Training Student Kit	447
Touch Ministries Seminar	246, 256, 262, 369, 417
Touch Ministries Seminar Facilitator's Kit	446
Touch Ministries Seminar loose leaf workbooks	447
Touch of the Spirit, The	441
TOUCH Singers	261
Tracts: seed sowing, cultivating, harvesting	447
Trilogy groups	89, 260-261
Trinity	96-97
Type "A" unbelievers	216, 244, 249-251
Type "B" unbelievers	216, 244-245, 251
U.S. church membership	16
United States, cell group churches	34
Urban strategy, how to develop	336-357
Vanier, Jean	64
Way Home NIV New Testament	444
Wesley, Samuel	165
West Memorial Baptist Church	84
Wolf, Tom	82
Words of Knowledge	173-174
World *oikos* principle	252-253
World urbanization	15
Worship stage	225
Yoido Full Gospel Church	20, 23, 24-25, 107, 378 ff.
Yopougon Baptist Church	212, 367
Young Men	46, 195, 375
Zone Pastor	375-377
Zone Pastor Intern	
Zone Pastor Training Course	
Zone Servant: see Zone Shepherd	
Zone Shepherd (or, Zone Servant)	45, 195, 373, 430
Zone Shepherd Conferences	374
Zone Shepherd Formation Weekend	373-374